International Journal on Advances in Software

2016 vol. 9 nr. 1&2

Printed from e-media with permission by:

Curran Associates, Inc.
57 Morehouse Lane
Red Hook, NY 12571

Some format issues inherent in the e-media version may also appear in this print version.

Printed by Curran Associates, Inc. (2018)

International Academy, Research, and Industry Association (IARIA)
412 Derby Way
Wilmington, DE 19810

Phone: (408) 893-6407
Fax: (408) 527-6351

petre@iaria.org

Additional copies of this publication are available from:

Curran Associates, Inc.
57 Morehouse Lane
Red Hook, NY 12571 USA
Phone: 845-758-0400
Fax: 845-758-2633
Email: curran@proceedings.com
Web: www.proceedings.com

The *International Journal on Advances in Software* is published by IARIA.
ISSN: 1942-2628
journals site: http://www.iariajournals.org
contact: petre@iaria.org

Sponsored by IARIA
www.iaria.org

International Journal on Advances in Software
Volume 9, Number 1 & 2, 2016

Isabel Candal-Vicente, Universidad del Este, Puerto Rico
Juan-Vicente Capella-Hernández, Universitat Politècnica de València, Spain
Jose Carlos Metrolho, Polytechnic Institute of Castelo Branco, Portugal
Alain Casali, Aix-Marseille University, France
Yaser Chaaban, Leibniz University of Hanover, Germany
Patryk Chamuczyński, Radytek, Poland
Savvas A. Chatzichristofis, Democritus University of Thrace, Greece
Antonin Chazalet, Orange, France
Jiann-Liang Chen, National Dong Hwa University, China
Shiping Chen, CSIRO ICT Centre, Australia
Wen-Shiung Chen, National Chi Nan University, Taiwan
Zhe Chen, College of Computer Science and Technology, Nanjing University of Aeronautics and Astronautics, China PR
Po-Hsun Cheng, National Kaohsiung Normal University, Taiwan
Yoonsik Cheon, The University of Texas at El Paso, USA
Lau Cheuk Lung, INE/UFSC, Brazil
Robert Chew, Lien Centre for Social Innovation, Singapore
Andrew Connor, Auckland University of Technology, New Zealand
Rebeca Cortázar, University of Deusto, Spain
Noël Crespi, Institut Telecom, Telecom SudParis, France
Carlos E. Cuesta, Rey Juan Carlos University, Spain
Duilio Curcio, University of Calabria, Italy
Mirela Danubianu, "Stefan cel Mare" University of Suceava, Romania
Paulo Asterio de Castro Guerra, Tapijara Programação de Sistemas Ltda. - Lambari, Brazil
Cláudio de Souza Baptista, University of Campina Grande, Brazil
Maria del Pilar Angeles, Universidad Nacional Autonónoma de México, México
Rafael del Vado Vírseda, Universidad Complutense de Madrid, Spain
Giovanni Denaro, University of Milano-Bicocca, Italy
Nirmit Desai, IBM Research, India
Vincenzo Deufemia, Università di Salerno, Italy
Leandro Dias da Silva, Universidade Federal de Alagoas, Brazil
Javier Diaz, Rutgers University, USA
Nicholas John Dingle, University of Manchester, UK
Roland Dodd, CQUniversity, Australia
Aijuan Dong, Hood College, USA
Suzana Dragicevic, Simon Fraser University- Burnaby, Canada
Cédric du Mouza, CNAM, France
Ann Dunkin, Palo Alto Unified School District, USA
Jana Dvorakova, Comenius University, Slovakia
Lars Ebrecht, German Aerospace Center (DLR), Germany
Hans-Dieter Ehrich, Technische Universität Braunschweig, Germany
Jorge Ejarque, Barcelona Supercomputing Center, Spain
Atilla Elçi, Aksaray University, Turkey
Khaled El-Fakih, American University of Sharjah, UAE
Gledson Elias, Federal University of Paraíba, Brazil
Sameh Elnikety, Microsoft Research, USA
Fausto Fasano, University of Molise, Italy
Michael Felderer, University of Innsbruck, Austria
João M. Fernandes, Universidade de Minho, Portugal
Luis Fernandez-Sanz, University of de Alcala, Spain
Felipe Ferraz, C.E.S.A.R, Brazil
Adina Magda Florea, University "Politehnica" of Bucharest, Romania
Wolfgang Fohl, Hamburg Universiy, Germany

International Journal on Advances in Software
Volume 9, Numbers 1 & 2, 2016

CONTENTS

CommJ: An Extension to AspectJ for Improving the Reuse and Maintainability of Communication-related Crosscutting Concerns

Ali Raza
SaaS Cloud Engineer
ItsOn Inc.
Silicon Valley, California, USA
ali.raza@itsoninc.com

Stephen Clyde
Computer Science Department
Utah State University
North Logan, Utah, USA
Stephen.Clyde@usu.edu

Abstract—**This paper presents advances of research on CommJ, a framework for weaving communication-aware aspects into application code. Specifically, it presents a simplified *Universe Model for Communication* (UMC) and an enhanced implementation of CommJ. It also summarizes a preliminary experience that tests seven hypotheses about how CommJ might improve reusability and maintainability of software applications that rely on network communications. The summary includes a description of a quality model consisting of factors that impact reusability and maintainability, attributes that the factors depend on, and metrics for assessing those attributes. The experiment was a two-group study involving seven aspect-oriented programmers. Despite the small number of study participants, the experiment yielded encouraging results about CommJ's potential. Specifically, CommJ can improve reusability and maintainability of application code when there are communications-related crossing-cutting concerns.**

Keywords – aspect orientation; aspect-oriented programming languages; AspectJ; communications; cross-cutting concerns; software reuse; software maintainability.

I. INTRODUCTION

Inter-process communications are ubiquitous in today's software systems, yet they are rarely treated as first-class programming concepts. Consequently, developers have to implement communication protocols manually using primitive operations, such as connect, send, receive, and close. For many communication protocols, the sequencing and timing of these primitive operations can be relatively complex. For example, consider a distributed system that uses the Passive File Transfer Protocol (Passive FTP) to move large datasets between clients and servers. With Passive FTP, a server would enable communications by listening for connections requests on a published port, usually port 21. A client would then initiate a conversation, i.e., start an instance of the Passive FTP protocol, by sending a connect request to the server on that port. The server sets up a dedicated port, 2024 in this example, and sends its number back to the client. The client connects to that port and the server sends back an acknowledgment. At this point, two processes can start exchanging data on this dedicated communication channel. The arrows in Figure 1 illustrate this initial sequence of messages.

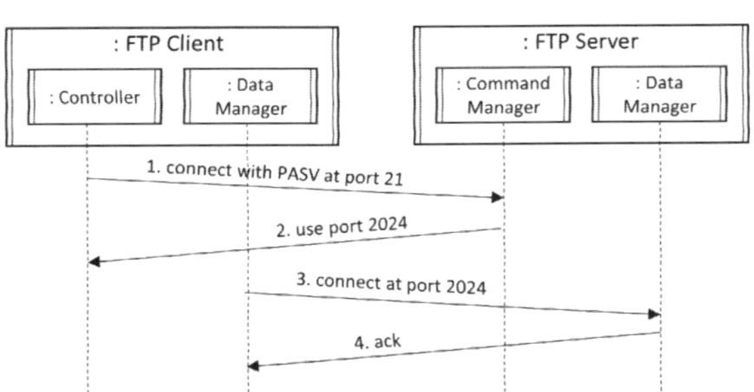

Figure 1. The Starting of a Passive FTP Conversation

Neither the client's nor the server's side of the conversation is trivial. In fact, both usually execute different parts of the conversation on different threads. For example, Figure 1 shows two threads for a FTP server and two threads for a FTP client. Although multi-threading has many advantages, it can create complexities while trying to follow a conversion's execution in the code because different parts of the conversation end up being handled by different components in the code.

A distributed system with concurrent conversations based on one or more non-trivial communication protocols may be further complicated by other communication-related requirements, such as logging, detecting network or system failures, monitoring congestion, balancing load across redundant servers, and supporting multiple versions of one or more of the protocols [1][2].

From a communication perspective, these concerns are examples of what Aspect Orientation (AO) refers to as crosscutting concerns, because they pertain to or cut through multiple parts of a core or base system. Implementing one or more of these concerns without careful attention to encapsulation, modularization, cohesion, and coupling can cause undesirable scattering and tangling of code.

AO, which first appears in the literature in 1997 [3][4], reduces scattering and tangling of code by encapsulating crosscutting concerns in first-class programming constructions, called aspects [5]. An aspect is an Abstract Data Type (ADT), just like classes in strongly-typed, class-based, object-oriented programming languages. However, an aspect can also contain advice methods that encapsulate logic for addressing crosscutting concerns and pointcuts for describing where and when the advice needs to be executed. A pointcut identifies a set of joinpoints, which are temporal points during the execution of the system when weaving of advice may take place. Each joinpoint corresponds to static place in the source code, called a shadow [5].

AspectJ is an extension to Java for aspects and, like many other AOPLs and Aspect-oriented Frameworks (AOFs) [5][6][7][8], it allows programmers to weave advice for crosscutting concerns into joinpoints that correspond to various programming construct, such as constructor calls/executions, methods calls/executions, class attribute references, and exceptions. For documentation on AspectJ, see *The AspectJ Project* website [5].

Since aspects are just special ADTs, it is possible for skilled software developers using traditional object orientation (OO) to implement classes that do basically the same thing. However, these classes would have to manage all the joinpoint contexts and weaving of crosscutting behaviors explicitly. Furthermore, hooks into crosscutting behaviors would most likely have to be introduced into the core application code. In other words, the real difference between AO and OO is that AO offers a convenient mechanism for separating crosscutting concerns from core functionality. It encourages obliviousness, which is the idea that core functionality should not have to know about crosscutting concerns [9][10]. With obliviousness, programmers should be able to add or remove the crosscutting concerns at build time without changing any source code.

The problem is that AspectJ and other AOPLs do not support the weaving of advice into core high-level application abstractions, such as conversations among processes in a distributed system, since those abstractions are based on run-time context information beyond code constructs, a single thread flow of execution, or its call stack. This paper introduces an extension to AspectJ, called CommJ [1][2] that allows developers to weave crosscutting concern into conversations in a modular and reusable way, while keeping the core functionality oblivious to those concerns.

We elaborate on the problem and review related literature in Section II. Then, in Section III, we formalize the notion of communication joinpoints and introduce CommJ. Next, Section IV demonstrates the feasibility and utility of CommJ by describing a library of reusable communication aspects and providing examples from a non-trivial sample application.

To explore CommJ's utility as a valuable extension to AspectJ, we conducted a preliminary experience that measured the quality of applications and extensions to applications built with CommJ compared to the same built with only AspectJ. Section V describes the quality model that we used for the comparison and evaluation of the application software. It is an adaption of the Comparison Quality Model by C. Sant'Anna et al. [11]. Sections VI & VII explain the hypotheses and experimental method, while Section VIII presents the results of the experiment along with our interpretations and conclusions for each hypothesis.

Overall, the experiment provides preliminary evidence that the applications written with CommJ are more cohesive and oblivious and that they have less scattering and tangling of cross-cutting concerns then their AspectJ-only comparison applications. Furthermore, those using CommJ were more loosely coupled, less complex, and smaller in size. The results are encouraging and provide ample motivation to continue work on CommJ and to pursue other opportunities for weaving aspects into application-level abstractions. Section IX summarizes the contributions of this paper and discusses future work.

II. Background and Related Work

To explain CommJ and its contributions, it is first necessary to establish a foundation of background concepts and related work in four areas: The AOP paradigm, AOP development tools (i.e, languages and frameworks), communications, and cross-cutting concerts with respect to communications.

A. The AOP Paradigm

In general, a skilled programmer can do anything in an OO programming language (OOPL) that could be done in an AOPL by making careful design decisions that encapsulate crosscutting concerns in well-modularized classes and hooking those features into the base application. To do this, a programmer could use software constructs, such as delegates, callbacks, and events, or apply various design patterns, like the Strategy, the Decorator, and the Template Method patterns [13]. However, the developer may still end up with code tangling and scattering, unnecessary coupling, lack of obliviousness, and compromised flexibility. AO provides an elegant way of weaving new behaviors into existing code, such that their functionality is less scattered, tangled, and decoupled from the base application, without compromising that functionality.

With AO, programmers should only need modular reasoning to discover the code and structure of the crosscutting concerns; whereas they would most likely need global reasoning when using traditional OO techniques [13]. Additionally, when using only OO techniques, separating out tangled code from core functionality can cause inheritance anomalies [14]. AO programmers, on the other hand, can refactor tangled code by moving it into loosely coupled aspects. So, the attraction of AO is not that a developer can do more, but that a developer can do certain things better, particularly in terms of modularizations or crosscutting concerns with less scattering and less tangling.

B. AOP Languages and Framework

Other techniques that address the same problems solved by OO, including Monads [15], Subject-oriented Programming [16][17], Reflection [18][19], Mixins [20], and Composition Filters [18]. The AO approach seems to have risen to the top as the most influential because it allows for better modularity of crosscutting concerns and it does not alter or violate principles of the OO paradigm.

There are many AOPLs and AOFs available today, such as AspectJ [5], AspectWorkz [6], Spring AOP [8] and JBoss AOP [7]. Though they are semantically similar in terms of their aspect invocation, initialization, access and exception handling routines, they differ in programming constructs, syntax, binding, expressiveness, approaches to advise weaving, static or dynamic analysis, and their overall acceptance in academia and industry. Currently, AspectJ (powered by IBM) is the de facto standard and the most widely used AOPL. Perhaps, this is because it is an extension to Java and takes advantage of Java class libraries and development environments.

None of the these AOPLs and AOFs allow developers to consider a conversation as a context into which cross-cutting concerns may be woven. They all focus on either compile-time contexts, like methods and classes) or primitive run-time contexts, like the objects and call stacks. To allow conversations to be contexts, without forcing programmers to create the necessary infrastructure manually as part of the application code, an AOF for communications would have to define model of communications and then automatically track individual conversations.

C. Communications, Conversations, and Protocols

In general, inter-process communications are either connection-oriented or connectionless. Connection-oriented communications require two concurrent processes to establish a communication link before exchanging data. This style of communication is very much like a person-to-person telephone call. In contrast, with connectionless communications, one process can send a message to another process without knowing whether that process is ready to receive the message or if it even exists yet. This style of communication is like traditional postal mail. Communication subsystems or libraries, like the JDK's Channels and Sockets, typically support both styles of communication.

A conversation is a series of interactions between two or more processes for some purpose. It may include the formation of a connection (only for connection-oriented communications), exchange of messages among the processes, and the termination of the connection (again, only for connection-oriented communications). A conversation is like a phone call with a doctor's office to setup an appointment or a series for postal mailings that were necessary for the signing of a contract. Conversations can last for just a millisecond or go on for days.

Like a formal interaction between two parties signing a contract, an electronic conversation between processes follows a protocol that governs the expected behavior of the participating processes. Some protocols are symmetrical, meaning that all participants follow the same rules. However, it is more common for protocols to be asymmetrical, meaning that each participant acts according to the role it is playing. Many protocols, like the Passive FTP example mentioned earlier, involve two roles: a conversation initiator and responder. Sometimes, these roles are simply referred to as client and server. However, these terms have broader meanings that imply other software architectural issues beyond communications, so we avoid them here.

Implementations of communication details can vary depending on the underlying communication libraries, e.g., Channels and Sockets. These differences are, however, only of secondary importance and can be easily supported by different adapters in CommJ implementation. So, further explanation of diversity and subtleties of the various communication implementation techniques are beyond the scope of this paper.

D. Crosscutting Concerns in Communications

Despite AspectJ's rich set of pointcut designators, there is still a weakness relative to weaving crosscutting concerns into communications. Specifically, AspectJ and any other similar AOPLs or AOFs do not work with conversations directly. Specifically, they do not track individual conversation contexts or link together messages of the same conversation. Consequently, programmers cannot weave behaviors directly into individual conversations. Furthermore, since the execution of conversation may be spread across multiple software components and multiple threads, tracking individual conversations is beyond what language-construct-based aspect weaving can accomplish.

Consider a communication-related crosscutting concern that involves tracking the total time for all connectionless conversations in a distributed application. If a programmer wants to implement crosscutting concern in AspectJ, he or she would have to implement some advice for the conversation's initiation that would capture the time when the first message was sent, as well as other advice that would capture the time when the last message was received and then compare the two times. However, send and receive logic for the conversation may be in separate code modules, may be separated in the execution flow by an unpredictable amount of time, and may even be handled on separate execution threads. Furthermore, a process may start or participate in many conversations at the same time, and the advice would have to manually correlate the first message of particular conversation with the last message of that conversation. In a nutshell, the programmer would have to build all of the message tracking and correlation objects into the aspect and its advice.

III. COMMJ

To enable the weaving of advice into individual conversations, we first define a general model, i.e., the Universe Model of Communication (UMC), for connection-oriented and connectionless communications and use it as a basis for formalizing the notation of communication joinpoints. We then implement CommJ according to the

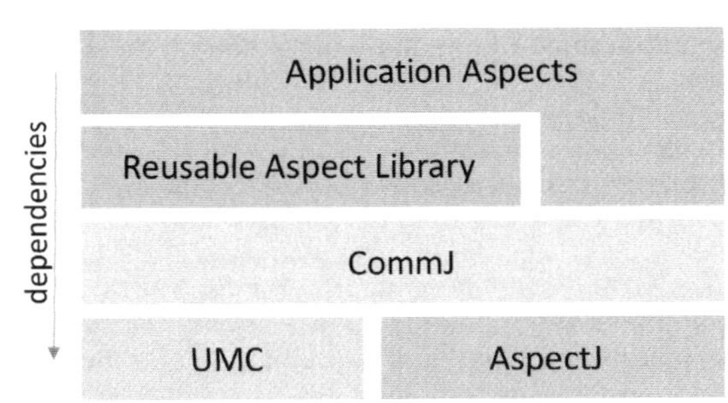

Figure 2. CommJ and its associated components

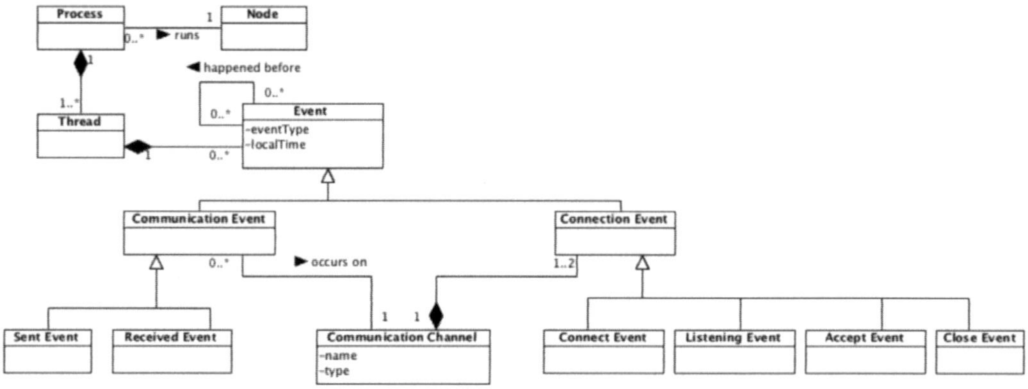

Figure 3. UMC for Events

UMC and on top of the aspect capabilities provided by AspectJ (see Figure 2). The CommJ implementation provides a) base aspects with abstract pointcuts for communications, independent of the underlying communications subsystem and b) behind-the-sense components to track individual conversation contexts at runtime. Application programmers simply include the CommJ library into their build and create their own communication aspects that inherit from the base CommJ aspects. To help them integrate common communication-related cross-cutting concerns into their application, we also provide a Reusable Aspect Library (RAL). The rest of this section describes the communications model, communication joinpoints, and the CommJ library in more detail. Then Section IV highlights some of the aspects in the RAL and shows how that can be used in a sample application.

A. A Universe Model of Communications

The UMC describes a minimal set of general concepts that cover both connection-oriented and connectionless communications provided by most communication systems. In doing so, it models events, threads, messages, conversations, and protocols, as well as the relationships among these concepts.

1) Events

An event can be described as the happening of something. The UMC contains three event types: Communication Event, Connection Event, and Exception Event (not shown in Figure 3). A Communication Event is the happening of something (related to send or receive) in message-based communications, at a particular point in time. It is further divided in two types: Communication Send Event and Communication Receive Event, respectively. The UMC states that every receive event must have a corresponding send event. In other words, a send event can exist without a receive event but not conversely. Communication Events also exhibit one more special characteristic, namely they can relate to each other; an event can contain or be associated with many other events. For example, in a distributed application, a thread T1 can send a message which corresponds to a send event. Eventually, that can lead to a receive-message event on some other thread T2. The relation between these two events is modeled by the "happened before" relationship on Event in Figure 3.

Connection Events are happenings related to the setting up of communication channels, and are specialized into four types:

- A Connect Event occurs when an initiator sends the connect request to a responder
- An Accept Event occurs when a responder accepts a connect request from an initiator
- A Listen Event occurs when a responder listens for incoming data
- A Close Event occurs when a responder or an initiator closes the connection

UMC does not need to include exception events explicitly because AspectJ already defines a rich set of pointcuts for defining crosscutting concerns that involve exceptions.

A Thread can instantiate and encapsulate multiple send or receives events. A Communication Event can be associated with at most one thread. One process can have multiple threads, and a node can host multiple processes. In communication systems, an application may be using multiple nodes, each with several processes, which in turn may have multiple threads.

2) Conversations

In general, a conversation from single process's perspective is a sequence of messages that follow communication rules that either comprise all or part of exchange with other process:

A. an entire conversion from a process's perspective (see the bracket sequence, A, in Figure 4)
B. any sequence of send or receive events in the conversation as seen by a process (see B in Figure 4)
C. a single send or receive event in a conversation (C in Figure 4)

In Figure 5, we see that each conversation in UMC can use a set of Communication Events. A Communication Event occurs on a Communication Channel and is indirectly

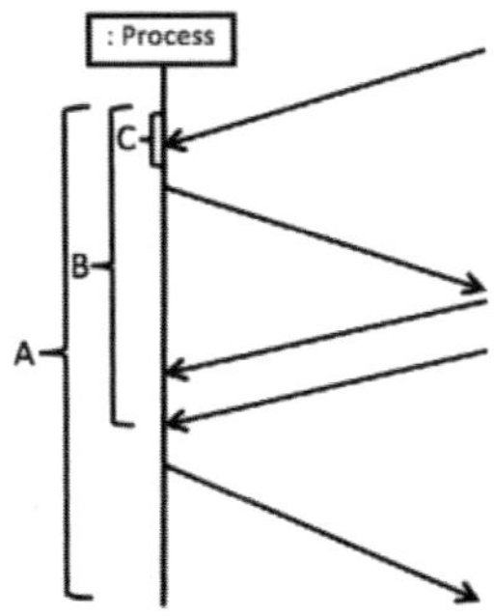

Figure 4. Conversations in *UMC*

associated with a protocol through it conversation to which the event belongs. A conversation is also capable of keeping track of Communication Events that occur in a multithreaded application with multiple channels.

With CommJ, a distributed application can consider a conversation all or just subset of the messages exchanged between specific processes, previously illustrated in Figure 4. This gives developer a freedom to organize the conversations in a manner that seems appropriate for the application and the freedom to use virtual any kind of communication protocol or pattern.

3) Channel

Every Conversation happens on a Channel (Figure 5). A Channel also acts as a way of connecting the Communication Events with the Connection Events. In addition, a Channel also abstracts the underlying network-specific components, e.g., JDK's Sockets and Channels, into higher level concepts that are consistent across platforms. In design pattern terms, the UMC's Communication Channel is like an Adapter [12] to underlying communication mechanisms, but for crosscutting concern.

4) Messages

A message is a class that encapsulates data exchanged during IPC. Processes or threads in communication systems exchange data through events invocations in UMC. Communication Events are strongly associated with Message instances in the model. Each Message can be associated with at most one send and one receive event. Further, Messages and Communication Events follow similar specialization hierarchies; from a process's perspective both are specialized into send and receive types. An instance of Message received keeps track of its Received Event, and a Message sent knows about its Sent Event.

All CommJ applications derive their specific message classes from the base Message class (see Figure 6), which is in the CommJ Infrastructure. The Message class contains getter and setter methods for the properties shown in Figure 6. Collectively, the first five properties are referred to Message Identifying Information (MIF). These five elements provide the necessary information to identify the context of any message, thus enabling CommJ to create and manage conversation metadata, represented by the Conversation class in Figure 5.

The CommJ Infrastructure implements abstract Message with an interface, call IMessage. CommJ then dynamically introduces it into the core software during aspect initialize (see Section IV.A). The interface IMessage is the only direct dependency between the core application and CommJ.

5) Connections

A process may be acting in the role of a sender or receiver while handling communication events and as an initiator or a responder while handling connection events. An initiator can handle only connect and close events, whereas a responder can handle listen, accept and close events, respectively. Figure 7 illustrates the connection-related concepts in UMC.

IV. COMMJ ASPECT LIBRARY AND SAMPLE APPLICATION

This section describes the general architecture of CommJ along with some fundamental concepts, mostly about low-level design and implementations. Finally, it discusses some sample applications, developed using CommJ.

A. Joinpoints

The UMC serves as a foundation for formalizing communication joinpoints, which fall into two general categories: communication joint points and connection-related join points, respectively.

1) Communication Joinpoints

Joinpoints represent places and times where/when advice can be executed. In *AspectJ*, they correspond to constructors, methods, attributes, and exceptions. Advice can be executed before, after, or around these various contexts. *CommJ* adds

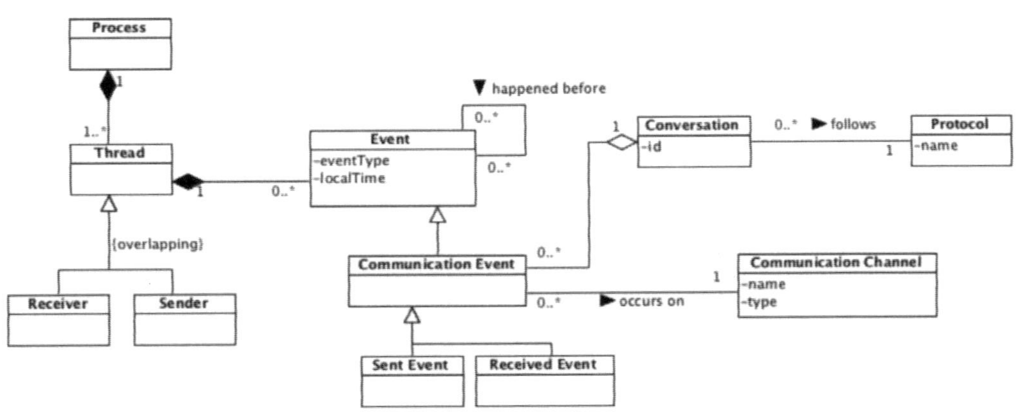

Figure 5. UMC for Conversations

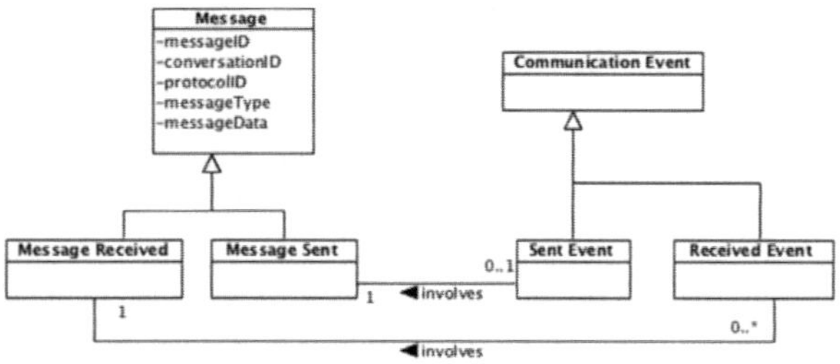

Figure 6. UMC for Messages

conversations to AspectJ as possible contexts. Unlike AspectJ contexts, however, a conversation is not tied to a single programming construct but to the runtime abstraction of an inter-process conversation.

Figure 8 represents different kinds of message related joinpoints in *CommJ*. A Send Event JP, is the region of code, where advice can be woven into, when a communication event related to sending of data, occurs in a process or thread, where as a Receive Event JP is related to receiving of data respectively. Request Reply Conversation JP, represents a joinpoint for complete conversations, but they follow basic request-reply protocols. It contains a Send Event JP and a Receive Event JP. A Send Event JP keeps track of message Id whereas a receive Event JP records a response Id for a request-reply type of conversation. An initialization aspect dynamically introduces MIF information for all CommJ joinpoints. While sending a message, CommJ creates an instance of a Send Event JP and adds it to the communication registry, which contains communication joint points. Similarly on receiving a message, it creates an instance of a Receive Event JP and finds a Send Event JP from the registry where the message Id of the former equals the response Id of the later. Finally, Multi-step Conversion JP, represents joinpoints for across multiple events or for entire conversations. Multiple send and receive events are modeled using a state machine in a Multi-step Conversation JP.

2) *Connection Joinpoints*

The other types of joinpoints are connection-related sequence of events such as connect, accept, listen, and close events. Connection joinpoints in CommJ are either owned by an initiator or a responder (see Figure 9 for more details about the following types of connection-related joinpoints in *CommJ*).

An initiator creates a Connect Event JP. It encapsulates the connection information related to underlying sockets and

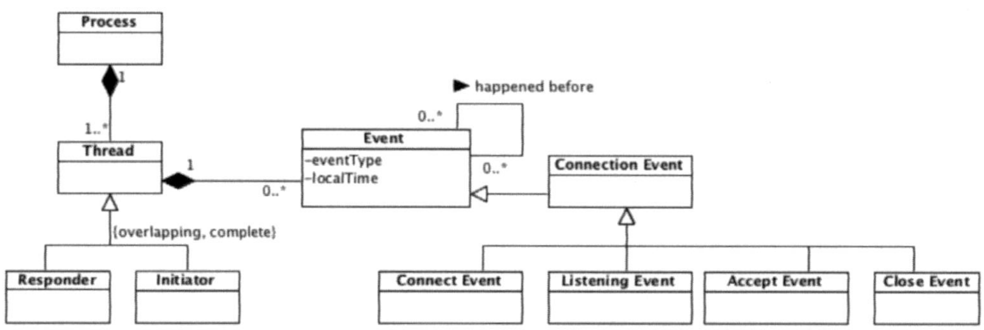

Figure 7. UMC for Connections

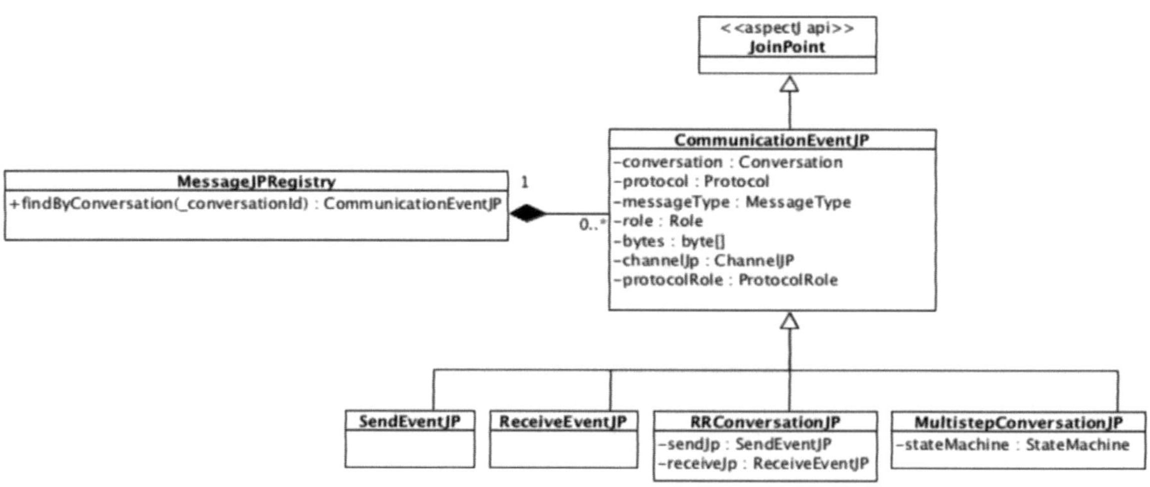

Figure 8. Communication Joinpoint and Registry

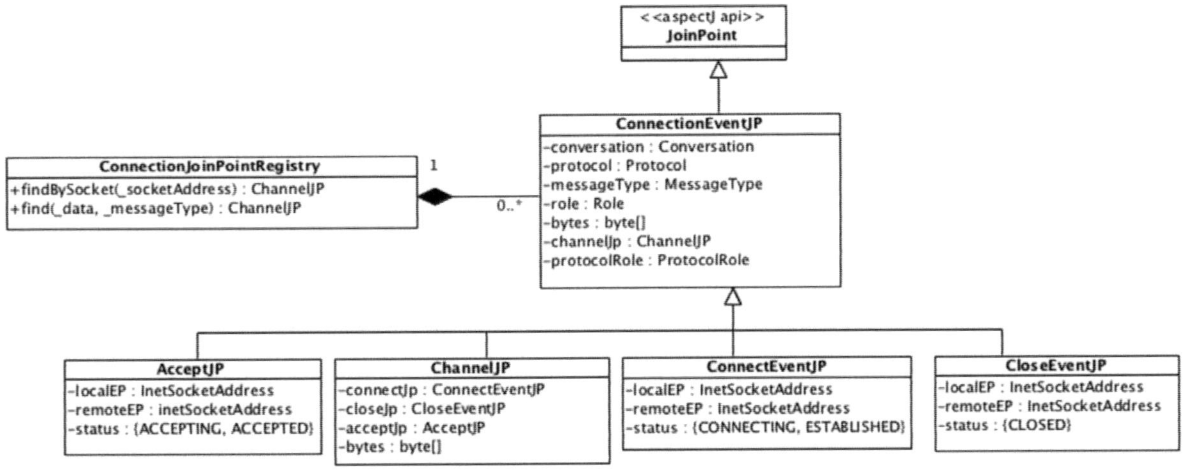

Figure 9. Connection Joinpoint and Registry

channels along with their local and remote addresses. Responder creates an Accept JP on receiving a connection request from the initiator. Both the initiator and responder instantiate a Close Event JP when a connection closes.

Channel JP acts like a bridge between communication joinpoints and connection joinpoints. It also maintains links between a responder Accept JP and an initiator Connect Event JP. Additionally, a Channel JP Registry is used to correlate different connection-related events that belong to the same conversation.

B. *Joinpoint Trackers*

Behind the scenes, CommJ relies on JoinpointTrackers, which are monitors [13] that perform pattern matching on communication events and connection events to track individual events and to organize them into high-level conversation contexts. Since the monitoring of communications is itself a crosscutting concern, Joinpoint Trackers are implemented as aspects that weave the necessary monitoring logic into places where a communication event may take place. In CommJ, there can be two types of event trackers: message-joinpoint trackers and connection-joinpoint tracker.

1) *Message Joinpoint Trackers*

The Message Joinpoint Tracker (see Figure 10) crosscuts the send and receive events for both reliable and unreliable communications in the core application and defines a set of pointcuts in the simple send and receive abstractions. Message Joinpoint Tracker is an aspect that hides communication related abstractions in the core application.

The Message Joinpoint Tracker aspect defines pointcuts in the send and receive abstractions (Figure 11) by overcoming the syntactic and semantic variations, defined in JDK Sockets and Channels libraries. It provides simple and elegant communication pointcuts, which are rich enough to encapsulate abstractions for both connection-oriented and connectionless protocols. Hence, Message Joinpoint Tracker creates two clean, well-encapsulated communications related

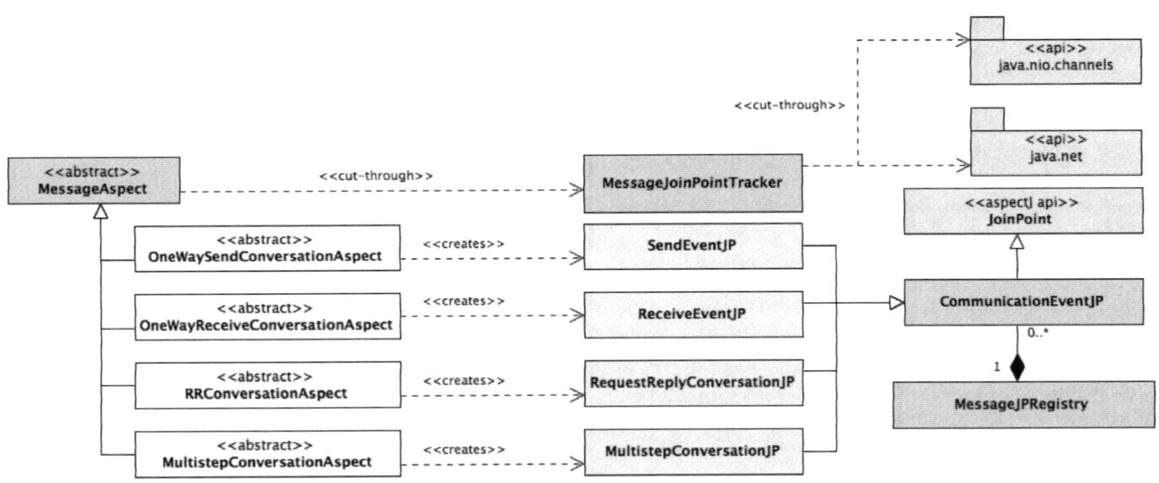

Figure 10. *CommJ* Message Event Join Points and Reusable Aspects

```
public aspect MessageJoinPointTracker {

  private pointcut SocketRead(Socket _socket, byte[] _buffer, int _len) :
    call(* Socket+.read(byte[], ..)) && target(_socket) && args(_buffer, _len);

  private pointcut ChannelRead(SocketChannel _channel, ByteBuffer _buffer) :
    call(* SocketChannel+.read(ByteBuffer)) && target(_channel) && args(_buffer) ||
    call(* DatagramChannel+.receive(ByteBuffer)) && target(_channel) && args(_buffer) ;

  public pointcut SocketWrite(Socket _socket, byte[] _data, int _length) :
    call(void Socket+.write(byte[], int)) && target(_socket) && args(_data, _length);

  public pointcut ChannelWrite(SocketChannel _channel, ByteBuffer _data) :
    call(* SocketChannel+.write(ByteBuffer)) && target(_channel) && args(_data);

  public pointcut DatagramChannelWrite(DatagramChannel _channel, ByteBuffer _data, SocketAddress _addr) :
    call(* DatagramChannel+.send(ByteBuffer, SocketAddress)) && target(_channel) && args(_data, _addr) ;

  private pointcut DatagramChannelRead(DatagramChannel _channel, ByteBuffer _buffer) :
    call(* DatagramChannel+.receive(ByteBuffer)) && target(_channel) && args(_buffer) ||
    call(* DatagramChannel+.read(ByteBuffer)) && target(_channel) && args(_buffer);
                                    ....
                                    }
```

Figure 11. *CommJ* Message Event Join Points and Aspects

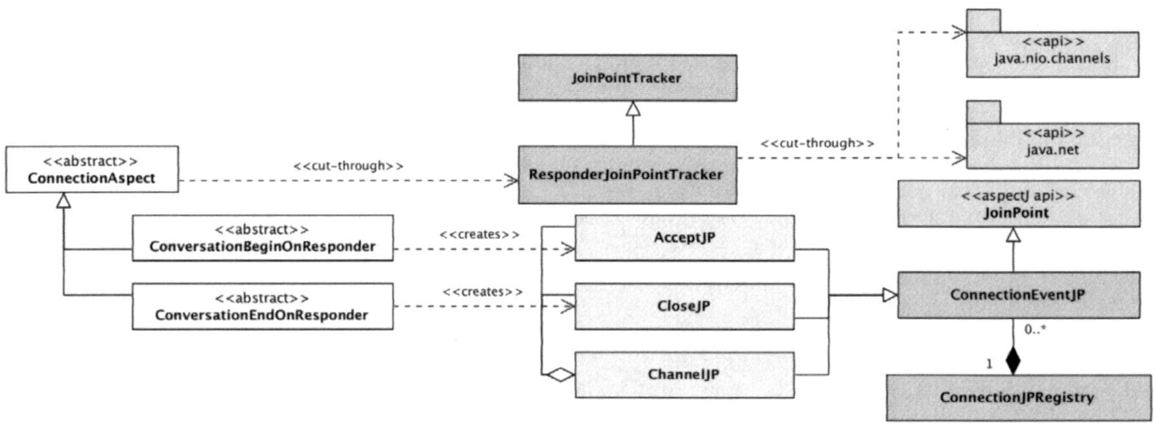

Figure 12. Responder Joinpoint and Base Aspects

abstractions for all types of read and write operations.

2) *Connection Joinpoint Trackers*

The Message Joinpoint trackers are categorized into Initiator Joinpoint Tracker and Responder Joinpoint Tracker, which crosscut the syntactic and semantic variations, exist in both reliable and unreliable communications, and unify them into a set of pointcuts in the abstractions of channel, connect, accept and close.

The Responder Joinpoint Tracker, defines two simple pointcuts, i.e., Accept and Close, where Initiator Joinpoint Tracker, defines three pointcuts, i.e., Channel Connect, Channel Connect Finish and Channel Close pointcuts. These two trackers manage all connection-related abstractions and styles related to both the responder and initiator for connectionless and connection-oriented communications. Figures 12 & 14 describe the general architecture of responder and initiator, and Figures 13 & 15 present their code snippets.

```
public aspect ResponderJoinPointTracker {
  private pointcut SocketAccept(Socket _socket, InetSocketAddress _remoteEP):
    call(* Socket+.accept(..)) && target(_socket) && args(_remoteEP);

  pointcut ChannelAccept(ServerSocketChannel _serverSocketChannel) :
    call(* ServerSocketChannel+.accept()) && target(_serverSocketChannel) ;


  pointcut ChannelClose(ServerSocketChannel _serverSocketChannel) :
    call(* ServerSocketChannel.close()) && target(_serverSocketChannel);


  public pointcut ChannelOpen(DatagramChannel _channel, SocketAddress _addr) :
    call(* DatagramChannel.bind(..)) && target(_channel) && args(_addr);
  ...
}
```

Figure 13. A Code Snippet of *ResponderJoinPointTracker*

C. *Base Aspects*

The CommJ Infrastructure implements high-level IPC abstractions as base aspects, which fall into two categories, i.e., Communication aspects and Connection aspects. They

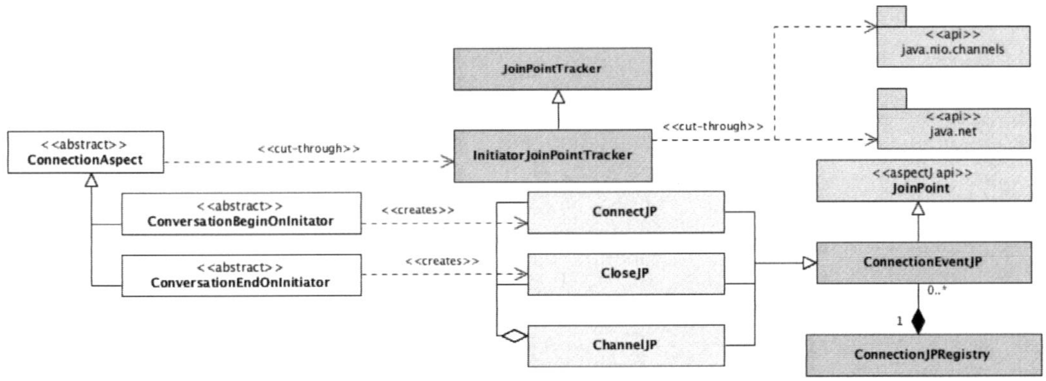

Figure 14. Connection Joinpoint and Base Aspects

```
public aspect InitiatorJoinPointTracker {

  private pointcut SocketConnectStyle1():
    call(Socket.new());

  private pointcut SocketConnectStyle2(InetAddress _address, int _port):
    call(Socket+.new(InetAddress, int)) && args(_address, _port);

  private pointcut SocketConnectStyle4(String _host, int _port):
    call(Socket.new(String, int)) && args(_host, _port);

  private pointcut SocketConnectStyle5(Socket _socket, InetSocketAddress _endPoint):
    call(void Socket+.connect(SocketAddress)) && target(_socket) && args(_endPoint);

  pointcut ChannelConnect(SocketChannel _socketChannel, InetSocketAddress _remoteEP) :
    call(* SocketChannel.connect(..)) && target(_socketChannel) && args(_remoteEP);

  pointcut ChannelConnectFinish(SocketChannel _socketChannel) :
    call(* SocketChannel+.finishConnect(..)) && target(_socketChannel);

  private pointcut SocketClose(Socket _socket):
    call(* Socket+.close(..)) && target(_socket);

  pointcut ClientChannelClose(SocketChannel _channel) :
    call(* SocketChannel.close()) && target(_channel);
  ...
}
```

Figure 15. A Code Snippet of *InitiatorJoinPointTracker*

cut through their respective joinpoint trackers and provide communication-related crosscutting concerns.

1) Message Aspects

All communication aspects are ultimately derived from the abstract Message Aspect class, which provides concrete pointcuts that dynamically track send and receive events (see Figure 16).

```
public abstract aspect MessageAspect {
   public pointcut MessageSend(SendEventJP jp) ...
   public pointcut MessageRecieve(ReceiveEventJP jp) ...
}
```

Figure 16. Pointcuts in *MessageAspect*

It is important to note that these pointcuts take CommJ joinpoint objects as parameters, because this is how advice is woven into these pointcuts, and can access conversation contexts.

The four specializations of Message Aspect correspond to four different kinds of conversation contexts. Developers can create their own application-level communication aspects that inherit from these aspects and include their own advice based on these pointcuts.

One-way send (OWS). An OWS conversation involves only one send event on the initiator's side. For the initiator, the conversation automatically ends after send event is finished (see Figure 17).

One way receive (OWR). An OWR conversation for a responder involves only one receive event. The conversation automatically ends for the responder after a receive event (see Figure 18).

Bi-directional (Request/Reply style of Conversation). Bi-directional conversations require a successful round-trip of a send and receive events. An RR Conversation Aspect, which applies to bi-directional conversations, defines pointcuts Start Conversation and End Conversation. The Start Conversation creates a Request Reply Conversation JP and starts a conversation when a sender invokes a sent event, the End Conversation retrieves the matching Request Reply Conversation JP from the Message JP Registry and ends a conversation when a Receiver invokes a receive event (see Figure 19 for more details).

Multi-step Conversation. It involves any combination of send and receive events without any specific order. For example, few variations in multi-step conversations are as follows: one send event and multiple receive events; multiple send events and one receive event; multiple send events and multiple receive events or any complex model of send and receive events.

We implemented the multi-step conversation aspect (see Figure 20) by deriving from Message Aspect class and thereby inheriting the Message Send and Message Receive

```
public abstract aspect OneWaySendAspect
                    extends MessageAspect {
   public pointcut ConversationBegin(SendEventJP jp)....
}
```

Figure 17. OneWaySend aspect in RAL

```
public abstract aspect OneWayReceiveAspect
                    extends MessageAspect {
   public pointcut ConversationEnd(ReceiveEventJP jp)....
}
```

Figure 18. OneWayReceive aspect in RAL

```
public abstract aspect RRConversationAspect
                    extends MessageAspect {
   public pointcut ConversationBegin(RRConversationJP jp) ....
   public pointcut ConversationEnd(RRConversationJP jp) ....
         ....
}
```

Figure 19. RRConversation aspect in RAL

```
public  abstract aspect MultistepConversationAspect
                    extends MessageAspect {
 public pointcut ConversationBegin(MultistepConversationJP jp)....
 public pointcut ConversationEnd(MultistepConversationJP jp)....
  ....
}
```

Figure 20. MultistepConversation aspect in RAL

pointcuts. A multistep conversation retrieves message, role, protocol and conversation information from Message class and creates a state machine instance if it does not already exist. During one application session, an aspect may apply several concurrent conversations for one type of state machine (i.e., a protocol as it applies to one role). The context for each conversation is maintained in terms of its own current state and associated state machine instance. In general, there are two types of state machines. Mealy and Moor state machines [19]. Mealy state machine is a finite state machine whose output values are determined both by its current state and the current inputs whereas in the Moore state machine, the output values are determined solely by its current state. Mealy state machines are better suited for CommJ because they can be defined in terms of transitions triggers, which correspond to message events and message types.

The design of the state machine for multistep conversation is shown in Figure 21 and code snippet is in Figure 22. A CommJ state machine has two components: State and Transition. A State encapsulates the state name, whether it is in initial or final state, and its list of transitions. Transition is defined using four basic elements: Action Type, Message Type, From State, and To State. The Action Type is transition trigger and can be either a send or receive action. The Message Type is a filter or guard that specifies what types of messages may trigger the transition. From State defines the state before transition and To State defines the target state after transition.

When an application is loaded into memory, all application-level state machine classes are initialized and stored in State Machine Types - a hash map between application classes and state machine types. The Register methods, declared in abstract state machine and implemented by each application-level state machine, are called when applications are loaded through a static initialization block.

2) Connection Aspects

A Connection Aspect derives from a CommJ base aspect, which crosscuts Responder Joinpoint Tracker and Initiator Joinpoint Tracker pointcuts. The base connection aspect defines the following four pointcuts (see Figure 22):

Connect pointcut. It crosscuts Initiator Joinpoint Tracker connection related pointcut and provides Connect pointcut.

Accept pointcut. It crosscuts Responder Joinpoint Tracker accept related pointcuts and provides an Accept pointcut.

Close Server pointcut. It crosscuts Responder Joinpoint Tracker and provides a Close Server pointcut.

Close Client pointcut. It crosscuts Initiator Joinpoint Tracker "close connection" pointcuts and provides Close Client pointcut.

Complete Connection Conversation. It inherits from Connection Aspect (Figure 23) and defines following

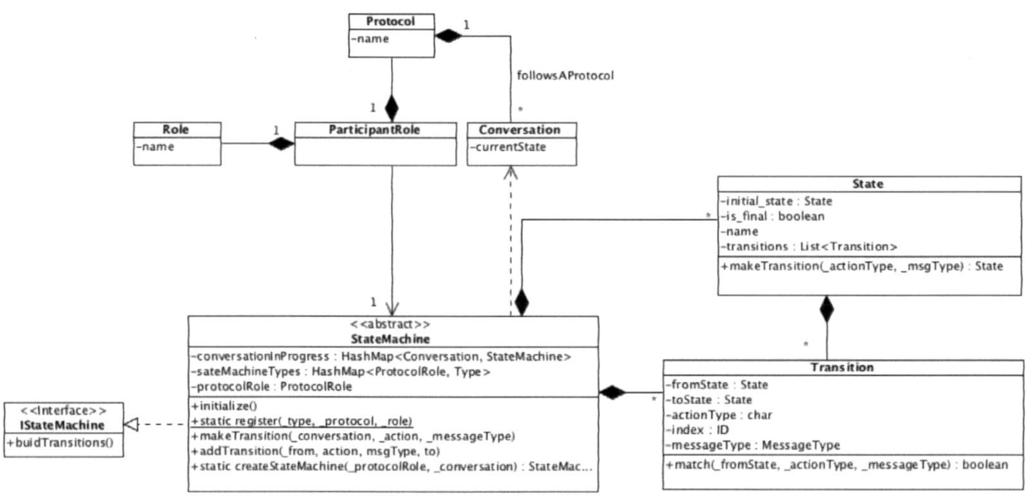

Figure 21. Design of Multi-step State Machine

```
public abstract aspect ConnectionAspect {

  public pointcut Connect(ConnectEventJP _connectJp) :
    within(InitiatorJoinPointTracker) &&
    execution(* InitiatorJoinPointTracker.ChannelConnect(..))
           && args(_connectJp);

  public pointcut Accept(ConnectEventJP _connectJp) :
    within(ListenerJoinPointTracker) &&
    execution(void ResponderJoinPointTracker.ChannelAccept(..))
           && args(_connectJp);

  public pointcut CloseServer(CloseEventJP _closeJp) :
    within(ResponderJoinPointTracker) &&
    execution(void ResponderJoinPointTracker.CloseServerEventJointPoint(..))
           && args(_closeJp);

  public pointcut CloseClient(CloseEventJP _closeJp) :
    within(InitiatorJoinPointTracker) &&
    execution(void InitiatorJoinPointTracker.CloseClientEventJointPoint(..))
           && args(_closeJp);
}
```

Figure 22. A Code Snippet of *Connection* Aspect

```
public abstract aspect CompleteConnectionAspect extends ConnectionAspect {

  public pointcut ConversationBeginOnInitiator(ChannelJP _channelJp) :
    execution(* CompleteConnectionAspect.BeginOnInitiator(ChannelJP)) &&
args(_channelJp);
  public pointcut ConversationBeginOnResponder(ChannelJP _channelJp) :
    execution(* CompleteConnectionAspect.BeginOnListner(ChannelJP)) &&
           args(_channelJp);

  public pointcut ConversationEndOnResponder(ChannelJP _channelJp) :
    execution(* CompleteConnectionAspect.EndResponder(ChannelJP)) &&
           args(_channelJp);

  public pointcut ConversationEndOnInitiator(ChannelJP _channelJp) :
    execution(* CompleteConnectionAspect.EndInitiator(ChannelJP)) &&
           args(_channelJp);

  ...
}
```

Figure 23. A Code Snippet of *Complete Connection* Aspect

```
public aspect TotalTurnAroundTimeMonitor
         extends MultistepConversationAspect{
  private long startTime = 0;
  private long turnAroundTime = 0;
  before(MultistepConversationJP jp): ConversationBegin(jp){
       startTime = System.currentTimeMillis();
       Begin(jp);
  }
  after(MultistepConversationJP jp): ConversationEnd(jp){
       long turnaroundTime = (System.currentTimeMillis() –
                startTime)/1000;
       End(multiStepJP);
  }
  public getTurnAroundTime { return turnAroundTime; }
  protected void Begin(MultistepConversationJP jp){
       // Specialization of this aspect should override the method
  }
  protected void End(MultistepConversationJP jp){
       // Specialization of this aspect should override the method
  }
  ...
}
```

Figure 24. A code snippet of *Total Turn Around Time Monitor*

pointcuts that help programmers to define conversations for total connection time on both responder and initiator sides.

The Conversation Begin On Initiator and Conversation End On Initiator pointcuts crosscut the state of request to establish and end a connection on the initiator.

The Conversation Begin On Responder and Conversation End On Responder pointcuts mark the start and end of connection related conversation on the responder.

We also define a helping initialization aspect, which loads application specific state machines and introduces conversation, role, protocol and message identity information before the application sends or receives any messages.

D. *Re-usable Aspect Library (RAL)*

Aspects in the RAL are also derived from the base aspects in CommJ. They represent general crosscutting concerns commonly found in applications with significant communication requirements. Figure 24 shows part of the implementation of first one, i.e., Total Turn Around Time Monitor. Note how the advice in this aspect follows the Template Method pattern [12]. This allows developers to quickly adapt it to the specific needs of their application by overriding the Begin and End methods. Other aspects in the RAL make use of this and other reuse techniques so developer can easily integrate them into existing or new applications. We expect that RAL will continue to grow as new generally applicable communication aspects are discovered, implemented, and documented.

E. *Application-level Aspects*

This section provides four examples of communication and connection related crosscutting concerns implemented with CommJ.

1) Measure Performance in Multi-step Conversation Process

This example discusses the design and implementation of measuring the total turnaround time for a multistep conversation. Consider a communication protocol involving three processes, *A*, *B*, and *C*, wherein A starts a conversation by sending a message to *B* and waits for a response. When *A* receives a response from *B*, it sends a message to *C* and waits for a response. When *A* receives a response from *C*, it sends a final message to both *B* and *C*. Figure 25 shows a finite state machine for the *A Process Role* of this protocol. The behaviors for *B* and *C Process Roles* are considerably simpler and are shown in Figures 26 and 27, respectively.

The CommJ State Machine class includes a Build Transitions method that allows developers to define state machines in terms of states and message-event transitions. Figure 28 shows the implementation of this method to define a State Machine for the A Process Role

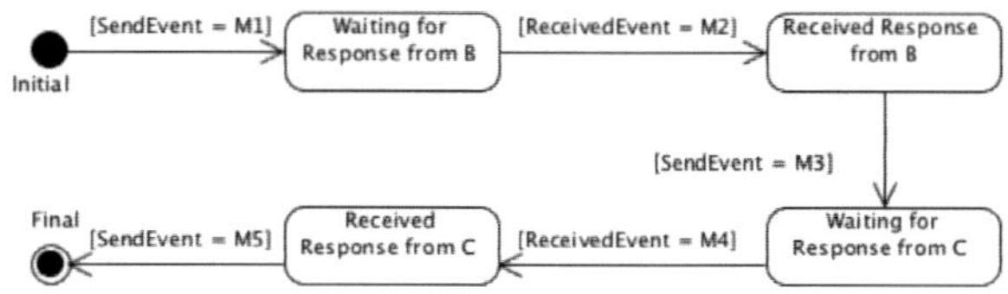

Figure 25. State Machine for the *A ProcessRole*

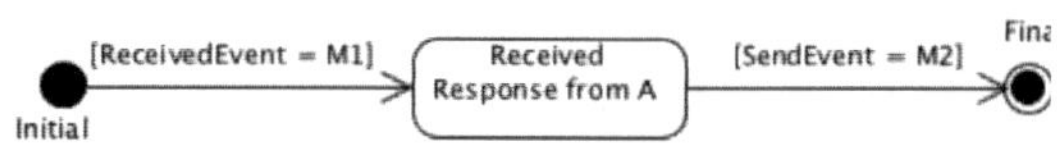

Figure 26. State Machine for the *B ProcessRole*

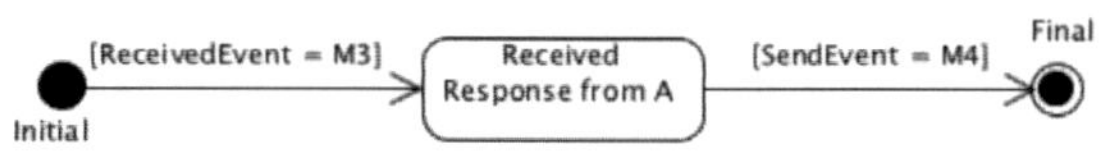

Figure 27. State Machine for the *C ProcessRole*

```
public aspect ProcessRoleA extends StateMachine{
....
 @Override
 public void buildTransitions(){
  addTransition("Initial", "S", "M1", "WaitingRspFromB");
  addTransition("WaitingRspFromB", "R", "M2", "ReceivedRspFromB");
  addTransition("ReceivedRspFromB", "S", "M3", "WaitingRspFromC");
  addTransition("WaitingRspFromC", "R", "M4", "ReceivedRspFromC");
  addTransition("ReceivedRspFromC", "S", "M5", "Final");
 }
 ....
}
```

Figure 28. State Machine Configuration for ProcessRoleA

For discussion purposes, assume that the performance measurements are a rolling window of throughput and average-conversation turn-around time statistics. Also, assume that the core application considers a unit of work to be the completion of a conversation that follows this protocol. So, throughput can be measured for a unit of time, say 1 minute, by simply counting the number of these conversations completed in 1 minute. The average turn-around time is the average of timespans from conversations start times to conversations end times. The rolling window keeps track of these statistics for the current minute and the 10 previous minutes. Figure 29 shows the key pieces of code for an aspect that implement this performance measure crosscutting concern.

First notice how the aspect is derived from Total Turn Around Time Aspect and in doing so, it can reuse its implementation of the conversation turnaround time concept directly. Then, it adds the Stats array for holding the rolling window of statistics and some additional behavior to the ending of a conversation to compute the statistics.

2) Version Control Aspect

This example discusses the design and implementation of an aspect that can coordinate communications when different processes are following different versions of a protocol. Imagine that the protocol discussed in the previous example has evolved over time, resulting in multiple versions of the messages' syntax. If process A is following the updated

```
public aspect MyAppPerformanceMonitor
        extends TotalTurnAroundTimeMonitor {

 private ArrayList<Stats> statsList = new ArrayList(11);
 private int currentStatsIndex = 0;

 @Override
 public void End(MultistepConversationJP jp) {
  //Get number of elapsed minutes since begining of current Stats
  long elapsedMinutes = Min(Stats[currentStatsIndex]
                             .getMinutesSinceStartTime(),
                             10);
  //Roll Stats window forward, if necessary
  for (int i=0; i<elapsedMinutes; i++) {
   currentStatsIndex++;
   if (currentStatsIndex>10){
    currentStatsIndex=0;
    Stats[currentStatsIndex].Reset();
   }
   currentStats.addCompleteConversation(getTurnaroundTime);
  }
 }

 class Stats {
  private long startTime;
  private int completeConvCount;
  private double avgTurnaround;
  public Stats() {Reset(); }
  public void Reset() {
   startTime = currentTime;
   completeConvCount = 0;
   avgTurnaround = 0;
  }
  public long getMinutesSinceStartTime() {
  //using current time, compute and return the number of minutes
  //since the start time of this Stats object. A zero means we still
  // in the  same minute.
  }
  public void addCompleteConversation(double turnaroundTime) {
   avgTurnaround = ((completeConvCount*avgTurnaround) +
    turnaroundTime)/(++completeConvCount);
  }
 }
}
```

Figure 29. Performance Measure Crosscutting Concern

```
public aspect SendVersionControlAspect
        extends OneWaySendAspect {
 ....
 void around(SendEventJP _sendEventJp):
        ConversationBegin(_sendEventJp){
  //code that check and update the most recent version
  //of messages being sent
  }
}
```

Figure 30. Version Control Aspect for Messages Sent

```
public aspect ReceivedVersionControlAspect
        extends  OneWayReceiveAspect {
 ....
 void around(ReceiveEventJP _receiveEventJp):
        ConversationBegin(_receiveEventJp) {
  //code that check and update the most recent version of
  // received message
  }
}
```

Figure 31. Version Control Aspect for Messages Received

syntax rules and trying to communicate with B or C processes that are following rules from prior versions, there will be communication errors. Ideally, it would be nice to allow seamless independent upgrading to any of the processes without effecting the communications.

The application-level version control aspects in Figures 30 and 31 extend RAL communication aspects discussed in Section IV.C. On sending the messages, One Way Send Aspect ensures that it is sending the most recent version of messages. Similarly, on receiving the messages, OneWayReceiveAspect verifies that received message is also in the most recent version.

3) Logging Responder and Initiator Connection Times for FTP

This section describes aspects for logging responder and initiator connection times for the processes using FTP for file transfer. Assume that an FTP client establishes a TCP connection to an FTP server. Then it requests the server for transferring a file. The server receives the request. If the file is too big to transfer in one send, it divides the file into smaller chunks of fixed block sizes and sends each chunk with its completion status. After sending the final chunk, both the server and client close the connections.

As mentioned above, with FTP, there are two processes: an FTP client and FTP server. The server and client communicate using two messages, i.e., File Transfer Request and File Transfer Response. FTP client sends a File Transfer Request message to FTP server, after a connection has been established between the two processes. The File Transfer Request message contains the requested file name. When FTP server receives the request, it starts sending the response message (File Transfer Response) to the client, which includes the file information, data chunk number and its completion status. Following paragraphs describe related application-level aspects for initiator and responder.

Aspect - Logging Initiator Connection Time. This is an application-level connection aspect, developed using the RAL connection aspect, i.e., Complete Connection Aspect in Section IV.C. It logs the time between initiating connection request to the responder (FTP server) and ending of connection on the initiator (FTP client) using Conversation Begin On Initiator and Conversation End On Initiator pointcuts (see Figure 32).

Aspect - Logging Responder Connection Time. This is an application-level connection aspect, developed using RAL connection aspect, i.e., Complete Connection Aspect in Section IV.C. It logs the time period between acceptance of connection request from initiator and ending of connection on the responder using Conversation Begin On Responder and Conversation End On Responder pointcuts (see Figure 33).

V. EXTENDED QUALITY MODEL

To measure the maintainability and reuse, we use Sant'Anna's Comparison Quality Model (CQM) [21] and extends it with new factors and internal attributes, forming the Extended Quality Model (EQM); see Figure 34. We use Sant'Anna's model because it is more generalized to measure different concerns of reuse and maintenance as compared to Lopes' work [22]. Additionally, this model is strong enough to be applied to different types of implementations, discussed in this paper.

Sant'Anna builds the CQM using Basili's General Quality Methodology (GQM) [23], which provides a three-step framework: (1) list the major goals of the empirical

```
public aspect InitiatorTimeAspect extends CompleteConnectionAspect {
  private long startTime = 0;
  static String timingInfo = "";

  before(ChannelJoinPoint _channelJp) : ConversationBeginOnInitiator(_channelJp) {
    startTime = Systems.currentTimeMillis();
  }

  after(ChannelJoinPoint _channelJp) : ConversationEndOnInitiator(_channelJp) {
    String Time = String.format("%.3g%n", bew Double(System.currentTimeMillis() - startTime)/1000);
    timingInfo = "Total Time of Initiator " + thisJoinPointStaticPart.getSignature().getName() + " localEP "
                    + channelJp.getConnectJp().getLocalEP()
                    + " turn-around time (nano seconds) : " + Time + "\n";
  }
}
```

Figure 32. Third Code Snippet of TurnAroundTimeAspect

```
public aspect ResponderTimeAspect extends CompleteConnectionAspect{
  private long startTime = 0;
  static String timingInfo = "";

  Object around(ChannelJoinPoint _channelJp) : ConversationBeginOnResponder(_channelJp){
    startTime = Systems.currentTimeMillis();
    return proceed(_channelJp);
  }

  Object around(ChannelJoinPoint _channelJp) : ConversationEndOnResponder(_channelJp){
    String Time = String.format("%.3g%n", bew Double(System.currentTimeMillis() - startTime)/1000);
    timingInfo = "Total Time of responder " + thisJoinPointStaticPart.getSignature().getName()
                    + " localEP turn-around time (nano seconds) : " + Time + "\n";
    return proceed(_channelJp);
  }
}
```

Figure 33. Fourth Code Snippet of TurnAroundTimeAspect

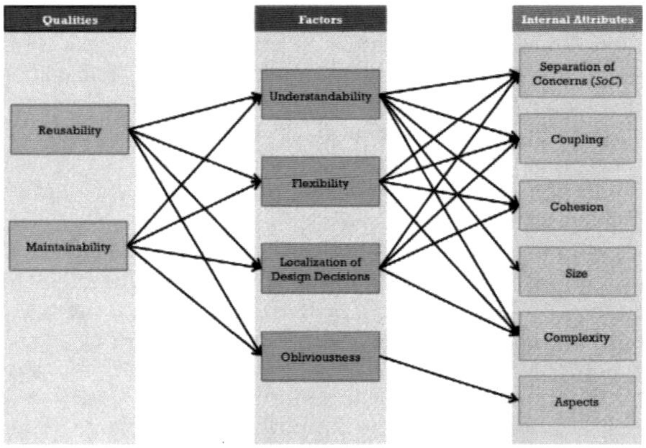

Figure 34. Extended Quality Model (*EQM)*

study, (2) derive from each goal the questions that must be answered to determine if the goals have been met, and (3) decide what must be measured to be able to answer the questions adequately.

Santa'Anna organized the CQM into four components: qualities, factors, attributes, and metrics. The qualities are the high level characteristics that we want to primarily observe in our software. Factors are the secondary quality attributes (more granular than qualities) that influence the defined primary attributes, i.e., qualities. Internal attributes are properties of software systems related to well-established software-engineering principles, which in turn are essential to the achievement of the qualities and their respective internal factors. Finally, the metrics are ways to measure the attribute.

We also made a few enhancements in EQM and believe that doing so will further strengthen the model. First, our model creates a dependency of maintainability and reusability upon flexibility and understandability factors. Secondly, because our experiment involves crosscutting concerns, so we introduced two important missing factors, i.e., code obliviousness [24] and localization of design decisions [25]. Research and practice also validate that modular code is more maintainable [26] when obliviousness and localization of design decisions are present.

A. Qualities

Qualities are the highest level of abstractions in EQM. For our experiment with CommJ, we considered maintainability and reusability would be the two most important qualities to focus on.

- Reusability: Reusability exists for a given software element, when developers can use it for the construction of other elements or systems [27].
- Maintainability: Maintainability is the activity of modifying a software system after initial delivery [28]. It is the ease with which software components can be modified.

B. Factors

Following are the list of factors in our EQM.

- Understandability: indicates the level of difficulty for studying and understanding a system design and code.
- Flexibility: indicates the level of difficulty for making drastic changes to one component in a system without any need to change others.
- Localization of Design Decisions: indicates the level of information hiding for a component's internal design decisions. Hence, it is possible to make material changes to the implementation of a component without violating the interface [29].
- Obliviousness: is a special form of low coupling wherein base application functionality has no dependencies on crosscutting concerns [21].

Localization of design decisions, and code obliviousness were not part of CQM. However, we introduced them into our EQM for two reasons. First, in his landmark paper [25], Parnas proposes three important characteristics of modular code: understandability, flexibility and localization of design decisions (information hiding). Hence, reasoning maintainability and reusability only in terms of understandability and flexibility is not complete. Introduction of localization of design decisions is also equally important. Second, by the time Parnas proposed the definition of modular code, obliviousness had not been invented as a fundamental design principle. However, in the context of our research experiment, which depends heavily on measuring crosscutting concerns, code obliviousness becomes critical.

C. Attributes

Following are the internal attributes in our EQM.

- Separation of Concerns (SoC): defines ability to identify, encapsulate and manipulate those parts of software that are relevant to a particular concern.
- Coupling: is an indication of the strength of interconnections between the components in a system. In other words, it measures number of collaborations between components or number of messages passed between components.
- Cohesion: is a measure of the closeness of relationship among the internal components of a method, class, subsystem, etc.
- Size: represents the length of a software system's design and code.
- Complexity: characterizes how and how much components are structurally interrelated to one another.
- Tangling: exists when a single component includes functionality for two or more concerns, and those concerns could be reasonably separated into their own components.
- Scattering: exists when two or more components include similar logic to accomplish the same or similar activities. The most serious causes of scattering occur when design decisions have not been properly localized.

D. Measurement Metrics

Figure 35 presents the metrics the EQM uses to measure each of the internal attributes. Detail descriptions of these metrics follow below.

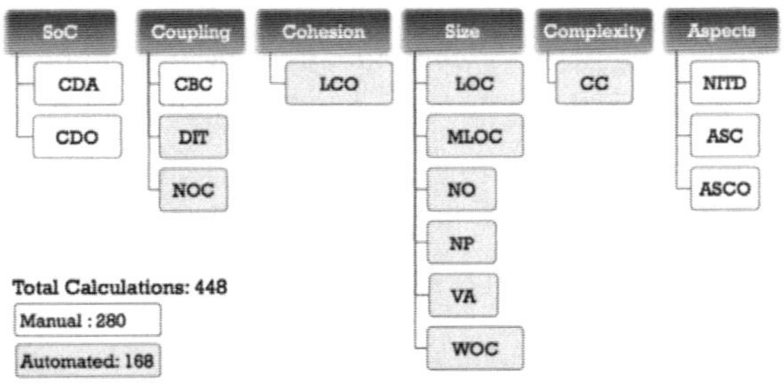

Figure 35. Measurement Metrics in *EQM*.

1) SoC Metrics

EQM includes the following metrics for SoC and code scattering: Concern Diffusion of Application (CDA) and Concern Diffusion over Operations (CDO). CDA counts the number of primary components (a class or aspect) whose main purpose is to contribute to the implementation of a concern. It counts the number of components that access the primary components by using them in attribute declarations, formal parameters, return types or method calls. CDO counts the number of primary operations whose main purpose is to contribute to the implementation of a concern. It also counts the number of methods and advices that access any primary component by calling their methods or using them in formal parameters, return types, and it throws declarations and local variables. Constructors also are counted as operations.

2) Coupling Metrics

The EQM uses the following metrics for measuring coupling: Coupling between Components (CBC), Depth Inheritance Tree (DIT) and Number of Children (NOC). CBC counts the number of other classes and aspects to which a class or an aspect is coupled. On the other hand, excessive coupling of AspectJ concerns increases to CBC, which can be detrimental to the modular design and prevent reuse and maintenance. DIT counts how far down in the inheritance hierarchy a class or aspect is declared. As DIT grows, the lower-level components inherit or override many methods. This leads to difficulties in understanding the code and design complexity when attempting to predict the behavior of a component. NOC counts the number of children for each class or aspect. The subcomponents that are immediately subordinate to a component in the component hierarchy are termed as its children. However, as NOC increases, the abstraction represented by the parent component can be diluted if some of the children are not appropriate members of the parent component.

3) Cohesion Metrics

The EQM uses the Lack of Cohesion in Operations (LCO) for measuring cohesion and tangling among components.

Specifically, LCO measures the lack of cohesion of a class or aspect by looking at lines of code within method and advice pairs, which do not access the same instance variables. If the related methods do not access the same instance variable, they logically represent unrelated components and hence should be separated.

4) Complexity Metrics

McCabe's Cyclomatic Complexity (CC) [30] is the EQM's chosen metric for measuring complexity. Mathematically, the cyclomatic complexity of a structured program is defined with reference to the control flow graph of the program, a directed graph containing the basic blocks of the program, with an edge between two basic blocks if control may pass from the first to the second. The complexity M is then defined as:

$$M = E - N + 2P$$

Where:
E = the number of edges of the graph
N = the number of nodes of the graph
P = the number of connected components (exit nodes).

CC measures the logical complexity of the program. The metric defines the number of independent paths and provides you with an upper bound for the number of test cases that must be conducted to ensure that all statements have been executed at least once. High value of CC affects program maintenance and reuse.

5) Obliviousness Metrics

The EQM introduces the following new metrics for obliviousness metrics: Number of Inter-type Declarations (NITD), Aspect Scattering over Components (ASC), and Aspect Scattering over Component Operations (ASCO). NITD counts the number of inter-type declarations. A higher value of NITD indicates a tighter coupling between the aspect and application components. ASC counts the number of aspect components scattered over application components. It measures the tangling of aspects in the application components. More tangling of aspects in the program makes the original application less reusable and maintainable. ASCO counts the number of aspect components scattered over application component operations. ASC (discussed above) gives a high-level overview of the application tangling in the aspect components but ASCO provides more insight on operations-level tangling of applications inside aspect components.

6) Size Metrics

The EQM uses the following size metrics: Lines of Code (LOC), Method Lines of Code (MLOC), Number of Operations (NO), Number of Parameters (NP), Vocabulary Size (VA) and Weighted Operations per Component (WOC).

LOC counts the lines of code. The greater the LOC, the more difficult it is to understand the system and harder to manage the software reuse and maintenance. MLOC counts the method lines of code. Kremer [31] states that the greater the average of MLOC for a component, the more complex the component would be. NO counts the number of operations in a component. Objects with large number of operations are less likely to be reused. Sometimes LOC is less but NO is more, which indicates that the component is more complex. NP counts the number of parameters for methods in each class or aspect. NP is an Operation-Oriented Metric. A method with more parameters is assumed to have more complex collaborations and may call many other method(s). VA counts the number of system components, i.e., the number of classes and aspects into the system. Sant' Anna [21] points out that if number of components increase, it is an indication of more cohesive and less tangled set of ADT.

Finally, WOC metric measures the complexity of a component in terms of its operations. WOC does not specify the operation complexity measure, which should be tailored to the specific contexts. The operation complexity measure is obtained by counting the number of parameters of the operation, assuming that an operation with more parameters than another is likely to be more complex. It is an object-oriented design metric, proposed by Kemerer [31] and sums up the complexity of each method. The number of methods and complexity is an indication of how much time and effort is required to develop and maintain the object. The larger the value of weighted operations, the more complex the program would be.

VI. Hypotheses

CommJ's theoretical foundation and design lead to the following seven hypotheses, with respect to comparing the reusability and maintainability of IPC software built with *CommJ* instead of just *AspectJ*.

- *Hypothesis 1:* If crosscutting IPC concerns are effectively encapsulated in *CommJ* aspects, then the software has better *separation of concerns* and less scattering (as described by CDA, CDO in Section V.D.1.) than equivalent systems developed with AOP design techniques.
- *Hypothesis 2:* If crosscutting IPC concerns are encapsulated in *CommJ* aspects, then the software has *lower coupling* (as described by CBC, DIT, NOC in Section V.D.2) than equivalent systems developed with AOP design techniques.
- *Hypothesis 3:* If crosscutting IPC concerns are encapsulated in *CommJ* aspects, then the software has *higher cohesion* and less tangling (as described by LCO in Section V.D.3. than equivalent systems developed with AOP design techniques.
- *Hypothesis 4:* If crosscutting IPC concerns are encapsulated in *CommJ* aspects, then the software is not significantly *complex* (as described by CC in Section V.D.4) than equivalent systems developed with AOP design techniques.
- *Hypothesis 5:* If crosscutting IPC concerns are encapsulated in *CommJ* aspects, then the software is significantly more *oblivious* (as described by NITD, ASC, ASCO in Section V.D.5) than equivalent systems developed with AOP design techniques.
- *Hypothesis 6:* If crosscutting IPC concerns are encapsulated in *CommJ* aspects, then the software is not significantly larger (as described by LOC, MLOC, NO, NP, VA, WOC in Section V.D.6) than equivalent systems developed with AOP design techniques.
- *Hypothesis 7:* If crosscutting communication concerns are encapsulated in *CommJ* aspects, then extension for new requirements touches fewer components or lines of code (as measured by Eclipse IDE diff function) than equivalent systems developed with AOP design techniques.

VII. Experiment Method

The following sections briefly describe the steps of a preliminary experiment that authors used to test the hypotheses.

A. Experimental Planning and Approval

In the first step, we developed a plan and submitted an application for conducting this Human Research Experiment to the IRB [32], and received approval. Each of us also had to pass an online human research experiment-training course offered through Collaborative Institutional Training Initiative (CITI) [33].

B. Selection of Applications and Crosscutting Concerns

We selected sample software applications (see Table I) that were multithreaded, distributed, and used either JDK sockets or channels for communications. The applications were diverse in the way they implemented IPC and therefore provide good coverage of different types of communication heterogeneities. Finally, each application supported more than one communication protocol.

Since the experiment would eventually require developers to modify or extend applications for requirements that represented communication-related crosscutting concerns, our methodology included a step, which systematically selected our representative crosscutting concerns. Developers would have to apply each of these to the applications, individually. Additionally, to minimize noise in our data, we wanted to make sure that these crosscutting concerns were sufficiently simple that novice programmers could understand them and come up with a

TABLE I. SELECTED SAMPLE APPLICATIONS

Application Name	Description
Levenshtein Edit-Distance Calculator (LD)	A server will calculate the LD between two input strings, provided by the client, over a connection-oriented communication.
File Transfer Program (FTP)	A file transfer protocol over connection-oriented communication.
Weather Station Simulator (WS)	A simple weather station simulator, supported by a Transmitter and a Receiver.

TABLE II. SELECTED SAMPLE CROSSCUTTING CONCERNS

Aspect Name	Description
*Version Compatibility***	This concern adapted one version of the message to another, so processes running different versions could still communicate with each other. The crosscutting concern included knowledge of converting one version to another and conversely
*Measuring Performance***	It measured some performance related statistics for message-based communications between a sender and receiver
*Symmetric-Key Encryption***	It encrypted the communication between a sender and receiver using symmetric-key encryption
NetworkNoiseSimulator	Allows developers to add noise, message log, and message duplication to network communications, which is useful for system testing
NetworkLoadBalancer	Helps programmers balance message loads across two more communication channels
MessageLoggingByConversation	Log messages by conversations in a developer-defined format and repository

** Selected cross-cutting concerns for the experiment

solutions in less than 10 hours. We also come up with a list of possible crossing concerns that the subject programmers would have to implement in the applications (See Table II). Those marked with "**" represent the ones selected for the experiment.

C. Recruitment and Training of Participants

To transparently recruit the candidates, we sent invitation letters and recruited seven volunteer developers who met the participation criteria, specifically they were experienced in object-oriented software development, Java, and with software-engineering design principles, such as modularity and reusability. We then randomly organized them into two study groups: A and B. Group A would use AspectJ only and Group B would use CommJ on top of AspectJ. Next, the participants completed a survey that assessed their background and skill levels. We also provided AOP training to developers in Group A, and worked through some practice applications with them. Similarly, we trained Group B developers in CommJ, and worked through some practice applications with them.

D. Experiment Phases

In the first phase, participants filled a pre-implementation questionnaire, developed the application using initial requirements, recorded hourly journals and completed a post implementation questionnaire. In the second phase, we requested enhancements (sample applications and crosscutting concerns), had them revised their implementation accordingly, and then collected those software systems. Participants again completed the pre and post questionnaire and wrote their experiences in the hourly journals.

Finally, after the second phase, we analyzed and evaluated the reusability and maintainability using various software artifacts, which included surveys, questionnaires, hourly journals, and actual code.

We used both manual computation and automated tools to compute measurements for all 16 metrics. Experiment generated a total of 28 software systems. With 16 code metrics in the EQM, we had a total of 448 measurements, 280 computed automatically with a tool [34] and 168 calculated manually.

VIII. EXPERIMENT RESULTS AND CONCLUSIONS

This section presents the data collected from the experiment and our results in context of the seven hypotheses. In the following graphs, the vertical axes represent the measurements, and the horizontal axes represent the activities of the experiment. For each activity there are two bars: a blue bar is for the results of AspectJ-only group and a green bar for CommJ group.

A. Separation of Concerns

Hypothesis #1 theorized that if crosscutting communication concerns are effectively encapsulated in CommJ aspects, the software has better separation of concerns and less scattering as measured by CDA and CDO than equivalent systems developed with AOP design techniques. In other words, the CDA and CDO metric values for CommJ should be less than AspectJ (See Section V.D.1. for details on metrics). We found CDA and CDO did decrease for the CommJ group. In Figure 36, the vertical axes represent the CDA and CDO measurements, and the horizontal axes represent the four activities of the experiment.

Not only were CDA and CDO values reduced using CommJ, but they were zero in all four activities of the experiment. The reason for phenomena is that CommJ pointcuts provide total obliviousness between the application and communication-related crosscutting concern. In AspectJ, components and their operations for crosscutting concern were significantly more diffused in the application because the pointcuts had to be tied to programming constructs instead of communication abstractions.

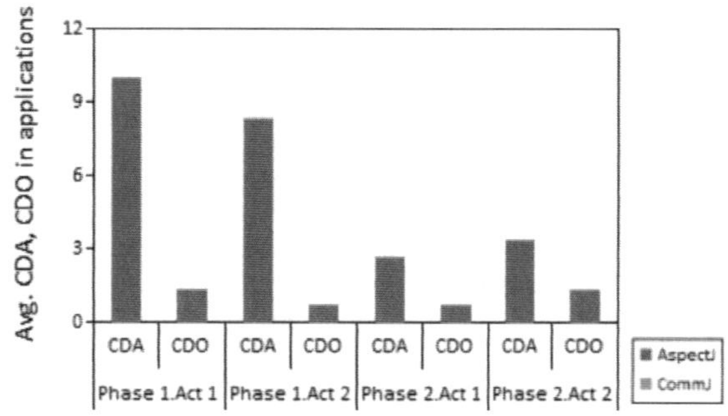

Figure 36. CDA, CDO coverage over phases.

From these results, we can conclude that Hypothesis#1 holds true for better separation of concerns in CommJ implementations than in AspectJ.

B. Coupling

Hypothesis #2 theorized that if crosscutting communication concerns are effectively encapsulated in CommJ aspects, the software has lower coupling as measured by CBC, DIT and NOC than equivalent systems developed with AOP design techniques. In other words, CBC, DIT and NOC metric values for CommJ should be less than AspectJ (see Section V.D.2. for details on metrics). Figure 37 indicates that CommJ implementations significantly reduced the values of CBC, DIT and NOC, respectively, as compared to AspectJ implementations in all the four phases of the experiment. CommJ crosscutting concerns did not maintain any direct relationship with the application components and thus had a lower CBC value. However, in AspectJ, excessive coupling of concern with the application increased CBC, which hindered reuse and maintenance.

The reason for higher DIT and NOC values in AspectJ was that the participants preferred to override parent methods in crosscutting concerns to share data structures across aspect and application components during message passing. However, CommJ provides a comprehensive set of pointcuts, which fully encapsulates the IPC abstractions, and thus participants did not need to override or inherit the aspect components. From these results, we can conclude that

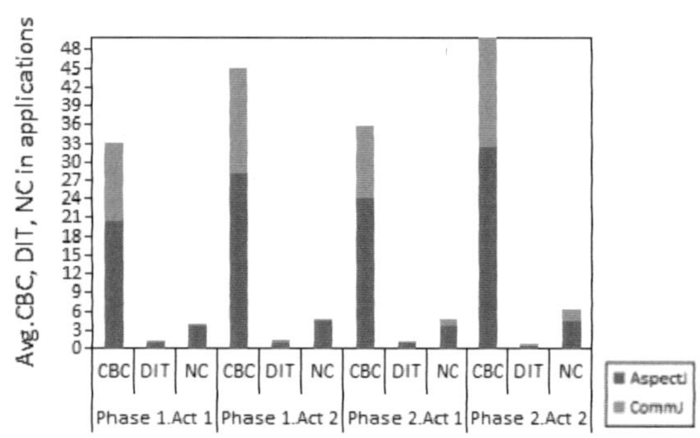

Figure 37. CBC, DIT, NC coverage over phases.

Hypothesis#2 holds true for reduced coupling in CommJ than in AspectJ.

C. Cohesion

Hypothesis #3 theorized that if crosscutting concerns are effectively encapsulated in CommJ aspects, the software has higher cohesion (as described by LCO in Section V.D.3.) than equivalent systems developed with AOP design techniques. In other words, the LCO metric value for CommJ should be less than AspectJ. The results shown in Figure 38 demonstrates that CommJ maintains a lower value for LCO than AspectJ in all four phases of the experiment. Sant'Anna [21] says that LCO measures the degree to which a component implements a single logical function. These results indicate that CommJ implementations were more cohesive and logical than AspectJ, hence have a lower LCO value. Therefore, we conclude that Hypothesis #3 holds true for increased cohesion in CommJ than in AspectJ.

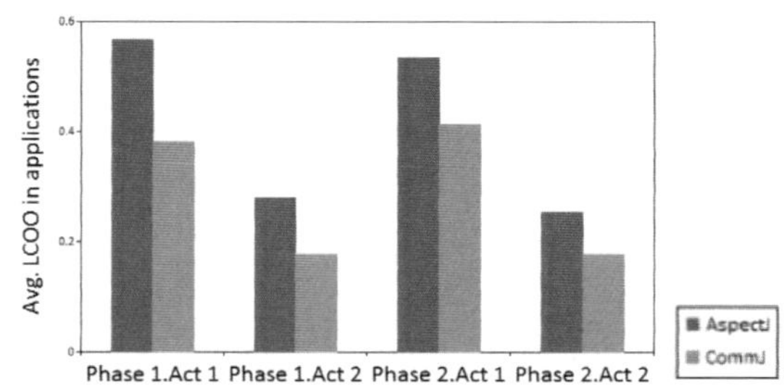

Figure 38. LCO coverage over phases.

D. Complexity

Hypothesis #4 theorized that if crosscutting communication concerns are effectively encapsulated in CommJ aspects, the software is significantly less complex (as described by CC in Section V.D.4.) than equivalent systems developed with AOP design techniques. In other words, the CC value for CommJ should be less than AspectJ. Figure 39 shows that the value of CC is smaller for CommJ than AspectJ, because CommJ hides complex IPC abstractions, which result in simple conditional statements and less tangled code.

From these results, we conclude that Hypothesis #4 holds true for less complex software in CommJ than AspectJ.

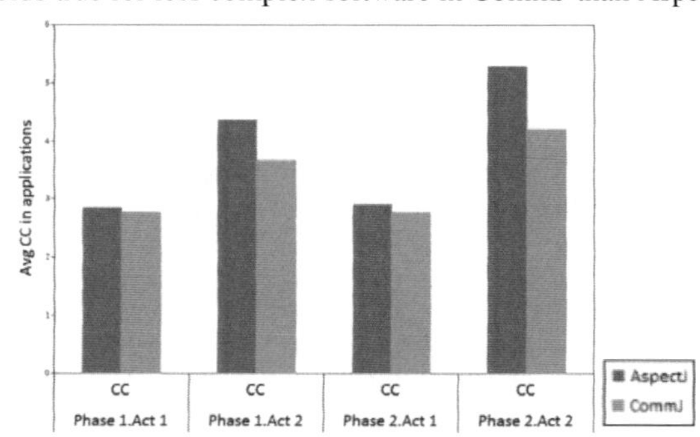

Figure 39. CC coverage over phases.

E. Obliviousness

Hypothesis #5 theorized that if crosscutting communication concerns are effectively encapsulated in CommJ aspects, the software will be more oblivious (as described by NITD, ASC, ASCO in Section V.D.5.) than equivalent systems developed with AOP design techniques. In other words, NITD, ASC, ASCO for CommJ should be less than AspectJ. Figure 40 shows that CommJ implementations significantly reduced the values of NITD, ASC and ASCO metrics.

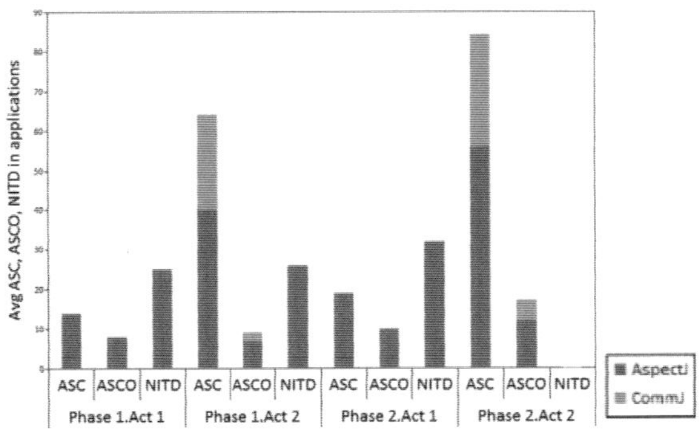

Figure 40. ASC, ASCO, NITD coverage over phases.

In comparison with AspectJ, the reason for having a zero value for NITD in CommJ was that the participants used IPC constructs and did not need to use inter-type declarations (ITD) for sharing of data structures between application and aspect component. Significant reduction in ASC and ASCO was due to the layers of indirection between the application and aspect components, which CommJ provides but are missing in AspectJ. Therefore, we conclude that Hypothesis #5 holds true for less oblivious software concerns in CommJ than AspectJ.

F. Reduced Size

Hypothesis #6 theorized that if crosscutting communication concerns are effectively encapsulated in CommJ aspects, the software is not significantly larger (as described by LOC, MLOC, NO, NP, WOC, VA in Section V.D.6.) than equivalent systems developed with AOP design techniques. In other words, LOC, MLOC, NO, NP, WOC metrics values for CommJ should be less and VA be more than AspectJ. Figure 41 shows that CommJ implementations significantly reduced the metrics values for LOC, MLOC, NP, NO and WOC in all phases of the experiment.

In comparison with AspectJ, CommJ participants found a more neat and clean set of pointcuts in IPC abstractions, which helped them to code the crosscutting concerns in less LOC. CommJ conceptually models various general network and distributed abstractions using UMC (Section III.A.) into rich set of communication and connection join points along with general purpose family of conversations, which helped the participants to implement the application crosscutting concerns in simpler and more logical method bodies, with no extra lines of code and less number of operations. Hence it reduced MLOC, NO, NP and WOC.

As predicted by the above hypothesis, results shown in Figure 41 gives sufficient evidence that average VA for all programs was more for CommJ than AspectJ. Although the number of components were more in CommJ implementations, they were more cohesive. Thus, from these results, we can conclude that Hypothesis#6 holds true for improved code size in CommJ than in AspectJ.

G. Reuse and Maintenance of Concern

Hypothesis #7 theorized that if crosscutting communication concerns are effectively encapsulated in CommJ, the crosscutting concern will require a smaller number of changes (as measured by CR, CM as follow) than equivalent systems developed with AOP design techniques, where CR and CM are as follows:

- *CR.* Number of changes required to reuse the concern for another application. The eclipse IDE calculates this metric.
- *CM.* Number of changes required to maintain the concern. The eclipse IDE calculates this metric.

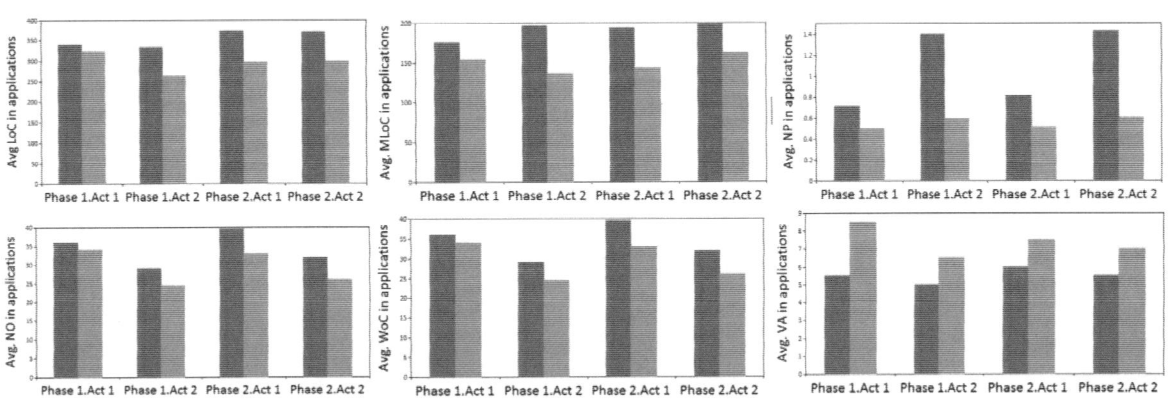

Figure 41. LoC, MLoC, NP, NO, WoC coverage over phases.

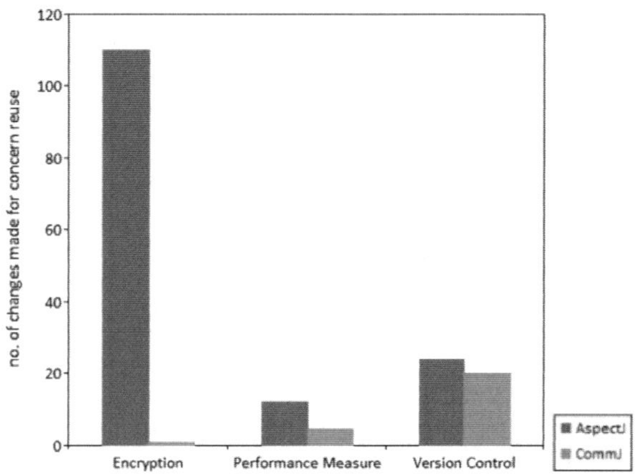

Figure 42. CR over Extensions

In other words, CR, CM values for CommJ should be less than AspectJ. From the results shown in Figure 42, we can see that CommJ implementation significantly reduced the changes required to reuse the previous implementations in the second phase of the experiment than AspectJ. CommJ aspects were overall more oblivious, logical and independent from the base application than AspectJ concerns and so they reduced the CR value in all four phases of the experiment.

Figure 43 provides another graphical representation to analyze reuse for AspectJ and CommJ. The light green colored-graphs represent scattering in CommJ (aspects only) and light blue colored-graphs represent AspectJ implementations. The scattered points in graph indicate the number of changes for reusing a concern with CommJ and AspectJ in different activities of Phases 1 and 2, respectively. The scattered points in blue represent ASC and in red represent ASCO metrics results. Overall, the results of the graph indicate that ASC and ASCO remained zero for all the activities of CommJ (highly reusable), but it was highly scattered in AspectJ. The reason for less scattering is discussed in Section VIII.A above.

Figure 44 shows the number of changes required to maintain the program in its initial activity (Activity 1 of Phase 1) to its maintenance activity (Activity 2 of Phase 2), reduced significantly for CommJ than AspectJ. The difference between CR and CM is that in CR we are only considering changes in the concern; however, in CM we are interested in number of changes both in the concern and application. We found that CommJ concerns were overall more oblivious, logical and independent from the base application than AspectJ concerns, and so they have reduced CM values in all four phases of the experiment.

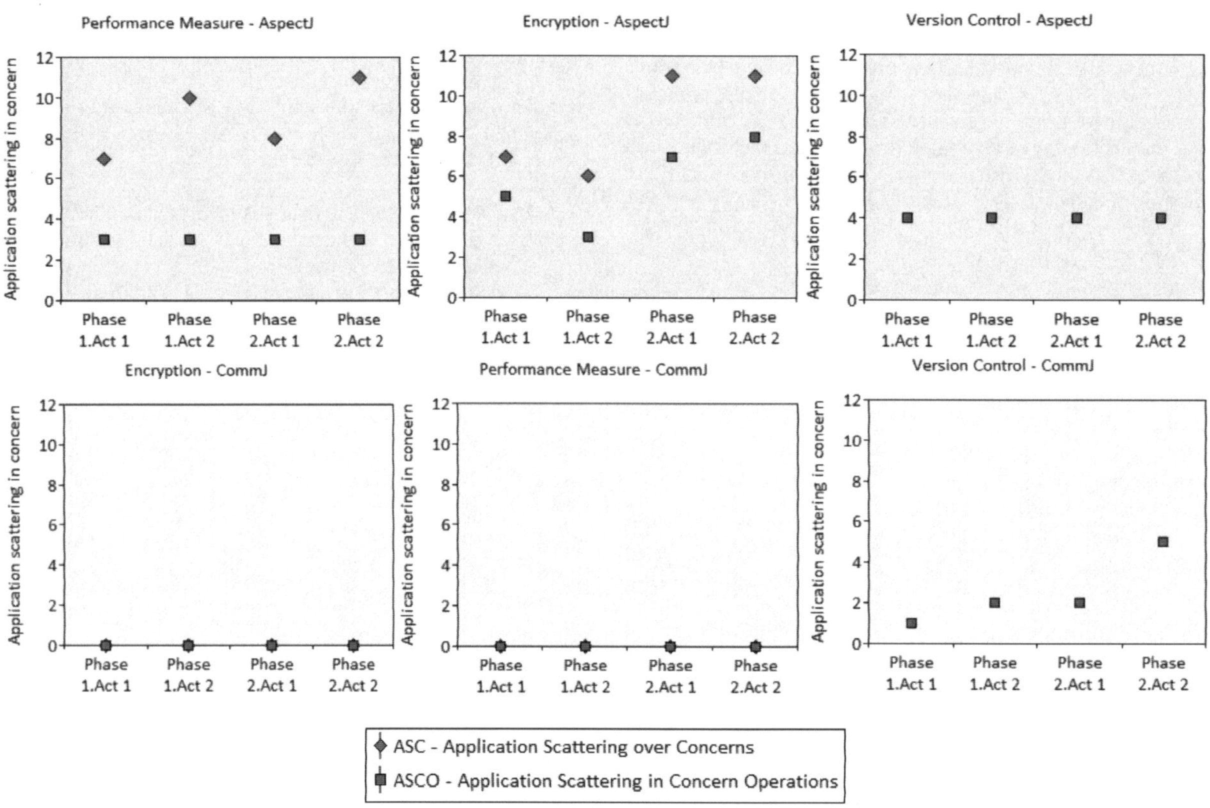

Figure 43. ASC and ASCO over Phases in AspectJ and CommJ

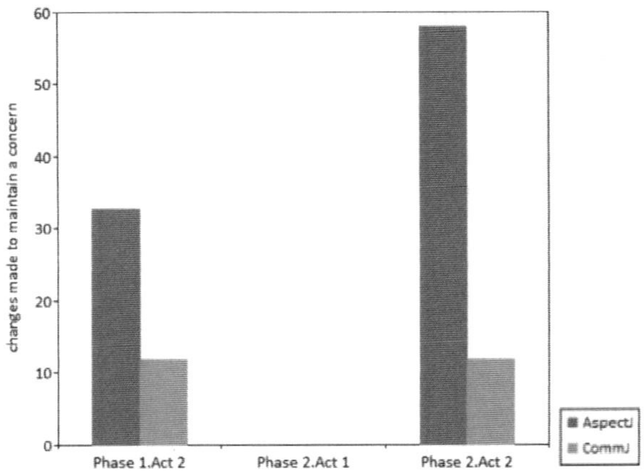

Figure 44. CM over phases

Figure 45 presents another representation for maintenance. The light green colored-graphs represent scattering in CommJ and light blue colored-graphs represent AspectJ respectively. The scattered points in blue, red and green represents CDA, CDO and NITD metrics results respectively. The points in the above graph indicate the number of changes for maintaining a program with CommJ and AspectJ in different activities of Phases 1 and 2, respectively. The results of the graph indicate that CDA, CDO and NITD were zero for all the activities of CommJ (highly maintainable) but were highly scattered in AspectJ. The reason for reduced values for CDA, CDO and NITD is already discussed in Section VIII.A and Section VIII.E, respectively.

From these results, we conclude that Hypothesis#7 holds true for more reusable and maintainable software in CommJ than AspectJ.

H. Other Useful Observations

Besides analysis of the hypotheses, we also collected a handful observations from participants' questionnaires and daily journals during each phase of the experiment.

In regards to understandable code, we found that 100% of AspectJ participants in the Phase 1 were confused in identifying pointcuts for implementing the given extension part, and 33% of the same participants were still confused during Phase 2. On the other hand, none of the CommJ participants struggled with identifying pointcuts during either phase. This tells us that CommJ implementation provides simple pointcuts with understandable IPC abstractions.

For reusability, we observed that 67% of the AspectJ participants in Phase 1 agreed that their applications might

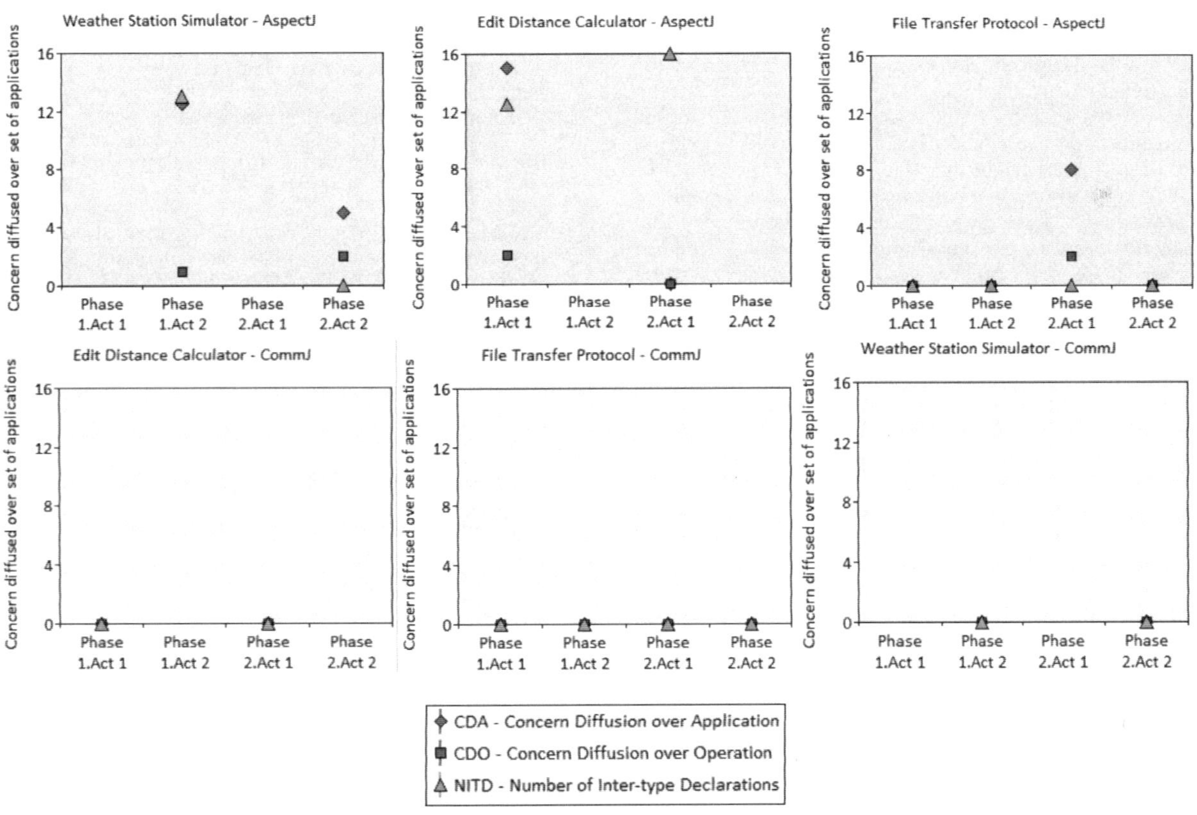

Figure 45. CDA, CDO and NITD in AspectJ and CommJ

not run after removing the extension part from the original application. This percentage further increased to 100% in Phase 2. On the other hand, none of the CommJ participants made this observation for either phase. This indirectly reconfirms Hypothesis #7, which states that CommJ implementations help in developing more reusable crosscutting concerns.

Similarly, for maintainability, 100% of the AspectJ participants said that their changes introduced new dependencies in the original sample application after both phases. However, none of the CommJ participants felt that they introduced any dependencies during either phase. So, this reconfirms our Hypothesis #7, which asserts that CommJ implementation helps in developing more maintainable programs.

The survey also provides information on frequency of bugs. Specifically, 67% of the participants in AspectJ group said that their extensions introduced new failures, i.e., bugs, into the application code during Phase 1. This percentage further increased to 100% for Phase 2. However, only 25% of the CommJ participants in Phase 1 and Phase 2 made this statement. This tells us that CommJ's modularization and obliviousness decreased the failures and debugging time.

IX. SUMMARY AND FUTURE WORK

Our research introduces the notation of communication and connection aspects and discusses an AspectJ framework, namely CommJ, for weaving aspects into IPC. It then describes the design and implementation of some of CommJ components, such as the base aspects. It also provides an overview of a toolkit, i.e., the RAL that consists of reusable communication aspects and doubles as a proof of concept, since these aspects can be directly applied to a wide range of existing applications. We believe that CommJ is capable of encapsulating a wide range of communication-related and connection-related crosscutting concerns in aspects. We hope to gather more empirical evidence of the CommJ's value by increasing the number of aspects in the RAL and by continuing to expand the number and types of applications that use CommJ. We also conducted a research experiment to compare AspectJ with CommJ for various software design attributes related to reuse and maintenance through an extended quality model. Findings from this initial experiment revealed that crosscutting concerns programmed in CommJ delivered more modular, reusable and maintainable programs. We hope to pursue larger and varied software-engineering productivity experiments to verify this belief.

We envision a number of extensions or spins off to CommJ. First, distributed transaction processing systems is another high-level programming concept that can be unnecessarily complex when crosscutting concerns, e.g., logging, concurrency controls, transaction management, and access controls, are scattered throughout the transaction processing logic or tangled into otherwise cohesive modules. We can use the same approach that we used for CommJ to extend AspectJ for the weaving of crosscutting concerns in transactions. Second, CommJ can also be extended for distributed pointcuts that would simplify the implementation of even more complex crosscutting concerns, such as object-replication, migration, or fragmentation in a distributed system.

Finally, CommJ has the potential to be very useful for testing various kinds of time-sensitive communication related errors in IPC. We plan to explore this potential and additional experiments focus on quality of service and timing issues related to IPC.

REFERENCES

[1] A. Raza, S. Clyde, and J. Edison, "Communication Aspects with CommJ: Initial Experiment Show Promising Improvements in Reusability and Maintainability," In ICSEA 2014, Nice, France.

[2] A. Raza and S. Clyde, "Weaving Crosscutting Concerns into Inter-Process Communication (IPC) in AspectJ," In ICSEA 2013, Venice, Italy, pp. 234-240.

[3] L.D. Benavides Navarro et al., "Invasive patterns for distributed programs," In OTM Confederated Int. Conf., Vilamoura, Portugal, 2007, pp. 772-789.

[4] G. Kiczales et al., "Aspect-oriented programming," (ECOOP), 1997, pp. 220-242.

[5] ApectJ, http://www.eclipse.org/aspectj/, last updated on May 13, 2016.

[6] AspectWorkz2, http://aspectwerkz.codehaus.org/ss, last updated on May 13, 2016.

[7] JBoss AOP, http://www.jboss.org/jbossaop, last updated on May 13, 2016.

[8] Spring AOP, org.springframework, last updated on May 13, 2016.

[9] Y. Coady et al., "Can AOP support extensibility in client-server architectures?" in Proc. ECOOP Aspect-Oriented Programming Workshop, Budapest, Hungary, 2001.

[10] C. Clifton and G T. Leavens, "Obliviousness, modular reasoning, and the behavior subtyping analogy," In Proc. 2nd Int. Conf. AOSD SPLAT Workshop, Boston, MA, 2003, pp. 1-6.

[11] C. Sant'Anna, A. Garcia, C. Chavez, C. Lucena, and A. Von Staa, "On the Reuse and Maintenance of Aspect-Oriented Software: An Assessment Framework," in 17th Brazilian Symposium on Software Engineering (SEES 2003), Manaus, Brazil (2003), PUC-RioInf.MCC26/03.

[12] E. Gamma, R. Helm, R. Johnson, and J. Vlissides, "Design Patterns: Elements of Reusable Object-Oriented Software," Addison-Wesley Longman Publishing Co., Inc., Boston, MA, USA. 1995.

[13] G. Kiczales and M. Mezini, "Aspect-oriented programming and modular reasoning," In Proc. 27th Int. Conf. Software Engineering, St. Louis, MO, 2005, pp. 49-58.

[14] R. Douence, D.L. Botlan, J. Noye, and M. Sudholt, "Concurrent aspects," In. Proc. 5th Int. Conf. GPCE, Portland, OR, 2006, pp. 79-88.

[15] W. De Meuter, "Monads as a theoretical foundation for AOP", In Int. Workshop on AOP at 11th ECOOP, 1997, Springer-Verlag. doi: 10.1.1.2.4757.

[16] P. Tarr, H. Ossher, W. Harrison, and S.m. Sutton, "N degrees of separation: Multi-dimensional separation of concerns," In Proc.21st Int. Conf. Software Engineering, Los Angeles, CA, 1999, pp. 107-119.

[17] H. Ossher and P.Tarr, "Multi-dimensional separation of concerns and the hyperspace approach," IBM, Yorktown Heights, NY, IBM Res. Rep. 21452, April,1999.

[18] W. Harrison and H. Ossher, "Subject-oriented programming - A critique of pure objects," In Proc. 8th Conf. on Object-

Oriented Programming Systems, Languages, and Applications, Oakland, CA,1993, pp. 411-428.

[19] S. Chiba, "Load-time structural reflection in Java," In Proc.14th ECOOP, Cannes, France, 2000, pp. 313-336.

[20] T.J. Brown, I. Spence, and P. Kilpatrick, "Mixin programming in Java with reflection and dynamic invocation," In Proc. 2nd Workshop on Intermediate Representation Engineering for Virtual Machines, Dublin, Ireland, 2002, pp. 25-34.

[21] C. Sant'Anna, A. Garcia, C. Chavez, C. Lucena, and A. Staa, "On the reuse and maintenance of Aspect-Oriented Software: An assessment framework," In Proc. 17th Brazilian Symp. Software Engineering, Manaus, Brazil, 2003, doi: PUC-RioInf, MCC26/03.

[22] C. Lopes, "D: A language framework for distributed programming," PhD. dissertation, Coll. Comp. Sci., Northeastern University, Boston, MA, 1997.

[23] R. Basili, G. Caldiera, and H. Rombach, "The goal question metric approach," In Encyclopedia of Software Engineering, vol. 2, J.J. Marciniak, Ed. Hoboken, NJ: Wiley, 1994, pp. 528-532.

[24] C. Kaewkasi and J. R. Gurd, "A distributed dynamic aspect machine for scientific software development," In Proc.1st Workshop on VMIL, 2007, ACM. doi: 10.1145/1230136.1230139.

[25] D. L. Parnas, "On the criteria to be used in decomposing systems into modules," Commun. ACM, vol. 15, no.12, pp. 1053-1058, Dec. 1972.

[26] G. Kiczales and M. Mezini, "Aspect-oriented programming and modular reasoning," In Proc. 27th Int. Conf. Software Engineering, St. Louis, MO, 2005, pp. 49-58.

[27] J. McCall, P.K. Richards, and G.F. Walters, "Factors in software quality," NTIS, Alexandria, VA, Tech. Rep. AD-A049-014, 015, 055, 1977.

[28] IEEE Standard for Software Maintenance, IEEE Standard 1219-1998, 1998.

[29] R.E. Filman and D. P. Friedman, "Aspect-oriented programming is quantification and obliviousness," IEEE RIACS Tech. Rep. 01.12, May 2001.

[30] T.J. McCabe, "A complexity measure," IEEE Trans. Softw. Eng., vol. 2, no. 4, pp. 308-320, Dec. 1976.

[31] S.R. Chidamber and C. F. Kemerer, "A metrics suite for object-oriented design," IEEE Trans. Softw. Eng., vol. SE-20, no. 6, pp. 476–493, June 1994.

[32] Institutional Review Board (IRB), http://rgs.usu.edu/irb, retrieved: Mayss 13, 2016.

[33] Collaborative Institutional Trainig (CIIT), https://www.citiprogram.org, retrieved: May 13, 2016.

[34] Metrics plugin, http://metrics2.sourceforge.net, retrieved: May 13, 2016.

Triangulation and Segmentation-based Approach for Improving the Accuracy of Polygon Data

Alexey Noskov and Yerach Doytsher
Mapping and Geo-Information Engineering
Technion – Israel Institute of Technology
Haifa, Israel
Emails: {noskov, doytsher}@technion.ac.il

***Abstract* — Often, same polygon objects are presented in Geoinformational Systems by distinct geometries with random positional discrepancies. It makes difficult to detect correspondences between data layers containing same object or parts of objects. The suggested method allows the user to improve the accuracy of one polygon layer by another more accurate polygon dataset by defining correspondences between polygons and parts of polygon boundaries. Two main techniques are applied: triangulation and segmentation. The triangulation is used to define correspondences between whole polygons by comparing triples of polygons. The segmentation approach is applied for the remaining polygons. Existing approaches do not work well in the case of partial equality of polygon boundaries. The main idea of the segmentation algorithm in this paper is based on defining correspondent segments of polygon boundaries and further replacing polygon boundary segments of the non-accurate layer with segments of the accurate data set; segments without pairs are rectified using ground control points. The resulting data contain parts of the accurate data set polygon boundaries, whereas the remaining elements are rectified according to the replaced boundary segments. From a review implemented by specialists it might be concluded that the results are satisfactory. The developed method could be applied to various types of polygonal datasets with similar scale.**

Keywords – Polyline and polygon similarity; geometry matching; shape descriptor; triangulation; topology.

I. INTRODUCTION

The same objects on different maps, which are on an equal scale, might be shown with small differences. In an ideal situation, accurate geometries of exiting maps should be used for preparing new data sets or for updating. Usually, in the real world, new maps are digitized without respect to existing data sets. Using geometries (e.g., river line) from an accurate topographic map for creating a thematic map (e.g., soil map), in many cases, is better than digitizing a new element. Often, data are unavailable, or available with significant restrictions, because of legal, technical, or other reasons. Additionally, even if an accurate data set is freely available, people usually do not want to spend time using an existing data set; in most cases they prefer to digitize new geometries on a satellite image or scanned map. These data should be aligned using accurate data sets [1]. This problem is especially sensitive for large-scale maps and plans [2].

The problem which is described in the paper refers to cadastral and city planning maps. A cadastral map is a comprehensive register of the real estate boundaries of a country. Cadastral data are produced using quality large-scale surveying with Total Stations, Differential Global Positioning System devices or other surveying systems with centimeter precision. Normally, the precision of maps based on non-survey large-scale data (e.g., satellite images) is lower. City planning data contain proposals for developing urban areas. Most city planning maps are developed by digitizing handmade maps, using space images. Almost all boundaries have small discrepancies in comparison to cadastral maps. It is very important to use exact boundaries, or their segments, on city planning data from a cadastral map, especially in central parts of cities. The approach described in the paper enables us to resolve this problem of matching two data types. Rectifying data using a set of ground control points is a popular way of improving the accuracy of a map [3]. The results of this approach are not satisfactory in many cases, because rectified objects cannot be identical to directly measured accurate objects. Another possibility is based on defining correspondent objects on an accurate data set by geometry or attributes and replacing objects from the non-accurate set with the accurate correspondent objects [4].

We present a triangulation approach. It enables us to define correspondent polygons of two datasets. It is achieved by dividing polygons into triples and comparing the triples of two datasets. A serious problem with this approach follows from the fact that objects could be partially similar (e.g., some segments of a polygon boundary are same, other parts are different). In contrast to existing approaches, the main idea of a segmentation approach is based on defining correspondent segments of polygon boundaries and further replacing polygon boundary segments of the non-accurate layer with segments of an accurate data set; segments without pairs are rectified by ground control points. The segmentation complements the triangulation algorithm. Triangulation is a fast process for defining correspondences between whole polygons. Segmentation is much slower. It enables us to define correspondences between boundary segments of polygons (excluding polygon pairs defined by triangulation). The triangulation is also used for evaluating results. The proposed algorithm could be applied to different sorts of polygon datasets with small boundary differences. The approach has not only been designed for city planning and cadastre datasets.

This paper is structured as follows: the related work is considered in Section II. Source datasets and the process of defining initial variables are described in Section III. The triangulation approach is proposed in Section IV. The algorithm of defining correspondent polylines is presented in Section V. The process of compiling the final map is described in Section VI. The results are discussed in Section VII. The conclusion is presented in Section VIII.

II. Related Work

In order to develop the proposed algorithm, various approaches were considered. The review of these approaches is presented in this section. Many of them were evaluated. We found several useful concepts for our task described in the considered papers. The papers are grouped. The groups appear in the order in which they influenced our research. Most of our ideas were taken from the feature-based matching group of approaches. The relational matching ideas also affected our approach, mainly in the sense of topological orientation of the developed approach. We have not found useful concepts for the context of the discovered datasets in the last category (attributes-based matching), but it discloses and raises many useful problems of attribute processing for data matching researchers. Additionally, several programming techniques are described at the end of the section, in order to improve the quality of the developed approach. Most of the techniques are applied.

Discrepancy problems on digital maps can be resolved in different ways. Common shape matching techniques are currently used in the raster and vector fields, and sometimes in combination with each other. Several common techniques in the field of Shape Similarity or Pattern Recognition could be applied to the various needs of the matched objects and relevant research questions.

Vector matching techniques can be divided into three main categories.

A. Feature-based matching

This group of methods is based on an object's geometry and shape. The degree of compatibility of objects is determined by their geometry, size, or area. The process is carried out by structural analysis of a set of objects and comparing whether similar structural analysis of the candidates fits the objects of the other data set [5][6]. In [4], comparison of objects is based on analysis of a contour distribution histogram. A polar coordinates approach for calculating the histogram is used. A method based on the Wasserstein distance was published by Schmitzer et al. [7]. A special shape descriptor for defined correspondent objects on raster images was developed by Ma and Longin [8]. Feature-based matching approaches do not allow for resolving our problem, because they have been developed mainly for single shapes; however, we can use them as part of our approach.

B. Relational matching

This group of methods takes objects' relationships into account. In [9], topological and spatial neighborly relations between two data sets, preserved even after running operations such as rotation or scale, were discovered. In relational matching, the comparison of the object is implemented with respect to a neighboring object. We can verify the similarity of two objects by considering neighboring objects. The problem of non-rigid shape recognition is studied by Bronstein et al. [10]; the applicability of diffusion distances within the Gromov-Hausdorff framework [10] and the presence of topological changes have been explored in this paper. A multiple-point geostatistical modeling based on cross-correlation functions is proposed by Tahmasebi et al. in [11].

C. Attributes-based matching

Matching two data sets' objects by attributes could be very effective if a similar data model is used. Two types of attribute matching could be mentioned: Schema-based [12] and Ontology-based. The concept of semantic proximity, which is essentially an abstraction/mapping between the domains of the two objects associated with the context of comparison, is proposed by Kashyap and Sheth in [13]. In [14], an approach based on both types is presented. An ontology-based integration of XML Web Resources focusing on the significance of offering appropriate high-level primitives and mechanisms for representing data semantics is described by Amann et al. in [15]. A technique for building approximate string join capabilities on top of commercial databases by exploiting facilities already available in them is described by Gravano in [16] and [17]. Attributes-based matching is a specific group of approaches; it can only be applied efficiently in special cases with special data. In most situations it is ineffective.

The merging and fusion of heterogeneous databases has been extensively studied, both spatially [18] and non-spatially [19]. The Map conflation method is based on data fusion algorithms; the aim of the process is to prepare a map which is a combination of two or more maps (often for updating an old map). Map conflation approaches are presented in [2] [20] [3]. In [21], three approaches for the linking of objects in different spatial data sets are described. The first defines the linking as a matching problem and aims at finding a correspondence between two data sets of similar scale. The two other approaches focus on the derivation of one representation from the other one, leading to an automatic generation of new digital data sets of lower resolution.

In order to resolve the described problem, the mentioned approaches have been considered. It has been concluded, that a new solution need to be developed.

Computer Vision algorithms are popular in the field of data matching [22]. The Open Computer Vision (OpenCV) framework [23] is widely used today; it provides a number of "out-of-the-box" functions enabling us to detect and compare objects and bindings for popular programming languages (e.g., Python [24]). This makes the OpenCV framework very useful for data-matching tasks. Delaunay Triangulation [25] and Voronoi Polygons [26] are very useful techniques for working with discrete vector data and neighbor analysis. We should also note that in practice, data is distributed in non-topological formats (e.g., Shape File format). That leads to complication of the analysis, because of a surplus number of objects and duplication of primitives, e.g., polygon boundaries, unexpected gaps between objects etc. We need to use one of the topological data formats presented by Landa [27] to avoid these obstacles. The topology in GIS context is described in detail by Blazek et al. in [28]. The main topological data types are presented: point, line (comprising nodes, vertices and segments), and polygons (consisting of boundaries and centroid). Many useful GIS definitions and techniques, including geometry relations, topology and operations (e.g., overlay), are described by Herring in [29].

Additionally, two perspective methods could be used in GIS data matching to reduce the time and computer resources required: Genetic Algorithms [30] help to avoid Brute-force operations in some cases; OpenCL technology [31] makes it possible to split a process into a huge number of parallel threads on a video card.

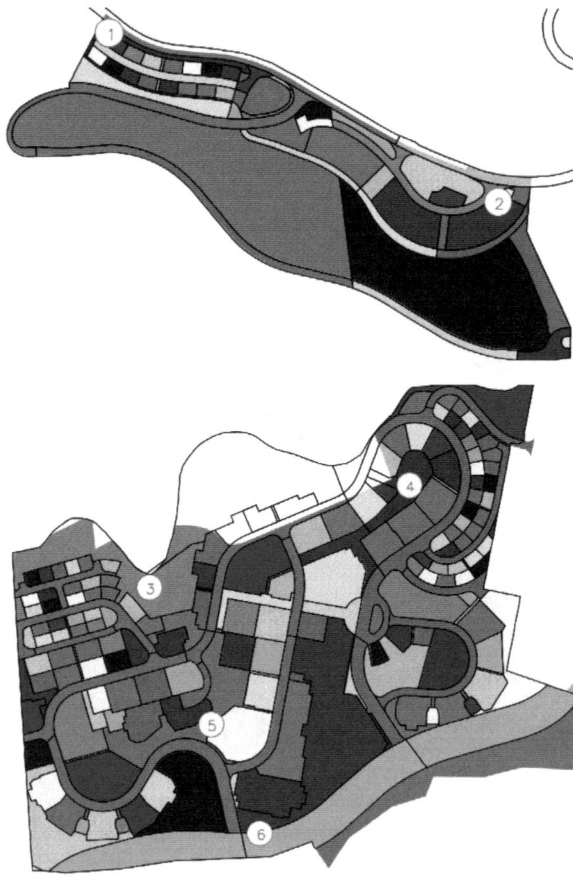

Figure 1. Source data: land-use city planning (color background) and cadastre (black polylines) of Nesher (upper) and Yokne'am (lower) datasets.

III. DEFINING INITIAL VARIABLES

For implementing and testing our approach, GIS data provided by Survey of Israel have been used. They contain cadastre and land-use city planning polygon shape files covering a part of Nesher and Yokne'am (towns in the Haifa District of Israel). Figure 1 depicts source data; red numbers in circles correspond to numbers of extents in Figure 21. Overlaid polygon boundaries of two data sets are presented in Figure 2. From the figure, one can conclude that transformation of lines would not yield positive results, because the gaps are extremely variable - the curved parts of lines consist of different numbers of vertices; thus, even with correct parameters of transformation, the result would not be satisfactory.

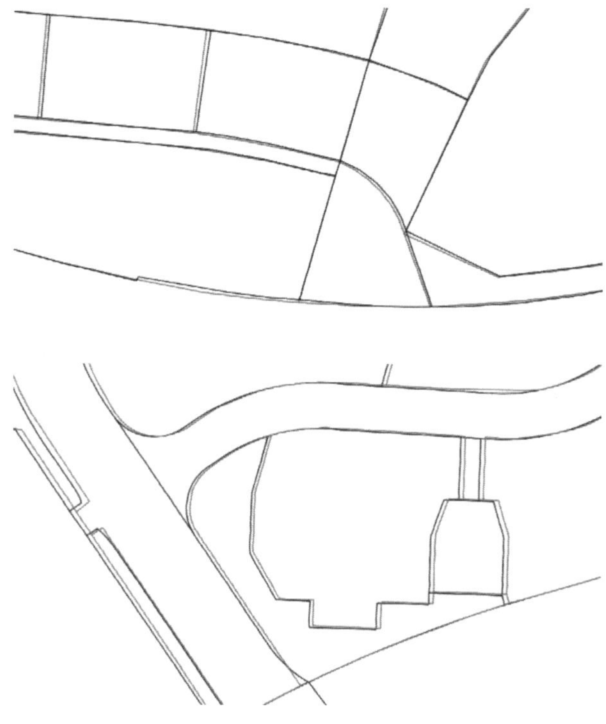

Figure 2. Positional discrepancies of city planning (red lines) and cadastre (black lines) datasets: Nesher (upper) and Yokne'am (lower).

Source shape files have been converted to GRASS GIS 7 topological data format [27]. Data preparation can be divided into 3 steps:

- Extracting polygon boundaries.
- Splitting polylines into a set of equidistant points. For depicting this parameter we will use the symbol d in the paper.
- Calculating an array of distances between the nearest points of two datasets. Setting of initial measures.

We have decided to use 2 meters between equidistant points. Using a greater distance makes impossible to detect small curves, whereas a smaller distance significantly increases the calculation time.

Several initial measures need to be calculated. Maximal distance (D_{max}) between the nearest points of two datasets and maximal standard deviation (σ_{max}) have been calculated. To calculate these parameters we need to create a list of 100 percentiles. Then we implement a loop from the first to the last percentile on the list. D_{max} equals percentile i and σ_{max} equals the double standard deviation of distance in the interval between percentiles number i and 100 if the standard deviation of distances between percentiles i-1 and i is more than 1. We calculate tail parameter (t) as follows: t= D_{max}/d, minimal tail parameter equals 4. Tail defines a starting or ending segment of polyline that can be ignored.

We have developed a special shape descriptor (S), based on the descriptor presented in [8]. The descriptor measures the similarity of polylines. Polylines are more similar if S is larger.

$$d = \log_{10}(1 + distA) - \log_{10}(1 + distB)$$
$$S = \frac{\sum \exp\left(-d^2 + \exp(-(angA - angB)^2)\right)}{(k \cdot k)^2} \quad (1)$$

In the equation, 1 means matrix of ones, distA – matrix of distances between all pairs of points laid on polyline a. distB – matrix of distances between all pairs of points laid on polyline b. If the number of points of a line is k, then matrix size is k×k. angA and angB are matrices of angles in radians between all pairs of points of lines a and b, correspondingly. The shape descriptor is calculated for the segments with equal length (k).

A list containing pairs of point sets has been prepared, where all points laid on line A are closest to points laid on line B of another dataset. For each element of the list, two shape descriptors of tails with t number of points have been calculated and collected into a list of shape descriptors of tails. St_min, St_max – minimal and maximal elements of the list. Also, we use maximal tail standard deviation of point distances (σt), and its (maximal tail) maximal value – σt_max.

The list of initial variables has been calculated:

Nesher datasets: Dmax=2.1, σmax=1.0, St_min=0,St_max=0.23; Yokne'am datasets: Dmax=7.9, σmax=1.5, St_min=0,St_max=0.25.

IV. Defining Corresponding Polygons of Datasets by Triangulation

As we can see in Figure 1, many polygons of city planning datasets have corresponding polygons in cadastre datasets. Thus, we can simply take attributes of these city planning polygons and link them to the geometry of correspondent cadastre polygons. To implement this idea we have developed a triangulation algorithm.

The triangulation consists of several stages: calculating of Delaunay triangulation based on polygon centroids; comparing all possible pairs of polygon triples and defining correspondent candidate pairs of polygon triples of two datasets by area and perimeter comparison; defining correct triple correspondence by considering distances between polygon centroids. Further in this section, the algorithm will be described in detail.

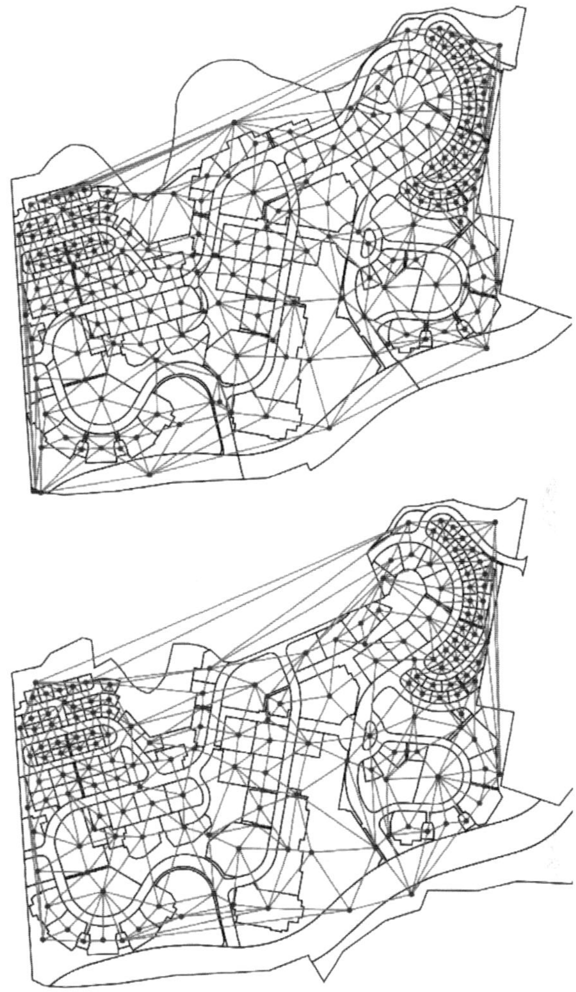

Figure 3. Delaunay triangulation (red lines) of cadastre (upper) and city planning (lower) datasets. Black lines are polygon boundaries, blue points are polygon centroids. Yokne'am.

Delaunay triangulation maps are presented in Figure 3. These maps enable us to select triples of polygons, where each triple belongs to one of the triangles (centroids of polygons are vertices of Delaunay triangles). Then, for each triple we try to find a candidate counterpart triple on a second dataset. A candidate counterpart is detected by comparing perimeters and areas of polygons as follows. A triple of first dataset polygons is the candidate counterpart of a triple of a second dataset, if for each polygon in the first triple we can find a polygon in the second triple (each polygon can only participate in one correspondence). The area and perimeter of the first polygon are more than the area and perimeter of the second polygon minus 20% and less than the area and perimeter of the second polygon plus 20%. The value 20% is empiric. It has been defined as optimal for the considered datasets, but it may be used with other datasets. It could be feasible to let the user modify the value.

At this time a list of candidate counterpart triples is prepared. The candidates are evaluated by distances between centroids of counterpart polygons to define the most likely correspondence of polygons in the triple pair (TripleB.GetTheMostSimilar() function in Figure 4). For each candidate triple of polygons, all possible combinations of polygon correspondences implemented by permutation are considered. For each combination, a sum of distances between correspondent polygons is calculated. A combination with the lowest sum describes the most likely correspondence of polygons in the current triple pair. The correspondence of polygons in the triple pair is correct if one of the two follows conditions is true. The first condition is valid if the sum of distances between centroids of correspondent polygons is less than D_{max} defined in the previous section. This condition does not work for incompact long curve polygons (e.g., road polygons), because even small changes in polygon boundary significantly changes centroid position. That is why another condition has been developed. This condition is valid if the mean distance between boundaries of all correspondent polygons in the triple pair is less than D_{max}. To calculate the mean distance between polygon boundaries, the boundaries have been split by equidistance points with intervals equaling d (2 meters) as defined in the previous section. For each point of the first polygon boundary, a distance to the closest point of the second polygon boundary is calculated. The mean distance between the polygon boundaries equals the mean value of the calculated point distance.

The described algorithm is presented as a pseudo code listing in Figure 4 and Figure 5. Figure 4 explains the process of preparing a candidate counterpart triples list. It mainly comprises standard geoprocessing operations like buffering, triangulating and overlaying. In order to improve the performance of the algorithms, we used a number of tricks for calculating a list of candidate counterpart triples, presented in Figure 4. In Figure 5, we consider a process of evaluating the candidate list by a number of conditions and loops. Each element of a result list contains polygon pairs of two datasets. The following text contains more detailed explanation of the listings.

Figure 4 starts from the definition of source polygon maps. PolsA and PolsB compare polygon maps. For each map several preparatory procedures are applied. Area, perimeter and centroid coordinates have been added to the attribute table for each polygon. Then, a map of centroids is created. An attribute table of source polygon is inherited. GetBuffer function returns the 0.1 m buffers around centroids. In our case, 0.1 m means the small value that we can ignore, i.e., we consider it as "almost 0". Another small value could be used; it depends on specific datasets and software. The attribute table is also inherited. GetDelaunay pseudo function generates a triangulation map based on centroids. OverayMap is the result of overlaying the buffer and triangulation map with an "and" operator. The three last described operations are illustrated in Figure 4. This approach of grouping polygons into triples works very fast. Many GIS applications have the described functions in the standard edition.

```
PolsA=first_polygon_map
PolsB=second_polygon_map
InitTriples=GetEmptyList()

Foreach map in [PolsA, PolsB] {

  CalculateAreaOfPolygons(map)
  CalculatePerimeterOfPolygons(map)
  CalculateXYOfPolygonsCentroids(map)
  CentroidMap=GetCentroidsAsPoints(map)
  BufferMap=GetBuffer(CentroidMap, buffer_size=0.1)
  TriangMap=GetDelaunay(CentroidMap)
  OverlayMap=GetOverlay(BufferMap, TriangMap)
  TempList=GetEmptyList()

  Foreach TriangleId in GetIds(TriangMap) {

    Attributes=GetAttribs(OverlayMap,get=map_perimeter,
map_area,map_centroidXY, where=TriangMap_id= TriangleId)
    TempList.append(Attributes)

  }

  InitTriples.append(TempList)

}

CandidateTriples= GetEmptyList()
Foreach TripleA in InitTriples[0] {
  Foreach TripleB in InitTriples[1] {
    Appropriate=True
    Foreach PolA in TripleA {
      PolB=TripleB.GetTheMostSimilar(PolA)
      TripleB.remove(PolB)

      If not (0.8*PolB.area < PolA.area < 1.2*PolB.area) and not
(0.8*PolB.perimeter < PolA. perimeter < 1.2*PolB. perimeter) {
        Appropriate=False
      }

    }

    If Appropriate==True {
      CandidateTriples.append([TripleA,TripleB]) }
    }
```

Figure 4. The first part of the triangulation algorithm: preparing of a list of candidate counterpart triples.

Now we can easily get a polygon triple belonging to any triangle. The first element of InitTriple contains all triples of polygons of the first polygon map; the second element contains all triples of polygons of the second polygon map. Then the triples of the two polygon maps are compared by area and perimeter and appropriate triples are added to the CandidateTriples list.

In Figure 5, an algorithm for evaluating candidate counterpart triples and defining correspondences between polygons is described. The combinations list comprises all possible correspondences of polygons in a triple pair. For each combination, a sum of distances between the centroids of correspondent polygons is calculated. A combination with a minimal sum of distances is kept in optimal variable for further processing.

```
Result= GetEmptyList()

 Foreach TripleA, TripleB in CandidateTriples {

  Combinations=getAllPossibleCombinations(TripleA, TripleB)
  DistList= GetEmptyList()

  For {i=0; i<length(Combinations);i++} {

       PolA1,PolB1,PolA2,PolB2,PolA3,PolB3=
Combinations.GetPolygonsAsList()

       DistList.append(              CentoidDistance(PolA1,PolB1)+
CentoidDistance(PolA2,PolB2)+ CentoidDistance(PolA3,PolB3)+)

  }

  MinDist= Minimal(DistList)
  Index=DistList.GetIndex(MinDist)

  Optimal= Combinations[Index]
  Foreach PolA, PolB in Optimal {

    If not (0.8*PolB.area < PolA.area < 1.2*PolB.area) and not
(0.8*PolB.perimeter < PolA. perimeter < 1.2*PolB. perimeter) {
        Continue
}

  Appropriate=True

  If MinDist < max_dist {
    Appropriate=True
  }

  Else {
   Foreach PolA, PolB in Optimal {
     Xa,Ya=PolA.CentroidCoords
     Xb,Yb=PolB.CentroidCoords
     AreaA=PolA.area
     Delta=Sqrt(AreaA)+max_dist

     If  (Xa-Delta  <  Xb  <Xa+Delta)  and  (Ya-Delta  <  Yb
<Ya+Delta) {

       EqdBoundsMapA= GetEquidistancePoints(PolA)
       EqdBoundsMapB= GetEquidistancePoints(PolB)
       DistArray=PointDistance(EqdBoundsMapA,
EqdBoundsMapB)

       If Mean(DistArray)>max_dist {
          Appropriate=False
       }

     }
     Else {
          Appropriate=False
     }
  } #end of Foreach PolA, PolB in Optimal

  If Appropriate == True {

    PolA1,PolB1,PolA2,PolB2,PolA3,PolB3=
Combinations.GetPolygonsAsList()

     Result.append([PolA1,PolB1])
     Result.append([PolA2,PolB2])
     Result.append([PolA3,PolB3])

  }
```

Figure 5. The second part of the triangulation algorithm: preparing a list of polygon correspondences.

All polygon correspondences are evaluated using areas and perimeters; if the condition is false, the triple pair is not considered and the next candidate is processed. If the sum of distances is less than D_{max} (max_dist in the listing; the parameter has been defined in the previous section), the polygon correspondences are correct and are added to the Result list. If the previous condition is false, then we calculate mean distance between polygon boundaries. It is implemented by calculating distances between equidistant points splitting boundaries. If the mean distance is less than D_{max}, a polygon pair passes the check. This condition has to be true for all polygon pairs in the combination. The performance of the described condition is quite low, which is why we use the Delta variable for filtering distant polygons. Delta equals to the square root of PolA's area plus D_{max}. Only if centroid PolB is placed inside a rectangle Xa-Delta, Ya-Delta, Xa+Delta and Ya+Delta (where Xa and Ya are PolA's centroid coordinates), we can calculate mean distance between polygon boundaries.

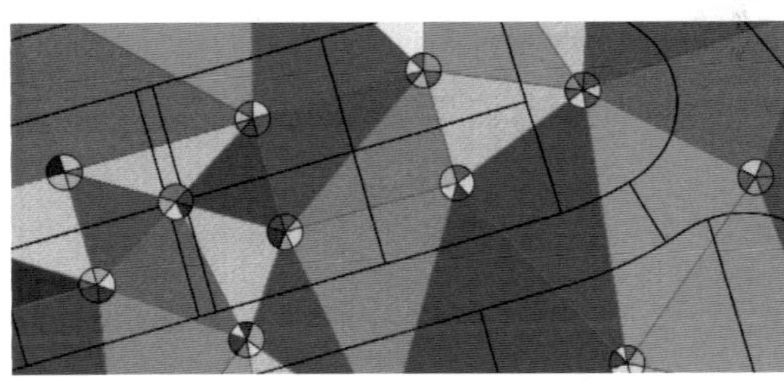

Figure 6. Grouping polygons into triples by triangulation (color background and red boundaries), buffering (circles) and overlaying (color sectors of the circles).Yokne'am.

The cadastre and city planning polygon datasets have been compared by the triangulation algorithm, and counterpart polygons have been detected. The result is presented in Figure 7 and in Figure 8: counterpart polygons are depicted by gray background and black boundaries, polygons without pairs are light gray areas with gray boundaries.

Almost all polygons of the Nesher datasets (see Figure 8) have correspondences; only several northern polygons do not have pairs. Many polygon correspondences have been defined on the Yokne'am datasets (see Figure 7). Several polygons look similar in the figure and have no defined correspondences. That means that either we do not see the differences because of the scale, or that polygons participate only in incorrect triples (triples with at least one polygon without correspondences).

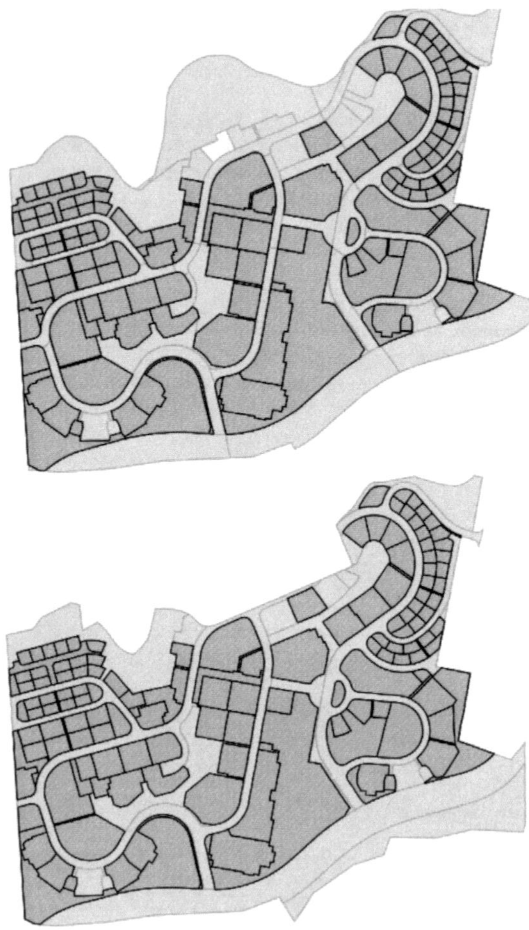

Figure 7. The result of triangulation. Upper – cadaster, lower – city planning. Yokne'am.

The counterpart polygons are excluded from further processing and will be involved in the processing only at the last stage of the approach. The polygons without pairs are extracted from the datasets for defining correspondences between boundaries and boundaries' segments.

V. DEFINING CORRESPONDING LINES OF DATASETS

To define corresponding lines, we have developed a special descriptor based on several measures: distances between points, standard deviation of distances, shape descriptor. Figure 9 depicts the main idea – using equidistant points on a polyline to detect corresponding polylines, or segments of polylines. In the figure, a polyline of cadastral data set with the nearest polylines of a city planning map are presented.

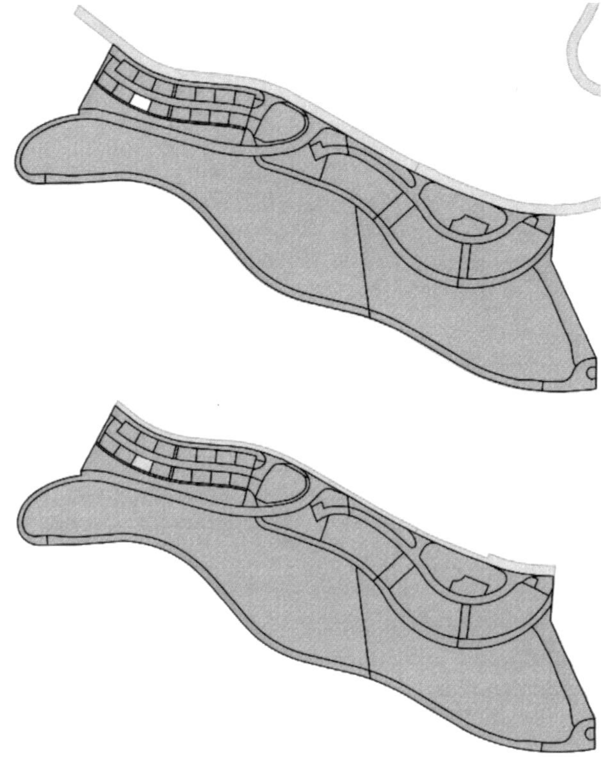

Figure 8. The result of triangulation. Upper – cadaster, lower – city planning. Nesher.

Figure 9. Equidistant points used to calculate similarity of polylines and polylines' segments. Red line – city planning dataset, black – cadastre.

The algorithm for line pairs searching is presented in pseudo code in Figure 10.

The pseudo-function gets the 'id's_of_closest_lines () and returns a pair of neighboring lines' ids points which are closest. Usually, for one line A, several pairs of ids can be defined (idA1-idB1, idA1-idB2, ...). All id pairs are processed. Pts_A – points of a city planning dataset are situated on a line with id idA; Pts_B – points of line idB (cadastral map). The pseudo function gets_segments (Pts_A, Pts_B) and splits lines into segments at intervals where the distance between the nearest points is more than D_{max}. In the first line of the pseudo function - finding_pairs (PtsA,PtsB) - we test distances from start point of line A to start and end points of line B. If start-start distance is more than start-end, we invert the order of points in line A. Then we set l,i,j variables: l – length of line, i - number of starting points on line A, j - number of starting point on line B.

```
Foreach idA,idB in get_ids_of_closest_lines(){
  Pts_A   = get_points('city planning',idA)
  Pts_B =   get_points('cadastre',idB)
  If min(len(Pts_A),len(Pts_B)) > tail {
    Foreach segm in get_segments(Pts_A,Pts_B){
      Pts_A_segm=segm['Pts_A']
      Pts_B_segm=segm[' Pts_B']
      Result_line_pair=find_pair(Pts_A_segm,Pts_B_segm)}}}

Function find_pair(PtsA,PtsB) {
  If (distance(PtsA[0],PtsB[0]) >
    distance(PtsA[0], PtsB[-1])){ PtsA=reverse(PtsA)  }
  Length=min(len(PtsA), len(PtsB))
  Global_measures=[ ]
  Foreach l in reverse([tail,...,length]){
   Local_measures=[ ]
   Foreach i in [0,...,len(PtsA)-tail]{
    Foreach j in [0,...,len(PtsB)-tail]{
      cur_measure=Calc_measures(PtsA,PtsB,i,j,l)
      if (cur_measure[0]<max_stand_dev and
         cur_measure[1]<max_distance){
        Local_measures.append(cur_measure)} } }
   Global_measures
.append(Find_local_indicator(Local_measures))
   If      Global_measures      and      (l==length      or
len(Global_measures)>tail){
     Gen_desc_list=[calculate_global_indicator(cur) for cur in
                    Global_measures]
     If max(Gen_desc_list[:-tail])> max(Gen_desc_list[-tail:]){
       Return
Global_measures[index_of_maximal(Gen_desc_list)]}}}

Function Calc_measures(PtsA,PtsB,i,j,l){

  cur_PtsA= PtsA[i:i+l]
  cur_PtsB= PtsB[j:j+l]
  dists=Distances(cur_PtsA,cur_PtsB)

  Return [stand_dev(dists),max(dists),
   min(dists),delta_x,delta_y,
   get_max_stddev_of_tailes(cur_PtsA,cur_PtsB),
   get_min_shape_descr_of_tails(cur_PtsA,cur_PtsB),
   get_shape_descriptor(cur_PtsA,cur_PtsB),   i, j, l]}
```

Figure 10. Searching for equal polylines or polylines' segments.

The function Calc_measures (PtsA, PtsB, i, j, l) and calculates a set of parameters (standard deviation of distances, shape descriptor, minimal shape descriptor of line tails, minimal and maximal distance between points). This enables us to define similarity of line A segment from i to i+l and for line B - from j to j+l. Variables i and j, which define the optimal segment (pseudo function Find_local_optimal (Local_measures)), have been found for each possible length l using (2).

$$Loc\_Ind = \frac{(d - D_{\max})}{-D_{\max}} + \frac{s - S_{t\_\max}}{S_{t\_\max} - S_{t\_\min}} \quad (2)$$

$$G\_Ind = \frac{\sigma_t - \sigma_{\max}}{\sigma_{\max}} + \frac{d - D_{\max}}{-D_{\max}} + \\ + \frac{s - S_{t\_\max}}{S_{t\_\max} - S_{t\_\min}} + (1 - l)/\mathrm{L} \quad (3)$$

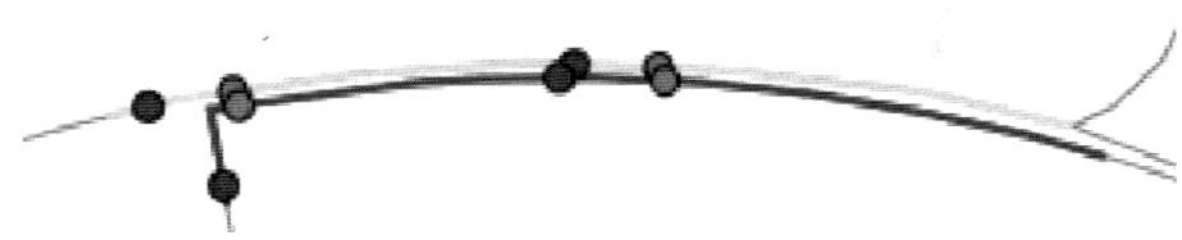

Figure 11. Segment of line A (city planning) – green; segment of line B (cadastre) – blue. Start and end point of the most similar line segments are red points (i=6,j=6, Loc_ind=0.86); blue points – i=2, j=1, Loc_Ind=0.026.

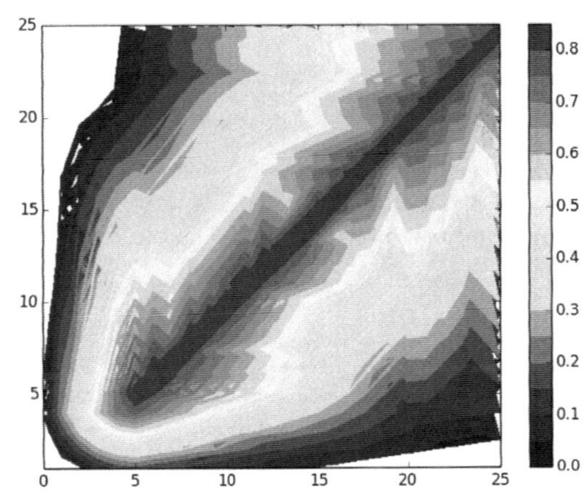

Figure 12. Plot of indicator Loc_Ind: X axis – i, Y axis - j. The segment with i=6 and j=6 is the most optimal.

The meaning of parameters in (2): d – maximal distance between points of lines A and B for (l,i,j), s - minimal tail shape descriptor. In this step, we have a Global_measures list containing elements that correspond to some l and contain measures of line segments with maximal indicator Loc_Ind derived from the list (Local_measures) with variable (i,j).

This process is illustrated in Figures 11 and 12 (segment length is 20 meters). Figure 11 depicts different segments with the same length; Figure 12 is a plot of indicator Loc_Ind depicted by color. The next stage is defining optimal segment length. In the previous stage, we defined optimal segments i,j for some length l by calculating local indicator Loc_Ind. To define optimal segment length we use global indicator G_Ind; its formula is presented as (3).

In the equation, σ_t means maximal standard deviation of point distances of line segments' tails; for more details see Section III and (2). The resulting optimal line length is defined by maximal global indicator G_Ind. The process is illustrated in Figures 13 and 14. Figure 13 depicts examples of optimal segments with different lengths. Figure 14 is a plot of indicator G_Ind. It is obvious that the optimal segment length is 41 meters (element with maximal G_Ind, according to the plot presented in Figure 14).

Figure 13. Segment of line A (city planning) – green; segment of line B (cadastre) – blue. Nodes of the most similar line segments with different lengths of segment: red points – l=41,i=5,j=5,G_Ind=2.35; green points – l=10,i=5,j=5 G_Ind=1.69; blue points – l=43,i=3,j=3 G_Ind=1.64.

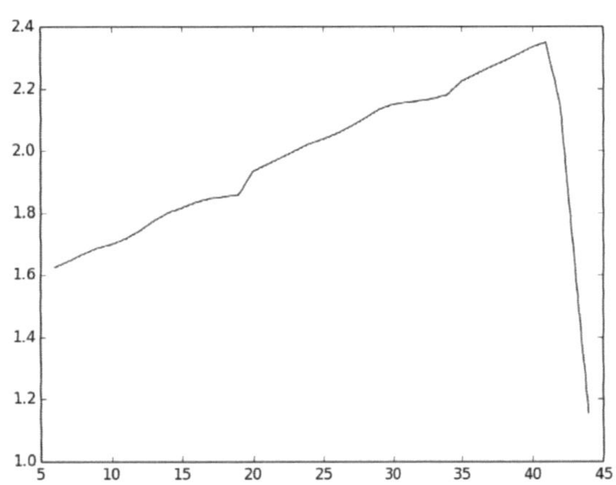

Figure 14. Plot of indicator G_ind: X axis – segment length (in meters), Y axis – G_Ind.

VI. COMPILING A FINAL MAP

At this point, we have the pairs of corresponding polygons and polygon boundary segments. Some segments are overlapped; to resolve conflicts, a special parameter was developed:

$$P = \frac{l - \min\_len}{range\_len + \frac{\sigma}{-\sigma_{\max}}} \quad (4)$$

where: l is length of line of one of the lines in a line pair, min_len – minimal length of line of all line pairs, range_len – range of length of all line pairs. A line pair with maximal P will be saved; others will be removed. The process is shown in Figure 15.

Figure 15. Overlaped line pairs: red line pair – P=1.23, green line pair – P=1.09 . Green line pair will be removed.

Figure 16. Moving segments without pairs and closing boundaries: green – lines that do not have pairs in cadastral dataset, blue – moved green lines, red – closing boundary by moving nodes, black – cadastral pair of city-planning line segments.

After removing overlapping line pairs, we can use a correspondent line segment of the cadastral dataset instead of the city-planning dataset. The boundaries of counterpart polygons are extracted from polygon maps calculated by triangulation. The pair segments are composed with the extracted boundaries. We will use nodes of pair segments and centroids of pair polygons as control ground points for transformation.

The lines and line segments of the city-planning dataset without corresponding lines of the cadastral dataset have been moved. Delta X and delta Y have been calculated as average delta X and delta Y of neighboring nodes of line pairs and centroids of pair polygons. Unclosed boundaries of polygons have been closed by moving the nodes of an unclosed line to the nearest node of a neighboring line (see Figure 16).

We now have a map containing closed boundaries. All legacy centroids have been removed. To create polygons we add a new centroid to each set of closed boundaries (see Figure 17). As mentioned above, we have prepared a list of control ground points. The list contains coordinates of correspondent polygons' centroids and line pairs' nodes. We use these control ground points to transform the original city planning dataset to its accurate position. The transformed city panning dataset could be used as a product by itself, because it is a more accurate dataset in comparison to the original map. But we will use it mainly for detecting attributes of the resulting dataset.

As mentioned earlier, the legacy centroids have been removed from the resulting map and new centroids have been added. In other words, we have removed all connections between result and original datasets. To define the final correspondences we need to apply the triangulation process one more time, but now we will compare the results (Figure 17) with the transformed city planning dataset. For each polygon a correspondence must be found, otherwise the polygon will be marked as an error polygon. We have applied the triangulation to both datasets. For each polygon a correspondence has been established; no error polygons have been detected.

Figure 17. Adding centroids to closed boundaries. Yokne'am.

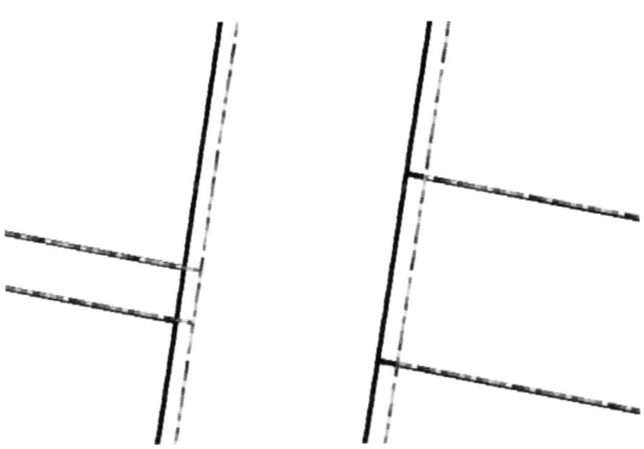

Figure 18. Calculation of minimal distances from segmented boundaries of the result dataset (color segments) to cadastre dataset (black lines).

VII. RESULTS

In order to evaluate the results, we use distances between the boundaries of the result and cadastre datasets as a main measure. As mentioned in the previous section, no error polygons have been defined by the triangulation, i.e., no semantic errors have been detected.

In order to evaluate the geometrical accuracy of the resulting map, the result boundaries have been split to 0.5 m segments and a minimal distance to the boundaries of the cadastre dataset is calculated. In Figure 18 the prepared color segments and black lines are presented. The minimal distance from each segment to the closest point on the nearest line is calculated.

TABLE I. GEOMETRIC ACCURACY OF THE RESULT DATASETS

Measures in meter	Nesher datasets compared with cadastre boundaries		
	Original	*Transformed*	*Result*
Mean distance	0.59	0.55	0.01
Standard deviation	0.55	0.54	0.05
	Yokne'am datasets compared with cadastre boundaries		
Mean distance	0.82	0.63	0.13
Standard deviation	0.81	0.84	0.77

Table I presents the geometric accuracy of the result datasets estimated by the distances between result boundary segments and cadastre (accurate) dataset. We can conclude that positional accuracy has been significantly improved for the result datasets. The accuracy of transformed maps has only slightly improved.

In addition to the table, the histograms of distances are presented in Figures 19 and 20. The vertical axis of the histogram is the number of segments, the horizontal axis depicts distance in meters. The histograms also prove the significant improvement in positional accuracy.

In contrast to the mean and the standard deviation values presented in the table, we cannot unambiguously conclude from the histograms in Figure 19 (Nesher dataset), that the transformed map is more accurate. The main reason for this is the fact that most polygons of the map have correspondences, and only several northern polygons do not. That leads to a situation of the presence of one type of control ground points (line pair nodes) in the northern part of the dataset only, with another type in the remaining area. For larger and more differentiate datasets this would not work. The histogram of result datasets depicts significant improvement of positional accuracy in comparison to original and transformed maps.

As mentioned earlier, in the case of a larger and more differentiate dataset, the contrast between the histograms of original and transformed datasets will be clearer. We can see this in Figure 19.

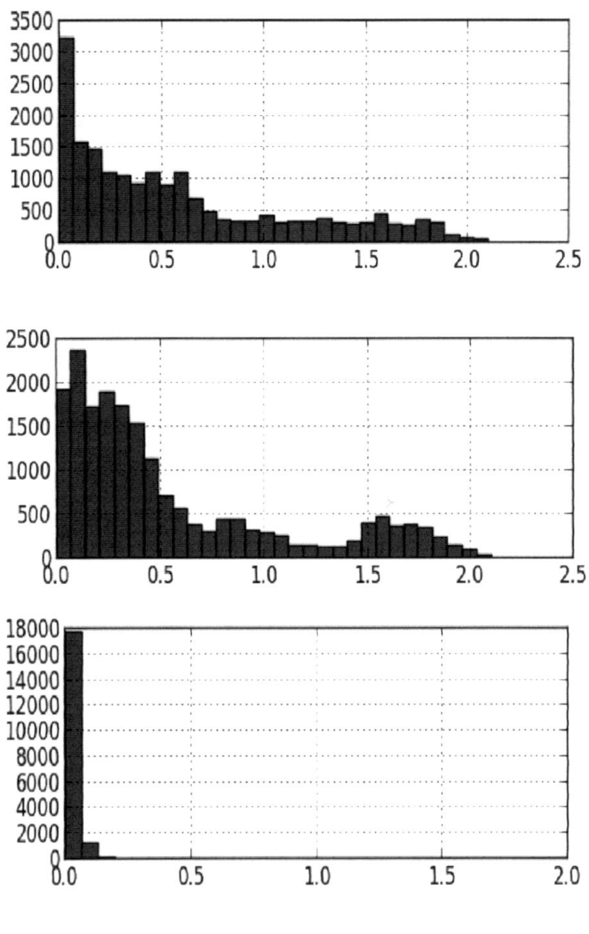

Figure 19. Histogram of distances. From top to bottom: original, transformed, and result datasets. Nesher. X axis – distance in meter, Y axis – number of segments.

Results are presented in Figure 21 for six extents. The extents correspond to the red numbers in circles in Figure 1. Color background is the result dataset. It is overlaid by red and black lines. Red lines are the original city planning dataset. Black lines are the cadastre dataset. We can conclude that most line segments have been taken from the cadastral dataset; others have been transformed to correspond with cadastral polyline segments. The result looks satisfactory; the final map is holistic and does not contain significant deficiencies. A review implemented by specialists enables us to state that the results are satisfactory and the approach could be used in real applications after fixing some lacks.

VIII. CONCLUSION

An approach for improving the accuracy of polygons' data is presented. Land-use city planning dataset locations have been corrected according to the cadastral dataset. The polylines' segments along the polygons have been split by equidistant points. Analysis has been performed using statistics based on the points of the neighboring polylines of the two datasets. A set of parameters has been used: shape descriptor of polyline segments, standard deviation of point distances, minimal and maximal point distances, standard deviation of segment tails, etc. A set of correspondent polyline segments using special indicators has been found. It enables us to find optimal segments from the list of polyline segments with different lengths and starting points.

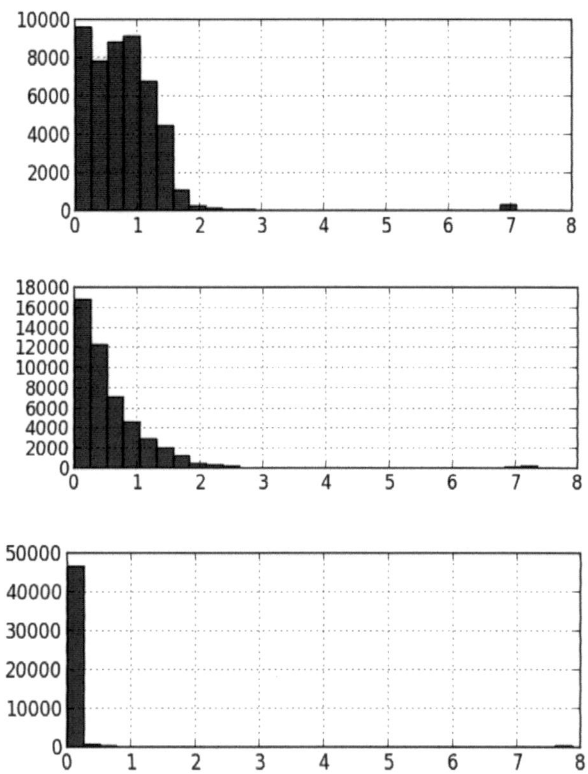

Figure 20. Histogram of distances. From top to bottom: original, transformed, and result datasets. Yokne'am. X axis – distance in meter, Y axis – number of segments.

The polyline segments of the city planning data with parameters similar/identical to the segments of the cadastral data were linked to these segments (defining counterpart segments). Segments without a counterpart were transformed. The triangulation process has been used to define correspondences between polygons. It enables us to find optimal segments from the list of polyline segments with different lengths and starting points.

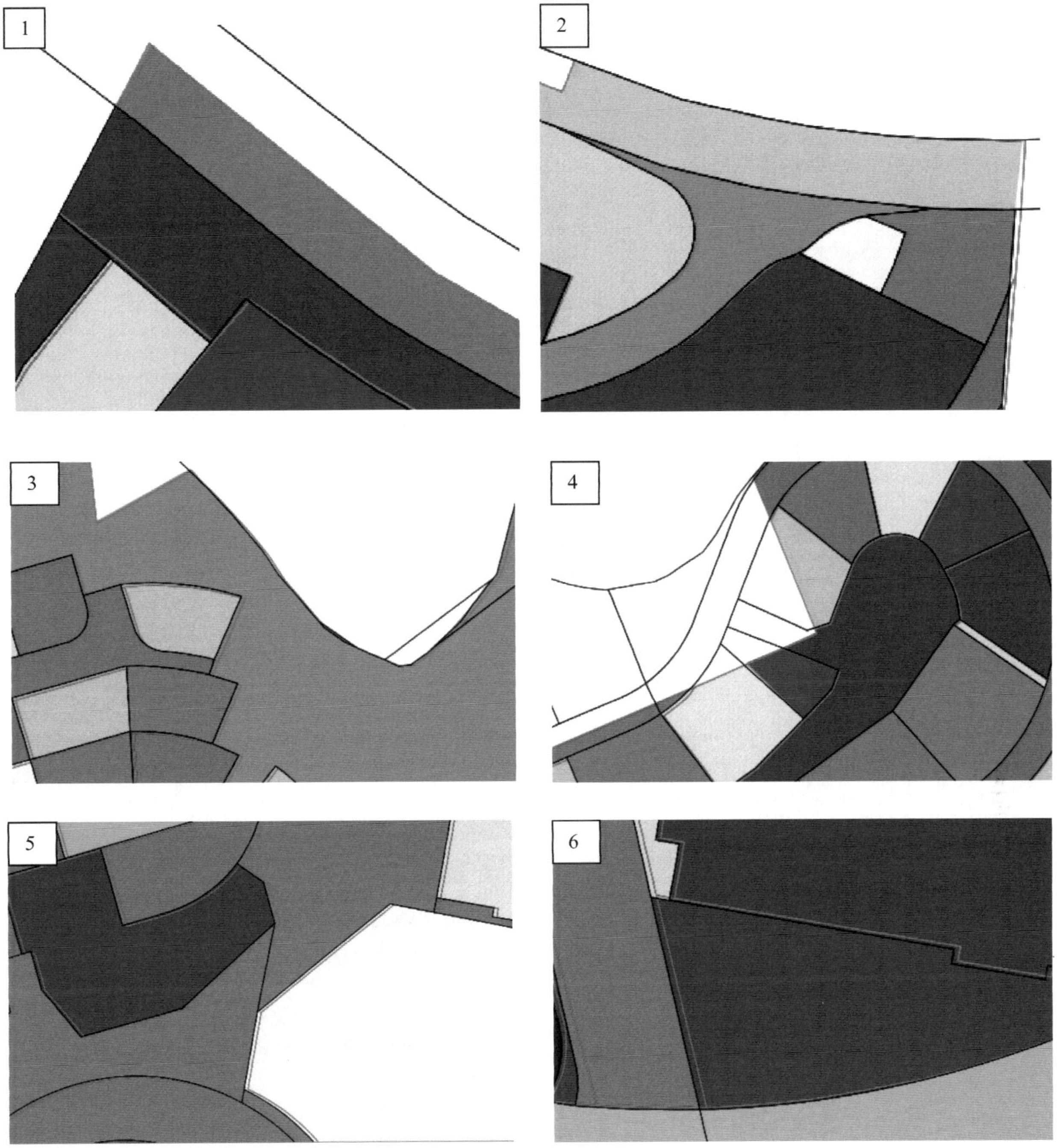

Figure 21. Results. Color background is result polygons. Red lines are original city planning polygons' boundaries. Black lines are cadastre polygons' boundaries. 1 and 2 - Nesher; 3-6 – Yokne'am. Figure 1 depicts the positions of the extents.

The polyline segments of the city planning data with parameters similar/identical to the segments of the cadastral data were linked to these segments (defining counterpart segments). Segments without a counterpart were transformed. The triangulation process has been used to define correspondences between polygons.

In the future, we need to test the approach with additional datasets and different parameters, to compare it with other approaches, and to improve calculation speed.

To implement the approach, we used Python 2.7 programming language (with numpy, scipy and matplotlib additional libraries), GRASS GIS 7.1, and Debian GNU/Linux 7 operating system.

ACKNOWLEDGEMENT

This research was supported by the Survey of Israel as a part of Project 2019317. The authors would like to thank the Survey of Israel for providing financial support and data for the purpose of this research.

REFERENCES

[1] A. Noskov and Y. Doytsher, "A Segmentation-based Approach for Improving the Accuracy of Polygon Data," GEOProcessing 2015, 2009, Portugal, pp. 69-74.

[2] S. Filin and Y. Doytsher, "The detection of corresponding objects in a linear-based map conflation," Surveying and land information systems, vol. 60(2), 2000, pp. 117-127.

[3] V. Walter and D. Fritsch, "Matching spatial data sets: a statistical approach," International Journal of Geographical Information Science (IJGIS), vol. 13 (5), 1999, pp. 445–473.

[4] X. Shu and X. Wu. "A novel contour descriptor for 2D shape matching and its application to image retrieval", Image and vision Computing, vol. 29.4, 2011, pp. 286-294.

[5] S. Belongie, J. Malik, and J. Puzicha, "Shape matching and object recognition using shape contexts," IEEE Trans. on Pattern Analysis and Machine Intelligence, 24(4), 2002, pp. 509-522.

[6] E. Safra, Y. Kanza, Y. Sagiv, C. Beeri, and Y. Doytsher, "Ad-hoc matching of vectorial road networks," International Journal of Geographical Information Science, iFirst, 2012, pp. 1–40, ISSN: 1365-8816, ISSN: 1362-3087.

[7] B. Schmitzer and S. Christoph, "Object segmentation by shape matching with Wasserstein modes," Energy Minimization Methods in Computer Vision and Pattern Recognition, Springer Berlin Heidelberg, 2013.

[8] T. Ma and J. Longin, "From partial shape matching through local deformation to robust global shape similarity for object detection," Computer Vision and Pattern Recognition (CVPR), IEEE Conference on. IEEE, 2011, pp. 1441-1448.

[9] X. Chen, "Spatial relation between uncertain sets," International archives of Photogrammetry and remote sensing, vol. 31(B3), Vienna, 1996, pp. 105-110.

[10] A. Bronstein, R. Kimmel, M. Mahmoudi, and G. Sapiro, "A Gromov-Hausdorff framework with diffusion geometry for topologically-robust non-rigid shape matching," International Journal of Computer Vision, vol. 89(2-3), 2010, pp. 266-286.

[11] P. Tahmasebi, A. Hezarkhani, and M. Sahimi, "Linking Objects of Different Spatial Data Sets by Integration and Aggregation," vol. 2(4), 1998, pp. 335-358.

[12] E. Rahm and P. Bernstein, "A survey of approaches to automatic schema matching," The International Journal on Very Large Data Bases (VLDB), vol. 10(4), 2001, pp. 334–350.

[13] V. Kashyap and A. Sheth, "Semantic and schematic similarities between database objects: a context-based approach," The International Journal on Very Large Data Bases (VLDB), vol. 5(4), 1996, pp. 276–304.

[14] P. Shvaiko and J. Euzenat, "A survey of schema-based matching approaches," Journal on Data Semantics IV, Springer Berlin Heidelberg, 2005, pp. 146-171.

[15] B. Amann, C. Beeri., I. Fundulaki, and M. Scholl., "Ontology-based integration of XML Web resources," 1st International Semantic Web Conference (ISWC), Sardinia, Italy, June 9-12 2002, pp. 117–131.

[16] L. Gravano, P. G. Ipeirotis, H. V. Jagadish, N. Koudas, S. Muthukrishnan, and D. Srivastava, "Approximate String Joins in a Database (Almost) for Free," Proceedings of the 27th International Conference on Very Large Data Bases, Italy, 2001.

[17] L. Gravano, P. G. Ipeirotis, N. Koudas, and D. Srivastava, "Text joins in an RDBMS for web data integration," Proceedings of the 12th international conference on World Wide Web. ACM, 2003.

[18] C. Parent and S. Spaccapietra, "Database integration: the key to data interoperability," Advances in Object-Oriented Data Modeling, M. P. Papazoglou, S. Spaccapietra, Z. Tari (Eds.), The MIT Press, 2000.

[19] G. Wiederhold, "Mediation to deal with heterogeneous data sources," Interoperating Geographic Information System, 1999, pp. 1–16.

[20] A. Saalfeld, "Conflation-automated map compilation," International Journal of Geographical Information Science (IJGIS), vol. 2 (3), 1988, pp. 217–228.

[21] M. Sester, K. Anders, and V. Walter, "Linking Objects of Different Spatial Data Sets by Integration and Aggregation," GeoInformatica, vol. 2(4), 1998, pp. 335-358.

[22] C. Steger, M. Ulrich, and C. Wiedemann, "Machine vision algorithms and applications", Weinheim: wiley-VCH, 2008, pp. 1-2.

[23] G. Bradski and A. Kaehler, "Learning OpenCV: Computer vision with the OpenCV library," O'Reilly Media, Inc, 2008.

[24] J. Howse, "OpenCV Computer Vision with Python," Packt Publishing Ltd, 2013, ISBN: 978-1-78216-392-3.

[25] J. Shewchuk, "Triangle: Engineering a 2D quality mesh generator and Delaunay triangulator," Applied computational geometry towards geometric engineering, Springer Berlin Heidelberg, 1996, pp. 203-222.

[26] F. Aurenhammer, "Voronoi diagrams - a survey of a fundamental geometric data structure," ACM Computing Surveys (CSUR), vol. 23(3), 1991, pp. 345-405.

[27] M. Landa, "GRASS GIS 7.0: Interoperability improvements," GIS Ostrava, Jan. 2013, pp. 21-23.

[28] R. Blazek, M. Neteler, and R. Micarelli, "The new GRASS 5.1 vector architecture," Open source GIS-GRASS users conference, University of Trento, Italy, 2002.

[29] J. Herring, "OpenGIS Implementation Standard for Geographic information-Simple feature access-Part 1: Common architecture," OGC Document 4, no. 21, 2011.

[30] I. Wilson, J.M. Ware, and J.A. Ware, "A genetic algorithm approach to cartographic map generalisation" Computers in Industry, vol. 52(3), 2003, pp. 291-304.

[31] B. Gaster, L. Howes, D. Kaeli, P. Mistry, and D. Schaa, "Heterogeneous Computing with OpenCL: Revised OpenCL1," Newnes, 2012.

Extending Interface Roles to Account for Quality of Service Aspects in the DAiSI

Dirk Herrling, Andreas Rausch and Karina Rehfeldt

Technical University Clausthal
Julius-Albert-Straße 4,
38678 Clausthal-Zellerfeld, Germany
email: dirk.herrling@tu-clausthal.de
andreas.rausch@tu-clausthal.de
karina.rehfeldt@tu-clausthal.de

***Abstract*—Dynamic adaptive systems are systems that change their behavior according to the needs of the user at run time. Since it is not feasible to develop these systems from scratch every time, a component model enabling dynamic adaptive systems is called for. Moreover, an infrastructure is required that is capable of wiring dynamic adaptive systems from a set of components in order to provide a dynamic and adaptive behavior to the user. To ensure a wanted, emergent behavior of the overall system, the components need to be wired according to the rules an application architecture defines. In this paper, we present the Dynamic Adaptive System Infrastructure (DAiSI). It provides a component model and configuration mechanism for dynamic adaptive systems. To address the issue of application architecture conform system configuration, we introduce interface roles that allow the consideration of component behavior during the composition of an application. Moreover, we extend the interface roles and application specifications by a quality of service concept. This enables a component to not only require a syntactical and semantical correct wiring, but also to demand the – from its viewpoint – best service.**

Keywords–dynamic adaptive systems; component model; adaptation; interface roles; application architecture awareness.

I. Introduction

This paper is an extended version of a paper presented at the Seventh International Conference on Adaptive and Self-Adaptive Systems and Applications (ADAPTIVE) [1].

Software-based systems are present at all times in our daily life. This ranges from our private life where nearly everyone owns and uses a smart mobile phone to large scale business applications and the public administration that are managed entirely by software systems. In every household, dozens of devices run software and a modern car will not even start its engine without the proper software. Some software systems have grown to be among the most complex systems ever made by mankind [2], due to their increase in size and functionality.

Through smaller mobile devices with accurate sensors and actuators and the ubiquitous availability of the Internet, the number of integrated devices in large scale applications has increased drastically within the last twenty years. These devices and the software running on them are used in organically grown, heterogeneous, and dynamic information technology (IT) environments. Users expect them to not only provide their primary services, but also to collaborate with each other to provide some kind of emergent behavior. The challenge is therefore to be able to build systems that are robust enough to withstand changes in their environment, deal with a steadily increasing complexity, and match requirements that might be defined in the future [3].

Due to the increasing complexity of large systems, be it in size or in functionality, those systems are no longer developed from scratch by one vendor. While the development usually takes place in a component-based way [4], it is usually split among a number of companies. Additional components for mobile devices are often developed against documented or reverse-engineered interfaces by independent developers.

To ease the development of dynamically integratable components, a common component model is called for. The development of DAiSI started in 2004 to address this issue [5]. Over the years, a component model was defined that allows developers to implement a component for dynamic adaptive systems easily. In contrast to adaptive systems, which adapt to changes in their environment only, dynamic adaptive systems can also integrate components into themselves, which were not known at design-time. DAiSI provides a component model and run-time infrastructure for such dynamic adaptive systems. The latter can run and integrate DAiSI components by linking required services with compatible provided services and thus forming one ore more DAiSI applications. Compatibility has been only syntactical at first, requiring that for every method in the required service, a method with the same signature (name, parameters, return types, etc.) is defined in the corresponding provided service [6]. The aspect was later extended to support semantic compatibility by additionally requiring equivalent behavior of each method [7].

Obviously, an application is more than just the sum of its components. This already becomes evident in very small examples. Consider cross country skiers and their trainer. A dynamic adaptive application connects vital data monitoring devices of the athletes to the management system of their trainer. In a competition with a competing team on the same track, athletes and trainers should only be connected to each other if they belong to the same team. While it is possible to work around this issue by, e.g., ensuring in the implementation of components that they only exchange data if they belong to the same team, this is just that – a work around.

An application architecture that is enforced by the infrastructure can define rules that can address the challenge our athlete– and trainer-components face. It can specify that only components of members of the same team are allowed to be connected to each other. More generically, the consideration of an application architecture during system configuration helps to ensure wanted, emergent behavior of dynamic adaptive systems. It does that by enabling application architects to limit the configuration space and thus prevent the connection of components that should not be connected. This paper will show the introduction of an application architecture into the field of dynamic adaptive system configuration and how we integrate it with the DAiSI infrastructure.

The rest of this paper is structured as follows: In Section II, we present an overview of other works in the field of dynamic adaptive systems. This is followed by an introduction to the DAiSI component model and the notation of DAiSI components in Section III. As a first step towards architecture conform configuration, we introduce interface roles and the consideration of local quality of service (QoS) aspects in Section IV. Afterwards, we briefly discuss the DAiSI configuration mechanism in Section V. In Sections VI and VII, an introduction of applications and application templates together with application-wide quality of service optimization follows. The paper ends with a conclusion in Section VIII.

II. Related Work

Component-based development is one of the state-of-the-art techniques in modern software engineering. Components as units of deployment and their component frameworks provide a well-understood, solid approach for the development of large-scale systems. This is not surprising, considering that components can be added to, or removed from the system at design-time easily. This allows high flexibility and easy maintenance [4].

If components should be added to, or removed from a system at run-time things get a little bit more difficult, as techniques for this were not implemented in early component models. However, service oriented approaches allowed the dynamic integration of components at run-time. Those systems usually maintain a service directory. Components entering the system register their provided– and query for candidates of their required services. Once a suitable service provider is identified for a required service, it can be easily connected to the component [8].

Service-oriented approaches are capable of handling dynamic behavior. Components that have not necessarily been previously known to the system can be integrated into it. However, they have the uncomfortable characteristic that the system itself does not care for the dynamic adaptive behavior. The component needs to register and integrate itself. Also, it has to monitor itself whether the used services are still available and adapt its behavior accordingly, if that is no longer the case. To address these issues a couple of frameworks have been developed to support dynamic adaptive reconfiguration.

CONIC was one of the first frameworks for dynamic adaptive, distributed applications. It provided a description technique that could be used to change the structure (and thus the architecture) of the integrated modules of an application. A CONIC application was maintained by a centralized configuration manager [9]. It allowed to spawn new component instances and to link them to each other.

Another framework, building on the knowledge gained through the research in CONIC, was a framework for Reconfigurable and Extensible Parallel and Distributed Systems (REX). It provided support for dynamic reconfiguration in distributed, parallel systems. It visioned those systems as component instances, connected through interfaces for which an own interface description language was defined. Components were considered as types, allowing multiple instances of any component to be present at run-time. The framework allowed the dynamic change of the number of running instances and their wiring [10], [11]. Both, the CONIC– and REX framework allowed the dynamic adaptation of distributed applications, but only through explicit reconfiguration programs for every possible reconfiguration.

This issue was addressed in [12]. They took a more abstract approach and defined sets of valid application configurations. Following this approach, a system can then adapt itself from one valid application configuration to another, whenever the system changes. The declaration of reconfiguration steps became obsolete.

Another framework to build dynamic adaptive systems upon is ProAdapt. It is set in the field of service-oriented architectures and reacts to four classes of situations:

- Problems that stop the execution of the application
- Problems that require the execution of a non-optimal system configuration
- New requirements
- Presence of services with a better service quality

ProAdapt is capable of replacing certain services and can, together with its service composition capabilities, replace composed services [13].

In [14], [15], a framework for the dynamic reconfiguration of mobile applications on the basis of the .NET framework was introduced. Applications are composed of components, and application configurations are specified initially in XML. A centralized configuration manager interprets this specification and instantiates and connects the involved components. The specification can include numerous different configurations which are distinguished by conditions under which they apply. The framework monitors its surroundings with the help of a special *Observer* component and evaluates which application configuration is applicable. The framework allows the dynamic addition and removal of components and connections.

In [16], the authors present a solution to ensure syntactical and semantical compatibility of web services. They used the Web Service Definition Language (WSDL) and enriched it with the Web Service Semantic Profile (WSSP) for semantical information. Additionally they allowed an application architect to further reduce the configuration space through the specification of constraints. While their approach is able to solve the sketched problem of preventing the wiring of components that should not be connected, they only focus on the service definition and compatibility. Our DAiSI approach defines an infrastructure in which components are executed that implement a specific component model. We do want to compose an application out of components that can adapt their behavior at run-time.

We achieve this by mapping sets of required services to sets of provided services and thus specifying which provided services depend on which required services. The solution presented in [16] does not offer a component model. All rules regarding the relation between required and provided services would have to be specified as external constraints. The authors in [17] provided a different solution to ensure semantic compatibility of web services. However, the same arguments as for [16] regarding the absence of a high level component model hold true.

With regard to the application architecture aware adaptation, Rainbow [18], [19] is one of the most dominant and well-known frameworks. Rainbow uses invariants for the specification of constraints in its architecture description language. For each invariant an operation for the adaptation of the system can be specified. The operation is then executed whenever the invariant is violated. However, this approach requires the knowledge of all component types at design-time, which is opposing our goal of an open system. Additionally, the developer has to implement the adaptation steps individually for every invariant. This imperative method for adaptation requires the component requiring the adaptation to have a view of the complete system and additionally introduces a big overhead at design-time as well as at run-time.

R-OSGi [20] takes advantage of the features developed for centralized module management in the OSGi platform, like dynamic module loading and –unloading. It introduces a way to transparently use remote OSGi modules in an application while still preserving good performance. Issues like network disruptions or unresponsive components are mapped to events of unloaded modules and thus can be handled gracefully – a strength compared to many other platforms. However, R-OSGi does not provide means to specify application architecture specific requirements. As long as modules are compatible with each other they will be linked. The module developer has to ensure the application architecture at the implementation level. Opposed to that, our approach proposes a high level description of application architectures through application templates that can be specified even after the required components have been developed.

III. THE DAiSI COMPONENT MODEL

This section will introduce the foundations of the DAiSI component model. As already briefly mentioned in the introduction of this paper, DAiSI components communicate with each other through services. Different component configurations map required– to provided services.

AS an example, we assume that a self-organizing system is to be developed, which supports the training of biathletes. A biathlon team consists of several athletes and trainers. Each trainer requires an overview of his athletes' performance data, which includes the current pulse and skiing-technique of the athlete. Based on this data, the trainer can give guidance to his athletes. Figure 1 shows a sketch of a DAiSI component with some explanatory comments for an athlete in the biathlon sports domain.

A component is depicted as a rectangle, in this example of a light blue color. Component configurations are bars that extend over the borders of the component and are depicted in yellow here. Associated to component configurations are the provided and required services. The notation is similar to the Unified Markup Language (UML) lollipop notation [21] with full circles resembling provided, and semi circles representing required services. A filled circle indicates that the associated service is directly requested by the end user and thus should be provided, even if no other service requires its use.

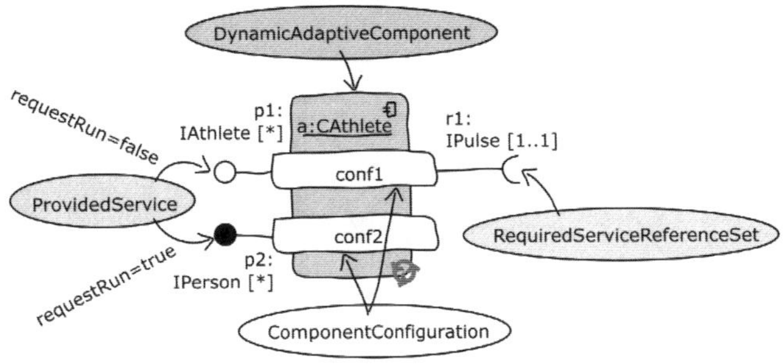

Figure 1. Example notation of a DAiSI component with explanatory comments.

Figure 1 shows the *CAthlete* component, consisting of two component configurations: $conf_1$ and $conf_2$. The first component configuration requires exactly one service variable r_1 of the *IPulse* interface. The second component configuration does not require any services to be able to provide its service p_2 of *IPerson*. The service could be used by any number of service users (the cardinality is specified as $*$). The other component configuration ($conf_1$) could provide the service p_1 of the type *IAthlete*, which could again be used by any number of users.

Figure 2 shows the DAiSI component model as an UML class diagram [21]. The component itself, represented as the light blue box in the notation example, is represented by the *DynamicAdaptiveComponent* class. It has three types of associations to the *ComponentConfiguration* class, namely *current*, *activatable*, and *contains*. The *contains* association resembles the non-empty set of all component configurations. It is ordered by quality from best to worst, with the best component configuration being the most desirable, e.g., because of best service qualities of the provided services. The order is defined by the component developer. A subset of the contained are the *activatable* component configurations. These have their required services resolved and could be activated. An *active* component configuration produces its provided services. At run-time, only one or zero component configurations per component can be active. The active component configuration is represented by the *current* association in the component model, with the cardinality allowing one or zero current component configurations for each component.

The required services (represented by a semi circle in the component notation in Figure 1) are represented by the *RequiredServiceReferenceSet* class. Every component configuration can declare any number of required services. Those that are resolved are represented by the *resolved* association. The cardinalities of the required service are stored in the attributes *minNoOfRequiredRefs* and *maxNoOfRequiredRefs*. Provided services (noted as full circles on the left hand side in Figure 1) are represented by the *ProvidedService* class. They can be associated to more than one component configuration, if more than one component configuration provides the same service. The *runRequestedBy* association is relevant at run-time and resembles the component configuration that actually wants the provided service to be produced.

Not all provided services can be used any number of times. The attribute *maxNoUsers* indicates the maximum number of allowed users. The flag *requestRun*, represented by the

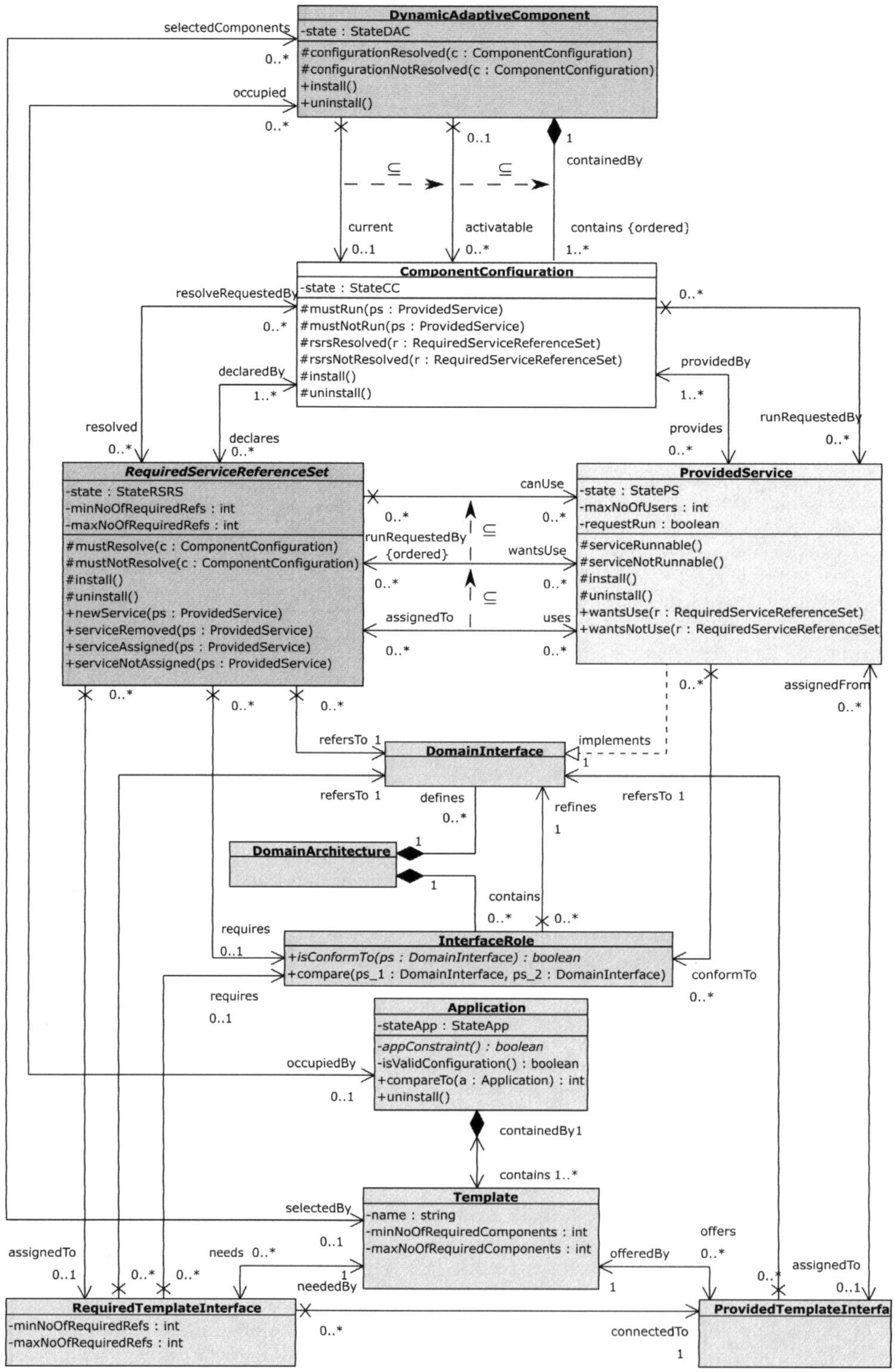

Figure 2. DAiSI component model.

full circle being filled with black in the component notation, indicates that the service should be produced, even if no other service requires its use. This is typically the case for services that provide graphical user interfaces or that provide some functionality directly requested by the end user.

The provided and required service, more precisely their respective classes in the component model, are associated with each other through three associations. The first association *canUse* represents the compatibility between two services. If a provided service can be bound to the service requirement of another class, these two are associated through a *canUse* association. A subset of the *canUse* association is *wantsUse*. At run-time, it resembles a kind of reservation of a particular provided service by a required service reference set. It does not already use the provided service, but would like to use it. After the connection is established and the provided service satisfies the requirement, they are part of the *uses* association which represents the actual connections. All classes covered to this point implement a state machine to maintain the state of the DAiSI component. If you want to know more about the state machines and the configuration mechanism, please refer to our last years paper [22].

To this point, we have covered the building blocks of a DAiSI component. An application in a dynamic adaptive environment is composed of any number of such components that are linked with each other through services. Those services are defined through *DomainInterfaces*. Required services (represented by the *RequiredServiceReferenceSet* class) refer to exactly one domain interface, while provided services (represented by the *ProvidedService* class) implement a domain interface. The set of all defined domain interfaces composes the *DomainArchitecture*. The interface roles, which will be presented in the next section, are contained by the domain architecture. They refine domain interfaces and are required by any number of required service reference sets. Any provided service can conform to an interface role. However, this is not a static information, but changes during run-time.

For our example, it is assumed that the component presented in Figure 3 is available.

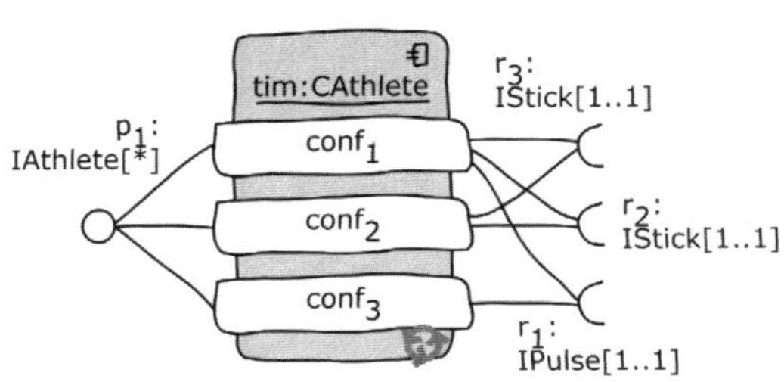

Figure 3. The CAthlete component.

The component defines three *ComponentConfigurations* with $conf_1$ specified as best configuration and $conf_3$ as worst. The $conf_3$ configuration can be activated if r_1 can be connected to a service that implements the interface *IPulse*. The $conf_2$ configuration can be activated, if r_2 and r_3 are each connected with a ski stick. The $conf_1$ configuration is activated if the dependencies of all three *RequiredServiceReferenceSets* can be resolved. In all three configurations, the component provides a service that implements the domain interface *IAthlete*. It defines a method *getPulse():int* to query the current pulse and also a method *getSkiingTechnique():String*, which returns the currently used skiing technique (double poling/diagonal technique). Additionally, it provides a method *getLocation():double[2]* to query the current location of the athlete. If the $conf_3$ configuration is active, the call *getSkiingTechnique* returns the value null. If, in contrast, the $conf_2$ configuration is active, the call *getPulse* returns the value -1.

The component presented in Figure 4 represents the trainer.

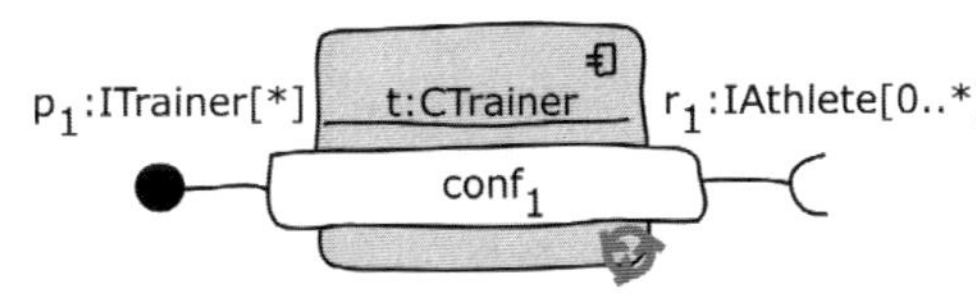

Figure 4. The trainer component available in the system.

The required functionality is provided by the service p_I, which implements the interface *ITrainer*. The service defines a dependency on services that implement the interface *IAthlete*. The individual athletes' performance data within the application are provided by components providing this interface. However, *ITrainer* can also be run when no athlete is available in the system.

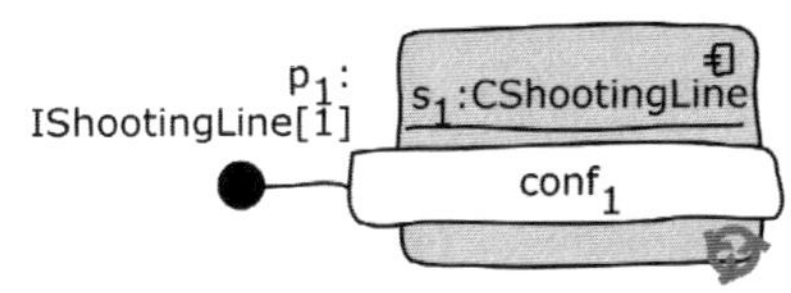

Figure 5. The CShootingLine component.

Shooting training is another requirement of our example system. Each shooting line is represented by a component, providing a service described by the domain interface *IShootingLine*. Figure 5 presents the DAiSI component *CShootingLine*.

Figure 6. The CSupervisor component.

The shooting line may be monitored by a supervisor. This is represented in the system by a service that implements the domain interface *ISupervisor*. The component presented in Figure 6 provides such a service. It can make use of a shooting line component.

All provided services of these components (trainer, shooting line, and supervisor) start, even if there is no other component requiring them. The flag *requestRun* is set, which is indicated by the filled circle.

IV. Interface Roles

With the *RequiredServiceReferenceSet* class many component local requirements can be specified. However, this is not sufficient for self-organizing systems.To illustrate the problem, let us consider Figure 7. It shows a simplified DAiSI component for an athlete. It specifies only one of the three configurations we defined in the previous section. The component provides a service of the type *IAthlete* and requires two *IStick* services to be able to do so. The provided service calculates the current skiing technique and needs measurement data of the sticks movements, which is provided by the two required services. However, with the component model as presented in Section III, a binding between only the left ski stick with both required service reference sets would be possible and allow the component to run. Of course the domain interface *IStick* provides a method to query at which side a ski stick is being used. However, this information is not considered in the configuration process. Obviously, the *IAthlete* service can not perform as expected as the measurement data of the right ski stick is missing.

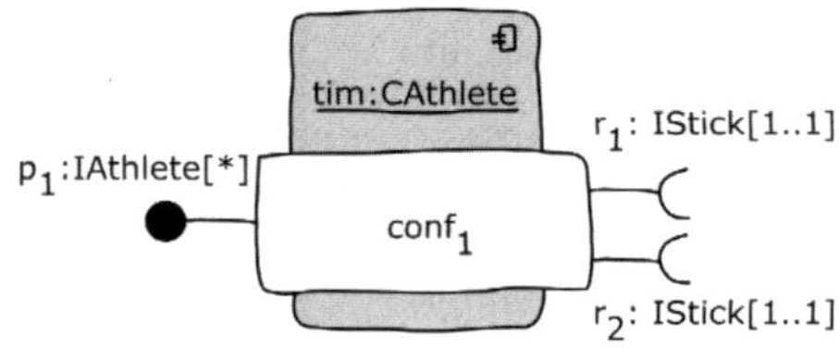

Figure 7. A DAiSI component for a biathlon athlete.

There are numerous other examples in which return values of operations of domain services have to be considered in order to establish the desired system configuration. For that reason, we extended the component model by the class *InterfaceRole*. In our previous understanding, provided and required services were compatible, if they referred to the same domain interface. Those interfaces can be seen as a contract between service provider and service user. We now extended this contract by interface roles. An interface role references exactly one domain interface and can define additional requirements regarding the return values of specific methods defined in that domain interface. A provided service only fulfills an interface role if it implements the domain interface and as well complies to the conditions defined in the interface role. Consequently, a required service reference set not only requires compatibility of the domain interface, but also of the interface role to be able to use a provided service.

Figure 8 shows the same DAiSI component as Figure 7, but with specified interface roles. With this addition it can be ensured that the athlete component in fact is connected with one left and one right stick. The *LeftStickRole* interface role refines the *IStick* domain interface and compares the return value of the method that returns the side of the ski stick is used on against a reference value for left ski sticks. This could be implemented by a method called *getSide():String* and the return value would be compared against the string "left". The interface role *RightStickRole* can be implemented accordingly.

This solution introduces new challenges for the configuration process of dynamic adaptive systems. Was it previously sufficient to connect a pair of required service reference set and provided service, this decision has to be monitored now. As the interface roles take return values of services into account, the fulfillment of an interface role is not static. The provided

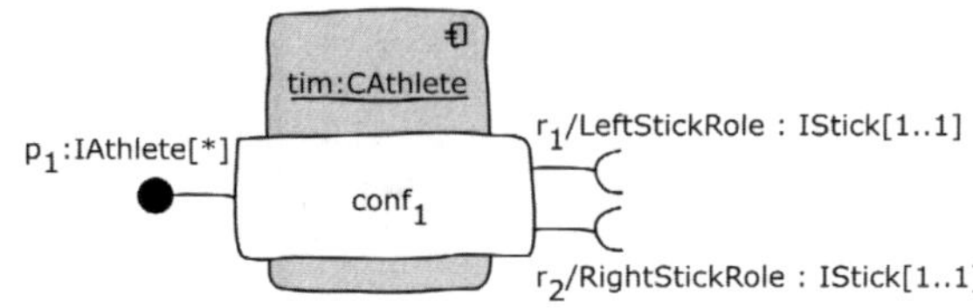

Figure 8. A DAiSI component for a biathlon athlete with interface roles.

service supposedly conforming to the interface role has to be evaluated either cyclically, or event based whenever relevant return values change. For our implementation, we took a cyclic approach, however, in [7] we described a way to re-evaluate the semantic compatibility of services whenever return values change equivalence classes.

The interface roles provide a possibility to include run-time information in the configuration process. But the true or false expressiveness of interface roles is not enough in some cases. Consider the following example: Every trainer is able to train three athletes at once. In addition, the energy consumption of the *IAthlete* service depends on the distance between trainer and athlete. To maximize the outcome of the training and minimize the energy consumption each trainer should see and analyze performance data of the three nearest athletes instead of the ones miles away. In Figure 9 the trainer should see the performance data of athletes A, B and C.

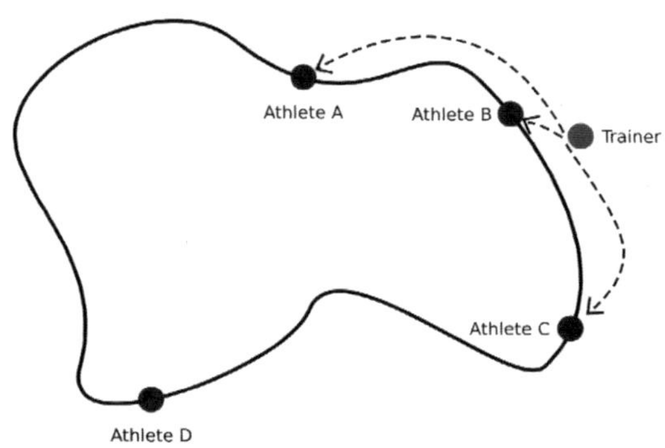

Figure 9. Locale optimization of energy consumption and training outcome.

The DAiSI component model and domain architecture presented above are not sufficient to express a constraint like this. There are other examples when the services referenced in *RequiredServiceReferenceSets* should be ordered by requirements of the component.

To achieve this, we expand the interface role by a comparator. The method *compare(DomainInterface* ps_1*, DomainInterface* ps_2*, DomainInterface req) : int* takes three domain interfaces as parameter. ps_1 and ps_2 are provided services which will be compared. The last domain interface req is an optional parameter, which may be used to take run-time information of the requiring component into account. It may be a provided service of the requiring component, which provides important run-time information for the comparator. In our example of trainer and athletes, the current position of the trainer is crucial for the ordering of *IAthlete* services.

The compare method returns either a negative integer, zero

or a positive integer. In the manner of known comparators, like Java's comparator, a negative value, zero, or a positive value mean the quality of ps_1 is less than, equal or greater than the quality of ps_2. Whether there are finer granularities in return values in the sense of -1000 is much worse than -1 depends on the particular implementation of the compare–method. It is important to notice that only provided services which are conform to the interface role are comparable. The standard implementation for the compare method treats every service as equal and returns always zero.

Now, the *RequiredServiceReferenceSet* of a component has the possibility to order the provided services by a chosen criterion. The available criteria are determined by the domain. Consequently, the configuration process has to take the order into account when configuring the system. All possibly usable services are represented by *canUse*. These are the services which implement the domain interface and which are conform to a required interface role. If there is a request for dependency resolution, the services in *canUse* are ordered with the help of *compare*. The resulting list of ordered services is then used to place a usage request for the currently best services. Their service references are copied to the *wantsUse* set. The configuration mechanism will be explained in more detail in the next section.

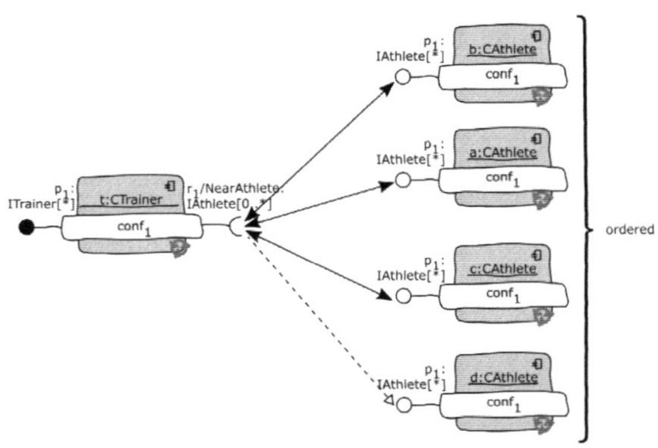

Figure 10. CAthletes components sorted by distance to CTrainer component.

Figure 10 shows our example from before with ordered components. The interface role *NearestAthlete* is now required by *t*, the *CTrainer* component. The compare method of *NearestAthlete* compares two *IAthlete* services with the help of one *ITrainer* service. Both *IAthlete* and *ITrainer* provide a method *getLocation():double[2]*, which returns the current GPS coordinates of the athlete or trainer. The compare method of *NearestAthlete* compares the distance of given athletes to the trainer. Of course, regarding our example a shorter distance is considered better, as a longer distance. To fulfill the specified meaning of the compare method's return value, ps_2's distance minus ps_1's distance is returned.

This results in the situation pictured in Figure 10. *t* can use all *CAthlete* components but in the end it uses b, a, and c, since this is the resulting order from sorting by distance to t. Concluding, the interface role comparator provides a rather simple method for the component to state which services it would like to use "the most".

V. CONFIGURATION MECHANISM

Beside the DAiSI component model and the DAiSI domain architecture model, a decentralized dynamic configuration mechanism was also already established in the DAiSI platform. Three types of relations between *RequiredServiceReferenceSets* and *ProvidedServices* exist, represented by the associations *canUse*, *wantsUse* and *uses*. The set of services that implement the domain interface referred by the *RequiredServiceReferenceSet* is represented by *canUse*. Note, this only guarantees a syntactically correct binding. Interface roles in addition provide a compatibility check with respect to a given common domain architecture.

The *wantsUse* set holds references to those services for which a usage request has been placed. Last, the *uses* set contains references to those services, which are currently in use by the component or by *RequiredServiceReferenceSet*. Each time a new service becomes available in the system, it is added to all *canUse* sets, if the corresponding *RequiredServiceReferenceSet* refers to the same *DomainInterface* as the *ProvidedServices*. The management of these three associations – *canUse*, *wantsUse* and uses – between *RequiredServiceReferenceSets* and *ProvidedServices* is handled by DAiSI's decentralized dynamic configuration mechanism. This configuration mechanism relies on the state machines, presented more detailed in [23] and sketched in the following paragraphs.

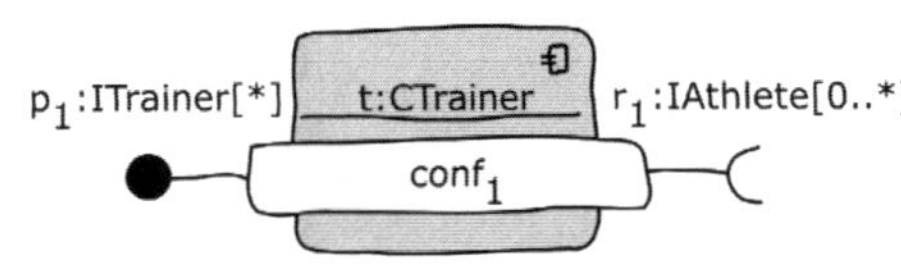

Figure 11. CTrainer component.

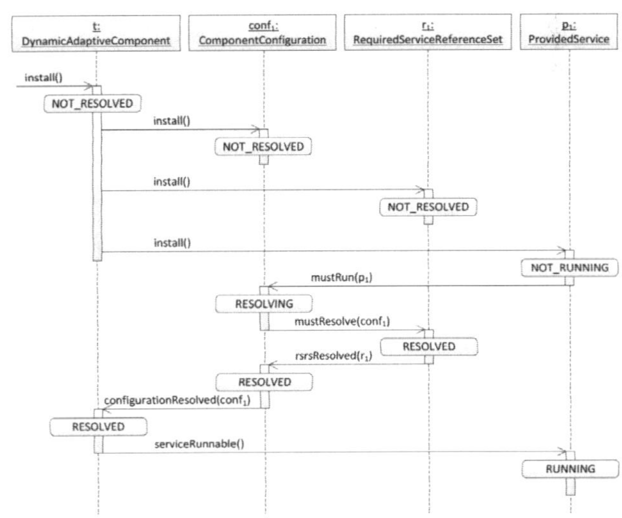

Figure 12. Sequence diagram showing the triggers and states of a standalone DAiSI component.

Consider again the biathlon example. Assume a given *CTrainer* component as shown in Figure 11. It has one single configuration and provides a service of type *ITrainer* to the environment, which can be used by an arbitrary number of other components. The component requires zero to any number of references to services of type *IAthlete*.

The boolean flag *requestRun* is true for the service provided. Hence, DAiSI has to run the component and provide the service within the dynamic adaptive system to other components and users. DAiSI can run the component directly and thereby provides the component service to other components and users as shown in the sequence diagram in Figure 12.

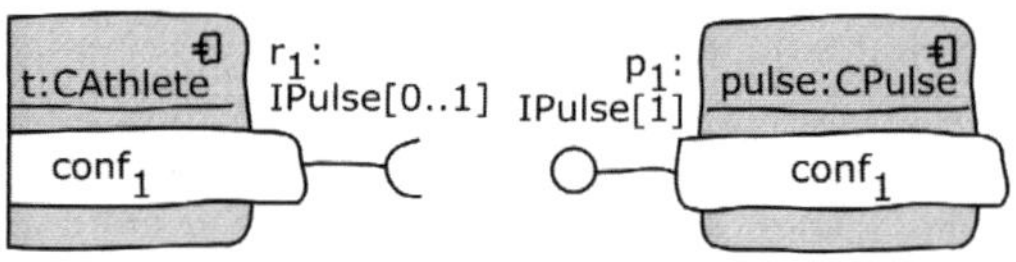

Figure 13. CAthlete and CPulse components.

Now assume two components: The *CAthlete* component, shown on the left hand side of Figure 13, requires zero or one reference to a service of type *IPulse*. The second component, *CPulse*, shown on the right hand side of Figure 13, provides such a service of type *IPulse*. Figure 14 shows the states and triggers of the involved state machines in a sequence diagram for this example.

Once the *CPulse* component is installed, DAiSI integrates the new service in the *canUse* relationship of the *RequiredServiceReferenceSet* r_1 of the component *CAthlete*. Then DAiSI informs the *CAthlete* component that a new usable service is available. DAiSI indicates that *CAthlete* wants to use this new service by adding this service in the set *wantsUse* of *CAthlete*. Once the service runs, it is assigned to the *CAthlete* component, which uses the service from now on (added to the set *uses* of *CAthlete*).

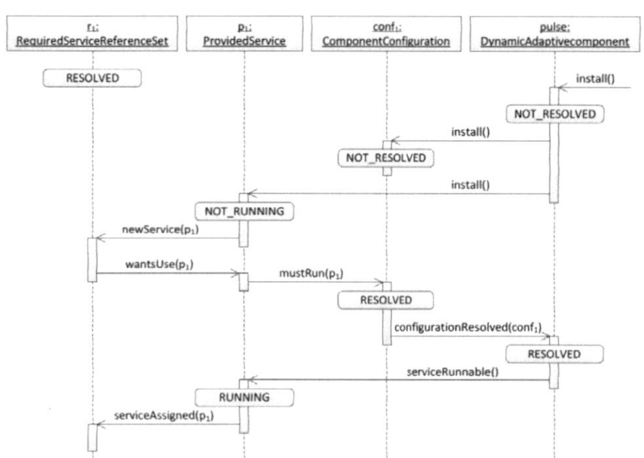

Figure 14. Inter-component configuration mechanism.

VI. Application Specific System Configuration

Imagine the following situation: the example biathlon application already introduced shall now fulfill a number of new requirements:

- The *ITrainer* service can only be run when it has access to at least one athlete service
- Each athlete must have access to a shooting line
- Shooting lines can only be used when they are supervised
- The skiing technique is to be analyzed in particular

Currently, the implementation of the components would have to be adapted in order to meet the requirements. For example, the attribute *minNoOfRequiredRefs* of r_1 from Figure 11 would have to be set to 1. However, a component's code cannot always be adapted in this way, for example because it is proprietary software and the source code not available. In addition, adapting it manually for the specific application purpose contradicts one of the original purposes of component based software development – reuse of components among different applications. The solution presented in the remainder of this section allows the application–specific specification of the minimum and maximum number of required references for *RequiredServiceReferenceSets* without having to adapt the component's source code.

Since the skiing technique is to be analyzed in particular, only the $conf_2$ *ComponentConfiguration* of the athlete component 'tim' of Figure 3 is relevant. Even if one pulse service and two ski stick services are available, the $conf_1$ configuration should not be activated. In this section, expansions of the existing framework are described, which enable such an application–specific influence on the activation of component configurations.

The system must guarantee that exactly one shooting line component is available for each athlete connected to the trainer component. This means that the number of those services used by the shooting supervisor component must be in accordance with the athlete components, which the trainer component accesses. One system configuration that meets all criteria described above is presented in Figure 15. A trainer component is connected with an athlete component, which in turn is connected to a left and a right ski stick. In addition, the application consists of a shooting supervisor component, which in turn is connected to a shooting line component.

In the DAiSI as it was presented on the previous pages, such system configuration requirements cannot be specified and, therefore, not be guaranteed. Moreover, further requirements would be relevant for this application, such as: if a new athlete component is added to the system in the configuration described above, it should only be integrated into the application when a shooting line component is available for this athlete. The application also needs to be stopped for example, when the athlete component from Figure 15 is only connected with one ski stick component.

To address these issues, we introduce application configurations. An application configuration consists of a number of components, as well as connections between these components. The primary task of DAiSI is to select the components that can be considered for a configuration conforming to the application architecture out of the number of all available components. In addition, the components must be connected in such a way that all specified requirements are met.

The criteria for the selection of suitable components for an application are defined with the assistance of so–called templates. An application specification consists of one or more of

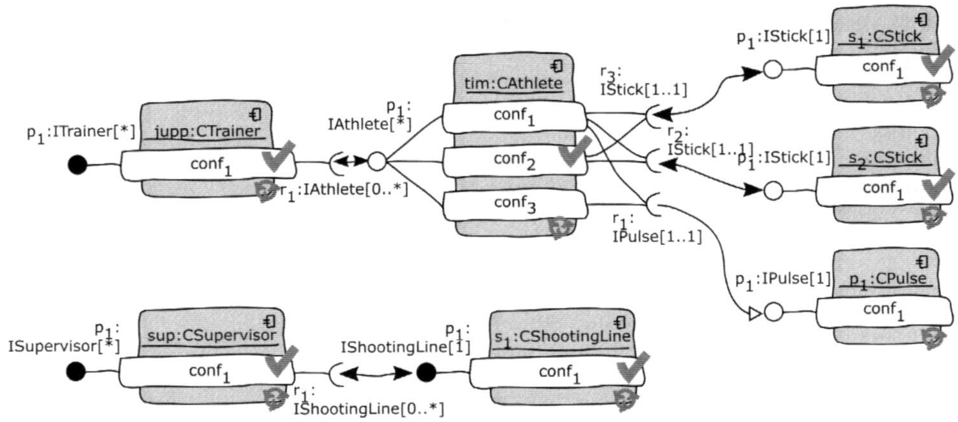

Figure 15. A system configuration that meets the requirements.

such templates. In this way, the biathlon application described above could, for instance, consist of a template for trainer components, and one for athlete components, one for shooting line components, etc. For each of these templates, requirements can be stored that specify under which circumstances a component is compatible with a template. The framework ensures that at runtime, only components matching the outline are allocated to the template. Graphically, a template is represented by a rectangle with dashed lines. Requirements related to required and provided component services are represented visually by circles and semi-circles with dashed lines (described in detail below). In Figure 16, two placeholders within an application template can be seen. One or two components can be allocated to the application, while one of the given components remains ignored, as it is not compatible.

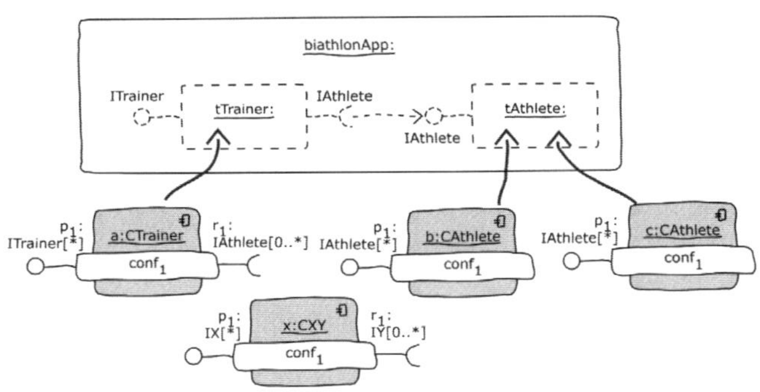

Figure 16. Suitable components for an application configuration.

The components selected must be connected with each other in order to obtain an executable system. For this purpose, in addition to the templates, the links between templates are defined, and represented as dashed arrows (see Figure 16). They provide information on how the allocated components are to be connected with each other. In this way it is possible to define that each component allocated to the *tTrainer* template in Figure 16 must be connected with at least one component, which is allocated to the *tAthlete* template. Later (during run–time), the framework ensures that the requirements related to the links between the components are considered. Figure 17 shows one possible resulting system configuration, while Figure 18 presents a possible application specification for the complete biathlon application.

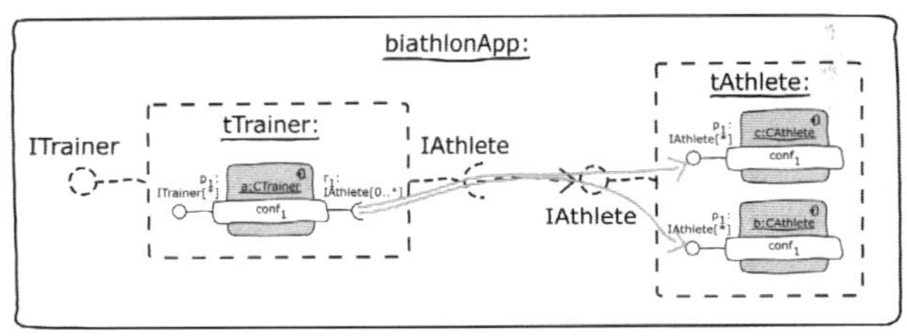

Figure 17. Generation of a valid configuration.

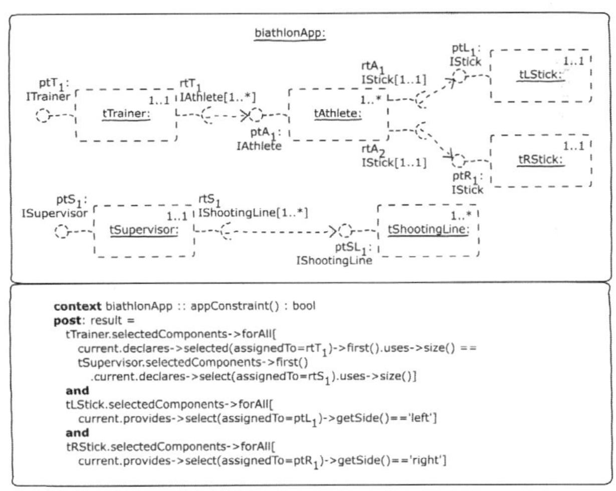

Figure 18. Graphical and textual application specification.

An application itself is graphically represented as a rectangle with the name of the application noted at the top. As stated before, each Template is represented as a rectangle with dashed outer lines and identified by a name. Within a template, the contents of the attributes *minNoOfRequiredComponents* and *maxNoOfRequiredComponents* are noted at the top right. A *ProvidedTemplateInterface* is represented as a dashed circle, which is labeled with its name, and the referenced domain interface. *RequiredTemplateInterfaces* are represented correspondingly as dashed semi-circles. They are also labeled with the referenced domain interface, the referenced interface role, if applicable, and a name. Links between *RequiredTemplateInterfaces* and *ProvidedTemplateInterfaces* (*connectedTo*) are visualized with a dashed arrow. The predicate specification (*appConstraint*)is specified in a separate area beneath the templates.

The aim of the DAiSI run–time infrastructure is to create an application configuration, which meets all specified requirements. As soon as this is achieved, the applications' state machine transitions from NOT_RUNNING to RUNNING. In other words: if an application is in the state RUNNING, the application configuration created conforms to the application architecture.

The following paragraphs describe how a valid application configuration can be generated automatically. The method suggested here follows a brute-force approach, which iteratively generates all possible configurations. It is sketeched in Listing 1 as pseudo code. While this is not optimal with regard to resources, it is sufficient to generate a valid system configuration.

```
1  boolean createValidConfiguration() {
2    while(possibleComponentAssignmentSets.hasNext()) {
3      possibleComponentAssignmentSets.next().
4        realize();
5
6      while(possibleInterfaceAssignmentSets.hasNext())
         {
7        possibleInterfaceAssignmentSets.next().
8        realize();
9
10       while(possibleUsageSets.hasNext()) {
11         possibleUsageSets.next().realize();
12
13         if(isValidConfiguration()) {
14           return true;
15         }
16       }
17     }
18   }
19   return false;
20 }
```

Listing 1. createValidConfiguration() method, pseudo code listing.

Since a valid configuration, which meets the requirements can change at any time in such a way that it no longer conforms to the application architecture, the application configuration is checked cyclically for conformance to the application architecture. As soon as the configuration no longer meets the defined application architecture–specific requirements, and therefore the predicate *isValidConfiguration* is evaluated as false, the applications' state machine changes back to the state NOT_RUNNING.

The algorithm is divided into two parts: the first part creates an application configuration (lines 2-9 in Listing 1), while the second checks the generated configuration for conformity with the requirements (lines 11-12 in Listing 1). Creating a configuration requires three steps. Firstly, selecting the components, then the *ProvidedService*– and *RequiredServiceReferenceSets* must each be allocated to a *ProvidedTemplateInterface* and *RequiredTemplateInterface*, respectively. Therefore, the two *assignedTo* quantities must be defined. Finally, the *uses* set must be determined for each *RequiredServiceReferenceSet*.

The initial situation of the configuration process is a set of available components. A selection must be made to obtain an application configuration. To accomplish this, an assignment of the *selectedComponents* set is created for each template, with the static properties already being considered. The configuration mechanism then calculates the set of all possible assignment combinations and makes them available via an iterator (*possibleComponentAssignmentSets* from Listing 1), based on the components available and the application specification, the method *realize* implements the specific assignment.

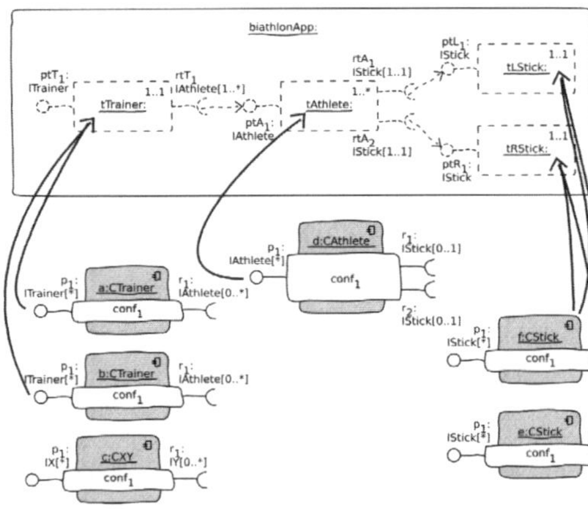

Figure 19. Allocation of components to templates.

In the example in Figure 19, the components *a* and *b* can be allocated to the *tTrainer* template. Only one component needs to be allocated to the template in order to fulfill the application requirements. Both components provide a service that implements the *ITrainer* domain interface and define a *RequiredServiceReferenceSet* that references the *IAthlete* domain interface. Only component *d* can be allocated to the *tAthlete* template since this component is the only one that meets the structural requirements of the template. A total of two components are available for the *tLStick* and *tRStick* templates and exactly one component must be allocated to each of these, in order to be able to meet the application requirements. This results in a number of possible allocations of components to templates. The configuration algorithm makes a selection, which is then realized by the configuration mechanism.

ProvidedServices of a component can fit to several *ProvidedTemplateInterfaces*. Since *ProvidedServices* must be allocated to *ProvidedTemplateInterfaces* during run–time, the framework needs to decide which to use. This applies accordingly to *RequiredServiceReferenceSets* and *RequiredTemplateInterfaces*. For example, the *RequiredTemplateInterface* of the *tAthlete* template in Figure 19, do not reference any interface roles but only the *IStick* domain interface as presented in Figure 20. In this example, the *RequiredServiceReferenceSet* r_1 can be allocated to *RequiredTemplateInterface* rtA_1 as well as rtA_2. The same applies to *RequiredServiceReferenceSet* r_2.

Within the algorithm in Listing 1, all possible allocation configurations, which result from the allocation of components to templates in the previous step are now iterated. In the

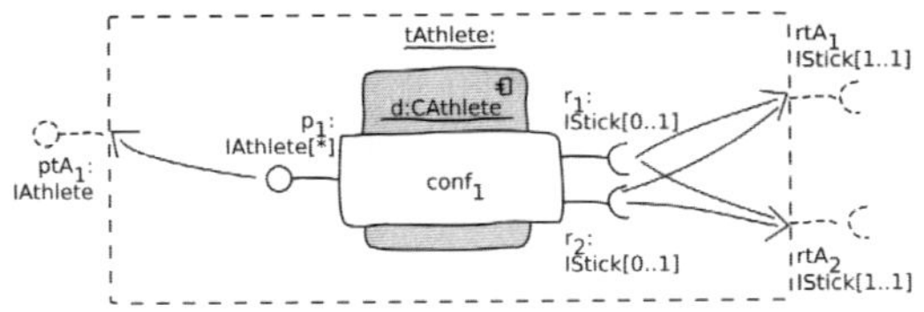

Figure 20. Allocation of component interfaces to template interfaces.

component model, the allocation between *RequiredServiceReferenceSet* and *RequiredTemplateInterface*, and between *ProvidedService* and *ProvidedTemplateInterface* are represented by the *assignedTo* association. All possibilities are iterated with the *possibleInterfaceAssignmentSets* iterator and a returned assignment is then realized by calling *realize*. In the next step, the *uses* set is assigned to the *RequiredServiceReferenceSets* of the components, which were allocated previously to the *selectedComponents*. As a last step, the configuration algorithm creates the *use* relations between the components.

After creating a component selection, subsequently allocating the services and then assigning the *uses* set of all *RequiredServiceReferenceSets* creates a running application configuration automatically. Every component that is part of the application is informed about their role in the application, i.e., which template they will fill, to which templates their services are assigned to, and to which provided services they should connect. The individual iterators of the algorithm are realized for individual components.

After creating a configuration with the algorithm described above, the remaining applications of the application specification can now also be checked for conformity. The predicate *isValidConfiguration* needs to be evaluated at this stage. Only if this predicate is evaluated to *true*, the application changes its state to RUNNING. Otherwise, a new configuration needs to be created. The algorithm presented here is only a sketch of the procedure for creating a configuration, which conforms to the defined application architecture-specific requirements.

VII. Application Specific Quality Criteria

In Section IV, we introduced a possibility for a component to sort its *RequiredServiceReferenceSets* by a quality criterion. This concept strives for local optimization. But consider again our biathlon training example. Each trainer wants to see the data of the nearest athletes to maximize the training outcome and minimize the energy consumption, but can at most train three athletes. Now, in contrast to our first example (see Figure 9), two trainers are available to the system instead of one.

Figure 21 shows the possible distributions of athletes and trainers if both *CTrainer* components require the interface role *NearestAthlete*. Situation I in the upper left corner of Figure 21 is optimal from the viewpoint of trainer 1, whereas situation II in the upper right is optimal from the viewpoint of trainer 2. In contrast to their individual views, the global optimum of energy consumption and training benefit is reached in situation III.

In this section, we present an extension to the previously introduced application configuration, which allows to define such global optimization criteria. The application from DAiSI's component model is extended by a compare method. The method *compareTo(Application a):int* compares the current application with the application given by a. As before, the return value is either negative, zero or positive meaning the current application's quality is less than, equal to, or greater than a's quality. The method is implemented by the application (and therefore the person defining the application template). The standard implementation treats all applications as equal.

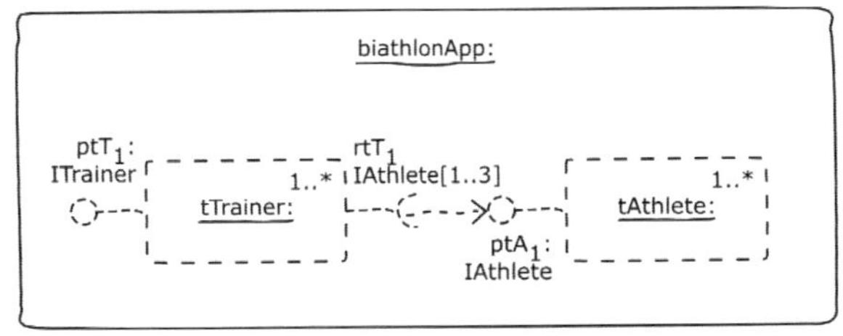

Figure 22. Simple graphical application specification for energy minimization scenario.

The biathlon application for minimized energy consumption is described by the application specification seen in Figure 22. Some parts like the pulse or stick services are missing but it shows the most important components. Listing 2 shows an implementation of *compareTo* for our desired energy minimization. Firstly, the overall distance between trainers and athletes in the current application is calculated. For all chosen *CTrainer* components in the template *tTrainer* the distance to its used *IAthlete* services is summed up. Afterwards, the same is done for the given application. The return value is the resulting difference between the compared and current application's sum of distances.

```
int compareTo(Application a) {

  distanceCurrent = 0;
  while(tTrainer.selectedComponents.hasNext()) {
    CTrainer t = tTrainer.
      selectedComponents.next();

    while(t.declares.uses.hasNext()) {
      distance += t.declares.uses.next().
        getLocation().distanceTo(t.getLocation());
    }
  }

  distanceOther = 0;
  while(a.tTrainer.selectedComponents.hasNext()) {
    CTrainer t = a.tTrainer.
      selectedComponents.next();

    while(t.declares.uses.hasNext()) {
      distance += t.declares.uses.next().
        getLocation().distanceTo(t.getLocation());
    }
  }
  return distanceOther−distanceCurrent;
}
```

Listing 2. compareTo method for biathlon application with minimized energy consumption, pseudo code listing.

Remember the *createValidConfiguration()* method from Listing 1. We will extend this algorithm with the *compareTo* method. Instead of realizing and accepting the first valid configuration, the algorithm will compare all possible valid configurations and realize the best one. Of course, this brute-force approach is not practical. The testing of sophisticated

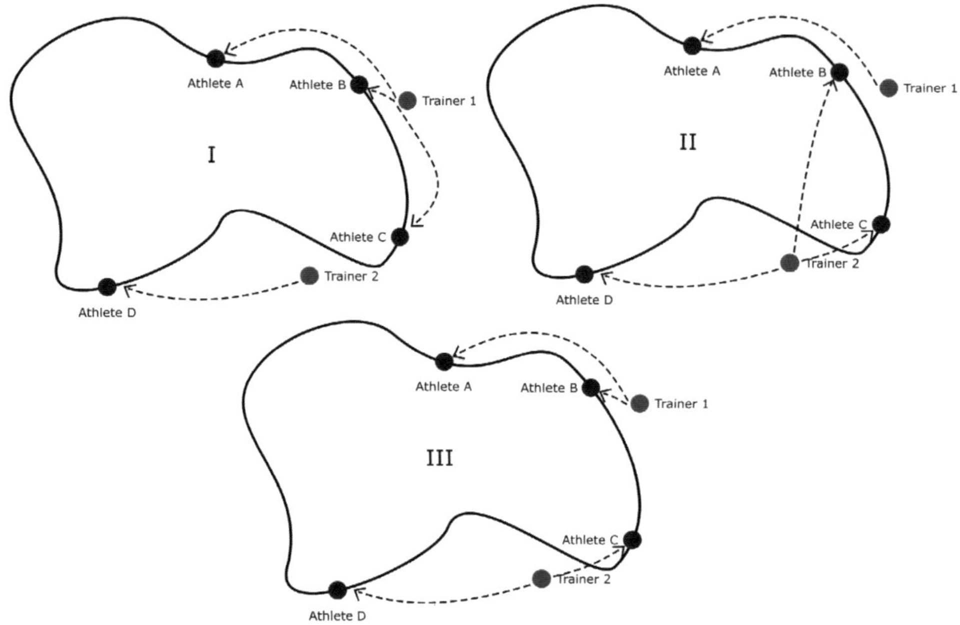

Figure 21. Possible distribution of athletes and trainers.

configuration algorithms and determining suitable heuristics are future work.

The extended configuration algorithm is sketched in Listing 3. It realizes the behavior described before. It is important to notice that lines 19 and 27 hide more complicated technical aspects. In line 19, the currently realized application configuration is saved. This could be done by saving all realized components, interfaces and usages, i.e., connections between components and services. This saved configuration is realized again in line 27.

```
1  boolean createValidConfiguration() {
2
3    Application best = null;
4
5    while(possibleComponentAssignmentSets.hasNext()) {
6      possibleComponentAssignmentSets.next().
7        realize();
8
9      while(possibleInterfaceAssignmentSets.hasNext())
       {
10       possibleInterfaceAssignmentSets.next().
11         realize();
12
13       while(possibleUsageSets.hasNext()) {
14         possibleUsageSets.next().realize();
15
16         if(isValidConfiguration()) {
17
18           if(compareTo(best)>0) {
19             best = this;
20           }
21         }
22       }
23     }
24   }
25
26   if(best != null){
27     best.realize()
28     return true;
29   }
30
31   return false;
32 }
```

Listing 3. createValidConfiguration() method expanded by usage of compareTo method, pseudo code listing.

This concludes the section about application specific quality criteria. The *compareTo* provides a tool to the application designer, which allows him to specify which (of a set of syntactically and semantically correct) application configuration is considered "best" and therefore should be realized. Since this depends on run–time information the configuration has to be checked whenever run–time information changes. Like before, a cyclical or more advanced approach could be taken.

VIII. Conclusion

This paper presented an extended version of the DAiSI framework. While the system configuration, more precisely the component wiring, in older versions of DAiSI and other dynamic adaptive system infrastructures were only considering syntactic and semantic compatibility, the newest findings enable developers to specify interface roles and application templates. These open the possibility to define local and application–wide constraints on the configuration.

We introduced a concept, which takes quality and service aspects into account. A service comparator defined on interface roles enables components to define not only which semantic domain interface they require, but also which quality criteria they prefer. Global quality of service is achieved on the application level.

Currently, DAiSI only supports service–oriented architectures. Upcoming technologies and paradigms, like the Internet of Things (IoT) or cyber–physical systems demand for other improvements, like pub/sub and message–based communication. We will extend concept and implementation of the DAiSI to account for these developments.

However, the extension presented in this paper provides a sustainable concept for the realization of decentralized, dynamic adaptive systems, while considering quality of service aspects.

REFERENCES

[1] H. Klus, D. Herrling, and A. Rausch, "Interface Roles for Dynamic Adaptive Systems," in The Seventh International Conference on Adaptive and Self-Adaptive Systems and Applications (ADAPTIVE), 2015, pp. 80–84.

[2] L. Northrop, P. Feiler, R. P. Gabriel, J. Goodenough, R. Linger, T. Longstaff, R. Kazman, M. Klein, D. Schmidt, K. Sullivan, K. Wallnau, and W. Pollak, "Ultra-Large-Scale Systems - The Software Challenge of the Future," Software Engineering Institute, Carnegie Mellon, Tech. Rep., Jun. 2006.

[3] J. Kramer and J. Magee, "A rigorous architectural approach to adaptive software engineering," Journal of Computer Science and Technology, vol. 24, no. 2, 2009, pp. 183–188.

[4] C. Szyperski, Component Software: Beyond Object-Oriented Programming, 2nd ed. Boston, MA, USA: Addison-Wesley Longman Publishing Co., Inc., 2002.

[5] D. Niebuhr, C. Peper, and A. Rausch, "Towards a development approach for dynamic-integrative systems," in Proceedings of the Workshop for Building Software for Pervasive Computing, 19th Conference on Object-Oriented Programming Systems, Languages and Applications (OOPSLA), Nov. 2004.

[6] H. Klus, D. Niebuhr, and A. Rausch, "A Component Model for Dynamic Adaptive Systems," in Proceedings of the International Workshop on Engineering of software services for pervasive environments (ESSPE), A. L. Wolf, Ed. Dubrovnik, Croatia: ACM, Sep. 2007, pp. 21–28.

[7] D. Niebuhr, Dependable Dynamic Adaptive Systems. Verlag Dr. Hut, 2010.

[8] M. P. Papazoglou, "Service-oriented computing: Concepts, characteristics and directions," in Proceedings of the Fourth International Conference on Web Information Systems Engineering (WISE). IEEE, 2003, pp. 3–12.

[9] J. Magee, J. Kramer, and M. Sloman, "Constructing distributed systems in CONIC," IEEE Transactions on Software Engineering, vol. 15, no. 6, 1989, pp. 663–675.

[10] J. Kramer, "Configuration programming – a framework for the development of distributable systems," in CompEuro'90, Proceedings of the 1990 IEEE International Conference on Computer Systems and Software Engineering. IEEE, 1990, pp. 374–384.

[11] J. Kramer, J. Magee, M. Sloman, and N. Dulay, "Configuring object-based distributed programs in REX," Software Engineering Journal, vol. 7, no. 2, 1992, pp. 139–149.

[12] I. Warren and I. Sommerville, "Dynamic configuration abstraction," in Software Engineering – ESEC'95. Springer, 1995, pp. 173–190.

[13] R. R. Aschoff and A. Zisman, "Proactive adaptation of service composition," in ICSE Workshop on Software Engineering for Adaptive and Self-Managing Systems (SEAMS). IEEE, 2012, pp. 1–10.

[14] A. Rasche and A. Polze, "Configurable services for mobile Users," in Proceedings of the Seventh International Workshop on Object-Oriented Real-Time Dependable Systems (WORDS). IEEE, 2002, pp. 163–170.

[15] ——, "Configuration and dynamic reconfiguration of component-based applications with microsoft.net," in Sixth IEEE International Symposium on Object-Oriented Real-Time Distributed Computing, 2003. IEEE, 2003, pp. 164–171.

[16] T. Kawamura, J.-A. De Blasio, T. Hasegawa, M. Paolucci, and K. Sycara, "Public Deployment of Semantic Service Matchmaker with UDDI Business Registry," in The Semantic Web ISWC 2004, ser. Lecture Notes in Computer Science, S. A. McIlraith, D. Plexousakis, and F. van Harmelen, Eds. Springer Berlin Heidelberg, 2004, vol. 3298, pp. 752–766.

[17] T. Haselwanter, P. Kotinurmi, M. Moran, T. Vitvar, and M. Zaremba, "WSMX: A Semantic Service Oriented Middleware for B2B Integration," in International Conference on Service-Oriented Computing. Springer, 2006, pp. 4–7.

[18] D. Garlan, S.-W. Cheng, A.-C. Huang, B. Schmerl, and P. Steenkiste, "Rainbow: Architecture-based self-adaptation with reusable infrastructure," Computer, vol. 37, no. 10, 2004, pp. 46–54.

[19] S.-W. Cheng, Rainbow: Cost-Effective Software Architecture-Based Self-Adaptation. ProQuest, 2008.

[20] J. S. Rellermeyer, G. Alonso, and T. Roscoe, "R-OSGi: distributed applications through software modularization," in Proceedings of the ACM/IFIP/USENIX 2007 International Conference on Middleware. Springer-Verlag New York, Inc., 2007, pp. 1–20.

[21] OMG, OMG Unified Modeling Language (OMG UML), Superstructure, Version 2.4.1, Object Management Group Std., Rev. 2.4.1, August 2011. [Online]. Available: http://www.omg.org/spec/UML/2.4.1

[22] H. Klus and A. Rausch, "DAiSI – A Component Model and Decentralized Configuration Mechanism for Dynamic Adaptive Systems," in The Sixth International Conference on Adaptive and Self-Adaptive Systems and Applications (ADAPTIVE), 2014, pp. 27–36.

[23] H. Klus, A. Rausch, and D. Herrling, "DAiSI – Dynamic Adaptive System Infrastructure: Component Model and Decentralized Configuration Mechanism," International Journal On Advances in Intelligent Systems, vol. 7, no. 3 and 4, 2014, pp. 595 – 608.

International Journal on Advances in Software, vol 9 no 1 & 2, year 2016, http://www.iariajournals.org/software/

A Framework for Big Metabolomic Data Management and Analysis

Xiangyu Li, Leiming Yu
and David Kaeli

Department of Electrical and
Computer Engineering
Northeastern University
Boston, MA, USA
Email:{xili,ylm,kaeli}@ece.neu.edu

Yuanyuan Yao, Poguang Wang
and Roger Giese

Department of Pharmaceutical Sciences and
Barnett Institute, Bouve College
Northeastern University
Boston, MA, USA
Email:yao.yu@husky.neu.edu, {p.wang,r.giese}@neu.edu

Vicent Yusa

Department of Analytical Chemistry
University of Valencia
Burjassot, Spain
Email:yusa.vic@gva.es

Akram Alshawabkeh

Department of Civil and Environmental Engineering
Northeastern University
Boston, MA, USA
Email:aalsha@neu.edu

***Abstract*—Preterm birth is one of the major contributing factors to infant death. In the Puerto Rico Testsite for Exploring Contamination Threats Center we explore a variety of risk factors for preterm birth in Puerto Rico, including environmental, genetic and demographic factors. Given the challenge of managing such a large amount data, we have constructed a customized database specifically designed for managing our data and for facilitating efficient analysis. In this paper, we present our database design and open source Mass Spectrometry Data Analysis Toolbox. Our design allows for the efficient handling of storage and computation during metabolomic analysis. The Toolbox enables supports and end-to-end analysis protocol, from data processing and feature selection, to machine learning and visualization.**

Keywords–preterm birth; database; MSDA Toolbox; machine learning.

I. INTRODUCTION

Preterm birth [1] has been identified to be a major cause of birth defects and infant deaths [2]. When an infant is delivered earlier than 37 weeks of pregnancy, the birth is considered as preterm. Research has shown that since 1990, the rate of preterm birth has been increasing worldwide, ranging from 5% to 18%. In 2010, preterm-related deaths were reported to be responsible for close to 35% of all infant deaths. A series of research findings suggests that environmental factors have a strong influence on preterm birth [3]–[8]. [9].

In our research, we focus on an area in northern Puerto Rico where the preterm birth rate is 50% higher than that in the rest of the United States. In the *Puerto Rico Testsite for Exploring Contamination Threats* (PROTECT) Center, we collaborate with a cohort of over 2000 women in northern Puerto Rico (presently 800 of the 2000 participant mothers have been recruited). We are analyzing many potential contributing factors, including environmental and biological factors, which could be linked to premature birth.

Our study is highly data driven. We collect and analyze data across a wide spectrum of sources, including:

- Environmental samples and measurements - soil samples, well and tap water samples, historical Environmental Protection Agency (EPA) data, Superfund site data,
- Biological samples - blood, urine, hair and placenta samples, and
- Human subjects information - medical history, reproductive health records, product use data surveys, and birth outcomes.

We have developed a carefully designed relational database system to manage this project. Up until now, we have collected over 400 million data entries and manage over 2467 data entities in our database. Since urine data presently dominates the volume of data collected in our database, we focus on the urine analysis.

In this paper, we provide an overview on PROTECT and present the database workflow for big data management. Particularly, we present our open source Toolbox for *Mass Spectrometry Data Analysis*, targeted for efficient machine learning and visualization on big datasets. We also provide a detailed description on each step of the metabolomic data analysis. Given the amount of data we need to work with, we discuss how we reduce the processing time by leveraging multi-core packages.

The rest of this paper is organized as follows. Section II presents background and related work. Section III provides an overview of PROTECT database, its current status and detailed workflow. Section IV describes the Mass Spectrometry Data Analysis Toolbox (MSDA), including discussions on performance tuning and lessons learned from our analysis. Section V concludes the paper and discusses areas for future work.

II. BACKGROUND

Preterm birth is a worldwide issue and its leading causes are still under investigation. P. Meis et al. identified a set of risk factors that could contribute to preterm birth [10]. These factors are categorized as: i) demographic factors, ii) medical history, iii) previous obstetric history and iv) current pregnancy. J. Meeker et al. correlated phthalate exposure with preterm birth by targeting specific phthalate metabolites, including MBP, MBzp and di(2-ethyl-hexyl) [11]. The contamination of groundwater has also been studied by T. Torres et al. [12]. They suggested a group of Chlorinated Volatile Organic Compounds (CVOCs), including trichloroethylene (TCE), tetrachloroethylene (PCE) and chloroform (TCM), could have a strong influence on preterm birth. Roca et al. proposed a strategy that combines a targeted approach for pesticide metabolites with a post-targeted screening for contaminant exposure, to determine the biomarkers in urine [13]. Their approach facilitates identifying biomarkers of exposure due to environmental pollutants.

In order to support a wide range of multidisciplinary studies, many Electronic Data Capture (EDC) systems have been developed to provide an automated workflow for data collection, reporting and exploration. EDCs are mainly designed to reduce the data retrieval cycle and to avoid errors during the data collection process. The StudyTRAX system can integrate data management with the process of generating academic outcomes (e.g., manuscripts, presentations, book chapters), which dramatically increases user productivity [14]. LimeSurvey is an open source package, providing a free and secured web-based interface to leverage the capability of customizable data collection [15]. Tools, such as Electronic Laboratory Notebooks (ELN), are designed to facilitate the documentation of experiments and procedures performed in a laboratory environment [16]. Among various web-based electronic data capture systems, REDCap is one of the most user-friendly tools that can stream captured data directly into the database [17]. The Environmental Quality Information System (EQuIS) from EarthSoft can integrate data collection with data management, provide automated web-based dashboards for the distributed environment, and support real-time data capturing and reporting schemes [18]–[20].

Based on the high quality data collected with these systems, previous studies have found that metabolites in urine could provides some clues, such as the residue of environmental pollutants in the human body that can trigger different clinical symptoms. W. Arlt et al. applied Generalized Matrix Relevance Learning Vector Quantization (GMLVQ) to discriminate adrenocortical adenoma (ACA) and malignant adrenocortical carcinoma(ACC), using urine steroid metabolomics as the biomarker [21]. Y. Kim et al. proposed using multivariate methods, decision trees and random forests, to diagnose breast cancer using urine metabolome profiles [22]. An efficient protocol for radiation metabolomics using urine samples was proposed by C. Lanz et al., which applies random forest techniques to gas chromatography, combined with mass spectrometry [23]. S. Reichenbach et al. proposed a new method to extract non-targeted chromatographic features from 2D chromatograms and showed that a Support Vector Machine (SVM) outperforms a k-Nearest Neighbor (kNN) clustering in their case studies [24]. In this study, we have developed a noncommercial *Mass Spectrometry Data Analysis Toolbox* and support a variety of machine learning techniques, including Principle Component Analysis (PCA) and hierarchical clustering to facilitate large-scale metabolomic analysis.

III. URINE SAMPLE DATABASE

The PROTECT database is built to handle terabytes of project data for our preterm birth study in Puerto Rico. We have designed an efficient framework for data import and cleaning, enabling the generation of detailed reports on specific queries to facilitate research activities. In terms of urine analysis, we store decoded raw urine data in the database and provide users with open source tools to extend their research ideas. Next, we will describe the goals of the PROTECT project, present current status of our data repository, demonstrate the workflow using proprietary software, and discuss details of our challenges with working with urine sample data in our study.

A. The PROTECT Center

The NIEHS Puerto Rico Testsite for Exploring Contamination Threats (PROTECT) Center studies the causal effects between exposure to environmental contamination and the high preterm birth rates recorded in Puerto Rico. We collect a wide range of data, including: blood, urine, ground water, tap water, placenta and medical records. Based on this rich range of data, we attempt to identify contributing factors associated with preterm birth. Domain specific analyses are applied, which include non-targeted chemical analysis, mechanistic toxicology, and targeted epidemiology. The organization of PROTECT is shown in Figure 1. An additional goal is to develop green remediation strategies to alleviate exposure and to reduce future preterm birth rates. For the PROTECT database, we support multiple research communities by facilitating data cleaning, data storage, data security and data reporting. We utilize software developed and marketed by EarthSoft called EQuIS. We are presently using EQuIS Professional and EQuIS Enterprise. Our backend database is Microsoft's SQLserver. We have developed a number of tools for data management and modeling to advance our preterm birth study.

B. Data Storage

In the current database we capture human subject data, environmental data and biological data. We currently have more than 400 million data points in our system. The structure of these data points is provided in Table I. In the near future, we expect to host more than 100 billion data entries in our system.

TABLE I. PROTECT database repository.

	Data Points (In millions)
Environmental	1.3
Human Subjects	1.5
Biological	0.2
Non-targeted	400

Since each data entry can be an indicator tied to an adverse reproductive outcome, we need the ability to carefully evaluate relationships between data entries across the millions of data points. Due to the sheer data volume, we leverage specialized software to facilitate the data management process. We also have the challenge that we are working is a geographically distributed team of researchers in PROTECT. Our researchers that need access to PROTECT data will have web-based dashboards to help them manage their data and perform customized

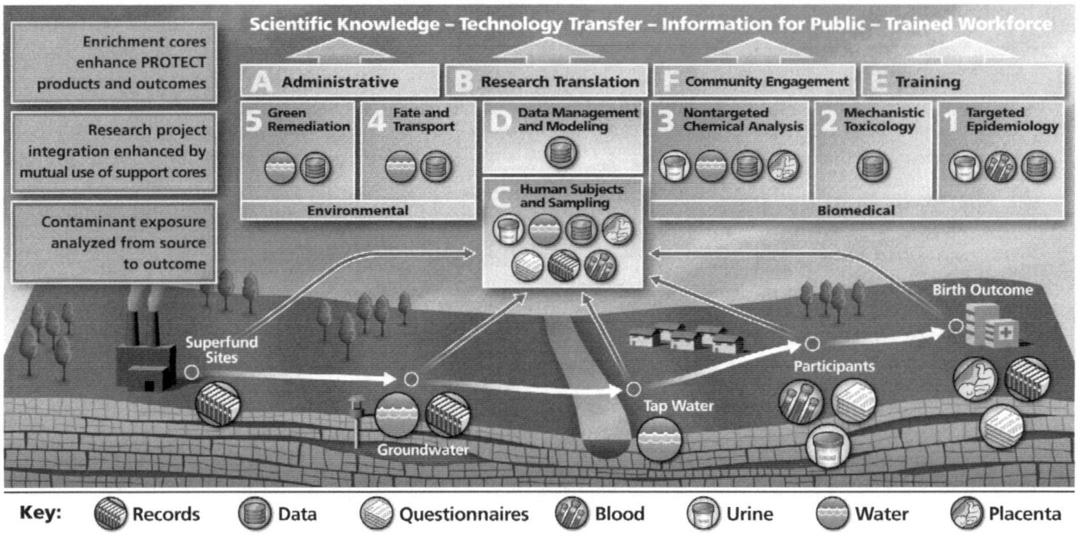

Figure 1. PROTECT collects source samples (white arrows, bottom) to analyze factors that contribute to preterm birth. Core C collects environmental and biological information. Core D handles data management and supports data analytics. Projects 1-5 utilize the collected data for their scientific studies.

queries. Our system helps to identify the linkages between pollutants and birth outcomes through the use of advanced machine learning algorithms.

C. Data Cleaning

After capturing the data, the integrity of each entity is inspected. This process is called *data cleaning*, and is fairly standard in any data collection campaign. The goal is to reduce errors in the data. The checking process needs to verify that each data field conforms to the data type and is within range for each field. Data dependencies between fields are also checked. This process is performed before incorporating any data into the database. To facilitate this checking, we have a complete data dictionary available for every entity stored in the database.

The data dictionary is developed by each domain expert. We abide by the rules present in the data dictionary when developing our schema, which in turn, helps to maintain a high level of data quality. Our cleaning tools can quickly highlight any detected anomalies in the data. Our comprehensive cleaning procedure can pinpoint corrupted data, and help to prevent errors from entering the database.

D. Software Stack

For the front-end of the PROTECT database, we use Microsoft Visual Basic to configure the schema for data cleaning. These scripts are used by EarthSoft's EQuIS Electronic Data Processor (EDP) to clean the input data according to the defined constraints. After data screening, EQuIS sends the cleaned data to Microsoft SQLserver. We leverage EQuIS Professional [25] and Enterprise [19] to support both standalone and distributed development environments, respectively. We use EQUIS's Electronic Data Processor (EDP) to import data into the database.

Users can customize data formats, also known as Electronic Data Deliverables (EDDs), for their individual study. EDDs can be stored in a number of popular documentation formats including Excel spreadsheets and Comma Separated values (CSVs). Typically, four files are needed to handle data cleaning: 1) format definition file, 2) a custom handler file, 3) an enumeration file, and 4) a reference value file. The *format definition file* follows the rules defined in the data dictionary. The *custom handler* applies the data checking scheme and generates discrepancy reports if mismatches are detected. Whenever a set of values need to be indexed based on their definition in the data dictionary, the *enumeration file* is used for this purpose, and so is an optional file. Users would use the reference value file to allow them check reference values remotely [18]. Errors are highlighted with detailed warnings to facilitate the debugging process. Only after all errors are resolved, then the input data values can be committed to the database.

This automated data cleaning process is handled through the EDP module in both EQuIS Professional and Enterprise. Distinct from the standalone development of EQuIS Professional, EQuIS Enterprise provides web-based dashboards to support distributed users [19]. Each dashboard is customized to include a set of widgets specific to the needs to the data researcher. For instance, data uploads and checking can be performed using the *EDD Upload* widget. The cleaning status can be configured to automatically inform a group of users through the *Notices* widget. The Environmental Information Agents (*EIA*) widget pushes reports to users on scheduled events or dates. Online data access is shared across the PROTECT center, providing access to researchers in Puerto Rico, Massachusetts, Michigan and West Virginia. The workflow from data collection to data reporting is shown in Figure 2.

E. Urine Samples

In our previous work, we have reported on a study of non-targeted analysis on 6 urine samples from Puerto Rico [1].

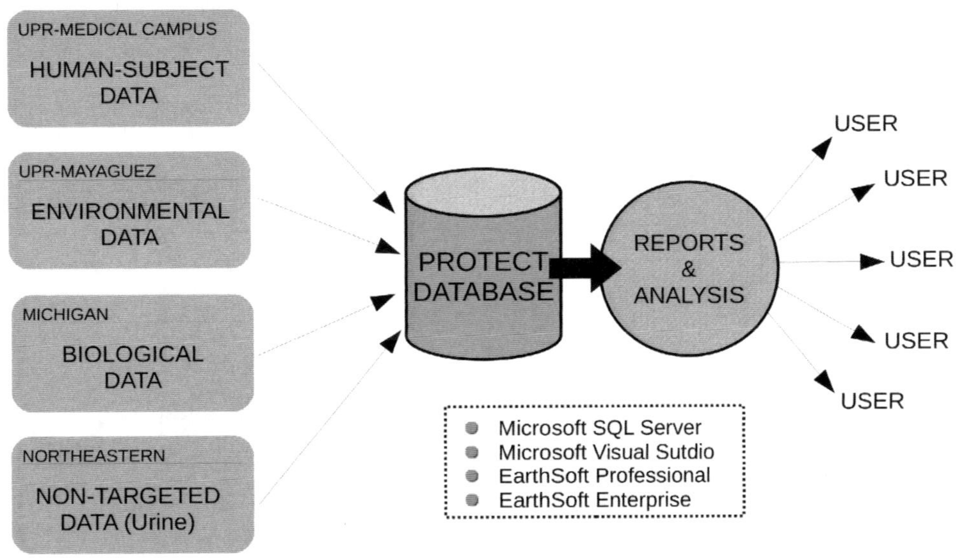

Figure 2. The PROTECT database collects data from different sources and includes data on: human subjects, environmental parameters, biological analysis and non-targeted chemical/biological data. Data is cleaned before it is imported into the database. The system supports both standalone analysis and distributed reporting capabilities through EQuIS Professional and Enterprise. Equipped with a distributed solution, users can query customized reports through the web server. The PROTECT database also supports data mining and modeling capabilities.

TABLE II. Urine samples from Developmental Neurotoxicity Assessment of Mixtures in Children (DENAMIC) project.

Country (Region)	Type	Resolution (FWHM)	Raw Data Samples		
			ESI+	ESI-	ESI+/-
Spain (Valencia)	Pregnant mothers	50,000	306	306	-
		25,000	-	-	143
	Children (4 years)	50,000	216	216	-
Spain (Sabadell)	Pregnant mothers	25,000	-	-	160
Slovakia	Pregnant mothers	25,000	-	-	52
	Children (4 years)	25,000	-	-	49

We discovered a range of clustering patterns present in these samples. Due to the limited sample data, the contributing chemicals remain to be identified.

To be prepared to compare results from our cohort to other cohorts of expectant mothers throughout the world, we have acquired an existing set of urine samples from the *Developmental Neurotoxicity Assessment of Mixtures in Children* (DENAMIC) Project [26] being carried out in Spain. The details for the DENAMIC urine samples are presented in Table II.

There are 661 mothers and 265 children across three different regions in the Spain study. The mass spectrum data is acquired using full scan mode (50-800 m/z), with a resolving power of 50,000 FWHM (full width at half maximum) (scan speed, 2 Hz), in both + and - modes of ESI (electrospray ionization), and with and without HCD (higher-energy c-trap dissociation fragmentation). Mass spectrum analysis is performed on the Orbitrap ExactiveTM mass spectrometer (Thermo Scientific, Bremen, Germany). Data acquisition is accomplished using Thermo Scientific's Trace Finder 3.1 software. The raw mzXML files for these samples are rather large (136 GB). Next, we will discuss how we work with this data in order to identify patterns in this data set. In the following section, we introduce our machine learning framework to deal with the data processing challenges with this large data set.

IV. MSDA

Our urine analysis procedure relies heavily on the accuracy of the mass spectrometer, and the supporting software. We could choose to use applications such as MarkerView [27], SIMCA-P+ [28] and SAS [29]. These packages provide black-box style analysis with limited flexibility and processing power. For example, MarkerView cannot handle large datasets efficiently; it takes more than 20 minutes to perform PCA on 6 urine samples, and is unable to process larger datasets due to memory storage issues. Meanwhile, there is free quantitative metabolomics software available, such as MetaboAnalyst [30] and MeltDB [31], which provides a comprehensive suite of analysis recipes. However, these packages, while free, come with a number of challenges, including limiting the maximum file (limited to 6 MB in MetaboAnalyst), and very poor

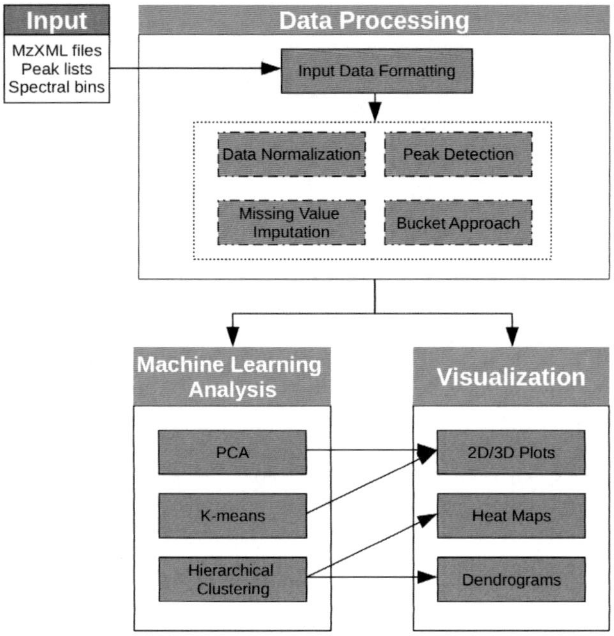

Figure 3. The Mass Spectrometry Data Analysis Toolbox.

runtime performance. In order to address these issues, we have developed our own open-source *Mass Spectrometry Data Analysis Toolbox* (MSDA), designed to efficiently carry out a number of different mass spectrometry (MS) data analyses tasks. Our MSDA Toolbox is able to analyze large datasets.

As shown in Figure 3, the Toolbox consists of three main components: 1) data processing, 2) machine learning analysis, and 3) visualization. The data processing component translates the input data to the required input format for the data analysis component. MSDA supports a wide variety of input data types, including raw mzXML files, peak lists and spectral bins. A set of data processing methods, such as peak detection/alignment, bucketing, missing value imputation and data normalization are supported. The machine learning analysis component provides a wide range of machine learning techniques, such as feature selection, clustering and PCA to provide insight into the data. The visualization component generates 2D/3D plots for PCA results, as well as heat maps and dendrograms for viewing hierarchical clustering results. The Toolbox is an open source software written in Python, which utilizes state of the art statistical and machine learning libraries written in Python, R and C. By integrating data analytics capabilities, the Toolbox can significantly reduce data processing time, providing researchers with a fast research toolset. We have modularized our design to facilitate future contributions from the open source community.

A. Data Processing

The data processing component filters the input data formats before passing the data on to other components for the further analysis. The first step is to check the input data formatting, which transforms input data files into a data matrix. Next, the user can choose to normalize the data, insert missing values, or perform peak detection and bucketing. In this paper we utilize the urine sample data from the DENAMIC project to demonstrate how our toolbox facilitates data discovery.

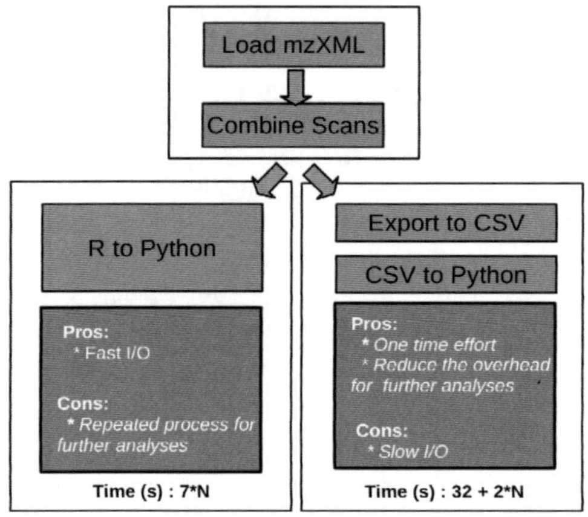

Figure 4. Compare memory exporting (bottom left) and disk (bottom right) exporting approach for formatting one mzXML file. N stands for the number of rounds of analysis. Reading data directly from R consumes 7 seconds / round, whereas reading from disk consumes 2 seconds / round, plus one time overhead of 32 seconds.

1) Input data formatting: This step converts input data into a data matrix, with samples in rows and features in columns. Three different data sources are supported: MS spectra raw files, peak list files and spectra bin files. The MS raw file should be in the *mzXML* format, while the rest are stored as CSVs. A peak list file should have either 2 columns (mass and intensities) or 3 columns (retention time, mass and intensities), with the first row reserved for column labels. A spectra bin file can have any number of columns, with the first row filled with labels for m/z buckets. The Toolbox also supports batch processing.

We utilize the *MALDIquant* [32] package in R and the *Panda* [33] library available in Python to transform mzXML and CSV files into data matrices, respectively. To seamlessly read the output of the *MALDIquant* package using Python, *rpy2* [34] is used to convert R objects into an accepted Python format, which avoids performing slow disk I/O operations. Since the mzXML files are frequently used, we convert them to CSV files and they are saved to disk for future analysis.

This data formatting is I/O bound, and so its performance depends on the size of the input file and output locations. To translate one urine sample file from the DENAMIC project, loading the mzXML file (83 MB) using *MALDIquant* takes 6 seconds and combining all of scans into a data matrix using *data.table* consumes 1 second. In MSDA, we provide two locations for data exporting, namely memory and disk. To export the data to memory, the *rpy2* package is used to facilitate the process, reducing runtime overhead to approximately 20 μs when offloading data (350 MB) in R to Python. On the other hand, we can export the data to disk first, which takes 25 seconds in R, then read it in as a Python object, which takes 2 seconds using *Pandas*. A comparison of both approaches is presented in Figure 4. Given the common case that we need to run many rounds (N being a big number) of analyses, the disk approach would be preferred by most users.

2) Data normalization and missing value imputation: Once a data matrix is generated, users can select whether to perform data normalization and missing value *imputation*. Many statistical and machine learning algorithms, such as PCA, do not work properly if features have a wide range of values or missing entries. Data normalization is used to modify the range of independent features so that they are normally distributed. Several data normalization methods are provided in MSDA, such as centering by mean or median values, scaling by the standard deviation, maximization, root square or logarithm. A variety of methods to treat missing values are also implemented in the Toolbox, including replacement by zero, mean, median and discarding the whole feature in the sample if the number of missing values is over a user-defined threshold. The *numpy* [35] library is used for data normalization and missing value imputation in our system. The resulting execution time is less than 50 ms for each urine sample.

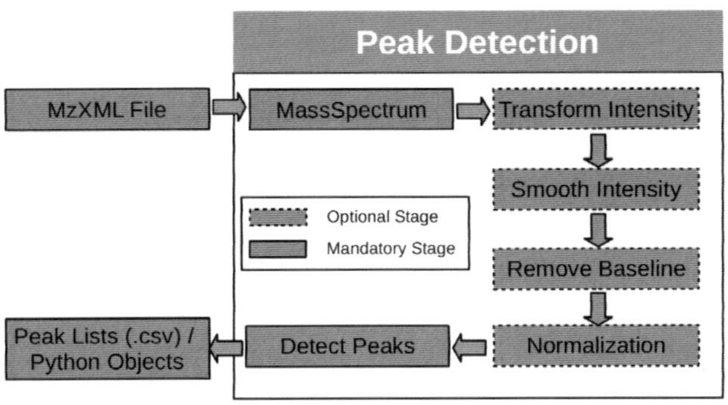

Figure 5. Peak detection pipeline. Dashed boxes represent optional steps and the solid ones stand for mandatory steps. A full peak detection pipeline includes all the stages, whereas a short one only includes the mandatory stages.

3) Peak Detection: Users can choose whether to select peaks for a given mzXML file or just leave the MS data unchanged in CSV format. *MALDIquant* is used to carry out the peak detection task. It provides a peak detection pipeline, as shown in Figure 5. The 4 stages of the pipeline include: i.) removing noise from the spectra, ii.) transforming intensities, iii.) correcting the baseline, and iv.) aligning the spectra.

At the beginning of the peak detection process, we read the mzXML data by calling the *importMzXml* function. Figure 6 (a) shows one scan of an input urine sample. The intensity values are then centered and scaled, as shown in Figure 6 (b). Several scaling methods are supported, including square root and logarithm. The smoothing stage can be implemented using either the *SavitzkyGolay* or *MovingAverage* method, and configurable to a half window size [36]. The *SavitzkyGolay* method with a half window size of 10 is applied in Figure 6 (c). Then, the spectra baseline can be estimated and removed by adopting *SNIP* [37], *TopHat* [38], *ConvexHull* [39] or *median* methods. These methods estimate the background signal, iteratively. Users can adjust the *iteration* parameter to achieve the best result. Figure 6 (d) shows the baseline estimation using the *SNIP* method with 10 iterations. Figure 6 (e) shows the spectra with the baseline removed. The resulting spectra can be normalized using either *Total-Ion-Current-Calibration* (TIC) or *Probabilistic Quotient Normalization* (PQN) [40]. Figure 6 (f) shows the normalized spectra using the TIC method. The last and most critical stage is the peak detection step. This step estimates noise using either the *media-absolute-deviation* or *Friedmans Super Smoother* method. Users can adjust the half window size and signal-to-noise ratio (SNR) to identify the local maximum intensities. The SNR can also be estimated automatically using the *estimateNoise* function. The baselines for SNR 1 and 2 are presented in Figure 6 (g). The results of using the full peak detection pipeline are plotted in Figure 6 (h), where an SNR 2 is applied. In addition, the short pipeline's results are shown in Figure 6 (i). This approach skips all the optional stages that were present in Figure 5. The output of the pipeline can be either directly fed to Python through *rpy2*, or saved to disk as a peak list file in CSV format for faster accesses in the future.

We show that different peak lists are generated by applying either the full or short peak detection pipeline in Figures 6 (h) and (i). Users can choose which pipeline to use, depending on the trade-off between the execution time and the peak resolution.

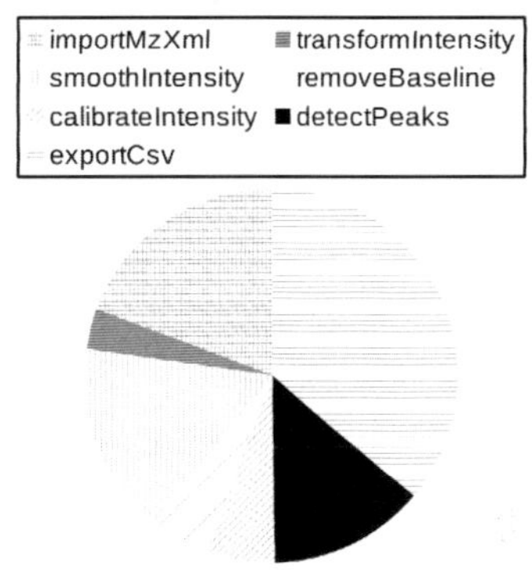

(a) Full pipeline execution time = 25.5 s. Three dominant factors: (1) exportCsv-36% (2) importMzXml-19% (3) smoothIntensity-16%.

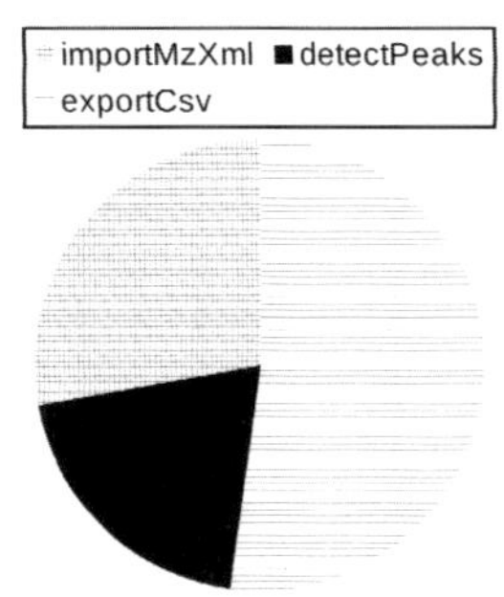

(b) Short pipeline execution time = 17.6 s. Three dominant factors: (1) exportCsv-52% (2) importMzXml-28% (3) detectPeaks-20%.

Figure 7. Performance breakdown for both the full and short pipelines. The 3 most timing consuming steps are presented in descending order.

4) Peak Detection Performance: We use an Intel i7-4790K (4 cores / 8 threads, using hyperthreading) to evaluate peak de-

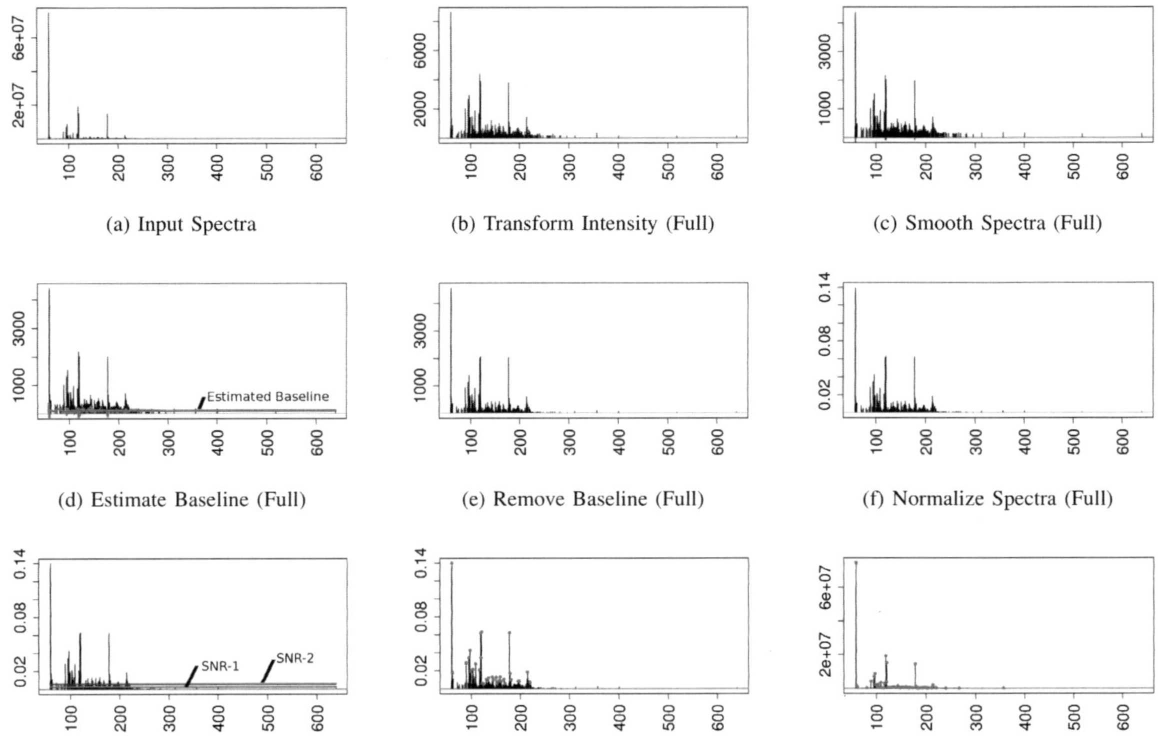

(a) Input Spectra (b) Transform Intensity (Full) (c) Smooth Spectra (Full)

(d) Estimate Baseline (Full) (e) Remove Baseline (Full) (f) Normalize Spectra (Full)

(g) Estimate SNR (Full) (h) Detect Peaks (Full) (i) Detect Peaks (Short)

Figure 6. A pipelined Peak Detection example. The spectral results after each stage in a fully pipelined peak detection are shown in Figure (b) to (h), whereas Figure (i) shows the detected peaks using a short pipeline. The x-axis is mass, the y-axis is intensity.

tection performance. In R, the average processing time for one urine sample is 17 and 25 seconds for the short and full peak detection pipelines, respectively. The detailed performance breakdown for each case is illustrated in Figure 7. Since there are 1448 urine samples in the *DENAMIC* datasets, it requires 7 hours for the short pipeline and 10 hours for the full pipeline to detect intensity peaks. To reduce the processing overhead, we identify the performance bottlenecks and explore multi-threading techniques to accelerate the process. We consider the aforementioned single-threaded performance as our baseline for comparison.

As shown in Figure 7, the dominant performance bottleneck lies in the *exportCsv* step, which merges a list of mass spectrometry data into a single matrix, and then exports the data to a CSV file. Due to the overhead of combining rows (*rbind*) and columns (*cbind*) in R, the merging step takes 9.1 seconds, as compared to 0.1 seconds to export the CSV file. In order to accelerate the merge step, we leverage the optimized *rbindlist* function in the *data.table* package [41]. First, for each peak scan, as a data frame object is appended to the pre-allocated list, the list is reduced into one data frame using *rbindlist*. We observed the execution overhead of the merge step drops from 9.1 seconds to just over 1 second. This is because *rbindlist* is highly optimized in C, whereas *rbind* is coded in a high level scripting language (R). We can reduce the execution time of *exportCsv* from the 9.2 seconds (baseline) to 1.1 seconds.

The next performance hot-spot is the *importMzXml* process. We leverage the *mzR* package from Bioconductor (an open software for bioinformatics) [42][43]. In our baseline approach, *importMzXML* in *MALDIquantForeign* reads the mzXML file (internally using *readMzXmlFile* from the *readMzXmlData* package) and creates the MassSpectrum class accordingly [44][45]. To improve performance, we utilize the *openMSfile* function from the *mzR* package to read the input file more efficiently, and apply the *peaks* method inside *mzR* to acquire the m/z and intensity values. We achieve a 2.6x speedup over the baseline, reducing the elapsed time from 4.9 seconds to 1.9 seconds.

Besides single-threaded optimization, we also utilize *parallel* packages (e.g., a multi-threaded implementation in R) to obtain more speedup [46]. The execution time for the three steps (*import, peak, export*) by varying the number of threads is shown in Figure 8. Here, the *peak* stage includes the steps from *transformIntensity* to *detectPeaks* in Figure 5.

In our optimization scheme, we use the *mclapply* function to parallelize the list operation on the *MassSpectrum* data. The *peak* operation is applied to every *MassSpectrum* data list using *mclapply*. The same operation is applied to the parallel creation of *MassSpectrum* objects in the *import* stage and the *export*

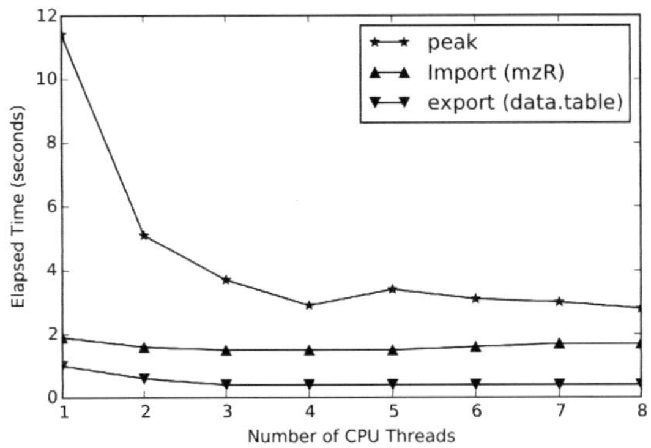

Figure 8. The performance for parallelizing three performance hotspots 1) import 2) peak 3) export for the full pipeline peak detection on an Intel i7-4790K.

stage. However, since the *parallel* package forks to create a new process by taking a complete copy of the master process, the overhead is very high for both *import* and *export* stages. Thus, the performance flattens out after two threads for *import* (red line) and *export* (yellow line), as shown in Figure 8. For the *peak* stage, only urine sample IDs are duplicated during the forking process. We achieved a 3.9x speedup using 4 threads. In summary, Figure 9 shows that by using *data.table* (rbindlist), we can achieve a 1.5x speedup on average. Adding *mzR* (openMSfile) to *data.table*, we can obtain on average 1.9x speedup. When using *parallel* (mclapply), and adding the benefits of the two previous optimization methods, we can achieve a 5.3x speedup by using 4 threads. Overall, we reduced the processing time for the full pipeline peak detection from 10 hours to 2 hours. Applying the same technique, we shortened the processing time from 7 hours to 1 hour for the short pipeline peak detection.

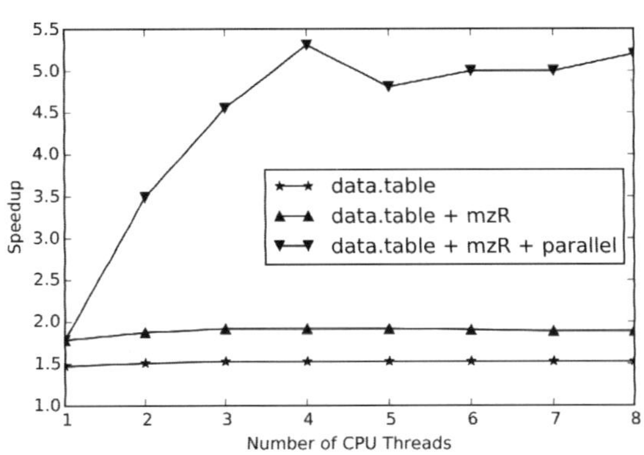

Figure 9. The total speedup achieved by parallelizing the full pipeline peak detection on Intel i7-4790K.

5) Bucketing Approach: The Bucketing approach is also implemented in MSDA. For each peak list, we group multiple

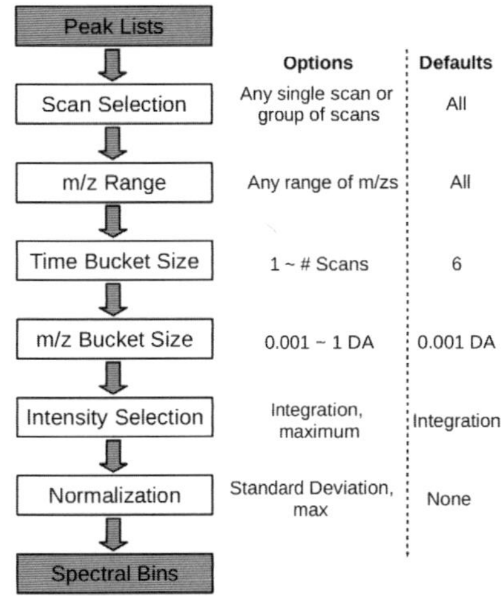

Figure 10. Workflow of the Bucketing approach. Users can specify the parameters.

scans together in a time-bucket, and multiple m/zs in a m/z-bucket. The time-bucket size and the m/z-bucket size are chosen based on the HPLC peak width, while considering the mass accuracy and the resolution of the mass spectrometer. The Bucketing approach essentially extracts the spectral features integrated over time in order to reduce the redundancy in the original MS data, and to improve our computational capabilities. As shown in Figure 10, the input is a set of peak lists in CSV format and the output is the spectral bins. The boxes between the input and the output represent the optional transformations that can be applied by the users. Users can choose from the listed options in Figure 10, or specify their own parameters. Otherwise, the default values are used. The first parameter allows the user to choose any combination of scans in a sample. A range of m/z sizes can be specified using the second parameter. Users can choose how many scans they want to put into one bucket by specifying the time-bucket size, and the size for m/z-buckets by the m/z bucket size. Users can also choose how to combine the bucketed scans, by either integrating all the intensity values, or by selecting the maximum intensity for each m/z bucket. In addition, users can also select the normalization method for the bucketed intensities.

To process one urine sample from the DENAMIC project, whose scan speed is 2 Hz with normal MS scans and HCD fragmentation scans interleaved, we choose the even-numbered scans in the range of 40 to 1200 and use 6 as the time-bucket size and 0.001 DA as the m/z-bucket size.

The generated spectral bins for the 306 urine samples (spanish mothers with ESI+) consist of 97 time-buckets and 750k m/z-buckets in each sample, corresponding to a 29,682 x 750,204 sparse matrix of 1.5% density. The *Scipy* [47] library is used to store the sparse matrix in the compressed column storage (csc) format to minimize the memory cost. The spectral bins, represented as in a data matrix, can be directly fed into the machine learning analysis component or stored on disk as a CSV file.

Figure 11 plots the execution time of the bucketing approach for one urine sample consisting 600 scans and 942,397

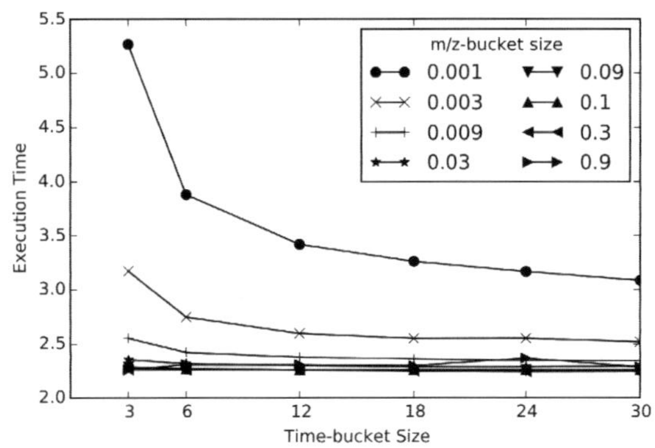

Figure 11. Bucketing performance while varying the bucket size.

(m/z, intensity) pairs. We vary the time and m/z-bucket sizes to compare their impact on the performance. It turns out that m/z-bucket size is the dominant factor as we can see two big jumps in the execution time when decreasing the m/z-bucket size from 0.009 to 0.003 and from 0.003 to 0.001. The time-bucket size, on the other hand, contributes little to the execution time, especially when the m/z-bucket size is large.

B. Machine Learning Analysis

A general set of machine learning techniques for mass spectrum analysis are implemented in MSDA. In this section, three different methods are discussed: i) Principal Component Analysis (PCA), ii) K-means clustering, and iii) Hierarchical clustering.

1) PCA: Principal Component Analysis (PCA) [48] is a commonly-used method to reduce a data matrix of n features to k ($k << n$) features, with much of the variability in the data preserved. The transformed k features are called *principal components*. The principal components are sorted by their variance, hence the first principal component has the largest variance and each subsequent component has the next largest variance. As noted by Worley and Powers, PCA is one of the most popular multivariate analysis methods used in metabolomics [49]. Because PCA can significantly reduce the dimensionality of a dataset, it is often used in compression algorithms as it provides an approximation of the original data using only k principal components. Another common use of PCA is visualization: datasets in high-dimensional space can be projected onto a 2D or 3D space, while most of the patterns in the dataset are preserved. Researchers can gain insight into complex data by just studying the 2D and 3D plots. In MS data analysis, the data matrix is usually a huge sparse matrix, especially when the m/z-bucket size is small. One of the data matrices from the DENAMIC project used in this work contains 306 urine samples, where each sample is represented by 97 time-buckets and 750,204 m/z-buckets. This results in a 29,682 x 750,204 sparse data matrix with ~ 350 million non-zero elements. Normal PCA methods that take a dense matrix as the input cannot be used in this case, hence MSDA uses a TruncatedSVD [50] from *scikit-learn* [51] for this task. The execution time of applying the TruncatedPCA on the aforementioned matrix is 34 seconds on average.

2) K-means Clustering: K-means [52] is one of the most popular clustering algorithms, especially given its simplicity and effectiveness. It is widely used in metabolomic studies due to its capability to perform rapid subset identification from the information-rich spectral datasets [53]–[55]. In MS analysis, K-means (and its variants) are heavily used to cluster urine samples to detect anomalies. It can either be applied on the original data matrix to calculate the pairwise distances in n dimensions, or directly on the dimensionality-reduced matrix generated by PCA.

3) Hierarchical Clustering: In K-means, the desired number of clusterers k must be specified by the user, and determining k is not an easy job. Hierarchical clustering is another widely used clustering algorithm that builds a hierarchy of clusters, so that the clustering results for all k (from 1 to n) are automatically generated [56][57]. MSDA uses an agglomerative clustering algorithm and displays the clustering results using a dendrogram.

C. Visualization

In this section, we showcase 2D/3D plots for the PCA results and the heat map / dendrogram for the hierarchical clustering results.

1) 2D/3D plots: Figures 12 and 13 show the 2D and 3D plots of the PCA results generated by MSDA using *matplotlib* [58] in Python. We are able to project 29,682 data points on a 2D and 3D space in 20 seconds and 25 seconds, respectively.

2) Heat map and Dendrogram: A heat map is a data visualization technique to reveal the relationships among data points, using a color scheme. A heat map applies a color-shared matrix display, and reorders the data matrix to disclose the underlying structure of the data [59]. It is widely applied in data visualization in the natural and biological sciences. This technique has been extensively used in previous urine studies [60]–[62].

A dendrogram is a tree-based diagram that illustrates how k clusters are grown out of n observations for any arbitrary k (from 1 to n). To view the clustering result for a specific k, a "cut" can be taken horizontally on the y-axis where k intersections are created. Each vertical line at the intersection then leads to a cluster.

Heat maps and dendrograms are often combined to illustrate hierarchical clustering results. MSDA uses *matplotlib* to generate the combined plot. An example of 306 urine samples is shown in Figure 14.

V. Conclusion and Future Work

In this paper, we have presented an overview of *Puerto Rico Testsite for Exploring Contamination Threats* Center, and highlighted many of the challenges faced during data management and analysis. We have developed a highly efficient solution based on the EQuIS, providing for efficient data cleaning and reporting given the diversity of the data sources.

In order to begin to understand how environmental factors can impact preterm birth, we have developed a number of Toolboxes. We discuss the development of a Toolbox to streamline metabolomic analysis of expectant mother's urine samples. The goal is to identify non-targeted compounds in the urine. Due to the computational challenges of this analysis, we have built an open source framework called the *Mass Spectrometry Data*

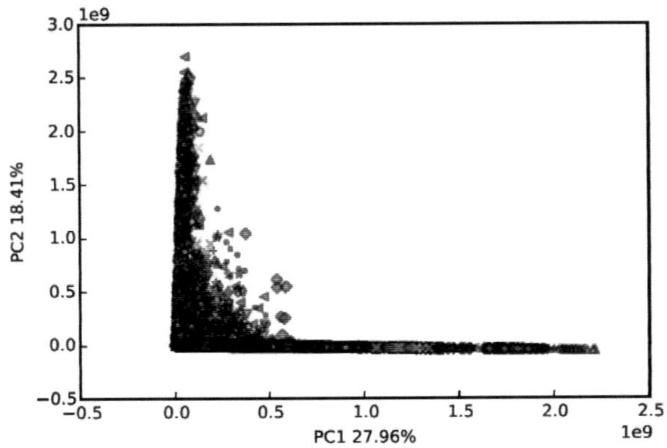

Figure 12. A 2-D PCA plot.

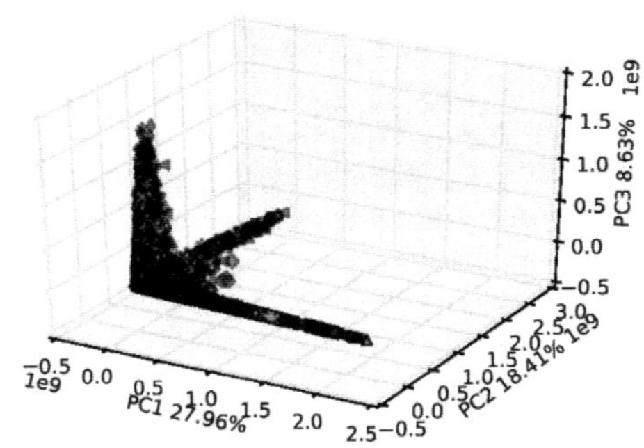

Figure 13. A 3-D PCA plot.

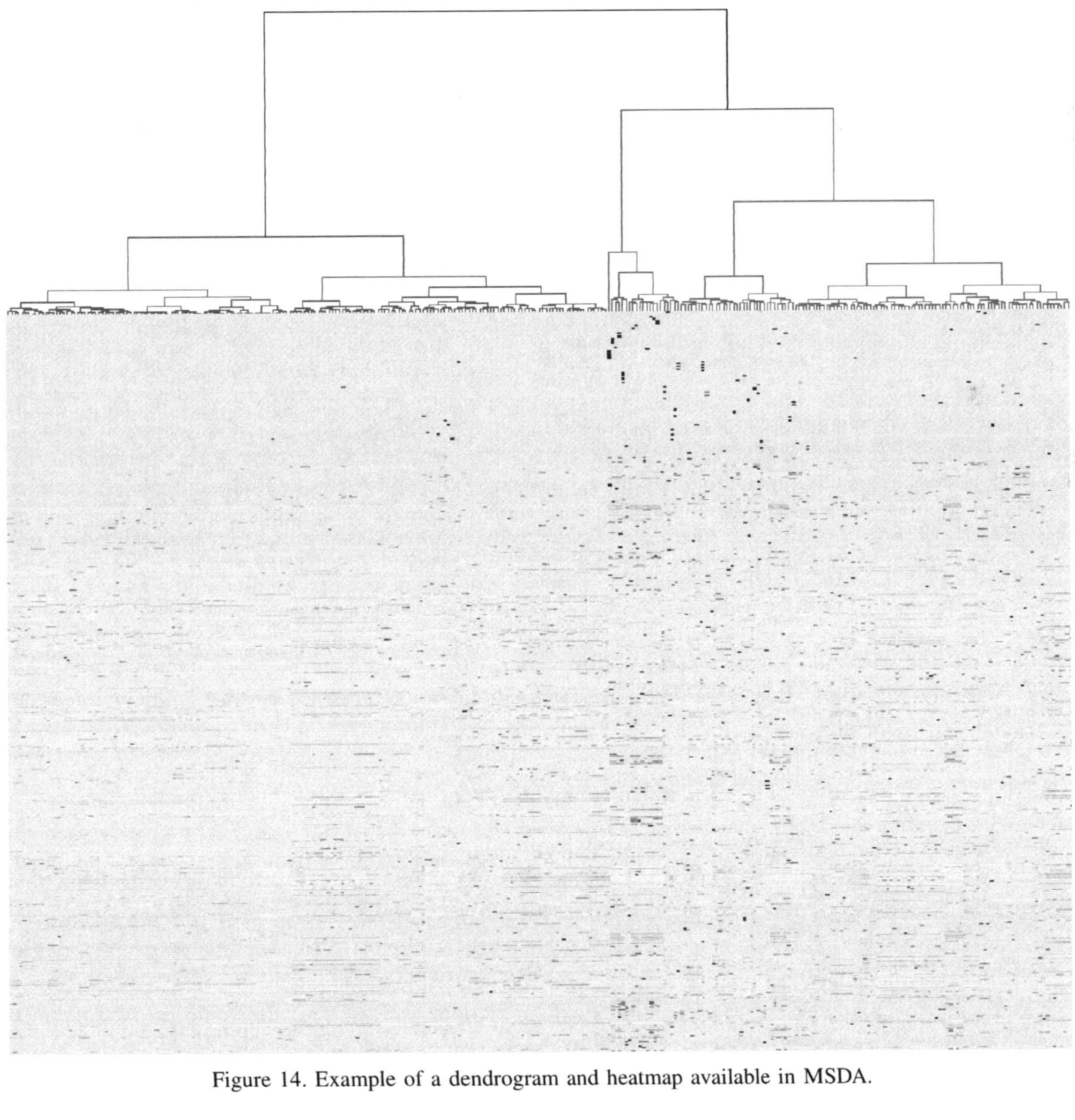

Figure 14. Example of a dendrogram and heatmap available in MSDA.

Analysis Toolbox. The Toolbox can signficantly accelerate metabolomic analysis. MSDA can handle a complete analysis pipeline ranging from data processing to machine learning. The Toolbox also provides visualization capabilities to help the user understand sample characteristics present in a high-dimensional feature space.

We have been able to demonstrate the saving provided by MSDA, enabling much faster processing utilizing parallelization, but also integrating a number of tools together into a single framework. We believe MSDA will have a strong impact on discovering biological patterns in the future.

To further improve the capability of MSDA, we plan to implement additional machine learning and statistical techniques, including PLS-DA, t-Tests and SVM capabilities. We also plan to enhance the performance and scalability of the Toolbox further, leveraging GPUs and the Spark [63] distributed computation framework.

ACKNOWLEDGMENT

This work is supported in part by Award Number P42ES017198 from the National Institute of Environmental Health Sciences. Authors would like to thank Ana Miralles-Marco for her collaboration. This study had the support of the FP7-ENV-2011 DENAMIC project (cod 282957). In addition, we would like to thank EarthSoft for their generous support.

REFERENCES

[1] X. Li, L. Yu, Y. Yao, P. Wang, R. Giese, A. Alshawabkeh, and D. Kaeli, "Big Data Analysis on Puerto Rico Testsite for Exploring Contamination Threats," in *ALLDATA'2015: The First International Conference on Big Data, Small Data, Linked Data and Open Data*, pp. 29–34, 2015.

[2] H. Blencowe *et al.*, "National regional and worldwide estimates of preterm birth rates in the year 2010 with time trends since 1990 for selected countries: a systematic analysis and implications," *The Lancet*, vol. 379, pp. 2162–2171, 2012.

[3] J. D. Meeker *et al.*, "Urinary phthalate metabolites in relation to preterm birth in mexico city," *Environ. Health Perspect.*, vol. 117, pp. 1587–1592, 2009.

[4] D. Cantonwine *et al.*, "Bisphenol a exposure in Mexico City and Risk of prematurity: a pilot nested case control study," *Environ. Health*, vol. 9, pp. 62–68, 2010.

[5] A. P. Mucha *et al.*, "Abstract: Association between pbde exposure and preterm birth," in *10 Annual Workshop on Brominated Flame Retardants*, (Victoria, BC Canada), p. 42, 2008.

[6] K. Tsukimori *et al.*, "Long-term effects of polychlorinated biphenyls and dioxins on pregnancy outcomes in women affected by the yusho incident," *Eniron. Health. Perspect.*, vol. 116, pp. 626–630, 2008.

[7] P. Z. Ruckart, F. J. Bove, and M. Maslia, "Evaluation of contaminated drinking water and preterm birth, small for gestational age, and birth weight at Marine Corps Base Camp Lejeune, North Carolina: a cross-sectional study," *Environ. Health*, vol. 13, pp. 1–10, 2014.

[8] J. D. Meeker, "Exposure to environmental endocrine disruptors and child development," *Arch. Pediatr. Adolesc. Med.*, vol. 166, pp. 952–958, 2012.

[9] G. Guennebaud, B. Jacob, *et al.*, "Eigen v3." http://eigen.tuxfamily.org, 2010.

[10] P. J. Meis, R. L. Goldenberg, B. M. Mercer, J. D. Iams, A. H. Moawad, M. Miodovnik, M. K. Menard, S. N. Caritis, G. R. Thurnau, S. F. Bottoms, *et al.*, "The preterm prediction study: risk factors for indicated preterm births," *American journal of obstetrics and gynecology*, vol. 178, no. 3, pp. 562–567, 1998.

[11] J. D. Meeker, H. Hu, D. E. Cantonwine, H. Lamadrid-Figueroa, A. M. Calafat, R. Loch-Caruso, M. M. Téllez-Rojo, A. S. Ettinger, and M. Hernandez-Avila, "Urinary phthalate metabolites in relation to preterm birth in mexico city," 2009.

[12] N. Torres Torres, J. Howard, I. Padilla, P. Torres, I. Cotto, and C. Irizarry, "Effects of hydrogeologic conditions on groundwater contamination of cvocs in the north coast karst aquifer of puerto rico," in *AGU Fall Meeting Abstracts*, vol. 1, p. 1251, 2012.

[13] M. Roca, N. Leon, A. Pastor, and V. Yusà, "Comprehensive analytical strategy for biomonitoring of pesticides in urine by liquid chromatography–orbitrap high resolution mass spectrometry," *Journal of Chromatography A*, vol. 1374, pp. 66–76, 2014.

[14] Y. Chen, P. J. McGrath, and J. W. Stewart, "Web-Based Electronic Data Capture System in Psychiatry Clinical Trials: A StudyTRAX Review,"

[15] C. Schmitz *et al.*, "Limesurvey: an open source survey tool," *LimeSurvey Project Hamburg, Germany. URL http://www. limesurvey. org*, 2012.

[16] C. Voegele, B. Bouchereau, N. Robinot, J. McKay, P. Damiecki, and L. Alteyrac, "A universal open-source Electronic Laboratory Notebook," *Bioinformatics*, vol. 29, no. 13, pp. 1710–1712, 2013.

[17] P. A. Harris, R. Taylor, R. Thielke, J. Payne, N. Gonzalez, and J. G. Conde, "Research electronic data capture (REDCap)a metadata-driven methodology and workflow process for providing translational research informatics support," *Journal of biomedical informatics*, vol. 42, no. 2, pp. 377–381, 2009.

[18] EarthSoft, "EarthSoft: Standalone EQuIS Data Processor (EDP) User Guide." http://www.dec.ny.gov/docs/remediation_hudson_pdf/edpuserguide.pdf, 2008.

[19] EarthSoft, "EQuIS 6 Enterprise: Workflow Automation & Dashboards." http://www.earthsoft.com/products/enterprise/, 2015 (accessed September 1, 2015).

[20] EarthSoft, "EarthSoft Corporate Overview EQuIS^{TM}." http://www.earthsoft.com/wp-content/uploads/2014/11/2014-Corp-Overview-Nov.pdf, 2014.

[21] W. Arlt, M. Biehl, A. E. Taylor, S. Hahner, R. Libe, B. A. Hughes, P. Schneider, D. J. Smith, H. Stiekema, N. Krone, *et al.*, "Urine steroid metabolomics as a biomarker tool for detecting malignancy in adrenal tumors," *The Journal of Clinical Endocrinology & Metabolism*, vol. 96, no. 12, pp. 3775–3784, 2011.

[22] Y. Kim, I. Koo, B. H. Jung, B. C. Chung, and D. Lee, "Multivariate classification of urine metabolome profiles for breast cancer diagnosis," *BMC bioinformatics*, vol. 11, no. Suppl 2, p. S4, 2010.

[23] C. Lanz, A. D. Patterson, J. Slavík, K. W. Krausz, M. Ledermann, F. J. Gonzalez, and J. R. Idle, "Radiation metabolomics. 3. biomarker discovery in the urine of gamma-irradiated rats using a simplified metabolomics protocol of gas chromatography-mass spectrometry combined with random forests machine learning algorithm," *Radiation research*, vol. 172, no. 2, pp. 198–212, 2009.

[24] S. E. Reichenbach, X. Tian, Q. Tao, D. R. Stoll, and P. W. Carr, "Comprehensive feature analysis for sample classification with comprehensive two-dimensional lc," *Journal of separation science*, vol. 33, no. 10, pp. 1365–1374, 2010.

[25] EarthSoft, "EQuIS Professional." http://www.earthsoft.com/products/professional/, 2015 (accessed September 1, 2015).

[26] DENAMIC, "Developmental Neurotoxicity Assessment of Mixtures in Children." http://www.denamic-project.eu/, 2015 (accessed September 1, 2015).

[27] "Marker view software." http://sciex.com/products/software/markerview-software.

[28] "Simca-p." http://umetrics.com/products/simca.

[29] "Sas." https://www.sas.com/en_us/home.html.

[30] J. Xia, N. Psychogios, N. Young, and D. S. Wishart, "Metaboanalyst: a web server for metabolomic data analysis and interpretation," *Nucleic acids research*, vol. 37, no. suppl 2, pp. W652–W660, 2009.

[31] H. Neuweger, S. P. Albaum, M. Dondrup, M. Persicke, T. Watt, K. Niehaus, J. Stoye, and A. Goesmann, "Meltdb: a software platform for the analysis and integration of metabolomics experiment data," *Bioinformatics*, vol. 24, no. 23, pp. 2726–2732, 2008.

[32] S. Gibb and K. Strimmer, "Maldiquant: a versatile r package for the analysis of mass spectrometry data," *Bioinformatics*, vol. 28, no. 17, pp. 2270–2271, 2012.

[33] W. McKinney, "Data structures for statistical computing in python," in *Proceedings of the 9th Python in Science Conference* (S. van der Walt and J. Millman, eds.), pp. 51 – 56, 2010.

[34] "rpy2 package." http://rpy2.bitbucket.org/.

[35] S. v. d. Walt, S. C. Colbert, and G. Varoquaux, "The numpy array: A structure for efficient numerical computation," *Computing in Science and Engg.*, vol. 13, pp. 22–30, Mar. 2011.

[36] A. Savitzky and M. J. Golay, "Smoothing and differentiation of data by simplified least squares procedures.," *Analytical chemistry*, vol. 36, no. 8, pp. 1627–1639, 1964.

[37] C. Ryan, E. Clayton, W. Griffin, S. Sie, and D. Cousens, "Snip, a statistics-sensitive background treatment for the quantitative analysis of pixe spectra in geoscience applications," *Nuclear Instruments and Methods in Physics Research Section B: Beam Interactions with Materials and Atoms*, vol. 34, no. 3, pp. 396–402, 1988.

[38] J. Gil and M. Werman, "Computing 2-dimensional min, median and max filters," 1996.

[39] A. M. Andrew, "Another efficient algorithm for convex hulls in two dimensions," *Information Processing Letters*, vol. 9, no. 5, pp. 216–219, 1979.

[40] F. Dieterle, A. Ross, G. Schlotterbeck, and H. Senn, "Probabilistic quotient normalization as robust method to account for dilution of complex biological mixtures. application in 1h nmr metabonomics," *Analytical chemistry*, vol. 78, no. 13, pp. 4281–4290, 2006.

[41] M. Dowle, T. Short, S. Lianoglou, R. Saporta, A. Srinivasan, and E. Antonyan, "data. table: Extension of data. frame," 2015.

[42] M. C. Chambers, B. Maclean, R. Burke, D. Amodei, D. L. Ruderman, S. Neumann, L. Gatto, B. Fischer, B. Pratt, J. Egertson, *et al.*, "A cross-platform toolkit for mass spectrometry and proteomics," *Nature biotechnology*, vol. 30, no. 10, pp. 918–920, 2012.

[43] R. C. Gentleman, V. J. Carey, D. M. Bates, B. Bolstad, M. Dettling, S. Dudoit, B. Ellis, L. Gautier, Y. Ge, J. Gentry, *et al.*, "Bioconductor: open software development for computational biology and bioinformatics," *Genome biology*, vol. 5, no. 10, p. R80, 2004.

[44] S. Gibb, "readMzXmlData: Reads Mass Spectrometry Data in mzXML Format," 2014.

[45] S. Gibb, "MALDIquantForeign: Import/export routines for maldiquant," 2015.

[46] D. Eddelbuettel, "Cran task view: High-performance and parallel computing with r," 2014.

[47] E. Jones, T. Oliphant, P. Peterson, *et al.*, "SciPy: Open source scientific tools for Python," 2001–. [Online; accessed 2016-02-28].

[48] I. Jolliffe, *Principal component analysis*. Wiley Online Library, 2005.

[49] B. Worley and R. Powers, "Multivariate analysis in metabolomics," *Current Metabolomics*, vol. 1, no. 1, p. 92, 2013.

[50] P.-G. M. Nathan Halko and J. A. Tropp, "Finding structure with randomness: Probabilistic algorithms for constructing approximate matrix decompositions," 2014.

[51] F. Pedregosa, G. Varoquaux, A. Gramfort, V. Michel, B. Thirion, O. Grisel, M. Blondel, P. Prettenhofer, R. Weiss, V. Dubourg, J. Vanderplas, A. Passos, D. Cournapeau, M. Brucher, M. Perrot, and E. Duchesnay, "Scikit-learn: Machine learning in Python," *Journal of Machine Learning Research*, vol. 12, pp. 2825–2830, 2011.

[52] T. Kanungo, D. M. Mount, N. S. Netanyahu, C. D. Piatko, R. Silverman, and A. Y. Wu, "An efficient k-means clustering algorithm: Analysis and implementation," *IEEE Trans. Pattern Anal. Mach. Intell.*, vol. 24, pp. 881–892, July 2002.

[53] K. H. Liland, "Multivariate methods in metabolomics–from preprocessing to dimension reduction and statistical analysis," *TrAC Trends in Analytical Chemistry*, vol. 30, no. 6, pp. 827–841, 2011.

[54] D. J. Vis, J. A. Westerhuis, D. M. Jacobs, J. P. van Duynhoven, S. Wopereis, B. van Ommen, M. M. Hendriks, and A. K. Smilde, "Analyzing metabolomics-based challenge tests," *Metabolomics*, vol. 11, no. 1, pp. 50–63, 2015.

[55] J. Xia, R. Mandal, I. V. Sinelnikov, D. Broadhurst, and D. S. Wishart, "Metaboanalyst 2.0ž014a comprehensive server for metabolomic data analysis," *Nucleic acids research*, vol. 40, no. W1, pp. W127–W133, 2012.

[56] X. Wang, A. Zhang, Y. Han, P. Wang, H. Sun, G. Song, T. Dong, Y. Yuan, X. Yuan, M. Zhang, *et al.*, "Urine metabolomics analysis for biomarker discovery and detection of jaundice syndrome in patients with liver disease," *Molecular & Cellular Proteomics*, vol. 11, no. 8, pp. 370–380, 2012.

[57] A. Miyagi, H. Takahashi, K. Takahara, T. Hirabayashi, Y. Nishimura, T. Tezuka, M. Kawai-Yamada, and H. Uchimiya, "Principal component and hierarchical clustering analysis of metabolites in destructive weeds; polygonaceous plants," *Metabolomics*, vol. 6, no. 1, pp. 146–155, 2010.

[58] J. Hunter, D. Dale, and E. Firing, "matplotlib: Python plotting," 2012.

[59] L. Wilkinson and M. Friendly, "The history of the cluster heat map," *The American Statistician*, vol. 63, no. 2, 2009.

[60] J.-Y. Moon, H.-J. Jung, M. H. Moon, B. C. Chung, and M. H. Choi, "Heat-map visualization of gas chromatography-mass spectrometry based quantitative signatures on steroid metabolism," *Journal of the American Society for Mass Spectrometry*, vol. 20, no. 9, pp. 1626–1637, 2009.

[61] X. Zhao, J. Fritsche, J. Wang, J. Chen, K. Rittig, P. Schmitt-Kopplin, A. Fritsche, H.-U. Häring, E. D. Schleicher, G. Xu, *et al.*, "Metabonomic fingerprints of fasting plasma and spot urine reveal human prediabetic metabolic traits," *Metabolomics*, vol. 6, no. 3, pp. 362–374, 2010.

[62] L. Mengual, M. Burset, M. J. Ribal, E. Ars, M. Marín-Aguilera, M. Fernández, M. Ingelmo-Torres, H. Villavicencio, and A. Alcaraz, "Gene expression signature in urine for diagnosing and assessing aggressiveness of bladder urothelial carcinoma," *Clinical Cancer Research*, vol. 16, no. 9, pp. 2624–2633, 2010.

[63] M. Zaharia, M. Chowdhury, M. J. Franklin, S. Shenker, and I. Stoica, "Spark: Cluster computing with working sets," in *Proceedings of the 2Nd USENIX Conference on Hot Topics in Cloud Computing*, HotCloud'10, (Berkeley, CA, USA), pp. 10–10, USENIX Association, 2010.

O|R|P|E - A Data Semantics Driven Concurrency Control Mechanism with Run-time Adaptation

Tim Lessner*, Fritz Laux†, Thomas M Connolly‡
*freiheit.com technologies gmbh, Hamburg, Germany
Email: tim.lessner@freiheit.com
†Reutlingen University, Reutlingen, Germany
Email: fritz.laux@reutlingen-university.de
‡University of the West of Scotland, Paisley, UK
Email: thomas.connolly@uws.ac.uk

***Abstract*—This paper presents a concurrency control mechanism that does not follow a 'one concurrency control mechanism fits all needs' strategy. With the presented mechanism a transaction runs under several concurrency control mechanisms and the appropriate one is chosen based on the accessed data. For this purpose, the data is divided into four classes based on its access type and usage (semantics). Class O (the optimistic class) implements a first-committer-wins strategy, class R (the reconciliation class) implements a first-n-committers-win strategy, class P (the pessimistic class) implements a first-reader-wins strategy, and class E (the escrow class) implements a first-n-readers-win strategy. Accordingly, the model is called O|R|P|E. The selected concurrency control mechanism may be automatically adapted at run-time according to the current load or a known usage profile. This run-time adaptation allows O|R|P|E to balance the commit rate and the response time even under changing conditions. O|R|P|E outperforms the Snapshot Isolation concurrency control in terms of response time by a factor of approximately 4.5 under heavy transactional load (4000 concurrent transactions). As consequence, the degree of concurrency is 3.2 times higher.**

Keywords*–*Transaction processing; multimodel concurrency control; optimistic concurrency control; snapshot isolation; performance analysis; run-time adaptation.

I. Introduction

The drawbacks of existing concurrency control (CC) mechanisms are that pessimistic concurrency control (PCC) is likely to block transactions and is prone to deadlocks, optimistic concurrency control (OCC) may experience a sudden decrease in the commit rate if contention increases. Snapshot Isolation (SI) better supports query processing since transactions generally operate on snapshots and also prevents read anomalies, but depending on the implementation of SI, either pessimistic or optimistic, it is also subject to the previously mentioned drawbacks of PCC or OCC. Semantics based CC (SCC) remedies some problems of PCC or OCC. It performs well under contention, reduces the blocking time, and better supports disconnected operations. However, its applicability is limited since data and transactions have to comply with specific properties such as the commutativity of operations. In addition to the previously mentioned drawbacks, neither PCC nor OCC nor SCC support long-lived and disconnected data processing. However, these properties are essential to achieve scalability in Web-based and loosely coupled applications. Another challenge is that in real-life scenarios often the data usage profile changes over time (e.g. stock refill in the morning, selling goods during business hours, housekeeping during closing hours) which calls for a dynamic CC-mechanism.

This paper extends a mechanism presented in [1] and originally introduced in [2] that combines OCC, PCC, and SCC and steps away from the **'one concurrency control mechanism fits all needs'** strategy. Instead, the CC mechanism is chosen depending on the data usage. While the original O|R|P|E model assigns the appropriate CC-mechanism statically, this paper addresses a dynamic adaptation of the CC-mechanism due to sudden changes of the system load. To address scalability, the mechanism was designed with a focus on long-lived and disconnected data processing.

Consider, for example, the wholesale scenario as presented in the TPC-C [3]. With PCC using shared and exclusive locks, the likelihood of deadlocks increases for hot spot fields such as the stock's quantity or the account's debit or credit. If transactions are long-lived, PCC is even worse since deadlocks manifest during write time and a significant amount of work is likely to be lost [4] [2]. With OCC, deadlocks cannot occur. However, hot-spot fields like an account's debit or credit would experience many version validation failures under high load causing the restart of a transaction. Like PCC, validation failures manifest during the write-phase of a transaction and a significant amount of work is likely to be lost. Both PCC and OCC cannot ensure that modifications attempted during a transaction's read-phase will prevail during the write-phase. Whereas PCC is prone to deadlocks, OCC is prone to its optimistic nature itself.

O|R|P|E resolves these drawbacks and data can be classified in CC classes. For example, customer data such as the address or password can be controlled by a PCC that uses exclusive locks only [5]. Such a rigorous measure ensures ownership of data and should be used if data is modified that belongs to one transaction. For example, account data or master data should not be modified concurrently and given the importance of this data a rigorous isolation is justified. The debit or credit of an account can be classified in CC class R, which guarantees no lost updates and no constraint violations. Such a guarantee is often sufficient for hot-spot fields. Class E can be used to access an item's stock, for example. Class E is able to handle use cases such as reservations. It should be used if during the read-phase a guarantee is required that the changes will succeed during the write-phase. Class O is the default class. It avoids blocking and under normal load it represents a good trade-off between commit and abort-rate.

Section II defines these four CC classes with different data access strategies used by our mechanism. In the case of a conflict, class O implements a **first-committer-wins** strategy, class R implements a **first-n-committers-win** strategy, class P implements a **first-reader-wins** strategy, and class E implements a **first-n-readers-win** strategy. The number n is determined by the semantics of the accessed data, e.g., by database constraints. According to the classes, the mechanism is called O|R|P|E. The "|" indicates the demarcation between data.

Section III proofs the correctness of the model. Section IV briefly describes the prototype implementation. Section V highlights some advantages of O|R|P|E, because it provides an application flexibility in choosing the best suitable CC mechanism and thereby significantly increases the commit rate and outperforms optimistic SI. The run-time adaptation mechanism and its adaptation rules are presented in Section VII. In the following Section V a prototype implementation is tested with various workloads. The results are discussed and the behavior is illustrated with time diagrams. Section VIII summarizes related work and compares it to our model. Finally, the paper draws some conclusions and provides an outlook (see Section IX) to future work.

II. Model

The model relies on disconnected transactions and 4 CC classes, which are defined in the following.

A. Transaction

To support long-lived and disconnected data processing, which both supports scalability, O|R|P|E models a transaction as a disconnected transaction τ, with separate read- and write-phase, i.e., no further read after the first write operation (see Definition 1, taken from [2]). To disallow blind writes, O|R|P|E guarantees that in addition to the value of a field, the version of a data field has to be read, too.

Definition 1: Disconnected Transaction:

1) Let ta be a flat transaction that is defined as a pair $ta = (OP, <)$ where OP is a finite set of steps of the form $r(x)$ or $w(x)$ and $<(\subseteq OP \times OP)$ is a partial order.
2) A disconnected transaction $\tau = (TA^R, TA^W)$ consists of two disjoint sets of transactions. $TA^R = \{ta_1^R, \ldots, ta_i^R\}$ to read and $TA^W = \{ta_1^W, \ldots, ta_j^W\}$ to write the proposed modifications back.
3) A transaction has to read any data item x before being allowed to modify x (no blind writes).
4) If a transaction only reads data it has to be labeled as read only.

B. CC Classes

Class O is the default class and is implemented by an optimistic SI mechanism, which is advantageous since reads do not block writes and non-repeatable or phantom phenomena do not happen. However, SI is not fully serializable [6] [7].

As stated, the drawback of optimistic mechanisms prevails if load increases, because many transactions may abort during their validation at commit time. An abort at commit time is expensive, because significant amount of work might be lost. A circumstance particularly crucial for long-lived transactions (see [2]).

Regarding the strategy, optimistic SI follows a "first-committer-wins" semantics revealing another drawback of O. It is the lack of an option allowing a transaction to explicitly run as an owner of some data. Consider, for example, the private data of a user such as its password or address. A validation failure should be prevented by all means, since it would mean that at least two transactions try to concurrently update private data. Although technically this is a reasonable state, for this kind of data a pessimistic approach that acquires all locks at read time is more appropriate. Such a mechanism follows a "first-reader-wins" (ownership) semantics and directly leads to class P. The acquisition of exclusive locks at read time prevents deadlocks during write time. To prevent deadlocks at all, a strict sequential access and preclaiming (all locks appear before the first read) or sorted read-sets are possible mechanisms. Which mechanism is chosen to prevent or resolve deadlocks is unimportant regarding the correctness of O|R|P|E (see Section III). Preclaiming has its drawbacks concerning the time a lock has to be acquired. Sorted read-sets may be unfeasible due to limitations of the storage layer or chosen index structure. The prototype (see Section IV) uses a Wait-For-Graph to prevent deadlocks during the read-phase of a transaction. Also, during our experiments (see Section V) the number of deadlocks was considerably small, because data classified in P should have no concurrent modifications by definition.

The decision if a data item is classified as O or P is based on the following properties [2]:

1) *Mostly read* (mr): Is the data item mostly read? If 'Yes', there is no need for restrictive measures and the data item should by classified for optimistic validation. A low conflict probability is assumed.
2) *Frequently written* (fw): fw is the opposite of mr.
3) *unknown* (un): It means neither mr nor fw apply, i.e., it is unknown whether an item is mostly read or written or approximately even.
4) *Ownership* (ow): if accessing a data item should explicitly cause the transaction to own this item for its lifetime?

Example 1: Classify data items in class O and P (taken from [2]).

This example is based on the TPC-C [3] benchmark and its "New-Order" transaction. Note that an additional table Account has been introduced to keep track about a customer's bookings (column debit and credit). It also defines an overdraft limit (column limit). The following tables are used in our example: Customer (id, name, surname), Stock (StockId, ItemId, quantity), Account (AcctNo, debit, credit, limit), and Item (ItemId, name, unit, price). Table I shows an initial classification.

Attributes *name*, *surname*, and *id* of a customer are expected to be mostly read, but if modified by a transaction it should definitively be the owner. The *id* of a customer, like all ids, is expected to become modified rarely. If the *id* becomes modified, ownership is required. In principal, all business keys should be classified in P, because they are owned by the application provider (see Rule 1, 1)).

Stock.quantity is expected to become modified frequently (fw) and to prevent the situation where an item was marked as available during the read phase, but at commit time the item is no longer available due to concurrent transactions, it is also marked as ow. For the time being, however, *quantity* will be classified as an ambiguity (see also Rule 1, 3)), which will be discussed below.

The *Account.credit* and *Account.debit* of a customer's account might be accessed frequently depending on a customer's activity and un is a good choice. However, since multiple transactions might concurrently update the balance, and an owner is hardly identifiable, $\neg ow$ is chosen. So, it is also an ambiguity (see Rule 1, 3)).

The *Account.limit* is the overdraft limit of a customer and expected to be mostly read, hence, mr is a good choice. Since it is neither owned by the customer nor by others, $\neg ow$ is a good choice (see Rule 1, 2)).

Assuming the application is a high frequency trading application, *Item.Price* might quickly become a bottleneck. An exact prediction is not possible though, hence, un is a good choice. Property ow would not be a good choice, because transactions of different components (dc) might simultaneously calculate the price (see Rule 1, 3)).

TABLE I. CLASSIFICATION OF EXAMPLE 1

x	mr	fw	un	ow	CC class
Customer.name	1	0	0	1	*P*
Customer.surname	1	0	0	1	*P*
Customer.id	1	0	0	1	*P*
Stock.StockId	1	0	0	1	*P*
Stock.ItemId	1	0	0	1	*P*
Stock.quantity	0	1	0	1	**A**
Account.debit	0	0	1	0	**A**
Account.credit	0	0	1	0	**A**
Account.limit	0	0	1	0	**A**
Item.name	1	0	0	1	*P*
Item.unit	1	0	0	1	*P*
Item.price	0	0	1	0	**A**

The ambiguities A of Example 1, see class A in Table I, highlight that classes O and P and their properties are not sufficient. Particularly, hot spot items such as *Stock.quantity* would benefit from a CC mechanism that allows many winners and resolves the drawbacks of OCC and PCC.

Laux and Lessner [8] propose the usage of a mechanism that reconciles conflicts –class *R*–. Their approach is an optimistic variant of O'Neil's [9] Transactional Escrow Method (TEM). Both approaches exploit the commutativity of write operations. If operations commute, it is irrelevant which operation is applied first as long as the final state can be calculated (see [8] [2] for further details) and no constraint is violated.

Unlike TEM, the reconciliation mechanism requires a dependency function. Consider, for example, two transactions that update an account and both read an initial amount of 10€, one credits in 20€ and the other debits 10€. Once both have committed, it is relevant that no constraint was violated at any time and the final amount has to be 20€. Usually, a database would write the new state for each transaction causing a lost update. A dependency function would actually add or subtract the amount (the delta!) and would always take the latest state as input. In other words, reconciliation replays the operation in case of a conflict. However, this is only possible if no further user input is required. In the example above this means the user wants to credit 20€ (or debit 10 €) independent of the account's amount as long as no constraint is violated! Another requirement is that each dependency function has to be compensatable (see also [2]).

The reconciliation mechanism [8] follows a "first-n-committers-win" semantics and the number of winners n is solely determined by constraints. The correctness of the mechanism is proven in [8], which also introduces "Escrow Serializability", a notion for semantic correctness.

TEM grants guarantees to transactions during their read-phase. For example, a reservation system is able to grant guarantees to a transaction about the desired number of tickets as long as tickets are available. The consequence is that transactions need to know their desired update in advance (see [9] for further details).

Whereas TEM [9] is pessimistic (constraint validation during the read phase) and works for numerical data only, Reconciliation [8] is optimistic (constraint validation during the write phase) and works for any data as long as a dependency function is known. The proof that E, like R, is escrow serializable can be found in [2].

The decision if an item is member of R or E is based on the following properties:

1) con: Does a constraint exist for this data item?
2) num: Is the type of the data item numeric?
3) com: Are operations on this data item commutative?
4) dep: Is a dependency function known for an operation modifying the data item?
5) in: Is user input independence given for an operation modifying the data item?
6) gua: Is a guarantee needed that a proposed modification will succeed?

RULE 1: Derivation of CC classes for data item x

1) $ow \rightarrow$ classify x in P (identify P).
2) $\neg ow \wedge mr \rightarrow$ classify x in O (identify O).
3) all other combinations of ow and mr: classify x in A (ambiguity).
4) $com \rightarrow$ classify x in $E \vee R$
   a) $(con \wedge num \wedge com \wedge gua) \rightarrow$ classify x in E (identify E).
   b) $(in \wedge dep \wedge com) \rightarrow$ classify $x \in R$ (identify R).
5) $x \in A \rightarrow$ item x will be eventually in O.

EXAMPLE 2 (Classification of data items in R and E)**:** The ambiguities of Table I are the input for this example. Table II shows the result of the classification of these ambiguities.

`Stock.quantity` has a constraint $value > 0$ and is numeric. The dependency function dep is known too. As stated above, a dependency function performs a context dependent write. For example, dependency function d would be $d(x, xread, xnew) = x + (xnew - xread)$. User input independence in is not given. If placing the order fails at the end, a replay would also fail. So, class R is not an option. Since an order requires a guarantee that the requested amount of items remains available, Rule 1, 4a) applies.

`Account.credit` and `Account.debit` are classified as R. Property dep is known, because operations are either

TABLE II. ILLUSTRATIVE CLASSIFICATION OF AMBIGUITIES OF EXAMPLE 1.

x	con	com	num	dep	in	gua	CC class
Stock.quantity	1	1	1	1	0	1	E
Account.credit	1	1	1	1	1	0	R
Account.debit	1	1	1	1	1	0	R
Item.price	0	0	1	1	0	0	O

additions or subtractions. Property in is given, because the account has to be updated if the order is placed and no constraint is violated. As the updates follow a dependency function they can be reconciled and should not raise an exception. Again, only a constraint violation such as an overdraft can cause the abort. Rule 1, 4b) applies.

`Item.price` depends on a variety of parameters including the last price itself. As a result, a price update might not be commutative. `Item.price` remains ambiguous and remains in O, because O is the default class. Rule 1, 5) applies.

III. CORRECTNESS

A transaction potentially runs under four different CC mechanisms. Due to the CC classes' individual semantics, each class has a different notion for a conflict, too. In any case, two read operations are never in conflict because read operations do not alter the database state and hence are commutative [10].

Usually, a conflict is given if two operations access the same data item and the corresponding transaction overlap in their execution time, and at least one operation writes the data item [5]. Whereas for O and P this is a correct definition of a conflict, for R and E it is not, because both can resolve certain write conflicts. The resolution of conflicts is a key aspect and advantage of SCC, and SCC questions the seriousness of a conflict. In other words, the meaning of a read-write or write-write conflict is interpreted. For R and E only a constraint violation is a conflict. Moreover, the state read by an operation is assumed to be irrelevant, otherwise commutativity is not given. It follows that any final serialization graph $SG-R$ and $SG-E$ for class R and E is non-cyclic because potential conflicts are reconciled (see [2] for a thorough discussion).

For P, the common definition of a conflict is correct. If a transaction wants to modify item p (let $p \in P$), it has to acquire a lock on p during its read-phase to become the exclusive owner. If not, the transaction does a blind write, which is disallowed according to Definition 1. Hence, every write in P cannot encounter a concurrent write or read, because if a transaction writes p it has to be the exclusive owner of P.

Consider the following (incorrect) schedule, for example ($disc_i$ and $disc_j$ denote the disconnect phase of transaction i (resp. j) and let $o \in O$ and $p \in P$):

$$r_i(o), r_j(p), r_j(o), disc_j, w_j(o), c_j, r_i(p), disc_i, w_i(p), c_i \quad (1)$$

In this schedule transaction i reads o before j modifies o and transaction j reads p ($r_j(p)$) before i writes p ($w_i(p)$). Usually, the ordering of transaction operations are visualized by a precedence graph as in Figure 1.

DEFINITION 2 (Serialization Graph (SG)): Let S be a schedule of transactions. The Serialization Graph (aka Conflict Graph) is a precedence graph where each node represents a transaction and each directed edge between two transactions represents a precedence of conflicting operations [11] [12] on a data item.

It is well known that a transaction schedule is conflict serializable if and only if the SG is acyclic [11] [13]. If the SG of a transaction schedule includes a cycle then no equivalent serial schedule exists and, therefore, this schedule is not serializable [11].

The above Schedule 1 leads to the following cyclic SG of Figure 1.

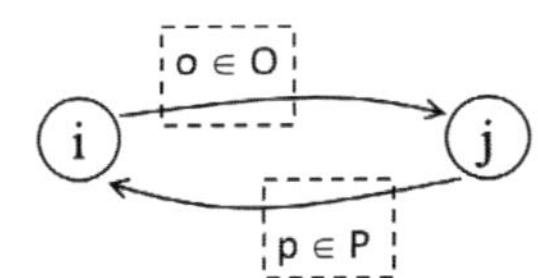

Figure 1. The cyclic serialization graph from Schedule (1).

Transaction i precedes j in class O and j precedes i in P. Having opposite orders, i.e., $i \rightarrow j$ in one, but $j \rightarrow i$ in another class violates serializability, because globally i precedes j, which in turn precedes i.

A transaction that reads a data item in O has to validate the value at write-time, even if the write is only for an item $p \in P$. The operation $w_i(p)$ causes a validation failure on item o because transaction i has read a value of o that transaction j has meanwhile updated. This is a conflict between transactions i and j in O and produces a validation failure. Commit c_i is wrong in the schedule above and would never happen in O|R|P|E. Hence, the above schedule looks as follows in O|R|P|E:

$$r_i(o), r_j(p), r_j(o), disc_j, w_j(o), c_j, r_i(p), disc_i, w_i(p), a_i \quad (2)$$

Even a deadlock in P cannot create a cyclic graph between O and P, because at least a write is required to create a conflict in P. However, since all deadlocks can only happen during the read phase of a transaction, no conflict cycle involving a deadlock can happen in P.

Based on these initial findings it is possible to state Theorem 1. The corresponding proof exploits that for R, P, and E the corresponding serialization graphs are non-cyclic.

THEOREM 1: Let $SG-G$ be the global serialization graph, which is the union of $SG-O$, $SG-R$, $SG-P$, and $SG-E$. The global serialization graph $SG-G$ is non-cyclic if $SG-O$ is non-cyclic.

Proof by contradiction:

Given that ta_i is serialized before ta_j ($i \rightarrow j$) in $SG-O$. In P, no other transaction can access an item in P if transaction ta_i has read this item. This is the consequence of x-locks during the read-phase used in class P. The same argument applies to ta_j as well and it is impossible to have a serialization order $j \rightarrow i$ in P. Since i and j can be arbitrarily changed there is a contradiction if $i \rightarrow j$ exists in one, and $j \rightarrow i$ in another class. $SG-R$ and $SG-E$ are negligible because any conflict is finally reconciled and both serialization graphs are non-cyclic. ■

COROLLARY 1: $SG - O$ sets the global serialization order for P.

If a ta does not modify data in O, then P sets the order. If a ta does not modify data in P, then R sets the order, because it is prone to validation conflicts as opposed to E that already has a guarantee to succeed.

IV. PROTOTYPE REFERENCE IMPLEMENTATION OF O|R|P|E

The prototype of O|R|P|E is not a full database system. From a fully operational database the backup and recovery functions are missing. Both functions do not functionally influence the CC mechanism. There is only a negative effect on the performance during backup or recovery. This applies in a similar way for any database management system with a single CC mechanism.

It was implemented using the JAVA programming language and Figure 2 illustrates its architecture. A client API provides access to the data and depending on the operation's type, read or write, the operation is executed by a dedicated pool. Pools "Reads" and "Writes" represent an read- and write-lane. In addition, a pool to handle the termination (commit and abort) has been implemented. Pools' reads and writes handle all incoming and outgoing operations and the classification has been placed directly into the index. Depending on an item's classification the corresponding CC mechanism is plugged in. This placement allows to decide about the CC mechanism with a single read operation, which imposes an negligible overhead. Once an item has been read or written, the additional pools' "read-callback" and "write-callback" deliver the results back to the clients. A Pool WFG (Wait-for-Graph) is used to handle access to the WFG. Deadlocks may occur during the read-phase of a transaction if the transaction accesses data items in class P. Deadlocks can only occur in class P during the read-phase, because lock acquisition is not globally ordered.

Having separate pools and callbacks to handle incoming and outgoing operations means that the prototype supports disconnected transactions, because the entire communication is asynchronous. Figure 3 illustrates the message flow within the prototype. A read operation is passed to the "Reads" pool. Each read is executed asynchronously and the complete read set is sent back to the client via a dedicated callback pool. To support asynchronous writes, a write operation is passed to the "Writes" pool and if all writes have been applied the write set is sent back to the client. Clients always sent their complete write-set.

Data is kept solely in memory and no data is written to disk unless the operating system needs to swap data to disk due to memory limitations. The only output to disk is to write logging events that are used for performance evaluation. Other functionality that has been implemented includes:

- CC mechanisms O, R, P and E,
- The prototype supports constraints,
- The prototype supports item selects, range-selects, updates, and inserts. The deletion of an item is implemented as update that invalidates a data item.
- A WFG implementation.

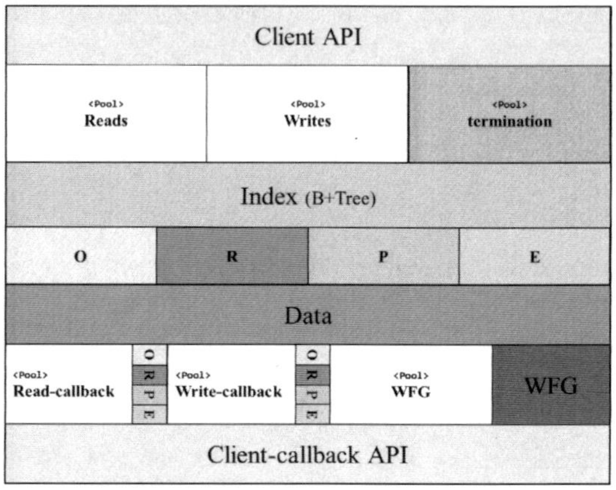

Figure 2. Architecture of the prototype.

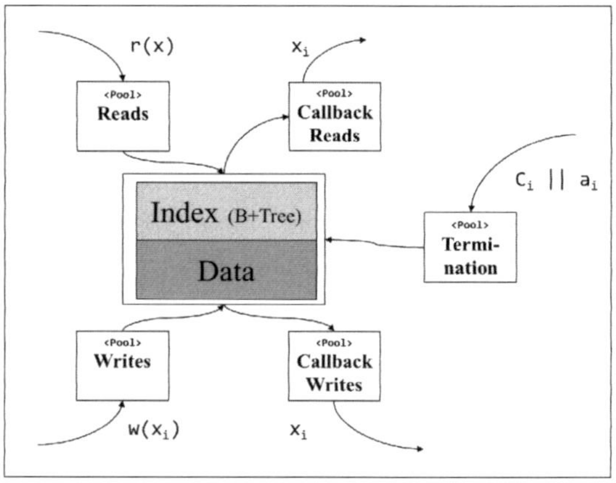

Figure 3. Message flow of the prototype.

V. PERFORMANCE STUDY WITH STATIC DATA CLASS ASSIGNMENT

The performance study has been carried out based on the prototype presented in the previous section (Section IV). As benchmark, the TPC-C++ benchmark [7] has been chosen, because we also conducted a study comparing O|R|P|E with Serializable SI, which is beyond the scope of this paper.

The data used for this study is similar to those of Examples 1 and 2. Each data item was statically assigned to a CC-Class as shown in Table III. Aspects of a dynamic assignment and its performance effects will be studied in the next section.

The performance study measures the response-time (resp. - time), the abort rate (ab-rate), the commits per second, and the degree of concurrency (deg. conc.). The degree of concurrency is the quotient of the serial estimated execution time over the elapsed time of the experiment. In addition, the arrival rate λ of new transactions has been varied to be set to the optimum (minimized abort rate and response time, maximized degree of concurrency). This optimum λ has been taken to conduct fair and calibrated comparisons. Each experiment has been repeated three times and the mean value is reported. Values refer to the execution of a transaction mix –deck– (42 New Order-, 42 Payment-, 4 Delivery-, 4 Credit check-, 4 Update

TABLE III. TPC-C: CLASSIFICATION OF DATA ITEMS.

Item	CC Class	operation
Customer	P	read
CustomerCredit	P	update
CustomerBalance	R	read
Customer	P	read
CustomerBalance	R	update
Customer	P	read
CustomerCredit	P	read
StockQuantity	E	update
Customer	P	read
CustomerBalance	R	update
WarehouseYTD	R	update
DistrictYTD	R	update
StockQuantity	E	read only
StockQuantity	E	update

Stock Level-, and 4 Read Stock Level - transactions see [7] [3] [2]).

Figure 4 illustrates the abort rate and degree of concurrency for SI under full contention and shows the drawbacks of optimistic SI: the higher the number of concurrent transactions, the higher the abort rate. Also, the system starts thrashing if the degree of concurrency drops below one, which is the point where a serial execution outperforms a concurrent. Table IV shows that for SI and O|R|P|E with the same λ (tests #1-6 and #10-15) the response-time increases with larger λ, which is expected and normal behavior. The direct comparison reveals that O|R|P|E has a $3 - 38$ times better response time, which shows that SI is over-strained for a workload of $\lambda \geq 200$. For $\lambda = 1000$ tas/sec the response time is about 3 times higher for SI and the degree of concurrency is only half compared to O|R|P|E. A good degree of concurrency with a low abort rate is given by $\lambda = 133$ (see Table IV #3).

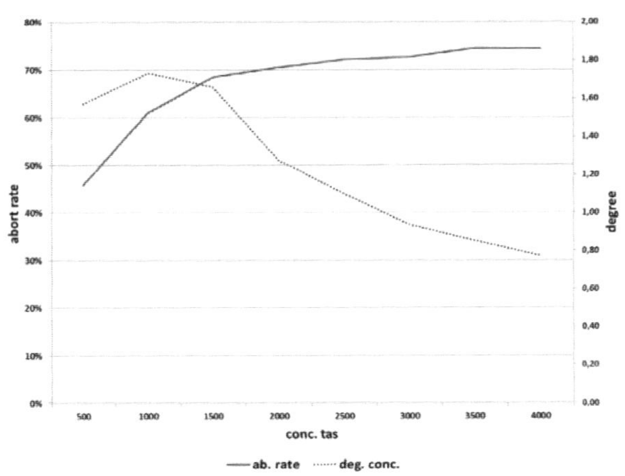

Figure 4. TPC-C++, optimistic SI (class O), abort rate and degree of concurrency.

Figure 5 shows the response-time and degree of concurrency for O|R|P|E for increasing λ. Unlike SI, O|R|P|E has no aborts caused by serialization or validation conflicts due to the classification of hot-spot data items in R or E, which prevents ww-conflicts. As shown by Figure 5, O|R|P|E has its best degree with $\lambda = 1000$ transactions per second achieving 227 commits per second (see Table IV, #15).

The comparison of O|R|P|E and SI uses $\lambda = 133$ (Table IV #3, and #7-9) for SI and $\lambda = 1000$ (Table IV #15-18) for O|R|P|E . For SI, $\lambda = 133$ was considered as being the best trade-off with respect to the degree of concurrency, $\lambda = 1000$ was considered as being the best trade-off for O|R|P|E.

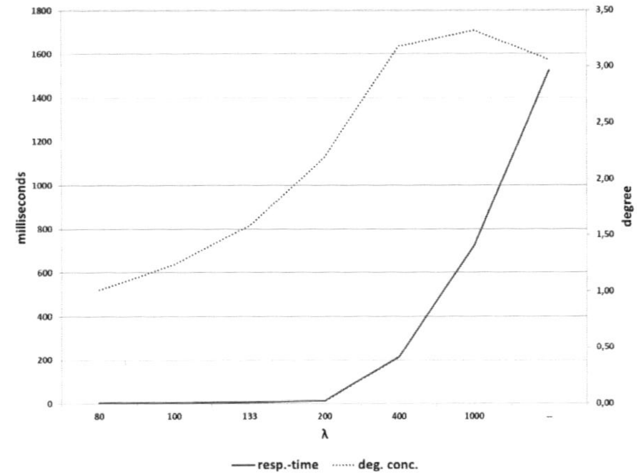

Figure 5. Response time and degree of concurrency for increasing λ for O|R|P|E .

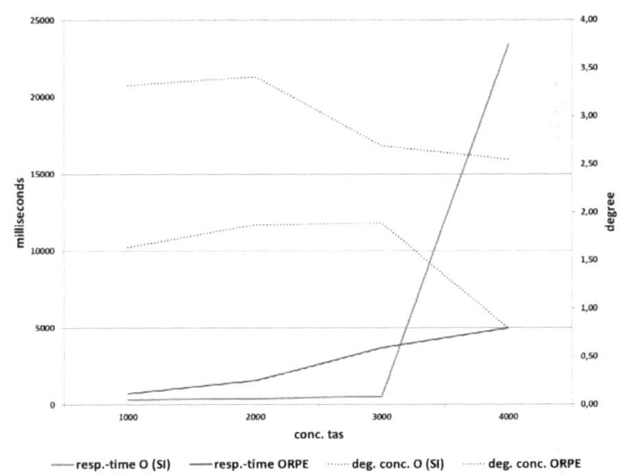

Figure 6. TPC-C++, SI and O|R|P|E : response-time and degree of concurrency for $\lambda = 133$ (SI) and $\lambda = 1000$ (O|R|P|E).

Figure 6 illustrates the degree and the response-time for data of class O with SI and O|R|P|E if both use the λ which reflect the best trade-off. As the figure shows, SI has a better response-time for 1000, 2000, and 3000 concurrent transactions, but then suddenly undergoes thrashing and the response-time grows exponentially. However, O|R|P|E shows a moderate and stable increase of the response-time even for 4000 concurrent transactions.

With a workload of 2000 transactions the degree of concurrency is 3.41 for O|R|P|E versus 1.87 for SI. The average response time is only 388 msec for SI and 1551 msec for O|R|P|E. It would be wrong to conclude that SI has a better performance than O|R|P|E because for a comparison λ has to be taken into account. In the test O|R|P|E had a 7.5 times higher transaction arrival rate than SI ($\lambda = 1000$ as opposed to $\lambda = 133$ for SI). At 4000 concurrent transactions O|R|P|E

TABLE IV. MEASURED VALUES OF EXPERIMENTS #1-18.

#	tas	λ	resp.-time	ab. rate	commits /second	deg. conc.
SI						
1	1000	80	43	2%	71	1,39
2	1000	100	84	3%	80	1,57
3	1000	133	309	5%	82	1,63
4	1000	200	1640	20%	62	1,50
5	1000	400	2091	26%	61	1,57
6	1000	1000	2464	27%	62	1,61
7	2000	133	388	9%	90	1,87
8	3000	133	522	8%	91	1,89
9	4000	133	23416	46%	22	0,79
O|R|P|E						
10	1000	80	5	4%	69	1,01
11	1000	100	5	4%	85	1,24
12	1000	133	8	4%	108	1,58
13	1000	200	14	4%	150	2,19
14	1000	400	213	4%	217	3,18
15	1000	1000	724	4%	227	3,32
16	2000	1000	1551	4%	234	3,41
17	3000	1000	3704	4%	184	2,69
18	4000	1000	4968	5%	174	2,55

outperforms SI in terms of response time by a factor of 3.7 (see Figure 6) and the degree of concurrency is 2.6 times better. Hence, under high contention O|R|P|E has the lowest abort rate and considering the trade-off between concurrency and response time, O|R|P|E outperforms SI significantly. Furthermore, its abort rate is nearly independent of the contention.

VI. Run-time Adaption

The attempt to manually classify data may finally result in ambiguous classification where default class O applies (see Rule 1, 5)). But, high contention can quickly cause performance issues for data classified in O. Even if class P is more expensive, because P requires locking during the read-phase it will lead to a better performance in this situation as the locking will queue the transactions and process them successfully.

An automatic and dynamic adaptation of the classification when transactional load or data usage changes would make the initial classification less critical and O|R|P|E could choose the optimal CC-mechanism based on the current situation.

A solution for automatic run-time adaptation is presented in this section. It re-classifies a data items of default class O to class P if the commit rate drops below an adjustable threshold. With this measure the commit rate increases again for the price of a longer response time. When the transactional load decreases and after the commit rate exceeds the threshold again it switches back to its original class O.

Data originally classified in P will not be re-classified to O when the load is low. This is not feasible, because an item initially in P has to remain in P due to the item's ownership semantics. An adaption at run-time that results in O would contradict the ownership semantics since a transaction would no longer request locks during its read-phase. This is, however, mandatory to comply with the ownership semantics (see Rule 1, 1)).

At a first glance, an adaption between $E \rightarrow R$ seems reasonable if the probability of an invariant violation (*PIV*) is low. It would save additional overhead, because invariant conditions in R have not to be validated at read-time, but in E. However, this is only a good decision if contention is low. To take this decision at high workload will result in a much longer response time because the response time for class R grows much faster than for class E. With high contention, the probability of constraint violations increases, but the exact determination is application dependent. Classifying a data item in E is only justified if an aborted transaction is more costly than to retry the transaction, i.e., the transaction needs a guarantee to succeed which leads to class E from the beginning (Rule 1, 4a)).

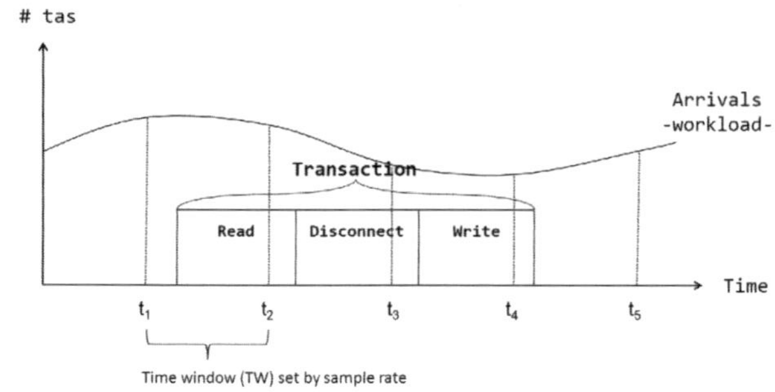

Figure 7. Arrivals (workload) and time windows.

A. Adaptation Criteria

The run-time adaptation is based on the commit rate cr. To measure and analyze cr a statistical model for the transactional system is necessary. According to [14] [15] [16], a transactional system is modeled as an open system whose transactional arrival rate is a Poisson process. The time between arrivals of transactions is assumed to be independent in Poisson, which has the advantage that the conflict rate (the term conflict is stated more precisely below) can be modeled around a single variable λ that represents the number of arrivals in relation to the time window. A Poisson process has a conflict probability density function $PC_x(X = k)$ given by Equation (3):

$$PC_x(X = k) = \frac{\lambda^k}{k!} e^{-\lambda} \quad (3)$$

For example, if on average 100 transactions arrive within one Time Window (TW), the probability that $k = 50$ transactions access item x within a TW is given by Formula (3). The arrival rate λ is in relation to time, for example, within one second; i.e., for a transaction that accesses x during that second, it means that the probability is $PC_x(X >= 2) = \sum_{k=2}^{\infty} \lambda^k / k!\, e^{-\lambda}$ to encounter other conflicting concurrent transactions.

Figure 7 illustrates the usage of TW as well as the arrivals –workload– in relation to time. The workload is, however, not constant over the lifetime of a transaction. A constant workload ignores that the workload, and hence, λ might suddenly change in particular if transactions are long running. Measuring the number of transactions terminating or committing during a time window are means to detect and react to sudden changes in the workload, which is an idea borrowed from [14]. The length of the TW defines the sample rate and its sensitivity.

The commit rate cr is used as indicator for the performance of the optimistic CC-mechanism of class O. If the cr drops below a threshold, there are more aborts due to validation failures and that class P would be a better choice to increase cr.

$$cr := \frac{\#\text{committed tas}/\text{TW}}{(\#\text{terminated tas} - \#\text{re-class. aborts})/\text{TW}} \qquad (4)$$

For each TW the commit rate cr is calculated as fraction of the committed transaction divided by all terminated transaction without those that were aborted due to a re-classification. The commit rate cr is identical to the effective commit rate cr_{eff} (see Definition 5) if no adaptation occurs. Formula (4) is apparently insensitive to the length of the TW. But, a longer TW tends to compute smoother cr and it saves measuring overhead. We used a TW of 100 msec which delivered a good trade off for the prototype implementation.

The adaptation policy is given by Rule 2, which uses a threshold γ for the target commit rate and an hysteresis δ to avoid constant switching (thrashing) between both classes. When a data item is re-assigned during an active transaction, the transaction is aborted when the change is from O to P. In the opposite case, the transaction can continue without conflicts, because the write-phase will succeed since the data item is already exclusively locked for that transaction.

RULE 2: General Adaptation $O \rightarrow P$

Let cr be the commit rate, δ the hysteresis, and γ the target commit rate. Adaptation is according to the following rules:

1) When cr decreases and O is the current class for an item x: If $cr < \gamma - \delta$ then P is the new classification of x
2) When cr increases and P is the current class for an item x: If $cr > \gamma + \delta$ then O is the new classification of x.
3) Reclassification during a transaction:
   a) If a ta reads at the time when O is the current class, but will write at a time when P is the current class, ta is aborted (non-avoidable crash) to maintain consistency.
   b) If a ta reads at a time when the data item is in P and writes when it is in O, the success of the write is guaranteed because the data is exclusively locked since read-time.

Adaptation solely relies on the commit rate cr. The arrival rate λ and hence the conflict probability are not measured which would be much more difficult. This leverages the decision to use a Poisson distribution for the transaction arrivals.

Figure 8 illustrates how the adaptation works if the commit rate decreases and later increases again. During the first TW $(t_2 - t_1)$ the commit rate cr drops to $1/8$ because only one out of 8 transactions was successful. Two transactions (ta_9, ta_{10}) have not terminated yet.

At the end of epoch 1 the commit rate is compared to $\gamma - \delta$ and as cr is below the threshold data x is re-classified to P. The transaction ta_9 will later abort due to a constraint violation and ta_{10} has to abort because of the re-classification to P. Now, for the following transactions the locking mechanism for P applies. One consequence is that ta_{11}, ta_{12}, and ta_{13} execute mostly sequentially. The commit rate grows in the following TW to $3/4$, but, this is not sufficient to switch x back to class O. During the third TW $(t_4 - t_3)$ the commit rate rises to $cr = 2/2 > \gamma + \delta$ and the (initial) optimistic CC (class O) is re-established.

The following history describes the example of Figure 8 more formally:

$$\begin{aligned} H = (&\underbrace{r_1(x), r_2(x), r_3(x), \ldots, r_{10}(x), w_1(x), c_1}_{\text{commit rate decreases}} \\ &\underbrace{w_2(x), a_2, w_3(x), a_3, \ldots}_{\text{commit rate decreases}}, \text{adapt to P}, a_{10}, a_9, \\ &\underbrace{l_{11}(x), r_{11}(x), w_{11}(x), c_{11}, l_{12}(x), r_{12}(x),}_{\text{commit rate increases}} \\ &\underbrace{w_{12}(x), c_{12}, l_{13}(x), r_{13}(x), w_{13}(x), c_{13} \ldots}_{\text{commit rate increases}} \end{aligned}$$

The history H shows in the first phase 10 transactions $ta_1, ta_2, \ldots, ta_{10}$ accessing x. They first read x $(r_1(x), r_2(x), r_3(x), \ldots, r_{10}(x))$ and then try to write x $(w_1(x), w_2(x), \ldots)$. In the given scenario only ta_1 can commit (c_1), all others have to abort $(a_2, a_3, \ldots)$ because too many transactions try to concurrently update x. This leads to a sudden decrease in the commit rate $cr = 1/8$ because only ta_1 was successful and ta_9 and ta_{10} have not yet updated x, i.e., it is still pending. If we assume a threshold γ of 0.8 and an hysteresis δ of 0.1, then $cr < \gamma - \delta$ which triggers the adaption according to Rule 2, 1).

After adaptation has been carried out, ta_{10} has to abort (Rule 2, 3a)) if it tries to update x. The abort a_{10} appears in the history after the adaptation even though the item x is now classified in P. Transaction ta_{10} has to abort, because it has not locked x before reading x $(r_{10}(x))$. If ta_{10} would not abort it would risk a lost-update, because ta_{10} would overwrite the last committed state since P does no version validation. Even with version validation, ta_{10} is very likely to abort, because the probability for a validation failure is high in this situation.

Let assume that transaction ta_9 accesses other data beside x and validation fails due to a constraint violation. This leads to an abort of ta_9. The distinction of the abort reason is important here as it will be counted for the commit rate.

After the adaptation to P newly arriving transactions apply a locking scheme for data x which is indicated by $l_{11}, l_{12}, \ldots$. The commit rate increases again because transactions $ta_{11}, ta_{12}, ta_{13}$ succeed and commit c_{11}, c_{12}, c_{13}. In fact, all following transaction succeed except those which violate a constraint.

If we choose the Time Window TW to start just before ta_{11} arrives the commit rate cr rises with each committed transaction. Class O is not reestablished at the end of this TW despite that the next 3 transactions succeed because $cr = 3/4 \leq \gamma + \delta = 0.9$. The class assignment remains unchanged and the following TW $(t_4 - t_3)$ will reestablish class O because $cr = 2/2$.

The adaptation mechanism proposed in Rule 2 maximizes the commit rate as seen in the previous example. But due to the restrictive locking policy the response time increases

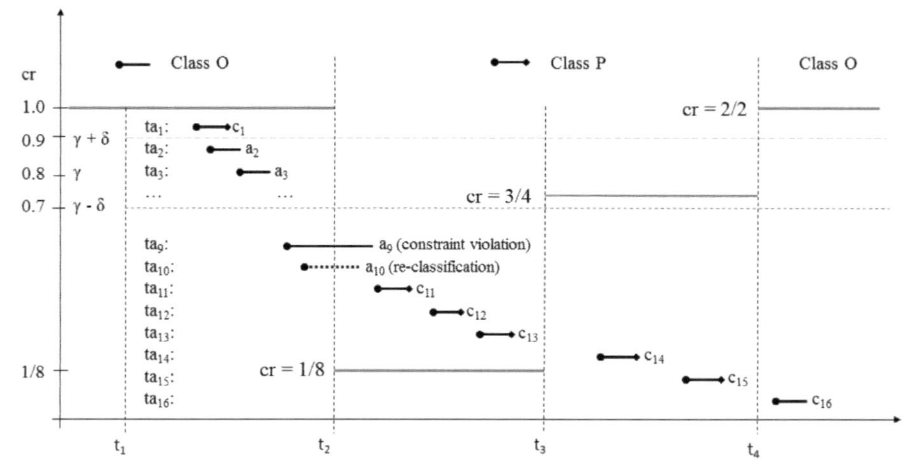

Figure 8. Example run-time adaptation scenario with decreasing cr in TW (t_1, t_2), reclassification at t_2 to P and increasing cr in TW (t_2, t_3) and (t_3, t_4) and switch back to class O at t_4.

as the execution tends to be serial. In the worst case, enduring contention, the growth is exponential. But, what if the maximum response-time is limited, for example, by Service Level Agreements (SLA) and penalties apply for exceeding the maximum acceptable response-time? The SLA penalties may outweigh the costs for aborts.

In this case maximizing the commit rate as only criteria is not a good strategy since it increases costs. To prevent unacceptable response times a barrier (denoted as β) is used that regulates the adaptation; i.e., once β is reached re-classification to O takes place despite a low commit rate and the abort rate starts to increase which in turn leads to shorter response times for the remaining successful transactions. The concrete value of β is application dependent. Its general purpose is to minimize costs, i.e., if the abort costs are lower than the costs for exceeding the response-time, more aborts are acceptable until the ratio turns over.

Application specific requirements that set β are out of the paper's scope, but to allow applications to limit the adaptation, β is incorporated in O|R|P|E (see Rule 3). Applications can now set β to limit the response time and, at run-time, continuously monitor and adapt the achieved commit rate as well as the response time as measured by the applications themselves. Further, applications can increase β at run-time appropriately. This way, applications can determine their own equilibrium between commit rate and response-time.

The challenge is the estimation of the expected mean response-time rt_{est}, which implies to predict the workload. As stated in the previous section, this is complicated if not impossible in a general and dynamic way. O|R|P|E circumvents this problem and measures the time between a read and the corresponding write if the current classification is P. Furthermore, adaptation does no longer calculate cr at the end of the current TW, instead each termination (commit and abort) triggers the adaptation. A useful fixed TW is difficult to choose. If TW is too short, the overhead is considerable and degrades performance. If the TW is too long the adaptation is too slow.

To estimate the future workload the terminating transaction snapshots the lock queue's size if P is the current class. The current queue size together with the average time between read and write give a good indication for the expected workload. Because the transaction has to notify all waiting transactions about the ongoing unlock and already is the current owner of the lock-queue, there is no need for further synchronization and the overhead is considerably low, but of course exists. It is a price that has to be paid to get run-time adaptation.

Finally, the number of notified transactions multiplied by the average time distance between a read and write is used as an approximation for rt_{est}. The rationale is that if q transactions are waiting to execute and the mean time between read and write is $\text{ø}(mt)$ then for newly arriving transactions rt_{est} is expected to be $rt_{\text{est}} = \text{ø}(mt) \times (q+1)$ because of the mostly sequential execution. Following this approach O|R|P|E can balance commit rate and response time.

Transaction termination triggers adaptation, however, it is important to note that the adaptation is not executed as part of a transaction. This prevents the situation where a failed adaptation would cause the transaction to abort, too.

RULE 3: Adaptation $O \rightarrow P$ with barrier

Let cr be the commit rate, δ the hysteresis, γ the target commit rate, and β the response time barrier. Adaptation is according to the following rules:

1) $(O \rightarrow P)$: If O is the current class for an item x and $cr < \gamma - \delta$ and $rt_{\text{est}} < \beta$ then P is the new classification of x.
2) $(P \rightarrow O)$: If P is the current class for an item x and cr is low $(cr < \gamma - \delta)$ and $rt_{\text{est}} > \beta$ then O is the new classification of x.
3) $(P \rightarrow O)$: If P is the current class for an item x and cr is high $(cr > \gamma + \delta)$ then O is the new classification of x.
4) Reclassification during a transaction:
a) If a ta reads at the time when O is the current class, but is about to write at a time when P is the current class, ta is aborted (non-avoidable crash) to maintain consistency.

b) If a ta reads at a time when the data item is in P and writes when it is in O the success of the write is guaranteed because the data is exclusively locked since read-time.

Rule 3, 1) takes care that the commit rate is sufficiently high as long as the response time is low. If the response time exceeds the limit β and cr is (still) low then Rule 3, 2) switches back to O. Rule 3, 3) ensures that when the commit rate is high the default CC-mechanism of class O is chosen. For all other situations the classification remains unchanged.

Rule 3, 4) is the same as before. It ensures that a reclassification can take place during ongoing transactions. Reclassification is now triggered by two parameters, the commit rate cr and the mean response time mrt.

VII. Performance under Adaptation

The performance study uses the implementation of O|R|P|E described in Section IV. Even if it is not a full database implementation with all features (no backup and no recovery functionality) it is sufficient for measuring the performance of O|R|P|E under different situations. Since backup and recovery are normally inactive there is no impact on the concurrency mechanism. Therefore, the performance measurements would also be valid for a fully featured database system. Clearly, if backup or recovery are active, this would impair performance. This would also apply to our prototype.

The study analyzes different workload profiles indicated by a sequence of workloads with a total life-span of one second each. The workload is held constant for one second (called *epoch*). The arrival rate λ for the workload ranges from 6.66 tas/sec up to a heavy overload of over 300 tas/sec. These values have been chosen, to show the behavior of the overloaded system with frequent aborts and the behavior under moderate workload with a stable commit rate.

During one epoch (1 sec) the commit rate is measured 10 times (sample rate $sr = 10$/sec). For simplicity, all transactions read and write only one data item, i.e., the worst case is simulated where an item in O suddenly becomes a bottleneck. The time unit in all simulations is milliseconds if not stated otherwise.

To obtain a preliminary understanding the first experiments study short living transactions with no disconnect time during three epochs. Afterwards long living transactions with a random disconnect time dt between 100 and 1000 milliseconds are analyzed over seven epochs. A disconnect time dt within these bounds simulates typical situations.

Finally, barrier β is enabled for the next set of experiments. The set up of long living transactions and seven epochs is always the same except for the response time barrier β which varies between 1000 and 15000 msec. We study the effects on commit rate cr and response time rt. Each experiment was executed three times.

A. Short Living Transactions with Three Epochs

Table V lists our test scenarios and summarizes the result. The right column of the table refers to the corresponding figures for a detailed analysis. The four tests use a different arrival rate λ for each epoch (one second interval) as marked in the Epochs column. The first two test scenarios do not require a concurrency control adaptation to demonstrate the base performance without adaptation. In Tests #3 and #4 the workload is increased to trigger adaptation.

TABLE V. RESULTS FOR THREE EPOCHS WITH DIFFERENT WORKLOAD, $\gamma = 0.9$, $\delta = 5\%$ AND $dt = 0$.

Summary					
Test#	Epochs	$\varnothing(cr)$	$\sigma(cr)$	$\varnothing(rt)$	Figure
1	9,14,19	1,00	0,00	3,6	9 (a)
2	153,176,176	0,89	0,16	2	9 (b)
3	10,19,178	0,96	0,06	3,7	9 (c)
4	168,310,309	0,90	0,05	2824	9 (d)

The average response time $\varnothing(rt)$ is very high for test scenario #4. This is the result of an increasing overload, which quickly triggers adaptation at the beginning of the second epoch (see Figure 9 (d)). This leads to a mostly sequential execution of the transactions, which explains the very high $\varnothing(rt)$ and the high $\varnothing(cr)$ at the same time. This increase of cr is typical for scenarios after adaptation to P has taken place. It continues until the upper bound $\gamma + \delta$ is reached. Then the adaptation switches back to class O.

As the tests indicate later, it would be better to add an additional criteria for the re-adaptation from $P \rightarrow O$. If the workload is still high (wait queue > 1) the data should remain in P until the workload is low again before going back to O. This measure could avoid multiple re-adaptations that produce an unstable system behavior during a sudden transition of the workload from heavy overload to low workload.

Figure 9 shows the commit rate cr, lower and upper bounds (set by $\gamma \pm \delta$), and the accumulated number of aborts and commits of the four test scenarios.

Test #1 has a low workload in all three epochs. The load starts with 9 tas/sec, continues in epoch #2 with 14 tas/sec and in the last epoch the workload rises to 19 tas/sec. The transactions are executed as they arrive and no concurrent interleaving transactions occur. As expected, no adaptation takes place. From the corresponding Figure 9 (a) it can be seen that the commit rate is 1 and no aborts occur. After 3.1 sec (31 time units) all transactions have successfully terminated and the number of commits remain constant. Test #1 is the only scenario without contention but surprisingly not the shortest rt. The reason for this is that a commit is more expensive than an abort for an optimistic CC. Compared to the other tests, Test #1 has no aborts and a commit rate of 100%.

For Test #2 the load is high (≈ 160 tas/sec) and nearly constant for three seconds. The load is heavy and contention is present as can be seen from the number of aborts and the decreasing commit rate. Figure 9 (b) shows that the commit rate does not fall below the re-classification limit, hence no adaptation occurs. The data remains in class O and the optimistic CC has low overhead which results in a short response-time of only 2 msec.

Part (c) of Figure 9 (Test #3) shows the results for an increasing workload where finally in the third epoch the adaptation is triggered. The workload starts with $10 - 19$ tas/sec for two seconds and continues with 178 tas/sec for the third epoch. The commit rate drops under the minimum threshold ($\gamma - \delta$) at the blue vertical line (2.2 sec after start). The CC-mechanism immediately switches to locking and the number of aborts decreases (the accumulated abort

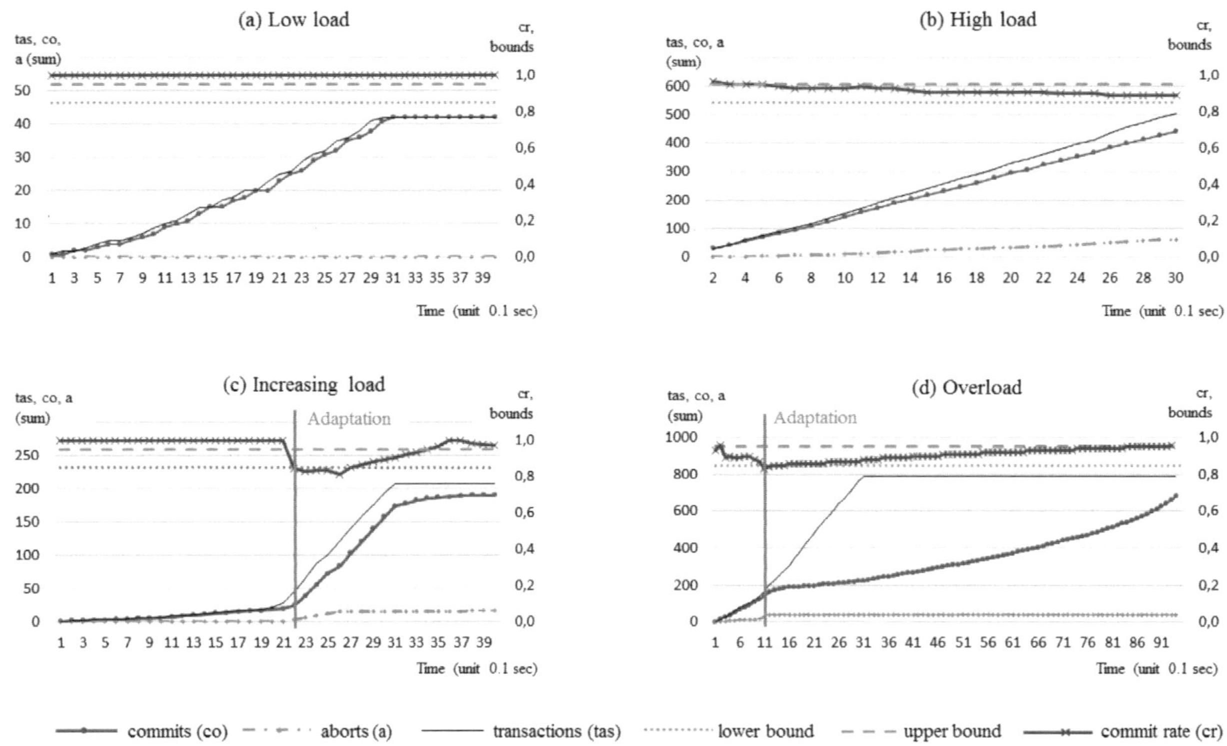

Figure 9. Various short workloads to demonstrate Run-time Adaptation; (a) low $9 - 19$ tas/sec , (b) high ≈ 160 tas/sec, (c) increasing load $10 - 180$ tas/sec, (d) increasing overload $170 - 310$ tas/sec, $\gamma = 90\%$, $\delta = 5\%$, $sr = 10/sec$, and $dt = 0$.

graph makes a sharp bend to a lower gradient). During the third epoch the workload is slightly higher than the system can immediately execute. This can be seen from the slowly growing gap between the accumulated transaction arrival (tas) and the accumulated committed transactions (co). The average response time $ø(rt)$ stays low since during the first two seconds the transactions were executed under O with short rt.

It is interesting to compare Tests #2 and #3. Test #2 has a constant high workload, but not high enough to trigger the adaptation, hence, the data remains in O. This is the reason for the very short response time. Test #3 has initially a low workload, but in Epoch #3 the workload just exceeds the threshold and adaptation to P applies. This leads to a higher rt even if the average workload is below the workload of Test #2.

Also, a start with low load (Tests #1 and #3) reduces the response-time because all transactions of the first epoch are executed under optimistic CC with a short rt.

Test #4 produces a heavy and increasing overload which triggers adaptation at the end of epoch 1. The gap between committed and arrived transactions grows until the arrival ends after 3 seconds. The adaptation to P allows to increase the commit rate until after 10 sec all queued transactions have terminated. The system needs 7 sec to process the queued transactions after the arrival of transactions has stopped before it becomes resilient. This explains the high mean response time $ø(rt)$.

It can be noted that run-time adaptation under heavy workload achieves an average commit rate $ø(cr)$ of approximately 90%, which was preset by γ. The price for improving cr is clearly a longer response-time rt which grows to 2.8 seconds for continuous overload in test-case #4.

The commit rate cr is the basis for adaptation. When cr drops below the lower bound $\gamma - \delta$ the adaptation is triggered and cr increases again. The commit rate cr increases until the upper bound $\gamma + \delta$ is reached which again triggers reclassification.

Summarizing, for sudden increases and decreases of cr, adaptation ensures a good response-time and a high commit rate if transactions are short lived ($dt = 0$) and the system is not permanently overloaded. If contention constantly remains high, adaptation has severe effects on the response-time.

B. Long Living Transactions, Seven Epochs, and β disabled

Long living transactions are characterized by a certain time interval between the read phase and the write phase where no data access occurs. Some authors [17] [18] [19] [20] [21] [22] call this interval "think time" when a typical transaction reads and displays data, then the user thinks about it, and finally modifies or adds some values. We prefer to call this time "disconnect time", because Web based transactional systems tend to logically disconnect from the database during this period.

For the tests a disconnect time dt from 100 - 1000 msec was randomly chosen. Each test consisted of seven epochs with different workloads. Workload W1 starts with $\lambda = 7 - 14$

tas/sec and rises the workload in epochs $3-7$ from 80 tas/sec continuously to 106 tas/sec. Workload W2 stresses the system with an increasing overload from $66-460$ tas/sec.

The detailed workload profiles are as follows:

- W1=(7,14,80,87,93,100,106) and
- W2=(66,132,200,265,332,400,460).

Each number denotes the transactions arriving during the respective Epoch of one second each. The tests were executed with two target commit rates $\gamma = 0.9$ and 0.7. Table VI shows a summary of the results.

TABLE VI. RESULTS OF SEVEN EPOCHS WITH WORKLOAD W1= $(7, 14, 80, 87, 93, 100, 106)$, W2= $(66, 132, 200, 265, 332, 400, 460)$, $\gamma = (0.9, 0.7)$, RANDOM DISCONNECT TIME $dt = 100 - 1000$ MS, AND BARRIER β DISABLED.

Workload	γ	$\o(rt)$	#Tas	$\o(cr_{\text{eff}})$	Figure
W1	90%	4561	487	82%	10
W2	90%	24104	1845	82%	11
W1	70%	927	483	57%	
W2	70%	18957	1845	46%	12

Adaptation from $O \rightarrow P$ causes a systematic abort of pending transactions originating in O. To take these aborts into account the effective commit rate is defined as:

$$cr_{\text{eff}} := \frac{\text{\# committed tas}}{\text{\# terminated tas}} \quad (5)$$

The effective commit rate cr_{eff} measures -as the name suggests- the performance of the system as shown to the user and the previously defined commit rate cr is used to trigger adaptation, because this indicator is more sensitive to the workload. The effective commit rate cr_{eff} reached our tests 82% for the first and $\approx 50\%$ for the second value of γ. Note that without adaptation all experiments would have a commit rate between 1 and 3 percent only due to the long living nature of the transactions and the higher conflict potential. This is also the reason why the performance in this test scenario is lower than in the previous subsection without disconnect time.

W1 has the shortest response-time due to the comparatively low workload. In Epoch 3 with high workload (80 tas/sec) quickly lets cr drop under the lower boundary $\gamma - \delta = 0.85$ (see Figure 10). The adaptation to P is triggered and in the following epochs cr rises again until the upper boundary is reached. The data is reclassified in O after 11 epochs and again the cr drops, but recovers faster as before, because the arrival of new transactions stopped after 7 epochs and after 12 epochs all pending transaction have terminated.

The adaptation profile for workload W2 (permanent contention) shown in Figure 11 is similar to W1. Due to the heavy workload starting in Epoch 1, the adaptation is already triggered at the end of Epoch 1. The permanent overload leads to a significantly longer mean response-time due to locking and queuing in P.

For workload W2 (permanent contention, second row), the mean response-time is significantly longer due to the queuing effect under P. Taking the same workload with a target commit rate of γ = 70% the adaptation behavior shows an instability (Figure 12). After adaptation to P, the upper boundary for cr is reached very quickly during the third epoch (time = 27 units = 2.7 sec) and the data is reclassified again in O (Rule 2, 2)) with the result that the commit rate cr drops to 40%. After this decrease, the system recovers slowly and reaches the upper boundary in epoch 14 again. At this point the arrival of transaction has already stopped but the remaining (queued) transactions cause another jitter for cr.

The reason for this oscillating effect is that Rule 2, 2) does not look at the number of queued transactions it only takes criteria $cr > \gamma + \delta$ to re-classify the data in O again. But in this situation all pending transactions except one will fail due to concurrency violation. This lets the commit rate cr drop as low as 40%.

It takes now longer for the adaptation mechanism to reach the upper boundary because many transactions have already aborted and accordingly more transaction have to commit to rise cr. The upper boundary is reached after 14 sec when the arrival of transaction has already stopped.

Summarizing, despite a sudden increase in contention, adaptation keeps the commit rate stable even if transactions are long living. If contention remains high, the response-time is getting longer since P queues transactions. With a low γ the mechanism tends to become unstable and an oscillating behavior can be noticed. Having γ close to 100% is recommended since adaptation is triggered earlier. To prevent an excessive increase in response-time, β has to be enabled as discussed in the next section.

C. Long Living Transactions, Seven Epochs, and β enabled

The following experiments study the effects on the workloads of the previous subsection if barrier β is enabled and γ is high (=90%) as recommended before. Table VII summarizes the results and shows barrier β, mean cr_{eff}, and the mean response-time $\o(rt)$ for workloads W1 and W2. It further links to Figures 14 and 15 showing sample graphs of one run of an experiment at a time.

TABLE VII. RESULTS OF SEVEN EPOCHS WITH WORKLOAD W1= $(7, 14, 80, 87, 93, 100, 106)$, W2= $(66, 132, 200, 265, 332, 400, 460)$, $\gamma = (0.9)$, RANDOM DISCONNECT TIME $dt = 100 - 1000$ MS, AND BARRIER β ENABLED.

Workload	β	$\o(rt)$	$\o(cr_{\text{eff}})$	Figure
W1	1000	187	17%	Figure 14 (a)
W1	3000	343	18%	Figure 14 (b)
W1	5000	355	29%	–
W1	8000	1960	36%	Figure 14 (c)
W1	15000	3758	39%	–
W2	1000	136	3%	Figure 15 (a)
W2	3000	248	16%	Figure 15 (b)
W2	5000	1219	18%	–
W2	8000	1172	25%	Figure 15 (c)
W2	15000	2625	31%	–

As Table VII shows, each workload was executed with different values $(1000, 3000, 5000, 8000, 15000)$ for β. All experiments show that the mean response-time is bounded by β and the effect of a very long response-time of 19 or 24 seconds (see Table VI of the previous section's experiments) with workload W2 no longer occurs. The table also shows that the value of β does not allow to infer the actual mean response-time. However, it shows that for an increasing β, the response-time and the commit rate increase and β correlates with these values.

Barrier β does not directly match with the maximum response-time as given, for example, by Service Level Agreements (SLA). The response time depends on the workload

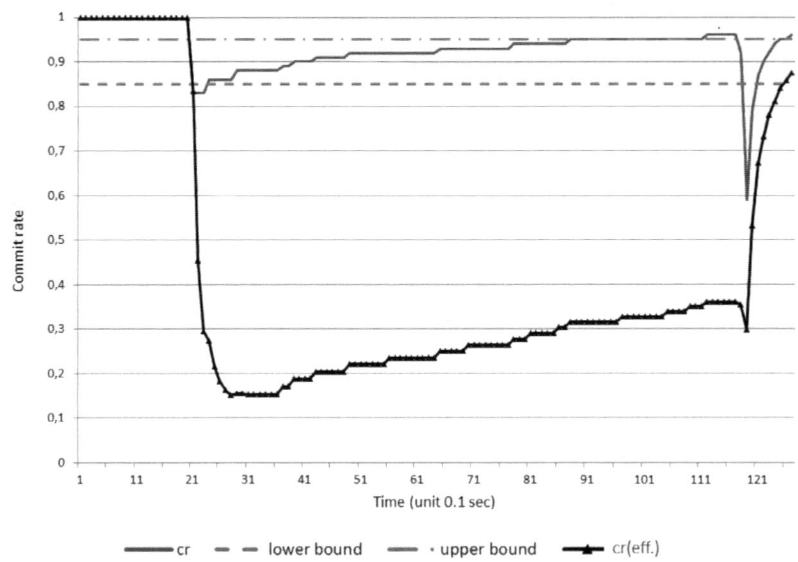

Figure 10. Run-time adaptation for W1 $= (7, 14, 80, 87, 93, 100, 106)$, $\gamma = 0.9$, random disconnect time $dt = 100 - 1000$ ms, and barrier β disabled.

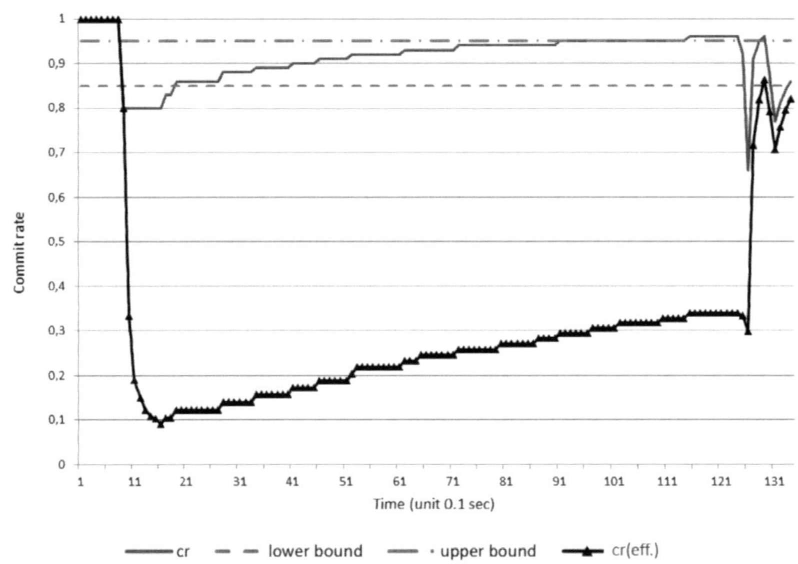

Figure 11. Run-time adaptation for W2 $= (66, 132, 200, 265, 332, 400, 460)$, $\gamma = 0.9$, random disconnect time $dt = 100 - 1000$ ms, and barrier β disabled.

and is directly influenced by the transactions' arrival rate. The distribution of the response time depends additionally on the concurrency model. For a queuing system like the concurrency model of class P a Poisson arrival process is assumed. The response time rt is calculated as wait time wt in the queue plus transaction processing pt time. Even in the simplest queuing system, the P/P/1, with Poisson arrival and one service process, only statements about the mean response time $ø(rt)$ can be made. To estimate the expected response time rt_{est}, the arrival and service rate is necessary. But in the present case both rates are heavily changing. If the arrival rate would only change due to statistical variation no adaptation would be necessary. But if a systematic change happens, e.g., because the data access type changes, the original class assignment is not any more suitable. Adaptation changes the service time and hence the service rate as well. The service time st in the case of P is the time between read and write. The only indicators for the estimated response time are the wait queue length $|Q_w|$ and the past average $ø(st)$. This leads to Formula (6):

$$rt_{\text{est}} := ø(st) \times (|Q_w| + 1) \tag{6}$$

The calculation takes into account the transactions that are already queued for execution and the average time to process

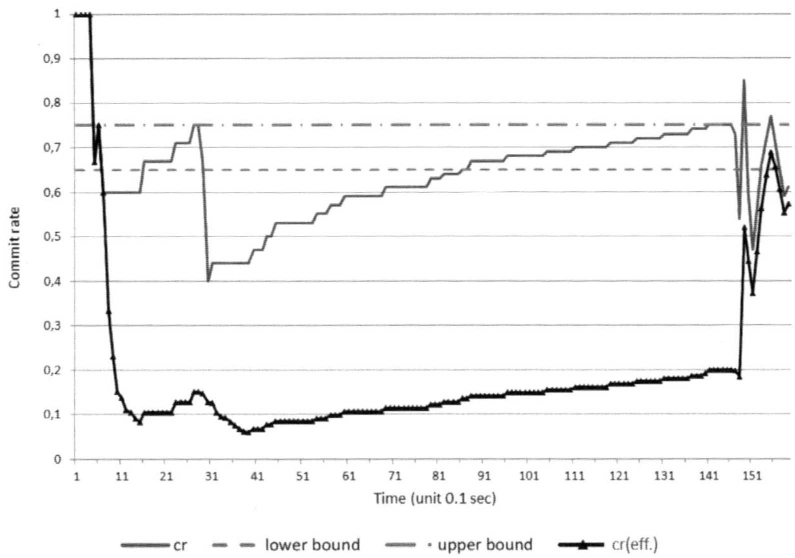

Figure 12. Run-time adaptation for W2 = $(66, 132, 200, 265, 332, 400, 460)$, $\gamma = 0.7$, random disconnect time $dt = 100 - 1000$ ms, and barrier β disabled.

a transaction. The processing time includes a possible waiting time due to locking.

The SLA defines a limit for the response time rt and in the case of an SLA violation, a penalty has to be paid. There is a trade off between loosing transactions or having excessive response time. Assuming an average price of r for each lost transaction and a penalty of p for every transaction exceeding the response time limit β the trade-off is given at the intersection of two cost functions that depend on the commit rate cr and the number of transactions tas:

$$ca := r \times (1 - cr) \times tas \tag{7}$$

$$cp := p \times tas_{rt>\beta}(cr) \times tas \tag{8}$$

If the functions are normalized with the number of transactions tas then Figure 13 shows the principal graph for this trade off. The break even point for this normalized example is given at commit rate $cr = 0.72$. In practice, the database system will measure the actual and number of aborts and the application should monitor these values and calculate the break even based on the costs for SLA violation and failed transactions.

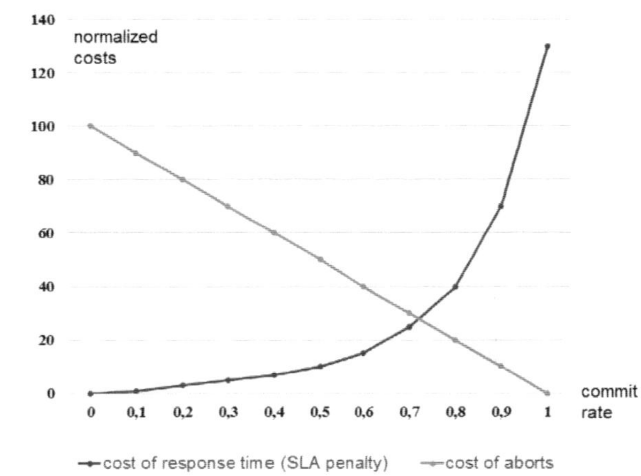

Figure 13. Example trade off between aborts and response time in terms of costs.

In the case of a fast changing workload it is difficult to estimate the workload profile. If the calculation is based on the past workload, the system may not react fast enough to sudden changes of the arrival rate.

The situation is more promising if a workload profile is known in advance. This is often the case if employees have clear routines during their workday. Assume, for example, the following tasks: order processing in the morning, stock administration after lunch, and master data management from 5 pm to 6 pm. In this scenario data access to product data in the morning and afternoon will be classified O while the product data will be re-classified to P from 5 - 6 pm.

Figures 14 and 15 illustrate the run-time adaptation profile if β is set. The time of the estimated response time rt_{est} is shown on the right vertical axis. The left ordinate shows the commit rate and the target boundaries. The horizontal axis shows the transactional time which is given by a sequence of time ordered events. The time interval from one event to the next is not constant and hence the time scale is not linear.

In Figure 14 (a) the commit rate cr is 1 during the first two seconds when the workload is low. When the overload begins after two seconds the commit rate cr drops quickly below the lower bound $\gamma - \delta = 0.85$ and adaptation to P takes place. The effective commit rate cr_{eff} (green line in Figures 14 and 15) always stays below cr because cr does not count aborts due to the adaptation $O \rightarrow P$, but cr_{eff} does. After adaptation to P the system stabilizes the commit rate cr as shown by the red graph. This appears in all test runs and can be seen more

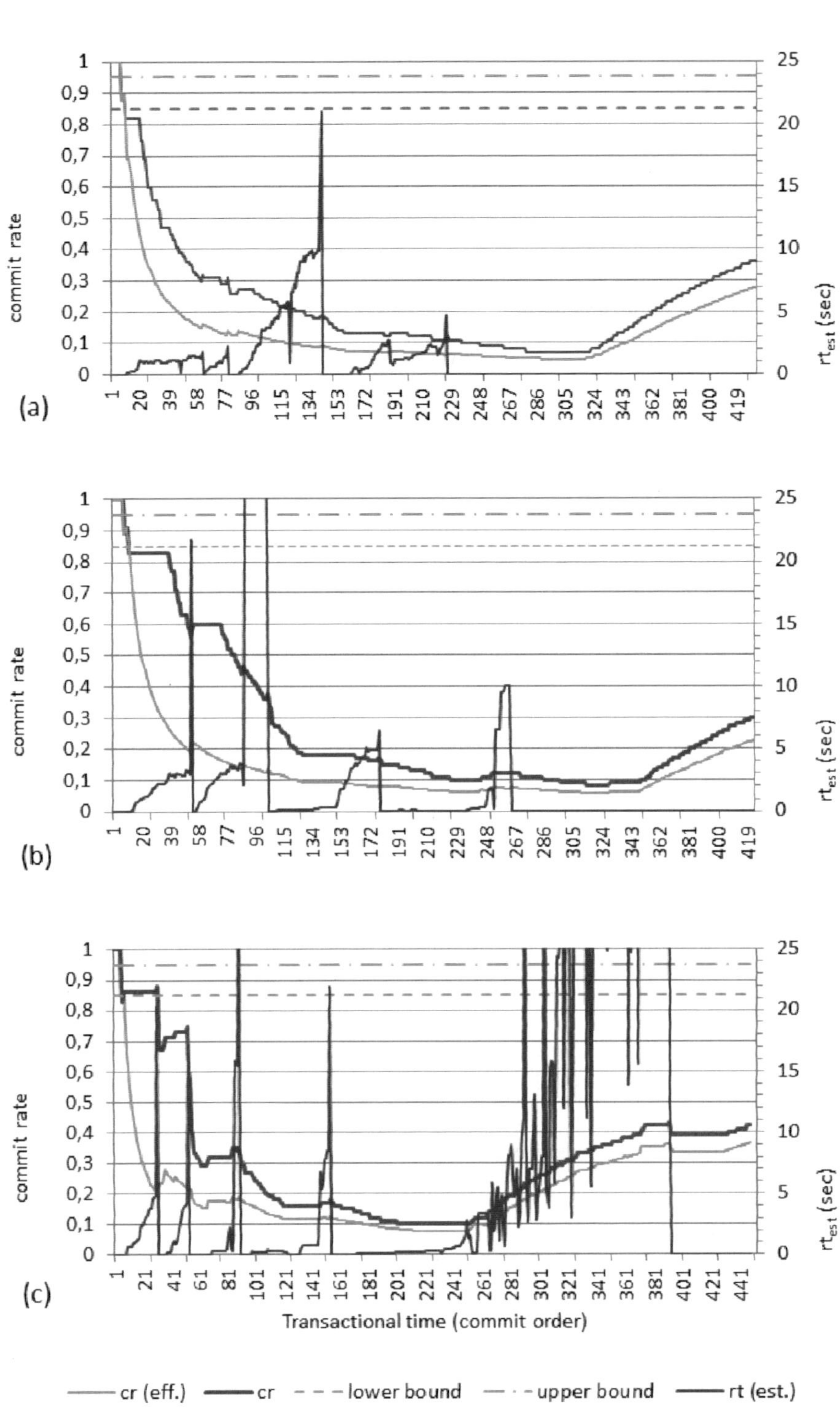

Figure 14. Run-time adaptation profile for target commit rate $\gamma = 0.9$: (a) workload W1 with $\beta = 1000$, (b) Workload W1 with $\beta = 3000$, and (c) Workload W1 with $\beta = 8000$.

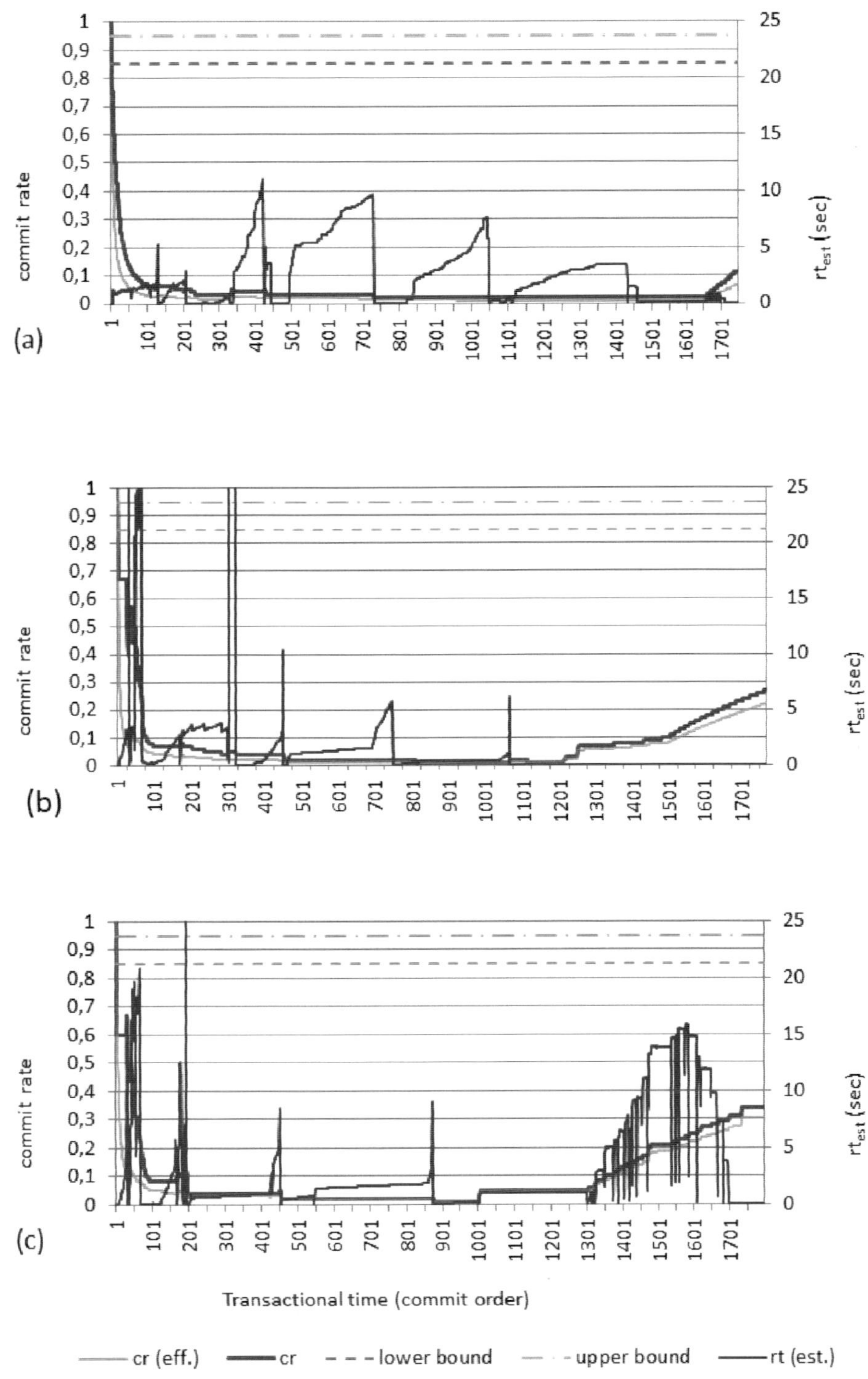

Figure 15. Run-time adaptation profile for target commit rate $\gamma = 0.9$: (a) workload W2 with $\beta = 1000$, (b) Workload W2 with $\beta = 3000$, and (c) Workload W2 with $\beta = 8000$.

clearly when we have a higher response time limit β as in part (b) and (c) of Figure 14.

In the case of $\beta = 8000$ (part (c)) the commit rate increases until the estimated response time exceeds the preset limit β. If $rt_{\text{est}} > \beta$ the re-adaptation to O is triggered by Rule 3, 2) because cr is still below the lower bound. The result is that pending transactions abort and in the following the commit rate decreases. Run time estimation works for P only because a wait queue Q_w is needed for Formula (6). If there is no wait queue then the number for rt_{est} is set to 0. Hence, as soon as rt_{est} exceeds β the systems switches to O and the rt_{est} drops to 0, which explains the saw tooth figure of rt_{est}.

A low limit for the response time as in Figure 14 (a) causes a low cr and many transactions run in O, which can only be observed indirectly by the low rt_{est}. If β increases (Figure 14 (b) and (c)), the number of aborts reduces because the system remains longer in P, which causes more waiting transactions which in turn cause more and higher peaks in the rt_{est}.

For workload W2, Figures 15 (a) - (c) illustrate the workload profiles for $\beta = 1000$, $\beta = 3000$, and $\beta = 8000$. The graph of rt_{est} for $\beta = 1000$ shows regularly appearing peaks of longer duration caused by the permanent contention. This effect nearly disappears for larger values of β (≥ 8000) because after adaptation to P much more transactions are allowed to queue up and commit later. This is indicated by higher and shorter rt_{est} peaks, which move to the beginning of the test run. As a result the cr_{eff} is slightly higher if β is high.

When the workload ends after 7 seconds and the rt_{est} drops below β Rule 3, 1) applies and the concurrency class switches to P which lets cr and cr_{eff} rises until all transactions have terminated.

Part (c) of Figures 14 and 15 show an effect of instability. This happens after the arrival of transactions has ended and before all transactions have terminated. The system has switched to P because rt_{est} was below the limit β and now the high number of remaining transactions in the queue leads to $rt_{\text{est}} > \beta = 8000$ and the re-adaptation to O lets rt_{est} drop below β, which again triggers Rule 3, 1) and forces the data to class P. The oscillation between P and O continues until most transactions have terminated and the queue is short enough to keep rt_{est} below the limit β.

In part (a) and (b) this effect shows up in a moderate form during the workload but not after its termination because the lower β does not allow many transactions to be queued and delayed for a longer time.

Summarizing, the usage of β keeps the mean response-time bounded, but compared to having $\beta = \infty$, a higher abort rate is the price that has to be paid. The exact determination of β demands a continuous adjustment and has to be carried out by applications. In particular in the case of a mixed workload a greater β causes short peaks in the rt_{est} since more transactions are allowed to commit in P. A lower β causes longer peaks since many transactions wait and their abort is not yet known. They continue in O and abort at write-time at the earliest.

Generally, it is important to know that O|R|P|E classifies hot spot items (HSIs) in classes R and E, if possible. This is the better choice if the semantic of the data allows this classification. Adaptation is only provided to handle a sudden, but impermanent increase of the contention for items classified in default class O. Permanent contention is likely to cause any system to become overloaded. O|R|P|E is at least able to protect itself by trading off response-time and commit rate.

VIII. Related Work

This paper extends the findings of [1] and is based on the Ph.D. thesis [2] of the main author, which introduces O|R|P|E. A vast amount of work [5] [11] has been carried out in the field of transaction management and CC, but so far no attempt was undertaken to use a combination of CC mechanisms according to the data usage (semantics). Most authors use the semantics of a transaction to divide it into sub-transactions, thus achieving a finer granularity that hopefully exhibit less conflicts. Some authors [23] use the semantics of the data to build a compatibility set while others try to reduce conflicts using multiversions [24] [25]. The reconciliation mechanism was introduced in [8] and is an optimistic variant of "The escrow transactional method" [9]. Escrow relies on guaranties given to the transaction before the commit time, which is only possible for a certain class of transactions, e.g. transactions with commutative operations. Optimistic concurrency control was introduced by [26], which did not gain much consideration in practice until SI, introduced by [27], has been implemented in an optimistic way. SI in general gained much attention through [6] [7], and also in practice [28]. Its strength lies in applications that have to deal with many concurrent queries but has only a moderate rate of updating transactions. O|R|P|E, however, is designed for high performance updating transactions processing, especially with data hot spots.

IX. Conclusion and Outlook

The paper presented a multimodel concurrency control mechanism that breaks with the *one concurrency mechanism fits all needs*. The concurrency mechanism is chosen according to the access semantic of the data. Four concurrency control classes are defined and rules guide the developer with the manual classification. When the access semantic is unknown the default class O with an optimistic snapshot isolation mechanism is chosen. For those data the model is extended to dynamically change the class assignment if the performance suggests a pessimistic mechanism P. The simulations with the prototype demonstrated that the mechanism is working and tests with the TPC-C++ benchmark resulted in a 3 to 4 times superior performance. The adaptation mechanism provides a response time guaranty to comply with Service Level Agreements for the price of a lower commit rate.

The tests revealed an instability in the form of an oscillating adaptation. This occurs only under an abrupt change of the workload from overload to inactive system. However, a refinement of the adaptation rule could possibly avoid the oscillation when the re-classification from $P \rightarrow O$ is executed. This could be achieved if the re-classification is only triggered when the wait queue is small or empty.

A dynamic algorithm for an automatic classification of data would be desirable and would relief the developer from manual classification. The same mechanism could then be used to dynamically adapt the data according to a changed usage profile.

Also, comprehensive performance tests that consider replication, online backup and a study of run-time adaptation under real-life conditions is still missing.

References

[1] T. Lessner, F. Laux, and T. M. Connolly, "O|R|P|E - a data semantics driven concurrency control mechanism," in *DBKDA 2015, The Seventh International Conference on Advances in Databases, Knowledge, and Data Applications*, 2015, pp. 147 – 152.

[2] T. Lessner, "O|R|P|E - a high performance semantic transaction model for disconnected systems," Ph.D. dissertation, University of the West of Scotland, 2014.

[3] *TPC BENCHMARK C, Standard Specification, Revision 5.11*, Transaction Processing Performance Council Std., February 2010.

[4] A. Thomasian, "Concurrency control: methods, performance, and analysis," *ACM Comput. Surv.*, vol. 30, no. 1, pp. 70–119, Mar. 1998.

[5] J. Gray and A. Reuter, *Transaction Processing: Concepts and Techniques*. Morgan Kaufmann, 1993.

[6] A. Fekete, D. Liarokapis, E. O'Neil, P. O'Neil, and D. Shasha, "Making snapshot isolation serializable," *ACM Trans. Database Syst.*, vol. 30, no. 2, pp. 492–528, Jun. 2005.

[7] M. J. Cahill, U. Röhm, and A. D. Fekete, "Serializable isolation for snapshot databases," *ACM Trans. Database Syst.*, vol. 34, no. 4, pp. 20:1–20:42, Dec. 2009.

[8] F. Laux and T. Lessner, "Transaction processing in mobile computing using semantic properties," in *Proceedings of the 2009 First International Conference on Advances in Databases, Knowledge, and Data Applications*, ser. DBKDA '09. IEEE Computer Society, 2009, pp. 87–94.

[9] P. E. O'Neil, "The escrow transactional method," *ACM Transactions On Database Systems*, vol. 11, pp. 405–430, December 1986.

[10] M. Kifer, A. Bernstein, and P. M. Lewis, *Database Systems: An Application Oriented Approach, Complete Version (2nd Edition)*. Boston, MA, USA: Addison-Wesley Longman Publishing Co., Inc., 2005.

[11] G. Weikum and G. Vossen, *Transactional Information Systems: Theory, Algorithms, and the Practice of Concurrency Control and Recovery*. Morgan Kaufmann, 2002.

[12] H. Garcia-Molina, J. D. Ullman, and J. Widom, *Database systems - the complete book (2. ed.)*. Pearson Education, 2009.

[13] Abraham Silberschatz, Henry F. Korth, and S. Sudarshan, *Database System Concepts (sixth edition)*. McGraw-Hill, 2011.

[14] T. Kraska, M. Hentschel, G. Alonso, and D. Kossmann, "Consistency rationing in the cloud: pay only when it matters," *Proc. VLDB Endow.*, vol. 2, pp. 253–264, August 2009. [Online]. Available: http://portal.acm.org/citation.cfm?id=1687627.1687657

[15] D. Gómez Ferro and M. Yabandeh, "A critique of snapshot isolation," in *Proceedings of the 7th ACM european conference on Computer Systems*, ser. EuroSys '12. New York, NY, USA: ACM, 2012, pp. 155–168. [Online]. Available: http://doi.acm.org/10.1145/2168836.2168853

[16] R. Osman and W. J. Knottenbelt, "Database system performance evaluation models: A survey," *Performance Evaluation*, vol. 69, no. 10, pp. 471 – 493, 2012. [Online]. Available: http://www.sciencedirect.com/science/article/pii/S0166531612000442

[17] F. Laux and M. Laiho, "Sql access patterns for optimistic concurrency control," in *Proceedings of the 2009 Computation World: Future Computing, Service Computation, Cognitive, Adaptive, Content, Patterns*, ser. COMPUTATIONWORLD '09. Washington, DC, USA: IEEE Computer Society, 2009, pp. 254–258. [Online]. Available: http://dx.doi.org/10.1109/ComputationWorld.2009.63

[18] A. Adya, R. Gruber, B. Liskov, and U. Maheshwari, "Efficient optimistic concurrency control using loosely synchronized clocks," in *Proceedings of the 1995 ACM SIGMOD International Conference on Management of Data, San Jose, California, May 22-25, 1995.*, M. J. Carey and D. A. Schneider, Eds. ACM Press, 1995, pp. 23–34. [Online]. Available: http://doi.acm.org/10.1145/223784.223787

[19] B. Ding, L. Kot, A. J. Demers, and J. Gehrke, "Centiman: elastic, high performance optimistic concurrency control by watermarking," in *Proceedings of the Sixth ACM Symposium on Cloud Computing, SoCC 2015, Kohala Coast, Hawaii, USA, August 27-29, 2015*, S. Ghandeharizadeh, S. Barahmand, M. Balazinska, and M. J. Freedman, Eds. ACM, 2015, pp. 262–275. [Online]. Available: http://doi.acm.org/10.1145/2806777.2806837

[20] J. Huang, J. A. Stankovic, K. Ramamritham, and D. F. Towsley, "Experimental evaluation of real-time optimistic concurrency control schemes," in *17th International Conference on Very Large Data Bases, September 3-6, 1991, Barcelona, Catalonia, Spain, Proceedings.*, G. M. Lohman, A. Sernadas, and R. Camps, Eds. Morgan Kaufmann, 1991, pp. 35–46. [Online]. Available: http://www.vldb.org/conf/1991/P035.PDF

[21] R. Agrawal, M. J. Carey, and M. Livny, "Concurrency control performance modeling: Alternatives and implications," *ACM Trans. Database Syst.*, vol. 12, no. 4, pp. 609–654, 1987. [Online]. Available: http://doi.acm.org/10.1145/32204.32220

[22] F. Laux, M. Laiho, and T. Lessner, "Implementing row version verification for persistence middleware using sql access patterns," *International Journal on Advances in Software, issn 1942-2628*, vol. 3, no. 3 & 4, pp. 407 – 423, 2010. [Online]. Available: http://www.iariajournals.org/software/

[23] H. Garcia-Molina, "Using semantic knowledge for transaction processing in a distributed database," *ACM Trans. Database Syst.*, vol. 8, no. 2, pp. 186–213, Jun. 1983.

[24] S. H. Phatak and B. Nath, "Transaction-centric reconciliation in disconnected client-server databases," *Mob. Netw. Appl.*, vol. 9, no. 5, pp. 459–471, 2004.

[25] P. Graham and K. Barker, "Effective optimistic concurrency control in multiversion object bases," in *ISOOMS '94: Proceedings of the International Symposium on Object-Oriented Methodologies and Systems*, ser. Lecture Notes in Computer Science, E. Bertino and S. D. Urban, Eds., vol. 858. London, UK: Springer-Verlag, 1994, pp. 313–328.

[26] H. T. Kung and J. T. Robinson, "On optimistic methods for concurrency control," *ACM Trans. Database Syst.*, vol. 6, no. 2, pp. 213–226, Jun. 1981.

[27] H. Berenson, P. Bernstein, J. Gray, J. Melton, E. O'Neil, and P. O'Neil, "A critique of ansi sql isolation levels," *SIGMOD Rec.*, vol. 24, no. 2, pp. 1–10, May 1995.

[28] D. R. K. Ports and K. Grittner, "Serializable snapshot isolation in postgresql," *Proc. VLDB Endow.*, vol. 5, no. 12, pp. 1850–1861, Aug. 2012.

Context-aware Mobile Security

Experimental Validation of Reliable and Secure Context Detection

Christian Jung, Denis Feth
Fraunhofer IESE
Kaiserslautern, Germany
Email: christian.jung@iese.fraunhofer.de, denis.feth@iese.fraunhofer.de

Abstract—**The exploitation of context-awareness, especially in mobile devices bears a huge potential. For example, mobile workers benefit from systems that adapt security settings or user interfaces to the current situation. However, the correct detection of contexts strongly relies on raw data from various context information sources that might be neither trustworthy nor authoritative. In this work, we present an extension to a context model that explicitly copes with trustworthiness of context information, i.e., its vulnerability to forgery, as well as their conduciveness denoting the source's decisive impact on context detection. Context descriptions based on this model can, for example, be used in security-critical environments to enforce security policies. We show the applicability of our approach in an industrial setting. In addition, we present the results of our experiments with respect to precision and recall of the context detection.**

Keywords–Context-Awareness; Context-Modeling; Security

I. Introduction

Context-awareness of software applications is still in its infancy [1], [2], although it has been researched since the beginning of the nineties [3]. Recently, the rise of mobile technologies introduced a new class of devices with various sensors providing context information. For such devices, context-awareness can be particularly useful to adapt user interfaces or security measures to the current situation, in order to relieve the user. For example, context-awareness enables more flexible control by limiting the applicability of security measures only to situations where they are indispensable (e.g., display timeout for mobile devices is set to fifteen minutes in the office, thirty minutes at home, and to two minutes elsewhere).

An important building block for enabling context-aware security is context modeling. The user's contexts (i.e., her current activity and device situation) have to be determined by aggregating low-level contextual information, such as current location, battery consumption, or connectivity of her mobile device. However, in order to provide reliable decision support, context descriptions have to be trustworthy, reliable, and accurate, especially to support security decisions. Thus, the context evaluation must consider information about how easy it is to counterfeit contextual information.

To this end, a methodology for eliciting and modeling contextual information is needed that yields reusable and comparable context descriptions. In particular, this method must support the identification of suitable context information sources and the aggregation of low-level pieces of context information into an overall context description.

Contribution. In [1], we present our context model and context descriptions that explicitly include a relevance and a security rating for each context information source. The two quality attributes are used to improve the recognition accuracy, which is an open challenge in activity recognition [4], [5]. These ratings enable us to provide quality statements for the accuracy of context detections. Security decisions benefit from the quality statements within a context description, aggregated during run-time. We extend [1] by showing the applicability of our approach in an industrial setting. In addition, we present the results of our experiments with respect to precision and recall of the context detection.

Paper Structure. The paper is structured as follows: Our context modeling approach is presented in Section II, followed by Section III addressing uncertainty of context information sources. In Section IV, we apply our approach to an industrial scenario from a large German company. We present our evaluation with respect to the quality of our context detection in Section V. Section VI addresses related work in the area of context definition and context information modeling. Finally, Section VII provides a summary and an outlook on future work.

II. Context Model

Our work uses a combination of existing definitions and descriptions of context, which are further described in our related work section (Section VI). We partition context sources into virtual and physical information sources, depending on the origin of the information, and we logically link them (similar to Hofer et al. [6]). As this work focuses on mobile devices and their users, activities of the user are an important aspect, as well as the operational state of the device. Thus, we define context as:

> *Context is the state of all virtual and physical information sources that characterize the activity of the user and the operational state of the mobile device in a specific situation at a certain time.*

Figure 1 presents a macroscopic view of the core parts of our model and their interrelations. The model mainly describes relations between the user, the mobile device, and the context. The context is broken up in a user context (user-centric context) and a device context (mobile device-centric context). We assume that a user can have one or more mobile devices and that a user has always her own mobile device, which she will not share with other users.

A user can perform several activities in a specific situation at a certain time. The user context depends on the activity and

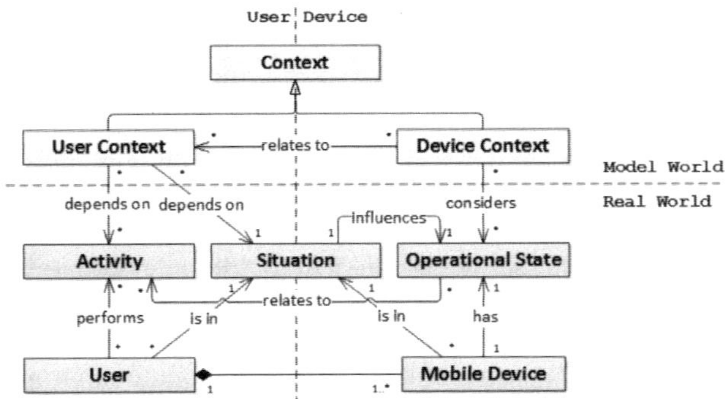

Figure 1. Context Model (Macroscopic Viewpoint).

the current situation of the user. In an ideal world, the user context would include all information about the activities and the situation. Hence, the information in the model world would be congruent with the information in the real world. However, due to technical constraints of the context information retrieval, the detection capabilities (e.g., environment sensors) are limited. In addition, the boundaries between certain activities are fluid and often cannot be determined by context information sources. Accordingly, the differentiation between activity, situation, and user context will persist. Hence, the relations between activity, situation, and user context depends on the granularity of the modeled user contexts. Our context model has to cope with such uncertainties.

A mobile device has an operational state and acts within a specific situation. Hence, the situation of the device includes internal states of the device and attributes of the environment. The overall device context considers the operational state, which may be influenced by the current situation. Similar to the relation between activity, situation, and user context, the device context would always match the current situation and operational state in an ideal world. However, due to technical limitations, several distinct device situations lead to the same device context. Moreover, the operational state may relate to the activity of the user. This relation must not necessarily hold, as the user can also perform device-independent activities. However, for automatic context detection, we can only use the operational state. Finally, the device context also depends on the user context. Again, in an ideal world, the device context would include all information about the situation and the operational state.

It is apparent that the environment and internal states of the device can only be sensed by context information sources that are technically available. Thus, device context and user context must be detectable by existing context information sources, but are only approximations of the real world, neglecting unmeasurable information. In contrast, activity, situation and operational state strive to represent the world as it really is.

The core part of the context model is the context itself. The goal is to model the user and device context as an abstraction and aggregation of pieces of information obtained from various context information sources.

A. *Context Description Structure*

A context description can be a logical or arithmetic expression. The context description aggregates raw sensor data as evaluators and combines them to a tree structure. For example, we can specify the context "LowBattery" as shown in Figure 2.

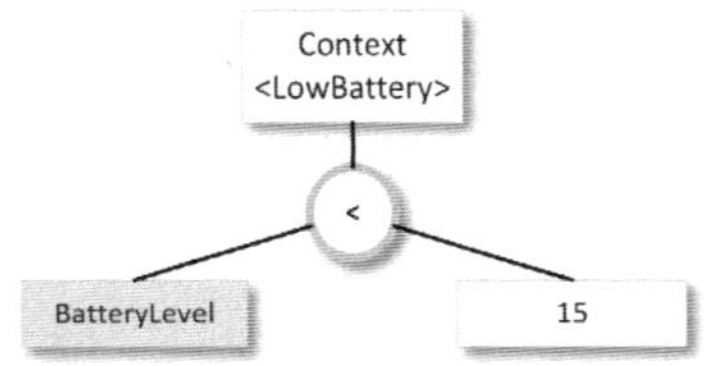

Figure 2. Example Context Tree "LowBattery"

To model contexts, *Expressions* can be combined to form arbitrarily complex descriptions (see Figure 3). Expressions can be combined and nested in a way that the respective overall result is a Boolean value with additional ratings for security and relevance (see Section III). *GenericExpression* forms the basis for all other types of Expressions (arithmetic, comparison, and logic) and a *ConstantExpression* holding a constant value. The Expression interface has a method for evaluating itself and a method for retrieving the return type. For type safety, it is important to have these type assignments, as a context description, at least in theory, could combine any expression type. However, there is a check whether the relation is allowed. For instance, a comparison between a Boolean type and a list of values would be rejected.

A specialization of the GenericExpression is the BinaryExpression, which allows exactly two subordinated expressions. *ComparisonExpressions*, for instance, take exactly two subexpressions for their evaluation.

ArithmeticExpressions are expressions for addition, subtraction, multiplication and division. For evaluating the expression, all assigned sub-expressions are joined by the appropriate operation. In general, ArithmeticExpressions can contain an unlimited number of nested expressions.

Similar to ArithmeticExpression, a *LogicExpression* can take an unlimited number of nested expressions for evaluation. For the moment, *and*, *or*, and *not* with their usual semantics

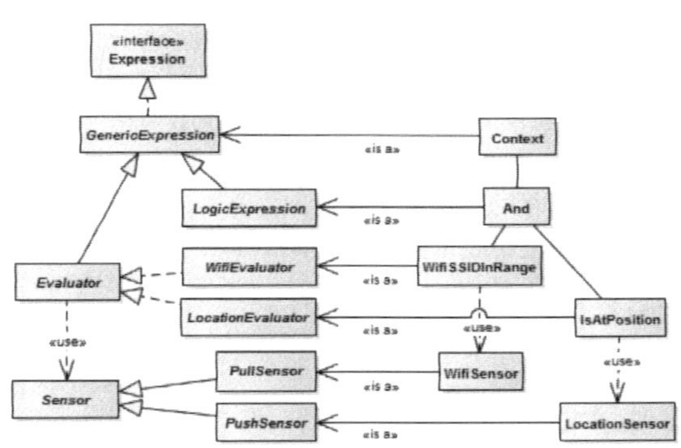

Figure 3. Excerpt of Expression Model.

have been implemented. Future extensions could include fuzzy logic or other evaluation capabilities.

The *Evaluator* can express various behaviors, for example, aggregation or temporal changes of information. Every functionality that cannot be expressed by arithmetic or logic expressions has to be provided by evaluators. Each evaluator implementation encapsulates a specific operation of *Sensor* data, which means, it is one possible abstraction of the operative behavior of the information source and performs a first aggregation of raw values from the measurement (if needed). Evaluators can be included as sub-expressions at arbitrary locations within the presented structure.

Sensors provide an abstract representation for context information sources, which usually deliver low-level information, such as the current coordinates of the Global Positioning System (GPS) or acceleration values. In general, we distinguish between push and pull behavior, based on the characteristics of the underlying information source. Some sensors can be configured to provide (i.e., push behavior) new information as soon as new data is available (e.g., acceleration or location sensors). Such push sensors usually contain parameters to configure conditions when data updates will be delivered. For example, the location sensor will only deliver new information if the mobile device location changed by at least 50 meters. Other sensor information has to be queried regularly (i.e., pull behavior) to obtain current information (e.g., mobile device settings, calendar). Pull sensors contain a *scheduleInterval* parameter specifying the frequency of data updates. For example, wireless network information can be requested every five minutes.

Our preferred format for a context description is XML (see Figure 4). In general, a configuration can contain several expressions of types arithmetic, comparison, or logic (future extensions could extend the list of available expression types).

The specification in Figure 4 includes two different evaluators: a GenericLocation evaluator for checking a specific location and a WiFiIsSSIDInRange-Evaluator to scan for specific wireless Service Set Identifiers (SSID). The location evaluator consumes the following parameters: location values (i.e., *latitude* and *longitude*), *distance* (specifying the data delivery and distance accuracy), *provider* (location information from network and/or GPS) and *maxAge* (allowed data age for evaluation). The wireless evaluator uses the parameter *ssid* to scan for this specific wireless SSID. In addition, the parameter *keepEnabled* prevents the user from disabling the wireless network sensing. The listing also shows an example of arithmetic expressions and comparisons. Evaluators may contain a relevance and a security rating, which are described next.

III. Dealing with Uncertainty

The basic question when building a context-aware system is: "To which extent is the context detection reliable?" We distinguish three major uncertainties to deal with: trustworthiness, relevance, and accuracy.

Accuracy information is typically already provided by sensors used in mobile systems. Therefore, we focus on other two uncertainties and introduce two quality metrics: a *security rating*, denoting the difficulty for an adversary to counterfeit the measurement of the context information source and a *relevance rating*, expressing the value of the context information source for the identification of the overall context.

```
<context id="example-context">
  <logic:and>
    <logic:or>
      <evaluator name="GenericLocation" relevance="5">
        <param name="latitude" value="49.431479"/>
        <param name="longitude" value="7.7520288"/>
        <param name="distance" value="15.0"/>
        <param name="provider" value="0"/>
        <param name="maxAge" value="3600"/>
        <param name="resultType" value="boolean"/>
       </evaluator>
       <evaluator name="WiFiIsSSIDInRange" relevance="3">
         <param name="maxAge" value="60"/>
         <param name="keepEnabled" value="true"/>
         <param name="scheduleInterval" value="15"/>
         <param name="ssid" value="wlan-home"/>
         <param name="resultType" value="boolean"/>
       </evaluator>
    </logic:or>
    <!-- Arithmetic demo: 2*2*4 >= 10+(36/6) -->
    <comparison:greaterEqual>
      <arithmetic:multiply>
        <constant type="double" value="2"/>
        <constant type="double" value="2"/>
        <constant type="double" value="4"/>
      </arithmetic:multiply>
      <arithmetic:add>
        <constant type="double" value="10"/>
        <arithmetic:divide>
          <constant type="double" value="36"/>
          <constant type="double" value="6"/>
        </arithmetic:divide>
      </arithmetic:add>
    </comparison:greaterEqual>
  </logic:and>
</context>
```

Figure 4. Evaluator Example.

For both quality metrics, we have to find suitable thresholds and combine them to trust the context detection in the given usage scenario. For example, a context based on low ranked context information sources only, can easily be counterfeited and might not be trustworthy. Similar, some context information sources are more supportive to detect the current context than others. For example, the wireless network information is well suited to detect the context "home", while it is rather bad for detecting activities such as "running".

A. Security Rating

Every evaluator has a security rating assigned to it. The rating takes the values from one (very low) to five (very high). Basically, the security rating denotes the trustworthiness of the context information, i.e., its vulnerability to forgery. The security rating within our work is defined as follows:

> *The Security Rating is a global indicator expressing difficulty and challenge for an adversary to counterfeit a context information source.*

The following aspects have to be considered, when rating an evaluator. A security expert or group of experts have to perform this task based on an attacker model when an evaluator is developed. The experts have to assess the necessary preconditions for successfully counterfeiting an information source:

(i) insider knowledge or configuration details
(ii) special expertise or knowledge to perform the operation
(iii) special software or application

(iv) special hardware or equipment
(v) influence on information source (backend or environment change)

Based on these prerequisites, the metric to determine the rating for every evaluator is defined as follows:

- **1 (very low)**: 0 out of 5 prerequisites needed
It is easy to counterfeit the measured values (e.g., just change or enter the value). An example for such a rating is the time of the mobile device or calendar entries of the user.
- **2 (low)**: 1 out of 5, but not prerequisite (iv)
The manipulation of the sensed value can be done with little effort. An example is to simulate a high light intensity with a torch or to shake the device to forge acceleration values.
- **3 (medium)**: 2 out of 5 OR 1 out of {(iii), (iv), (v)}
Some preparations are required, but they are not really challenging. An example would be faking the SSID or BSSID of a WiFi hotspot, which can directly be done by using a second smart mobile device.
- **4 (high)**: 3 out of 5 OR 2 out of {(iii), (iv), (v)}
The required measures are challenging for an adversary, and without special knowledge, it would not be possible to perform the attack. An example is to simulate that the device is connected to an encrypted (mobile) network.
- **5 (very high)**: 4 out of 5 OR 3 out of {(iii), (iv), (v)}
Forging of context information sources requires deep knowledge about the internal configuration and significant expertise; moreover special equipment is needed, such as software and hardware. An example is the GPS sensor or cell phone tower information, for which an attacker would need special hardware and knowledge how to use it.

The security rating has to be defined once, and it has a global scope for every instantiated context tree. However, it is possible to manually change the rating by explicitly setting it in the evaluator tag of the context description. For example, the security rating of a virtual context information source can vary according to its trustworthiness. A read-only enterprise calendar will be much harder to counterfeit than the personal calendar maintained by the user itself. Hence, we can manually assign a higher security rating to the evaluator using the read-only enterprise calendar.

We rated all our evaluators by asking two security experts from our institute to assess the five preconditions. Figure 5 presents possible answers for their assessment.

✓	The precondition is necessary for a successful manipulation.
×	The precondition is not necessary for a successful manipulation.
/	The precondition is not important or not relevant for the rating.
-	The precondition is not applicable.
?	The decision cannot be made and needs further discussion.

Figure 5. Possible Answers for Assessing Security Rating Preconditions

In addition, the experts had to write a brief statement for every precondition for being able to reconstruct their assessment and for being used in later discussions with the other security expert. Figure 6 shows the filled table for the *Bluetooth-Evaluator* by one security expert. The security expert rates the *BluetoothEvaluator* with a security rating of 4 (high), as 3 out of 5 preconditions are necessary for a successful manipulation.

BluetoothEvaluator		
✓	(i)	Generally speaking the Bluetooth interface is safe. There are possible attacks in certain configurations but those are only applicable if the user has its Bluetooth device set to be visible. With proper equipment and knowledge it is possible to disguise a device as something else. If the profile of the connecting partner is known it is also possible to disguise as a specific device.
×	(ii)	The general attack path is to trick the device into thinking it is communicating with a known device and therefor the system takes physical this presence into account for a special context. However this is false since the attacked device is communicating with is just disguised as a known device.
✓|×	(iii)	Either special hardware or special software is needed to trick the attacked device into thinking it communicates with a known device.
✓|×	(iv)	Either special hardware or special software is needed to trick the attacked device into thinking it communicates with a known device.
/	(v)	Not applicable.
Security Rating: 4 (high)		

Figure 6. Security Rating Assessment for BluetoothEvaluator

Finally, we collected the information from the two security experts and determined a security rating for every evaluator based on their assessment. For instance, evaluators using the accelerometer values have been rated with very low, as a device user can easily manipulate these values. Contrary, evaluators using Android's location services are rated as very high, as the location services are using a multitude of location sources (i.e., GPS, Cell-ID, Wi-Fi) [7], which are hard to manipulate.

B. Relevance Rating

For each context, we assign a second rating to every evaluator, expressing the contribution of the information source to the overall context identification. Similar to the security rating, it accepts values from one (very low) to five (very high). The rating represents whether the provided information tends to be decisive or has a less authoritative impact on context detection. The relevance rating is defined as follows:

> *The Relevance Rating is a local indicator expressing the correlation of a context information source with an activity, or situation.*

The relevance rating depends on the modeled context, but also on the quality of a sensor and cannot be specified by just following generic guidelines. Thus, the retrieval of the relevance rating is part of an automatic derivation process, which has been described in [8]. This process yields context descriptions that can be used in operative environments.

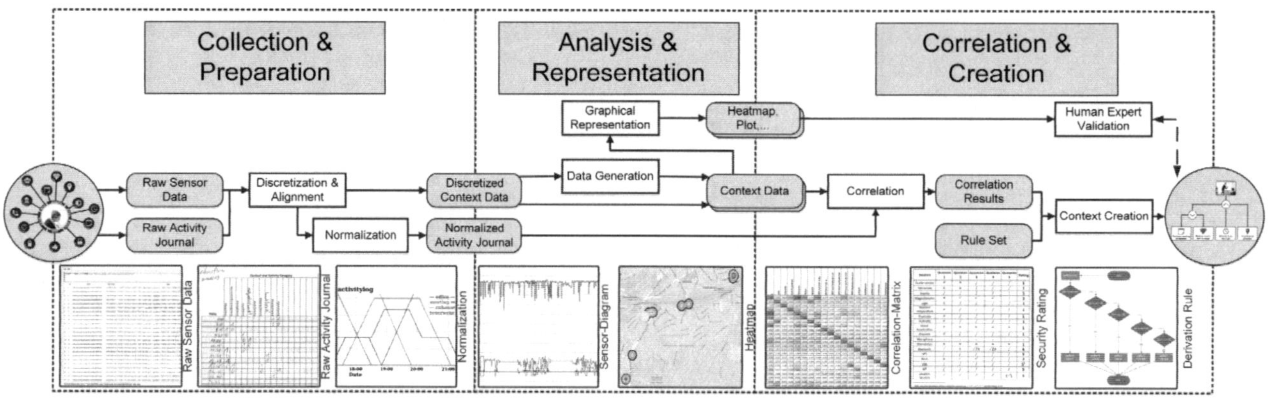

Figure 7. Detailed Process for Determining Context Descriptions

The entire process comprises three phases, depicted in Figure 7:

- Collection & Preparation,
- Analysis & Representation, and
- Correlation & Creation.

1) Collection & Preparation: In the first phase, we manually collect user activities/device situations and use mobile devices to automatically collect related contextual information (sensor data). The two data streams are fed into the process for further processing. We are using discrete time steps in the subsequent phase and therefore, we have to discretize the data collected. We have different strategies to transform the information, which depend on the nature of the given data. In addition, we consolidate the reported user activities and situations regarding their semantics (as users may use different verbalisms for reporting their activities and situations).

2) Analysis & Representation: The second phase has two objectives. First, the discretized context data can be analyzed to derive new information from it. For example, changes in battery level over time can be derived from absolute battery levels at specific points in time. Second, we create graphical representations of the data sets. For example, geolocation over time can be visualized via heatmaps. The graphical representations is used to allow human experts to validate context descriptions in the end.

3) Correlation & Creation: In the third phase, context descriptions are derived. Towards this end, the normalized activity journals are first correlated with contextual data. We use different statistical methods (see [8]) to correlate sensor data with activities/situations and use the results (e.g., a correlation matrix) to determine the relevance of a sensor for the characterization of an activity or situation. Derivation rules are then applied, producing context descriptions that correspond to user activities.

The evaluation result of a context is obtained by evaluating the tree structure of the context description. The logical operators have their standard meaning.

The calculation of the relevance and security rating for a context is as follows:

- **AND/OR**-relation: All fulfilled quality attributes of the elements in an AND/OR group affect the overall relevance or security rating. They are summed up to the denominator. The quality attributes of all evaluators that are actually fulfilled in the system under evaluation are summed up to the numerator.
- **NOT**-relation: The quality attribute of the element is propagated to the parent node, if the subordinated expression is false.

The quality attributes ensure that the fulfillment of those evaluators with highest relevance or security rating has the strongest impact on the overall result. For example, let us assume a context description c with three evaluators e_1, e_2, e_3 linked with a logical or: $c = e_1 \vee e_2 \vee e_3$. Assume further that evaluator $e_1(true,\ sec = 1,\ rel = 1)$ is fulfilled and has a relevance and security rating of one, and that $e_2(false,\ sec = 3,\ rel = 4)$ and $e_3(false,\ sec = 4,\ rel = 5)$ are not fulfilled and have a relevance rating of four and five, respectively. Then, the overall result of the context is fulfilled, but the relevance rating is only $1/10 = 0.1$ and the security rating is $1/8 = 0.125$. The security policy specification bears responsibility for defining suitable thresholds for the security and relevance ratings that are sufficient to trigger a change of the security settings. Furthermore, the decision strongly depends on whether to tighten or to ease security restrictions.

IV. Application Scenario

To demonstrate how such an approach can be used in an industrial setting, we applied it in cooperation with a large German company that administrates mobile devices via the mobile device management (MDM) solution *MobileIron*®. Via MobileIron®, they adjust security settings (e.g., to impose password restrictions or storage encryption, to install or revoke certificates for virtual private networks, or to disable camera or microphone), and perform actions such as sending messages to the user or wiping the device. However, these settings and actions are rather static and cannot be adapted according to the current operational state of the device or the user activity. In this setting, context-awareness can provide more flexibility. For example, camera and microphone usage can be prevented within company premises, but allowed elsewhere. However, when used for security purposes, context detection has to be accurate and reliable in order to comply with company regulations.

In our application, we analyzed the security demands of the company and identified the needed flexibility. We created appropriate context descriptions and connected our context detection with the MDM solution of the company. Unfortunately, we were not allowed to run the evaluation with productive users and had to evaluate it with researches from our institute.

A. Setup & Execution

Security policies in MobileIron® control security behavior such as password restrictions of the mobile device (cf. Table I). *Lockdown policies* limit the use of the mobile device such as disabling Bluetooth, camera, or microphone (cf. Table II). We specified two security policies ($security1$ and $security2$) and three lockdown policies ($lockdown1$, $lockdown2$, and $lockdown3$), which are briefly described in the following.

TABLE I. SECURITY POLICIES

	security1	security2
Maximum Inactivity Timeout:	30 min	2 times
Maximum Number of Failed Attempts:	3 min	5 times

TABLE II. LOCKDOWN POLICIES

	lockdown1	lockdown2	lockdown3
Bluetooth:	Disable	Enable (Audio only)	Enable
Camera:	Disable	Enable	Enable
Microphone:	Disable	Enable	Enable
NFC:	Disable	Enable	Enable
Screen Capture:	Disable	Enable	Enable
Lockscreen Widgets:	Disable	Enable	Enable
USB Debug:	Enable	Disable	Enable

In Table I, security policy $security1$ has a higher priority than security policy $security2$. Hence, if both policies are activated, security1 would be used and the maximum inactivity time would be 30 minutes. In Table II, the lockdown policy $lockdown1$ has a higher priority than $lockdown2$, which in turn has a higher priority than $lockdown3$.

MobileIron® allows the definition of labels and the assignment to security and lockdown polices. In our case, we defined four labels, namely $default\_label$, $work1\_label$ where security is tightened, $work2\_label$ where security is eased and $home\_label$. These labels have been assigned to our policies as depicted in Figure 8.

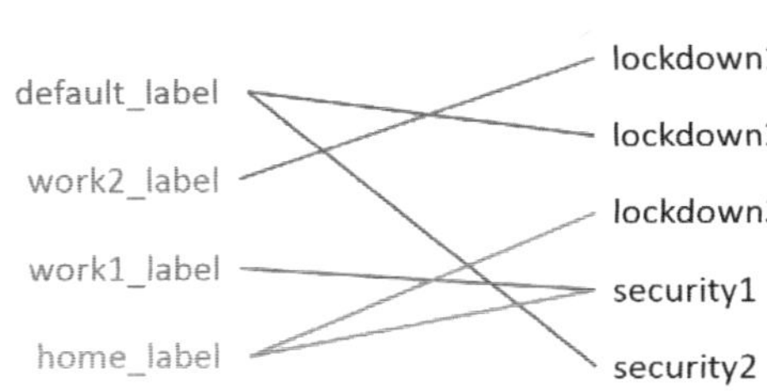

Figure 8. Mapping between Labels and Policies.

In the described setting, two contexts are of relevance: "Home" and "Work". Both contexts are modeled by using wireless, location, calendar, and time evaluators. Figure 9 illustrates the context tree for the "Work" context c_1, including all assignments for the security and relevance ratings. As the security rating has a global scope for each evaluator type, the value does not change within the same type of evaluator. In contrast, the relevance rating changes, depending on the results from the statistical calculation.

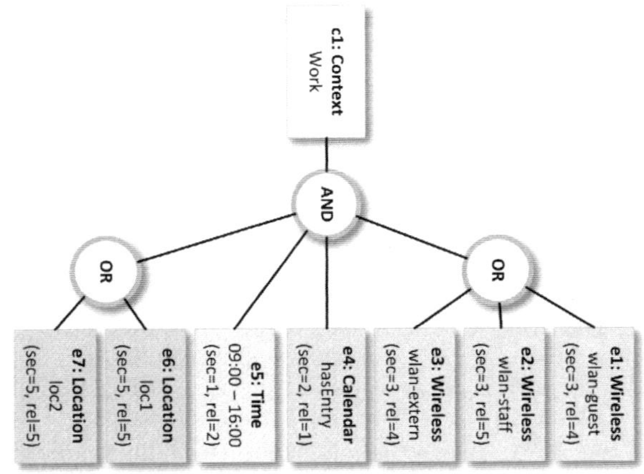

Figure 9. Context Tree Example for Context "Work".

For example, the wireless network *wlan-staff* has the highest statistical significance (correlation result), followed by *wlan-guest* and *wlan-extern*. This is reflected in the final relevance ratings of the wireless evaluators. *wlan-staff* is the employer's wireless network and has the highest relevance. The calendar seems to be a relevant context factor, but as users usually do not schedule their entire working day in the calendar, the calendar evaluator has the lowest relevance. Similar behavior holds for the time evaluator. The company has flexible working hours, but the core working hours are between 09:00am to 4:00pm. Hence, users arrive earlier or stay longer at work, to reach their daily working time. Nevertheless, the time evaluator is more relevant than the calendar evaluator.

The company has defined several policies assigned to the "Work" context, on which we focus in the following. On the one hand, there are policies easing security restrictions of the mobile device at work (in favor of usability). For example, the company increases the display timeout at work to thirty minutes for usability reasons ($work1\_label \rightarrow security1$). On the other hand, there are policies tightening the security at work. For example, the company prohibits the usage of camera, microphone, etc. at work to meet organizational policies ($work2\_label \rightarrow lockdown1$). The idea is now to define appropriate thresholds to reflect company needs.

To tackle this, we calculated the following cases:

- Context c_1 is $true$ with highest relevance $\rightarrow 1.00$
- Context c_1 is $true$ with lowest relevance e_1, e_4, e_5, e_6 are $true \rightarrow 0.46$
- Context c_1 is $false$ with highest relevance $e_1, e_2, e_3, e_5, e_6, e_7$ are $true \rightarrow 0.96$
- Context c_1 is $false$ with lowest relevance $\rightarrow 0.00$

Hence, the relevance range for c_1 $is\ true$ is between 0.46 and 1.00, and for c_1 $is\ false$ is between 0.00 and 0.96. Analogously, we calculated the security rating for c_1. Figure 10 shows our policy state chart and the state change criteria to activate and deactivate the policies. To change the states by using the relevance and security rating, as well as the fulfillment of the context, allows us to model hysteresis behavior. For example, changing from the state $work1\_label$ (inactive) to $work1\_label$ (active) is harder than changing from the state $work1\_label$ (active) to $work1\_label$ (inactive).

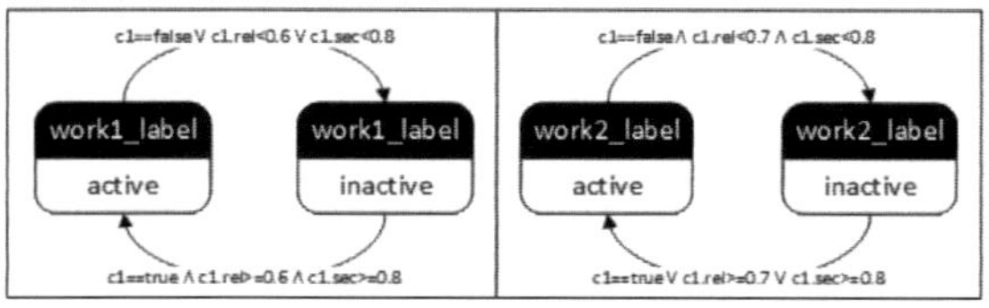

Figure 10. Policy Statechart.

For instance, assume that $work1\_label$ is inactive, the evaluators e_1, e_4, e_5, e_6 are true, and the evaluators e_2, e_3, e_7 are false. This results in context c_1 to be true. However, the relevance is only 0.46 and the security is only 0.50, which would prevent the change from inactive to active. Hence, we need at least one more evaluator changing its state to true for reaching the relevance threshold and even one more for reaching the security threshold. Vice versa, let us suppose that $work1\_label$ is active and the evaluators have the same state as before. Although c_1 is still fulfilled, we would make the change as the ratings are below the defined thresholds of 0.60 (relevance) and 0.80 (security).

B. Lessons Learned

The practical application was performed by two of our internal researchers, as they had to manually observe the mobile devices. For our case study, we used a Samsung Google Nexus 10 running Android 5.1 and a Samsung Galaxy Tab (SM-P600) running Android 4.4.2. Both devices were added to the MDM solution and had to adhere to the company-specific security policies. We made several observations in our practical application, which we describe next.

Some sensors have uncertainties and inaccuracies in their measurements. In our scenario these are the location and the wireless sensors. We configured the wireless sensor to scan for specific wireless networks every five minutes and prevented the user from disabling by setting the *keepEnabled* flag. However, the sensor occasionally misses some wireless networks although the networks are available. If we measure for a specific wireless network ten times, the sensor will miss this specific network one to two times. Hence, we have a failure rate of 10 to 20 percent in our measurements. Let us assume our context "work" c_1 is fulfilled and $work1\_label$ is active as well as $work2\_label$ is active. The affected wireless evaluators are e_1, e_2, e_3. All other evaluators are assumed to be fulfilled, i.e., working correctly. As they are in OR-relation (cf. Figure 9), all three have to provide a wrong measurement to yield an overall evaluation result of c_1 that is wrong, which did not happen during our evaluation period. Evaluator e_2 has the highest impact on the relevance and security ratings. If the evaluation of e_2 fails, the relevance rating is at 0.81 and the security rating is at 0.86. Both ratings are above the specified thresholds to trigger a state change for the labels $work1\_label$ and $work2\_label$. The failure of an additional wireless evaluator, for instance e_1 or e_3, puts the ratings to 0.65 (relevance) and 0.73 (security), which are below the thresholds. Such ratings result in a change of $work1\_label$ from active to inactive, which is uncritical as it tightens our security settings. Regarding $work2\_label$, we will stay in the active state, as the overall context c_1 is still true, which is also uncritical. To trigger a state change, we would need all three evaluators to fail, which did not happen during our evaluation period, as already mentioned.

Regarding the location evaluation, we observed that we have some uncertainties in the location evaluation of e_6 and e_7 when people are entering the specified locations. Such location changes usually happened in the morning, when people arrived at work, and after noon, when people came back from lunch outside the company. The reason for detection failures is the inaccurate location fix after a location change. The Android location services return a coarse grained location, which is outside our specified locations for the evaluators. Let us assume our context "work" c_1 is not fulfilled and $work1\_label$ is inactive as well as $work2\_label$ is inactive. The affected wireless evaluators are e_6, e_7. All other evaluators are assumed to be fulfilled, i.e., to work correctly. To trigger a state change, both evaluators have to be evaluated to true. Regarding $work1\_label$, it is uncritical as we are remaining in the high security settings; however, $work2\_label$ is critical. As we configured to receive a location fix latest every five minutes and after location changes greater than fifteen meters, we may stay five to ten minutes in a wrong state. However, as the Android location services pushes new information after the location fix, we observed to stay less than five minutes in the wrong state.

We modeled all evaluator groups in AND-relation, which was a bad decision regarding the time and calendar evaluators. As the working hours was given between 09:00am and 04:00pm, e_5 was also configured to be true in the specified interval. However, people usually do not completely stick to these working hours. We observed that $work1\_label$ stayed too long in state inactive (starting working before 09:00am) or changed from active to inactive too early (working longer than 04:00pm). Similar observations were made for the calendar evaluator e_4. We learned to model evaluators with lower relevance in an OR-relation rather than in an AND-relation. However, we have to gain more experience to make a final decision.

Overall, we conclude that our approach is feasible to adapt security settings provided by the MDM solution in our given scenario. Future work has to analyze the performance, focusing on the latency between the context detection and the effective enforcement of the security settings on the mobile device.

V. Experimental Evaluation

In our practical application, we evaluated our approach in a company setting. However, we run tests with two researchers in our premises and were not allowed to monitor the behavior in the company. In addition, our researchers did not use the mobile devices for their daily work. Hence, we did not evaluate the correctness of the context detection.

We started another experiment to evaluate precision and recall of our context detection in a real world setting. The following steps have been performed:

- **Preparation 1 - Data Collection:** Automated collection of contextual data and manual reporting of user activities and situations. This data is required for the context description generation.
- **Preparation 2 - Context Description Generation:** Derivation of context descriptions by using the process depicted in Figure 7. The derived context descriptions are used for the real world context detection.
- **Execution - Real World Context Detection:** Detection of context by using the generated context descriptions to adapt mobile device behavior (for convenient and security reasons) in a real world application.
- **Analysis & Discussion:** Analysis of the reported context detections with respect to precision and recall.

A. Preparation 1 - Data Collection

We first performed some data collection experiment before our actual evaluation experiment. In our first experiment, seven voluntary participants collected their contextual real-life data over a period of four weeks. The collection has two main parts: Subjects manually report their activities and situations in a context journal. Concurrently, mobile devices automatically collect contextual information from different sources; for example, physical sources such as built-in sensors (e.g., accelerometer, wireless networks) and virtual sources such as calendar entries.

For data collection, we use a mobile application, the funf framework [9]. The funf team implemented the application for sensing and processing contextual information on smart mobile devices. We use the "funf Journal" app from Google's PlayStore [10]. It allows a flexible sensing, processing, and storing of contextual information. We can configure the mobile application to collect data from different context information sources. The mobile app allows flexible scheduling based on time constraints and configurable triggers. Funf supports 38 different context information sources for data collection, so-called probes. Funf divides them into the following categories: device, device interaction, environment, motion, positioning, and social. After configuring and starting the funf application, it autonomously collects data as background process and stores the results in a SQLite database on the mobile device. The user can export the database to the local file system or upload the data to a server. Overall, we configured fourteen different sensors that collected about 110 million data entries in four weeks.

Besides raw context data, we also need information about the current activity/situation, in which the subject acts during the measurements for determining the relation between raw sensor data and user activities/device situations. Hence, our participants manually report their perceived context during the data collection phase in a context journal. The participants reported their activities paper-based or using the mobile application "Gleeo Time Tracker" [11].

During the automated context data collection, the participants are also reporting their activities. We tell the participants to check whether there are still active activities when they report a new activity. This is only important for the reporting on paper as the Gleeo Time Tracker app automatically stops running tasks when the user starts another task. Overall, the participants manually reported 65 different activities and situations during the measurement. Most of the activities occurred only a few times and could not be used in our process, as we are using statistical methods to calculate the correlation between contextual information and activities/situations. The three most relevant contexts for our experiment and further evaluation are "home", "work" and "sleeping".

B. Preparation 2 - Context Description Generation

In this step, the contextual and the journal data are fed to the derivation process to produce context descriptions. To determine the correlation, we choose binary correlation as statistical method. The method produces a correlation matrix considering all variables. Figure 11 shows binary correlations of reported activities followed by wireless networks. The values range from -1, denoting maximal anti-correlation, to +1, denoting maximal correlation. For instance, we take the first line with the activity "Office (Work)", which has a high correlation with "X" (0.87) and "WLAN mab" (0.94). Contrary, "Office (Work)" has a high anti-correlation with "Home (Private)" (-0.76) and "Cherrynetz" (-0.69). The anti-correlation between the two activities "Home (Private)" and "Office (Work)" is an obvious result.

	Office (Work)	Out of the Office Meeting (Work)	Travel (Work)	Home (Private)	Visiting Friends (Private)	X	AGSE	AndroidAP	BOLD PC_Network	Cherrynetz	ChriSim	WLAN mab
Office (Work)	1,00	-0,05	-0,03	-0,76	-0,08	0,87	-0,05	-0,04	-0,23	-0,69	-0,37	0,94
Out of Office Meeting (Work)	-0,05	1,00	0,00	-0,10	-0,01	0,12	0,77	0,00	-0,03	-0,09	-0,05	-0,05
Travel (Work)	-0,03	0,00	1,00	-0,06	-0,01	0,08	0,17	0,00	-0,02	-0,06	-0,03	0,01
Home (Private)	-0,76	-0,10	-0,06	1,00	-0,18	-0,78	-0,12	0,03	0,29	0,76	0,33	-0,76
Visiting Friends (Private)	-0,08	-0,01	-0,01	-0,18	1,00	-0,09	-0,01	0,04	-0,05	-0,16	-0,08	-0,08
X	0,87	0,12	0,08	-0,78	-0,09	1,00	0,14	0,08	-0,25	-0,73	-0,39	0,92
AGSE	-0,05	0,77	0,17	-0,12	-0,01	0,14	1,00	-0,01	-0,04	-0,11	-0,06	-0,05
AndroidAP	-0,04	0,00	0,00	0,03	0,04	0,08	-0,01	1,00	-0,03	-0,08	-0,04	-0,04
BOLD PC_Network	-0,23	-0,03	-0,02	0,29	-0,05	-0,25	-0,04	-0,03	1,00	0,33	0,09	-0,23
Cherrynetz	-0,69	-0,09	-0,06	0,76	-0,16	-0,73	-0,11	-0,08	0,33	1,00	0,52	-0,69
ChriSim	-0,37	-0,05	-0,03	0,33	-0,08	-0,39	-0,06	-0,04	0,09	0,52	1,00	-0,37
WLAN mab	0,94	-0,05	0,01	-0,76	-0,08	0,92	-0,05	-0,04	-0,23	-0,69	-0,37	1,00

Figure 11. Correlation Matrix (Binary Correlation)

The correlation matrix is used to generate operative context descriptions for the three relevant contexts: "home", "work" and "sleeping". In general, the generation process can optimize the produced context descriptions in terms of precision and recall. Precision is the relation of true positives to true positives and false positives. It denotes that if our context test detects a specific context, it will be correct or not. Contrary, recall is the relation of true positives to true positives and false negatives. It denotes that if a context is happening in the real world, our test will detect it. For our evaluation, we decided to choose context descriptions optimized in terms of precision for the transition $0 \rightarrow 1$. Hence, the precision should be high for detecting the entering into a specific context.

C. Execution - Real World Context Detection

In the actual experiment four voluntaries participated (out of the seven voluntaries for the first experiment). For these four participants, we take precision-optimized context descriptions to detect "home", "work", and "sleeping" (based on the data from the collection experiment). The voluntaries used the following private mobile devices to participate in the evaluation:

- Participant P1, Nexus 5 running Cyanogenmod 12.1
- Participant P2, Nexus 5 running stock ROM 4.4.4
- Participant P3, Nexus 4 running Cyanogenmod 12.1
- Participant P4, HTC One (M7) running Cyanogenmod 11

We equipped their private mobile devices with the Integrated Distributed Data Usage Control Enforcement (IND^{2}UCE) framework for Android [12] where the following features were used in our evaluation:

- **Device Administration:** The framework acts as device administrator for Android [13]. Hence, it supports device administration features such as changing security related settings, wiping, or locking the device, and disabling the camera.
- **Volume Control:** The framework supports controlling settings related to the volume control of the mobile device (i.e., setting the ringtone volume).
- **Captive Portal Login:** One extension addresses the automated login to a captive portal for granting access to the internet (without having to manually login via a webpage)
- **Network Settings:** We are able to control network settings with the framework. A simple example is the activation or deactivation of Bluetooth or Wifi.

We created policies for the IND^{2}UCE framework to react on context changes. Hence, we created a security policy for every possible context transition:

- Context was not fulfilled and is now fulfilled: $0 \rightarrow 1$-Transition
- Context was fulfilled and is now not fulfilled: $1 \rightarrow 0$-Transition

Such a context transition is modeled as depicted in Figure 12. The condition is checked every five minutes, as configured in the *timestep*-tag. In the condition, we resolve the actual context by using a so-called Policy Information Point (PIP) with the name "context". As parameter, we add the context id, which is "P1_home" in our case for participant P1. We link this request with a *before*-operator by using a logical *and*. Within the *before*-operator, we have a negated PIP request with the same parameters as our first one. To sum it up, if the first PIP request is now true and the second PIP request has been false in the timestep before, the condition will be true. Hence, we can phrase it as follows: We had a context change for the context "P1_home" from being not fulfilled to being fulfilled within the last five minutes.

We had two meetings with the participants to elicit convenient and security functions, they wanted to have depending on their current context. The focus was set to the three contexts: "home", "work", and "sleeping". Hence, every participant stated wanted behavior when, for instance, she is coming home or leaving home. Here are some examples we elicited:

- "When I am leaving Fraunhofer IESE [work], I would like to set my ringtone volume to 100%."
- "When I am at Fraunhofer IESE [work], I would like to set my ringtone volume to 20%."
- "When I am at home, I would like to activate the Wifi."

```
<timestep amount="5" unit="MINUTES" />
<condition>
 <and>
  <pip:boolean name="context" default="true">
   <param:string name="value" value="P1_home" />
  </pip:boolean>
  <before amount="1" unit="TIMESTEPS">
   <not>
    <pip:boolean name="context" default="true">
     <param:string name="value" value="P1_home" />
    </pip:boolean>
   </not>
  </before>
 </and>
</condition>
```

Figure 12. Transition Example for $0 \rightarrow 1$-Transition for Context "P1_home"

- "When I am not at home and not at work, I would like to deactivate the Wifi."
- "When I am at home, in my bedroom, and the time is between 10pm - 7am, then activate FlightMode."
- "When I am leaving my home, I would like to set my ringtone volume to 100%."

We elicited 29 rules to be applied based on the context detection. However, we are only able to fulfill the requirements of 20 rules with the IND^{2}UCE framework.

```
<detectiveMechanism name="home_0->1">
  <description>
  Context change from false to true
  </description>
  <timestep amount="5" unit="MINUTES" />
  <condition>
   <and>
    <pip:boolean name="context" default="true">
     <param:string name="value" value="P1_home" />
    </pip:boolean>
    <before amount="1" unit="TIMESTEPS">
     <not>
      <pip:boolean name="context" default="true">
       <param:string name="value" value="P1_home" />
      </pip:boolean>
     </not>
    </before>
   </and>
  </condition>
  <!-- setRingToneVolume to 50% -->
  <executeAction name="urn:action:local:volume">
   <param:int name="level" value="3"/>
  </executeAction>
  <!-- setDisplayTimeout to 30min -->
  <executeAction name="urn:action:local:SecuritySettings">
   <param:int name="display" value="30"/>
  </executeAction>
  <!-- feedback for context change -->
  <executeAction name="urn:action:local:feedback">
   <param:string name="mode" value="context" />
   <param:string name="value" value="P1_home" />
   <param:string name="flag" value="1" />
  </executeAction>
 </detectiveMechanism>
```

Figure 13. Policy Mechanism Example for $0 \rightarrow 1$-Transition for Context "P1_home"

We created for every participant appropriate rules, which we call policies in the IND^{2}UCE framework. Figure 13 illustrates a policy for the handling of the $0 \rightarrow 1$-Transition for context "P1_home". In other words, it handles what will happen when the participant is coming home. There are four execute actions to be performed by the IND^{2}UCE framework: First, the framework will set the ringtone volume to about 50%, which is done by the execute action "volume". Second, IND^{2}UCE sets the display timeout to 30 minutes by performing the execute action "SecuritySettings". Third, we will trigger our feedback app. When the feedback app is triggered in mode "context", it displays a sticky notification to the user and possibilities for the user to confirm or reject (cf. Figure 14):

Verify context detection 15:25
"*atWork*" is now active
Yes / No

A "yes"-button means, the context detection was right and the user confirms the correctness. By clicking on the "yes"-button, we count the context detection as correct. A "no"-button means, the context detection was wrong and the user is forwarded to a list of already recorded other contexts. If the context is not in the list, the user can add a new context. We count the context detection as wrong and add a new entry to the table with the context entered by the user. Doing so, we are capable to count all true positive and false positive context detections and can easily calculate the precision of the context detection.

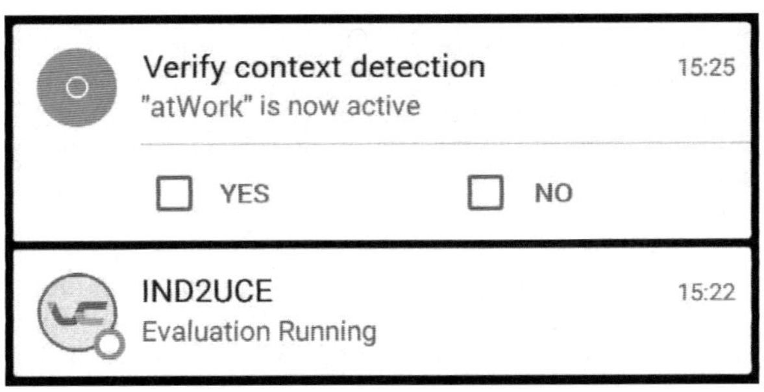

Figure 14. Context Check PXP: Notification

If the user misses to process the notification, we store all information in a list of unanswered context detection entries (see Figure 15). The user has the possibility to answer the questions later. By clicking on the "yes"-button or "no"-button, the app behaves as in the notification interaction.

We conducted the experiment over a period of two weeks, in which the participants had their usual working times (no vacation, no business trips, etc.). Unfortunately, we experienced technical difficulties for one participant and had to continue the experiment without him. For the three other participants, everything worked as expected.

D. Analysis & Discussion

The participants reported 243 context detections in two weeks, which results in about six context detections per day (in average). This is a plausible value, as it can be seen in the following reported feedback schedule of one of the participants (counting eight context detections):

However, the feedback occurrence distribution is 96 for P1, 44 for P2, and 103 for P3. P1 and P3 are nearly equal, P2 has much less context changes detections. There are two explanations for this behavior: First, P2 usually stays at work for having lunch and is not leaving the institute. Second, there are less changes for the context "home" in contrast to the other two participants.

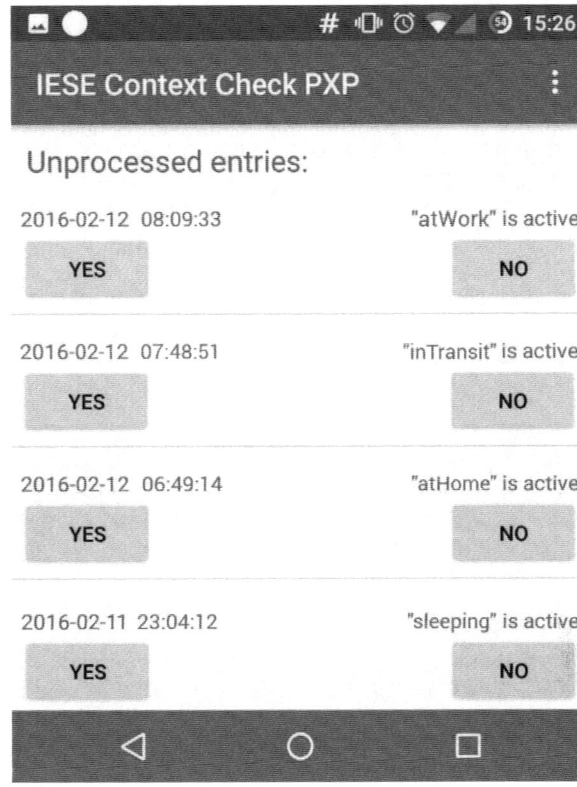

Figure 15. Context Check PXP: Unprocessed Entries

TABLE III. Excerpt of Feedback Result

No.	Time	Context	Transition	Description
1	15.10.2015 07:08	sleeping	$1 \to 0$	waking up
2	15.10.2015 08:06	home	$1 \to 0$	leaving home
3	15.10.2015 08:38	work	$0 \to 1$	entering work
4	15.10.2015 11:58	work	$1 \to 0$	leaving work (e.g., lunch)
5	15.10.2015 12:36	work	$0 \to 1$	entering work
6	15.10.2015 16:41	work	$1 \to 0$	leaving work
7	15.10.2015 17:47	home	$0 \to 1$	entering home
8	15.10.2015 22:57	sleeping	$0 \to 1$	sleeping

Table IV illustrates the overall result of the context detection for every participant. The first identifies the participant. The second and third column represents whether the context detection was reported as correct or wrong. The fourth and last column indicates the user input, if the context detection was wrong. As shown in the table, participant P1 and P2 always corrected the context detection, participant P3 missed it two times.

TABLE IV. Context Detection Results

Participant	Context Change Detected		
	Correct	Wrong	User Input
P1	53 (55.21%)	43 (44.79%)	43
P2	32 (72.73%)	12 (27.27%)	12
P3	76 (72.38%)	29 (27.62%)	29

The correctness of the context detection is between 55.21% and 72.73%. The result is not very convincing for being used in security related settings. However, the figures represent the overall correctness of the context detection. As we created precision-optimized context descriptions for the $0 \rightarrow 1$-transitions, we have to split up the data. The result is presented in Table V.

TABLE V. Context Detection Result (split)

Part.	Context Change Detected ($0 \rightarrow 1$)			Context Change Detected ($1 \rightarrow 0$)		
	Correct	Wrong	Sum	Correct	Wrong	Sum
P1	44 (95.65%)	2 (4.35%)	46	9 (18.00%)	41 (82.00%)	50
P2	18 (100.0%)	0 (0.0%)	18	14 (53.85%)	12 (46.15%)	26
P3	51 (98.15%)	1 (1.85%)	54	23 (45.10%)	28 (54.90%)	51

Now, we get a much better result regarding context detection precision for the $0 \rightarrow 1$-transitions. All values are above 95%, which fulfills our expectations. Moreover, we made no error for participant P2 and reached 100%. From our expectations, this is a good result and such context descriptions could be used to ease security mechanisms.

However, the precision for the context detection for the $1 \rightarrow 0$-transitions ranges from 18% to nearly 55%. In other words, the context detection would be wrong for every second detection in best case. This result cannot be used to adapt security mechanisms with high precision. We could improve the precision by either adapting the parameters for the hysteresis behavior (cf. Section IV) or using precision-optimized context descriptions also for the $1 \rightarrow 0$-transitions.

Obviously, there is a trade-off between these two kinds of context changes and we managed to optimize our context detection only in one direction (i.e., $0 \rightarrow 1$-transitions). Hence, we achieved a high precision for easing security mechanisms, but allow lower precision for tightening security mechanisms. In addition, we have to achieve a higher recall rather than having a high precision for tightening security mechanisms. Regarding the recall of our approach, we cannot provide reliable figures for this calculation as we have not monitored the real world behavior. Hence, we do not know how often or long the user was already in the specific context, but the context detection did not recognize.

VI. Related Work

This section provides an overview of the state of the art in context-awareness and context-aware computing. More specifically, the term *context* and its early definitions are introduced and different context modeling approaches are described.

A. Definitions of the term "Context"

The notion of *context* emerged over time, the earliest definitions in our sense originate in the early nineties. All of them share similarities, but they also show differences. We will present the most prevalent and influential definitions.

In 1994, an early definition was provided by Schilit et al. [3], stating that a context is characterized by three aspects: where you are, whom you are with, and what resources are nearby. Therefore, Schilit et al. infer that context-aware systems have to depend on the location of use, nearby people, hosts, and accessible devices, as well as on changes over time. Although they state that context is more than just location, location is apparently a very important information source for context-aware systems. Interestingly, although smart mobile devices did not nearly have the same capabilities in 1994 as today's devices have (especially the plethora of sensors), the authors already named today's sensors (e.g., light intensity, network connectivity) as additional context sources.

In 1997, Brown and Bovey [14] describe context similar to Schilit et al. but include temporal attributes, such as time of day, season, and temperature, as additional contextual information sources. In addition, the authors propose to enrich context by using additional (user-provided) information to obtain more valuable information for their application.

Hull et al. [15] describe context as "many aspects of a user's situation", such as "user identity, location, companions, vital signs, air quality, and network availability". Franklin and Flachsbart [16] focus on intelligent environments observing their users. They state that context-aware computing should consider the observed situation of the user. A similar description can be found in [17]. Ryan et al. [18] state that context should include location as well as states of external and internal sensors of the computer itself. Hence, they also consider virtual context sources such as the state of the software running on the device. Pascoe [19] also considers virtual context sources, but describes them as the states of the application and its environment rather than states of the computer itself. Pascoe et al. [20] reveal the more rich and complex nature of context and that context can be complex. Furthermore, in accordance with other publications, they state that context is more than just location.

In 1999, Abowd et al. [21] define context as any information that is used to characterize the situation of an entity. As mentioned in other publications, context is seen as additional information or as an attribute of an entity. They also state that context information has to be categorized in different context types, which makes it easier for context-aware computing. They introduce four primary context types for characterizing an entity's situation: location, identity, time, and activity.

Hofer et al. [6] partition context information regarding its origin and differentiate between physical, virtual, and logical context information. Physical context information, such as location, acceleration or light intensity, can directly be measured by sensors. Such physical measures are described as low-level context sources that are continuously updated. Virtual information stems from user data or internal system data. The latter context category, logical context information, is obtained by combining physical and virtual context sources according to some abstract logical rules.

B. Modeling Context Information

Context-aware systems strongly rely on the quality of the context information, which is usually represented in a context model. The modeling and provision of context information is very important to fulfill the desired task. In this work, context awareness aims at the enforcement and adaptation of flexible security policies on the mobile device and its applications. Different approaches for modeling context information have been suggested. In [22] and [23], the authors survey the most relevant approaches and classify them into five categories:

Key-Value Models are the simplest model for structuring context information. As such models provide no structuring of information, they are easy to manage. They are often used, although they provide only limited support for more sophisticated modeling [22][23]. Key-Value models allow easy querying by simple algorithms matching the key value pairs. The querying can be enriched by Boolean operators or wildcards for the matching algorithm.

Markup Scheme Models use a hierarchical structure of markup tags containing attributes and their values. A well-known example is the eXtensible Markup Language (XML). A markup scheme has been proposed, for instance, in [24]. In contrast to key-value models, markup scheme models provide a mechanism for structuring context information. However, querying such models becomes more complex than in the simple key-value model, but is essentially done similarly by matching the values of the markup tags or their attributes. In [25], Samulowitz et al. define "Context-Aware Packets (CAPs)" for storing context information. CAPs are organized in "context constraints, scripting, and data", where the context constraints part contains the modeled context information. This sub part is in turn subdivided into "abstract entities, relations, and events". Figure 16 illustrates a CAP example taken from [25]. The given CAP describes two entities (i.e., Printer and Florian) and a relation "inRoom" between the two entities. The relation describes the context "ContextC".

```
...
<CAP name="printing_locally" from="Florian"
put_to="Printer" duration="one-shot">

<ContextC>

  <Entity type="abstractDevice" name="Printer">
        <attrib lextype="colors">greyscale</attrib>
        <attrib lextype="papersize">a4</attrib>
        ...
        <interface>
         <put name="lpr">
          <param lextype="lpr_filter">no</param>
          <param lextype="MIMEtype">
                  stream/postscript
          </param>
           ...
         </put>
      </interface>

</Entity>

<Entity type="Person" name="Florian">
     <attrib lextype="date">02.02.2001 13:45</attrib>
     <attrib lextype="role">guest</attrib>
     ...
</Entity>

<Relation name="inRoom">
     <arg>Florian</arg>
     <arg>Printer</arg>
</Relation>

</ContextC>

<Data type="application/postscript">
  <![CDATA[ %!PS-Adobe-2.0
   ...  ]]>
</Data>

<Scripting>future use</Scripting>

</CAP>
```

Figure 16. Context-Aware Packets Example from [25]

Graphical Models can strongly vary in their representation. The best-known representative is probably the Unified Modeling Language (UML), which is also suitable for modeling context, as shown in [26] or [27]. Such models are easy to understand for human beings, but often lack formality.

Henricksen et al. [28] present a context extension for the Object-Role Modeling (ORM) approach, which describes context as collection of facts (as shown in Figure 17).

The model can directly be used to derive an entity relationship model as a basic structure for relational databases. An interesting aspect of their model is the differentiation between static context information (i.e., facts that remain unchanged as long as the entities they describe persist) and dynamic context information. They distinguish between contextual information that can be treated as property or constant attribute and changing contextual information such as location.

Object Oriented Models provide their information as a collection of objects that contain context information. Such models can employ all object-oriented modeling techniques

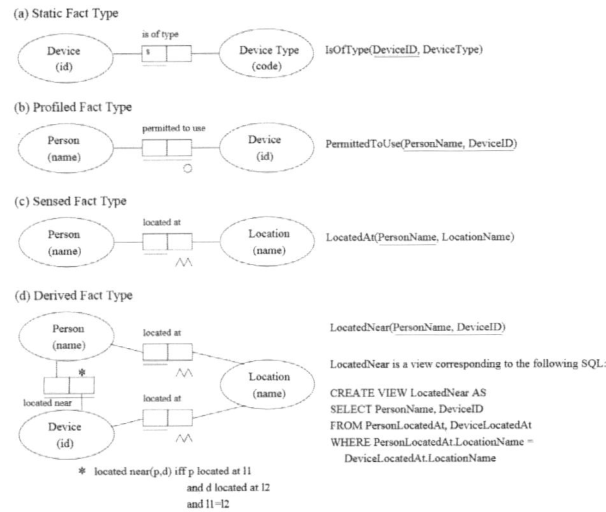

Figure 17. Excerpt from Context Extension for the Object-Role Modeling approach [28]

such as encapsulation, reuse, or inheritance. The objects can represent different context types and provide interfaces for the retrieval and processing of their context information. Hofer et al. used such object oriented models for the Hydrogen context framework [6].

In 2002, Henricksen et al. [29] presented an object-oriented approach which is the predecessor to their extension for the ORM approach. They already have a graphical representation, as depicted in Figure 18. Henricksen et al. use classifications for context modeling, such as "static" (i.e., "remain fixed over the lifetime of the entity") or "dynamic" associations. They split the dynamic associations into "sensed", "derived", and "profiled".

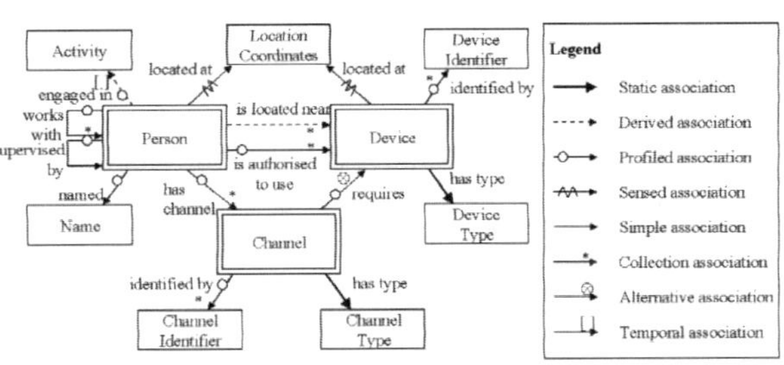

Figure 18. Example for an Object Oriented Context Model taken from [29]

Logic Based Models use formal methods to specify context information and rules that can be applied to them. Hence, they usually provide a high degree of formality. Typically, in the reasoning process new facts can be derived based on known facts and a given set of deduction rules. Albeit being very formal and precise, profound logic-based modeling is quite hard and modeling given facts can become very complex. One such approach has been published in 1994 by McCarthy and Buvac [30].

Ontology Based Models are used to represent concepts and interrelations. They are a very promising instrument for context modeling, especially with the option to apply ontology reasoning techniques and automatic derivation of new relationships. A representative of this class of models is the Aspect-Scale-Context (ASC) model (shown in Figure 19), which is based on the Context Ontology Language proposed by Strang et al. [31]. According to this model, an *Aspect* has one or more *Scales*, and a *Scale* has one or more *ContextInformation* items. These model elements are "interrelated via *hasAspect*, *hasScale* and *constructuredBy* relations" [31].

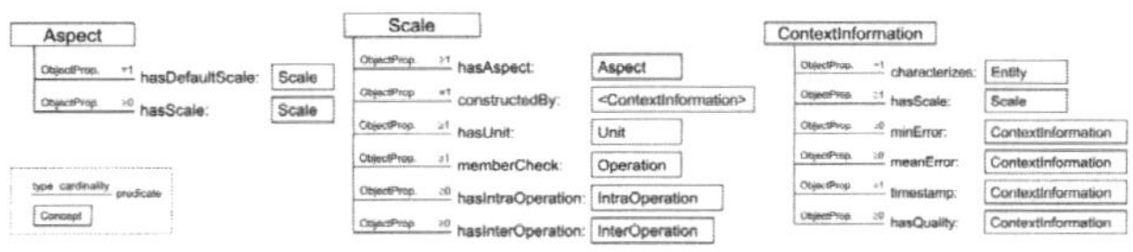

Figure 19. Example for an Ontology Based Context Model taken from [31]

For further details, the reader is referred to two surveys: Baldauf et al. [23] survey existing context systems and frameworks, including their respective context models. Another survey by Bettini et al. [32] describes the state of the art in context modeling and reasoning. In summary, the decision which kind of modeling approach to choose can only be made by investigating the underlying application scenario and the context to be modeled. Regardless of the presented approaches, none of them consider the uncertainty in context detection and are thus unsuited for security purposes.

In our work, we use a combination of the presented context modeling approaches (hybrid approaches) and extend them with two quality attributes to deal with uncertainty. The introduced quality attributes improves the context detection to be reliable and secure. Hence, our approach is also suited for security purposes and can improve security decisions.

C. *Context-awareness Enhancing Mobile Device Security*

There exist several frameworks for enhancing systems and especially Android with context awareness. We will provide an overview by presenting solutions especially for enhancing mobile device security.

Context-Related Policy Enforcement (CRePE), developed by Conti et al. [33], is a context-aware framework that enhances mobile device security. The approach is to hook into Android's permission checking mechanism and to take dynamic security decisions based on context information. Moreover, CRePE may perform different actions (e.g., system shutdown) specified in the user-definable policies. To enable dynamic permission checks, CRePE makes modifications to the Android system. The context check is done in the *PolicyManager* component that interacts with the *CRePE PermissionChecker* and the *ActionPerformer* component (see Figure 20).

CRePE offers no context model. However, Conti et al. define policies that include rules and context information (only location). In addition, priorities for rules and the handling of conflicts are described in [33].

CRePE improves security of the Android system by making permission checks context-aware, and it adds additional context-aware features, such as actions controlled by policies.

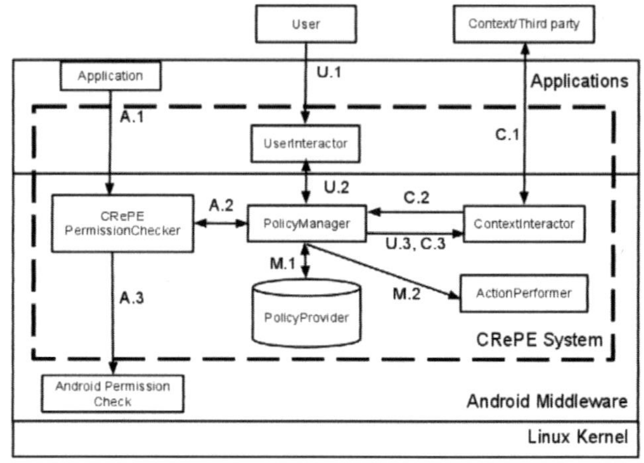

Figure 20. CRePE Architecture [33]

Context-Aware Usage Control for Android (ConUCON) by Bai et al. [34] is an extension of the UCON model [35] for Android. The framework consists of different components such as Policy Enforcement Point (PEP), Policy Decision Point (PDP), Policy Information Point (PIP) and a Policy Administration Point (PAP), as depicted in Figure 21. The components and their behavior relates to XACML [36], which is a standard describing declarative access control policies and a processing model for it.

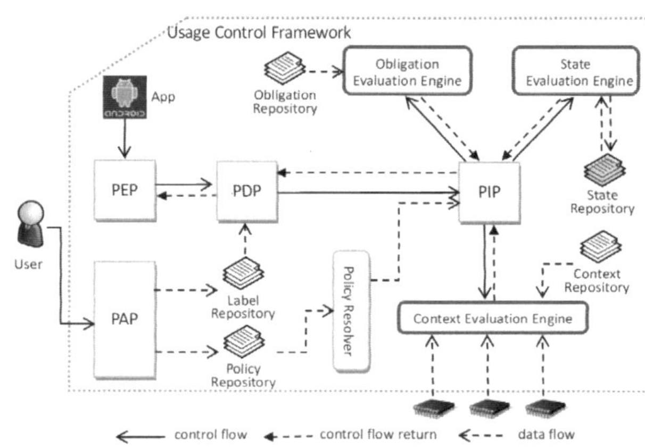

Figure 21. ConUCON Framework [34]

Contexts are part of these policies and are specified by using the tags *Context*, *ContextComposition*, and *Factor*. A context constraint is broken down into different *ContextCompositions*, which are always connected with a Boolean $\wedge$. The composition defines a logical operator (i.e., $\wedge$, $\vee$, $\neg$), which is used to aggregate the subordinated factor-tags. Finally, a factor specifies the context information such as time, battery, or Wifi state. A factor can have complex expressions such as "batteryPower $\geq$ 30%" or periodic expressions (cf. [34]). The model used can be described as Boolean logic with expressions. ConUCON also improves security of the Android system by using context-aware usage control policies.

Similar to our work, CRePE [33] and the ConUCON system [34] provide a technical solution to use context information to enhance security of mobile devices. However, CRePE uses only location as context information. Contrary to our approach, they do not address reliability and security of the context detection. In addition, they cannot deal with uncertainty of context information.

VII. Conclusion and Future Work

We presented a model for representing security-relevant contexts as context descriptions. The model contains a security rating for each evaluator to quantify the overall trustworthiness of the context description during runtime. In addition, the model provides a relevance rating expressing the conduciveness of a context information source to the overall context. The context descriptions enable context-aware security decisions by referencing them as a decision criterion in security policies.

We applied the context detection mechanism in an industrial scenario and showed its general applicability. The Mobile Device Management (MDM) solution can be enriched with contextual information to improve its decision making. We have taken some lessons learned from this industrial application, which we used to improve the generation of our context description.

In a second evaluation, we used the context-aware IND^{2}UCE framework for Android to analyze the improvement in context detection. The overall correctness of our context detection ranges from 55% to nearly 73%. But, the precision optimized context descriptions for the $0 \rightarrow 1$-transitions reached a correctness of 100% for one participant (best case) and nearly 96% for the participant with worst results. These values fulfilled our expectations and they are promising for being used in security related settings. However, the generalizability has to be shown in future work.

Future work will investigate potentials to return additional data types as an overall context result. Enriched context types facilitate the use of contextual information in the decision making process and improve expressiveness for security policy specifications. Presently, context descriptions are specified manually before being activated and are therefore rather static. Future work will investigate how context descriptions can be parametrized at runtime. This may include the use of context results as parameters for other context descriptions.

Regarding the security and relevance rating, we will further extend our evaluation criteria. We realized that faking the presence of contextual information can be easier in some cases then faking its absence (e.g., it is easier to simulate the SSID of a wireless access point than jamming the beacons from an existing one). Finally, we will explore the inclusion of accuracy information into our model as an additional quality attribute for judging the reliability of context information.

Acknowledgment

This paper is a result of the Software Campus project KoSiUX (Kontextsensitivität zur Steigerung der Sicherheit und User-Experience mobiler Anwendungen), which is funded by the German Ministry of Education and Research, grant number 01IS12053, and the European project SECCRIT, funded by the European Commission in the context of the Research Framework Program Seven (FP7), grant agreement number 312758. The authors are responsible for their content.

References

[1] C. Jung, A. Eitel, D. Feth, and M. Rudolph, "Dealing with uncertainty in context-aware mobile applications," in MOBILITY 2015: The Fifth International Conference on Mobile Services, Resources, and Users, June 2015, pp. 1–7.

[2] S. I. A. Shah, M. Ilyas, and H. T. Mouftah, Pervasive Communications Handbook, 1st ed. Boca Raton, FL, USA: CRC Press, Inc., 2011.

[3] B. Schilit, N. Adams, and R. Want, "Context-aware computing applications," in Proceedings of the Workshop on Mobile Computing Systems and Applications. IEEE Computer Society, 1994, pp. 85–90.

[4] Óscar D. Lara and M. A. Labrador, "A survey on human activity recognition using wearable sensors," Communications Surveys Tutorials, IEEE, vol. 15, no. 3, Third 2013, pp. 1192–1209.

[5] S. Wang and G. Zhou, "A review on radio based activity recognition," Digital Communications and Networks, vol. 1, no. 1, 2015, pp. 20 – 29. [Online]. Available: http://www.sciencedirect.com/science/article/pii/S2352864815000115

[6] T. Hofer, W. Schwinger, M. Pichler, G. Leonhartsberger, J. Altmann, and W. Retschitzegger, "Context-awareness on mobile devices - the hydrogen approach," in Proceedings of the 36th Annual Hawaii International Conference on System Sciences (HICSS'03) - Track 9 - Volume 9, ser. HICSS '03. Washington, DC, USA: IEEE Computer Society, 2003, p. 292.1.

[7] Android Developers. Location Strategies. http://developer.android.com/. [Online]. Available: https://developer.android.com/guide/topics/location/strategies.html [retrieved: May, 2016]

[8] C. Jung, D. Feth, and Y. Elrakaiby, "Automatic derivation of context descriptions," in 2015 IEEE International Inter-Disciplinary Conference on Cognitive Methods in Situation Awareness and Decision Support (CogSIMA), March 2015, pp. 70–76.

[9] MIT Media Labs. funf Open Sensing Framework. http://funf.org/. [Online]. Available: http://funf.org/developers.html [retrieved: January, 2016]

[10] funf.org. Funf journal. https://play.google.com/store/apps/. [Online]. Available: https://play.google.com/store/apps/details?id=edu.mit.media.funf.journal [retrieved: January, 2016]

[11] Gridvision Engineering GmbH. Gleeo time tracker. https://play.google.com/store/apps/. [Online]. Available: https://play.google.com/store/apps/details?id=ch.gridvision.pbtm.androidtimerecorder [retrieved: January, 2016]

[12] C. Jung, D. Feth, and C. Seise, "Context-aware policy enforcement for android," in Software Security and Reliability (SERE), 2013 IEEE 7th International Conference on, June 2013, pp. 40–49.

[13] Android Developers. Device Administration. http://developer.android.com/. [Online]. Available: http://developer.android.com/guide/topics/admin/device-admin.html [retrieved: January, 2016]

[14] P. Brown and J. Bovey, "Context-aware applications: from the laboratory to the marketplace," IEEE Personal Communications, vol. 4, no. 5, 1997, pp. 58–64.

[15] R. Hull, P. Neaves, and J. Bedford-Roberts, "Towards situated computing," in Proceedings of the 1st IEEE International Symposium on Wearable Computers, ser. ISWC '97. Washington, DC, USA: IEEE Computer Society, 1997, pp. 146–153.

[16] D. Franklin and J. Flachsbart, "All gadget and no representation makes jack a dull environment," In Proceedings of AAAI 1998 Spring Symposium on Intelligent Environments. AAAI TR SS-98-02, 1998, pp. 1–6.

[17] A. Ward, A. Jones, and A. Hopper, "A new location technique for the active office," Personal Communications, IEEE, vol. 4, no. 5, 1997, pp. 42–47.

[18] N. S. Ryan, J. Pascoe, and D. R. Morse, "Enhanced reality fieldwork: the context-aware archaeological assistant," in Computer Applications in Archaeology 1997, ser. British Archaeological Reports, V. Gaffney, M. van Leusen, and S. Exxon, Eds. Oxford: Tempus Reparatum, Oct. 1998, pp. 269–274.

[19] J. Pascoe, "Adding generic contextual capabilities to wearable computers," in Proceedings of the 2nd IEEE International Symposium on Wearable Computers, ser. ISWC '98. Washington, DC, USA: IEEE Computer Society, 1998, pp. 92–99.

[20] J. Pascoe, N. Ryan, and D. Morse, "Issues in developing context-aware computing," Handheld and ubiquitous computing, 1999, pp. 208–221.

[21] G. D. Abowd, A. K. Dey, P. J. Brown, N. Davies, M. Smith, and P. Steggles, "Towards a Better Understanding of Context and Context-Awareness," in HUC '99: Proceedings of the 1st international symposium on Handheld and Ubiquitous Computing. London, UK: Springer-Verlag, 1999, pp. 304–307.

[22] T. Strang and C. Linnhoff-Popien, "A Context Modeling Survey," in Workshop on Advanced Context Modelling, Reasoning and Management, UbiComp 2004 - The Sixth International Conference on Ubiquitous Computing, Nottingham/England, 2004, pp. 1–8.

[23] M. Baldauf, S. Dustdar, and F. Rosenberg, "A survey on context-aware systems," International Journal of Ad Hoc and Ubiquitous Computing, vol. 2, no. 4, June 2007, pp. 263–277.

[24] N. Ryan, "ConteXtML: Exchanging Contextual Information between a Mobile Client and the FieldNote Server," in Computing Laboratory, University of Kent at Canterbury, CT2 7NF, UK, August 1999, pp. 1–8.

[25] M. Samulowitz, F. Michahelles, and C. Linnhoff-Popien, "Capeus: An architecture for context-aware selection and execution of services," in New Developments in Distributed Applications and Interoperable Systems, ser. IFIP International Federation for Information Processing, K. Zieliński, K. Geihs, and A. Laurentowski, Eds. Springer US, 2002, vol. 70, pp. 23–39.

[26] Q. Z. Sheng and B. Benatallah, "Contextuml: A uml-based modeling language for model-driven development of context-aware web services development," in Proceedings of the International Conference on Mobile Business, ser. ICMB '05. Washington, DC, USA: IEEE Computer Society, 2005, pp. 206–212.

[27] J. Bauer, "Identification and modeling of contexts for different information scenarios in air traffic," 2003.

[28] K. Henricksen, J. Indulska, and A. Rakotonirainy, "Generating context management infrastructure from high-level context models," in In 4th International Conference on Mobile Data Management (MDM) - Industrial Track, 2003, pp. 1–6.

[29] K. Henricksen, J. Indulska, and A. Rakotonirainy, "Modeling context information in pervasive computing systems," in Proceedings of the First International Conference on Pervasive Computing, ser. Pervasive '02. London, UK, UK: Springer-Verlag, 2002, pp. 167–180.

[30] J. McCarthy and S. Buvac, "Formalizing context (expanded notes)," Computer Science Stanford University, Stanford, CA, USA, Tech. Rep., 1994.

[31] T. Strang, C. Linnhoff-Popien, and K. Frank, "Cool: A context ontology language to enable contextual interoperability," in LNCS 2893: Proceedings of 4th IFIP WG 6.1 International Conference on Distributed Applications and Interoperable Systems (DAIS2003). Volume 2893 of Lecture Notes in Computer Science (LNCS)., Paris/France. Springer Verlag, 2003, pp. 236–247.

[32] C. Bettini, O. Brdiczka, K. Henricksen, J. Indulska, D. Nicklas, A. Ranganathan, and D. Riboni, "A survey of context modelling and reasoning techniques," Pervasive and Mobile Computing, vol. 6, no. 2, 2010, pp. 161–180.

[33] M. Conti, V. T. N. Nguyen, and B. Crispo, "Crepe: context-related policy enforcement for android," in Proceedings of the 13th international conference on Information security, ser. ISC'10. Berlin, Heidelberg: Springer-Verlag, 2011, pp. 331–345. [Online]. Available: http://dl.acm.org/citation.cfm?id=1949317.1949355

[34] G. Bai, L. Gu, T. Feng, Y. Guo, and X. Chen, "Context-aware usage control for android," in SecureComm, 2010, pp. 326–343.

[35] J. Park and R. Sandhu, "The UCON ABC usage control model," ACM Trans. Inf. Syst. Secur., vol. 7, no. 1, February 2004, pp. 128–174.

[36] OASIS, "extensible access control markup language (xacml) version 3.0 - committee specification 01," http://docs.oasis-open.org/xacml/3.0/xacml-3.0-core-spec-cs-01-en.pdf, August 2010.

International Journal on Advances in Software, vol 9 no 1 & 2, year 2016, http://www.iariajournals.org/software/

A Software Application to Streamline and Enhance the Detection of Fraud in Published Financial Statements of Companies

Duarte Trigueiros
University of Macau, University Institute of Lisbon
Lisbon, Portugal
Email: dmt@iscte.pt

Carolina Sam
Master of European Studies Alumni Association
Macau, China
Email: kasm@customs.gov.mo

***Abstract*—Considerable effort has been devoted to the development of software to support the detection of fraud in published financial statements of companies. Until the present date, however, the applied use of such research has been extremely limited due to the "black box" character of the existing solutions and the cumbersome input task they require. The application described in this paper solves both problems while significantly improving performance. It is based on Web-mining and on the use of three Multilayer Perceptron where a modified learning method leads to the formation of meaningful internal representations. Such representations are then input to a features' map where trajectories towards or away from fraud and other financial attributes are identified. The result is a Web-based, self-explanatory, financial statements' fraud detection solution.**

Keywords–Fraud Detection; Financial Knowledge Discovery; Predictive Modelling of Financial Statements; Type of Information Mining.

I. INTRODUCTION

This paper describes a software solution to help detecting fraud in published financial statements. The objective is to streamline a widely researched but scarcely used application area. Parts of the paper were presented at the Fifth International Conference on Advances in Information Mining and Management (IMMM 2015) [1] as work-in-progress.

Fraud may cost US companies over USD 400 billion annually. Amongst different types of fraud, manipulation of published financial statements is paramount. In spite of measures put in place to detect fraudulent book-keeping, manipulation is still ongoing, probably on a huge scale [2].

Auditors are required to assess the plausibility of financial statements before they are made public. Auditors apply analytical procedures to inspect sets of transactions, which are the building blocks of financial statements. But detecting fraud internally is a difficult task as managers deliberately try to deceive auditors. Most frauds stem from the top levels of the organization where controls are least effective. The general belief is that internal procedures alone are rarely effective in detecting fraud [3].

In response to concerns about audit effectiveness in detecting fraud internally, quantitative techniques are being applied to the modelling of relationships underlying published statements' data with a view to discriminate between fraudulent and non-fraudulent cases [5]. Such external, *ex-post* approach would be valuable as a tool in the hands of users of published reports, such as investors, analysts and banks. Artificial Intelligence (AI) techniques are likewise being developed to the same end. Detailed review articles covering this research are available [6][7].

A discouraging fact is that analysts do not use tools designed to help detecting fraud in published reports. This is largely due to the fact that such tools are "black boxes" where results cannot be explained using their expertise [3]. Since analysts are responsible for their decisions, tools they may use to support decisions must be self-explanatory. Moreover, the required Extract, Transform and Load (ETL) tasks are time-consuming.

The paper aims at overcoming the above limitations. Web-mining is first employed to find, download and store data from published financial statements. Then fraud and two other attributes known to widen fraud propensity space are predicted by three Multilayer Perceptron (MLP) classifiers where a modified learning method leads to internal representations similar to financial ratios, readily interpretable by analysts. Such ratios then input a features' map where trajectories towards or away from fraud and other financial attributes are visualized. Diagnostic interpretation is further enhanced with the display of past cases where financial attributes are similar to those being analysed.

The most valuable contribution of the application described here is its strict adherence to users' requirements. The paper also offers a theoretical foundation for the prediction of financial attributes. Using such foundation, the paper then shows that it is possible to improve significantly the accuracy, robustness and balance of financial statements' fraud detection. Finally, the paper unveils an MLP training method leading to meaningful internal representations, which are capable of supporting analysts' financial diagnostic.

Section II characterizes the issue at hand, mentions previous research and lays down the foundations upon which the application is based; Section III describes the methodologies used; Section IV reports results and data used to obtain such results; Section V briefly describes the output and architecture of the application; finally, Section VI discusses limitations and benefits.

II. THEORETICAL FOUNDATIONS

Fraud detection covers many types of deception: plagiarism, credit card fraud, identity theft, medical prescription fraud, false insurance claim, insider trading, financial statements' manipulation and other types of fraud [8][9]. Conceptual frameworks used in the detection of, say, credit card fraud (such as Game Theory), are not necessarily efficient in detecting other types of fraud. Neural Networks are widely used in research devoted to the detection of published financial statements' fraud [10][11][12][13][14]. The latter citation contains an extensive and updated list of papers applying analytical AI algorithms, such as the nearest neighbour classifier, Back-propagation, the Support Vector machine and others, to the detection of financial statements' fraud and to other Financial Technology (Fin-Tech) tasks namely bankruptcy prediction.

It is pointless to compare accuracy results reported in the above-mentioned literature because samples used by authors to test such accuracy are extremely dissimilar, some being small and homogeneous while others are large and varied. Class frequencies are also imbalanced in one direction or in the other. Broadly, an out-of-sample overall classification accuracy of 65% to 75% is reported for large, non-homogeneous samples whereas for small, same-industry same-size samples, accuracy may be as high as 86% [14]. In all reported cases, accuracy is imbalanced: Type I and Type II errors differ by no less than 10% often being as high as 30% in both directions.

The increasing demand for Fin-Tech tools [15][16][17] has fostered the development of software to help detecting several types of fraud [18]. Tools which probe transactions for suspect patterns, as well as other internal auditing support software, are widely available but, as far as an exhaustive search may tell, the detection of fraud in published statements is not on offer, probably for the reasons already stated: "black boxes" fail to meet analysts' professional needs while the input task required by such tools would be cumbersome. Thus, evidence on published statements' fraud detection performance is the one summarized above. In any case, claims made by vendors, even when they exist, should not be taken as evidence, especially in areas, such as the wide and fast-growing Fin-Tech market, where products seldom are the object of scientific scrutiny.

Using large, non-homogeneous data and strictly balanced random sampling, the classification precision of the application described here is 87%–88% with an imbalance of 5%. Such result is indifferently attained when using Neural Networks, Logistic regressions, C5.0, or algorithms relying on Ordinary Least Squares (OLS) assumptions. While most authors emphasise comparisons between performances attained by different algorithms, in the present case the algorithm is important solely as a knowledge-discovery tool. The reported increase in performance should be credited to the use of input variables reflecting the cross-sectional characteristics of data found in financial statements. In the following, the nature of such variables is discussed.

A. Financial Analysis

Business companies, namely those listed in stock markets, are required, at the end of each period, to account for their financial activity and position. To this end, companies prepare and report to the public, a collection of monetary amounts with an attached meaning: revenues of the period, different types of expenses, asset values at the end of the period, liabilities and others. Such reports are obtained via a book-keeping process involving recognition, adjustments and aggregation into a standardised set of "accounts", of all meaningful transactions occurring during the period. The resulting "set of accounts" is made available to the public together with notes and auxiliary information, being known as the "financial statement" of the company for that period.

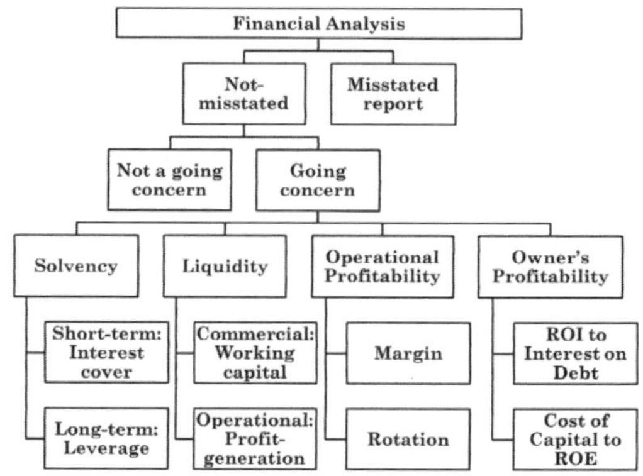

Figure 1. Hierarchical dependence of the topmost financial attributes.

After being published, financial statements are routinely scrutinised by investors, banks, regulators and other entities, with the object of taking decisions regarding individual companies or industrial sectors. Such scrutiny, and the corresponding diagnostic, is known as "Financial Analysis".

Financial Analysis aims to diagnose the financial outlook of a company. The major source of data for such diagnostic is the set of accounts regularly made public by the company and by other companies in the same industrial sector. The diagnostic itself consists of identifying and in some cases measuring the state of financial attributes, such as Trustworthiness, Going Concern, Solvency, Profitability and others. After being identified and measured, financial attributes convey a clear picture of a company's future economic prospects and may support the taking of momentous decisions, such as to buy or not to buy shares or to lend money. Financial attributes, therefore, are the knowledge set where investing, lending and other financial decisions are based.

In the hands of an experienced analyst, sets of accounts are extremely efficient in revealing financial attributes. It is possible, for instance, to accurately predict bankruptcy more than one year before the event [19]. The direction of future earnings (up or down) is also predictable [20]. Such efficiency in conveying useful information is the ultimate reason why accounts are so often manipulated by managers. Fortunately, manipulation may also be detected [4][5].

Financial analysis of a company is typically based on the comparison of monetary amounts taken from sets of accounts. The tool used by analysts to perform such comparison is the "ratio", a quotient of appropriately chosen monetary amounts. For instance, when a company's income at the end of a given period is compared with assets required to generate such income, an indication of Profitability emerges.

Since the effect of company size is similar in all accounts taken from the same company and period, size cancels out when a ratio is formed. Thus, by using ratios, analysts are able to compare attributes, such as Profitability, of companies of different sizes [21]. Besides their size-removal ability, ratios directly measure attributes, which are implicit in reported numbers: Liquidity, Solvency, Profitability and other attributes are associated with specific ratios. Thus, the use of ratios has extended to cases where size-removal is not the major goal. Indeed, ratios are used because they embody, to some extent, analysts' knowledge [23]. Most analytical tasks involving accounting information require the use of appropriately chosen ratios so that companies of different sizes can be compared while their financial attributes are highlighted.

Attributes examined by financial analysts are hierarchically linked: the significance and meaning of one depends on the state of others higher up in the hierarchy (Figure 1). The top attribute, which allows all the others to be meaningful, is Trustworthiness: whether a set of accounts is reliable or not. If accounts are free from manipulation, then it may be asked whether the company is a Going Concern (it is likely that the company will continue to exist) or not. Only in going concerns it makes sense to assess ratio-defined, numerical attributes, such as Solvency, Profitability and Liquidity, which also are at the root of hierarchies.

B. Ratios as model predictors

Knowledge-discovery in financial statements is the process of assigning each company in the database a set of logical classes/numerical values pertaining to attributes forming taxonomies similar to those of Figure 1. The assignment process is carried out using a corresponding set of models that, in turn, are built using "supervised learning" where algorithms learn to recognize classes from instances where diagnostics are already made; but unsupervised learning is also possible [14]. When completed, such process greatly facilitates the task of analysts, allowing them to concentrate on companies and conditions where algorithms may not be able to produce accurate diagnostics. If, however, for most of the attributes, modelling is unreliable, then knowledge-discovery is of little use. Such is the present situation, where only one of the many attributes analysts work with is accurately predictable.

As mentioned, in the hands of an experienced analyst, statements published by companies reveal their financial condition. If most attempts to extract knowledge from such rich content did not succeed, it is probably due to the very success of analysts. When trying to build knowledge-discovery algorithms, authors tend to imitate analysts, namely in the use of ratios. But, in spite of being the chief tool of analysts, ratios are inadequate for knowledge-discovery: first, because their random characteristics, together with constraints they are subject to, are both unfavourable for modelling purposes; and second, because ratios are themselves knowledge, not just data.

First, ratios are inadequate because monetary amounts taken from sets of accounts, as well as their ratios, obey a multiplicative law of probabilities, not an additive law.

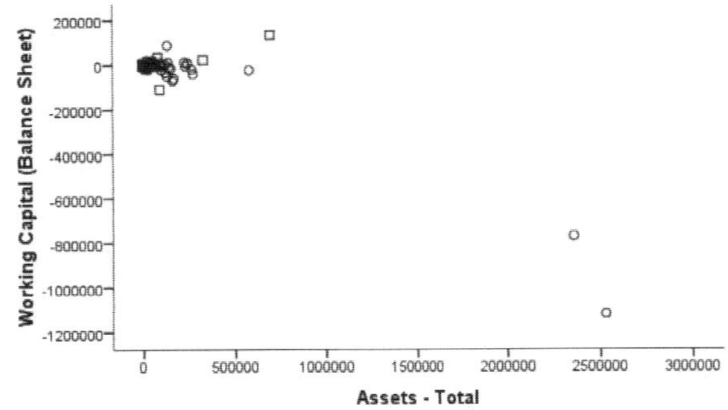

Figure 2. Influential cases in a scatter-plot of two typical ratio components.

Figures reported in a given set of accounts are accumulations. As such, they obey a specific generative mechanism where distributions are better described by the Lognormal and other similar functions with long tails (influential cases) and inherent heteroscedasticity [21], not by the Normal, symmetrical, well-behaved distribution. Where the multiplicative character of financial statements' data is ignored, any subsequent effort to model such data is fruitless, not so much because OLS or other modelling and estimation assumptions are violated but due to the distorting effect of influential cases (Figure 2). And when predictive performance is the issue, the use of robust algorithms is not recommended because the cost of such robustness is lessened performance. Amongst the three types of measurement, Nominal, Ordinal and Scalar, the latter is the richest in content. When scales are treated as ordered categories, as in most robust algorithms, such content is lost. Ratios are also affected by the interaction between their components, which are bounded together by book-keeping rules [22]. The numerator of several widely used ratios, for instance, is constrained to be smaller than the denominator. Such constraints, in turn, curb the variability made available to the predicting algorithm.

Second, the use of pre-defined ratios as input to most AI algorithms, namely those performing knowledge-discovery, entails a contradiction. When a ratio is chosen instead of other ratios, knowledge is required to make such choice. Each ratio embodies the analyst's knowledge that, when two monetary amounts are set against each other, a financial attribute is evidenced. Ratios, therefore, convey previous knowledge thus limiting knowledge that may be extracted from them. Analysts use ratios because they assess one piece of information at a time. They are unable to jointly assess collections of distributions, their moments and variance-covariance matrices, as algorithms do. Analysts need focus, machines do not. Predictive models can only lose by mimicking analysts' separation of knowledge in small bits in order to rearrange it in a recognisable way.

In the following, adequate knowledge-discovery algorithms are shown to be able to choose, amongst a set of monetary amounts, pairs that perform the same task as ratios. Algorithms build their own representations in a way that is similar to analysts' task of selecting, amongst innumerable combinations of monetary amounts, the ratio that highlights a desired attribute.

C. Cross-section characterisation of reported numbers

Studies on the statistical characteristics of reported monetary amounts brought to light two facts. First, in cross-section, the probability density function governing such amounts is nearly lognormal. Second, amounts taken from the same set of accounts share most of their variability as the size effect is prevalent [21]. Thus, variability of logarithm of account i from set of accounts j, $\log x_{ij}$, is explained as the size effect s_j, which is present in all accounts from j, plus some residual variability ε_i:

$$\log x_{ij} = \mu_i + s_j + \varepsilon_i \quad (1)$$

μ_i is an account-specific expectation. Formulations, such as (1), as well as the underlying random mechanism, apply to accumulations only. Accounts, such as Net Income, Retained Earnings and others, that can take on both positive- and negative-signed values, are a subtraction of two accumulations. Net Income, for instance, is the subtraction of Total Costs from Revenue, two accumulations, not the direct result of a random mechanism.

Given two accounts $i = 1$ and $i = 2$ (Revenue and Expenses for instance) and the corresponding reported amounts x_1 and x_2 from the same set, the logarithm of the ratio of x_2 to x_1 is

$$\log \frac{x_2}{x_1} = (\mu_2 - \mu_1) + (\varepsilon_2 - \varepsilon_1) \quad (2)$$

It is clear why ratios formed with two accounts from the same set are effective in conveying information to analysts: the size effect, s_j, cancels out when a ratio is formed. In (2), the log-ratio has an expected value $(\mu_2 - \mu_1)$. The median ratio $\exp(\mu_2 - \mu_1)$ is a suitable norm against which comparisons may be made while $\exp(\varepsilon_2 - \varepsilon_1)$ indicates the deviation from such norm observed in j. Ratios thus reveal how well j is doing no matter its size. For instance, if the median of Net Income to Assets ratio is 0.15, any company with one such ratio above 0.15, no matter small or large, is doing better than the industry.

In (2), upward or downward deviations from the logarithm of the industry norm are the result of subtracting two residuals, each of them account- and size-independent. The deviation $\varepsilon_2 - \varepsilon_1$ from industry norms plays the crucial role of conveying to analysts the size-independent, company-specific data they seek. It is clear, however, that $\varepsilon_2 - \varepsilon_1$ is only part of the size-independent, company-specific information available in x_1 and x_2. When the ratio is formed, all variability common to x_1 and x_2 is removed. Residuals ε_1 and ε_2 are uncorrelated and the size-independent, company-specific information contained in x_1 and x_2 but not conveyed by $\varepsilon_2 - \varepsilon_1$ is the variable orthogonal to $\varepsilon_2 - \varepsilon_1$, which is $\varepsilon_2 + \varepsilon_1$ [24]. Therefore, $\varepsilon_2 + \varepsilon_1$ is size-independent information not conveyed by the ratio. It is thus demonstrated that the use of ratios as model predictors curbs the information made available to the model. Only one dimension of the size-independent information, $\varepsilon_2 - \varepsilon_1$, is made available while the other dimension, $\varepsilon_2 + \varepsilon_1$, is ignored. This is yet another disadvantage associated with the use of ratios in predictive modelling.

D. An alternative to ratios

Given this fundamental limitation of pre-selected ratios, it is worth asking whether amounts directly taken from sets of accounts would not do a better job than ratios as predictors in statistical models. Such possibility is attractive because predictors obeying (1) behave exceedingly well: distributions are nearly Normal, relationships are homoscedastic and influential cases, when present, are true outliers. Log-transformed numbers allow the use of powerful algorithms, which make the most of existing content. In the downside, one obvious concern is how to deal with accounts that can take on both positive- and negative-signed values: logarithms apply only to positive values. Another, equally pressing concern is how to keep the influence of company size out of such models: ratios are size-independent variables but log-transformed account numbers are size-dependent, indeed, most of their variability reflects just the effect of size. Finally, the interpretation of coefficients of such models would not be straightforward.

Consider the usual linear relationship where y is explained by a set of predictors $x_1, x_2, \ldots$

$$y = a + b_1 x_1 + b_2 x_2 + \cdots \quad (3)$$

In the case of a Logistic regression, y may be seen as the linear score leading to the binary prediction. If, instead of $x_1, x_2, \ldots$ log-transformed predictors obeying (1) are included in (3), such relationship becomes

$$y = A + b_1 \varepsilon_1 + b_2 \varepsilon_2 + \cdots + (b_1 + b_2 + \cdots) s_j \quad (4)$$

where $A = a + b_1 \mu_1 + b_2 \mu_2 + \ldots$ is a constant value and residuals $\varepsilon_1, \varepsilon_2, \ldots$ now play the role of linear predictors. The term $(b_1 + b_2 + \ldots) s_j$ apportions the proportion of s_j (size) variability required by y. Coefficients $b_1, b_2, \ldots$ are under a constraint: their summation $b_1 + b_2 + \ldots$ must reflect the extent and sign of size-dependence in y; and where y is size-independent, $b_1 + b_2 + \ldots$ must assume the value of zero so as to bar information conveyed by s_j from entering the relationship.

Suppose, for instance, that y is indeed size-independent. Moreover, y is being predicted by two accounts only, x_1 and x_2. In this case $b_2 = -b_1 = b$ and (4) becomes $y = a + b(\mu_2 - \mu_1) + (\varepsilon_2 - \varepsilon_1)$ or

$$y = a + b \log \frac{x_2}{x_1} \quad (5)$$

In other words, a ratio is automatically formed so that size is removed from the relationship modelling y. Given the variety of companies' sizes found in cross-section relationships, the predictive power of s_j on y is, in most practical cases, small or non-existent. In such type of models $b_1 + b_2 + \ldots$ in (4) add to nearly zero. Size-related variability is allocated to a given predictor in order to counterbalance size-related variability from other predictors, so that y is modelled by size-independent or nearly size-independent variability. When building an optimal model, the algorithm assigns the role of denominator to some predictors (negative-signed b coefficients) and that of numerator to others (positive-signed b coefficients). Logarithmic representations similar

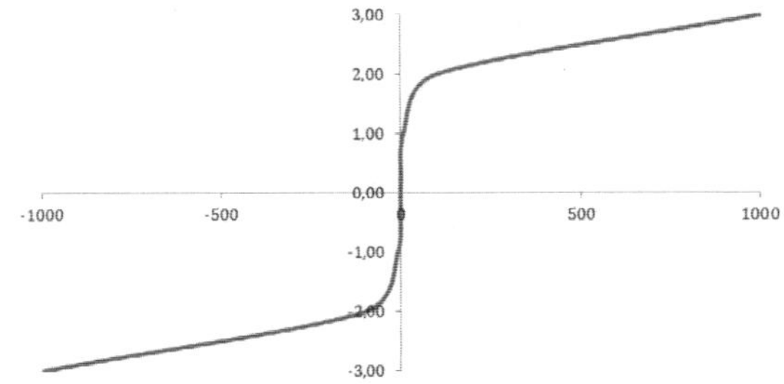

Figure 3. Graphical form where the Y-axis represents log-modulus of x.

to financial ratios are thus formed. In this way, financial attributes possessing optimal predicting characteristics, are unveiled without the intervention of the analyst. This is a notable trait of the methodology.

The above reasoning presupposes that y is size-independent. By forcing the modelling algorithm to obey $b_1 + b_2 + \ldots = 0$ in (4), it is possible to build models where y is explained solely by size-independent variability, even in cases where the relationship is size-related. Thus, ratios are not needed to build size-independent models. Ratios are needed solely because financial analysts, and other users, demand that predictors be interpretable.

The other concern, how to deal with accounts that can take on both positive- and negative-signed values, may be solved by using the "log-modulus" [25] or other similar transformation. The log-modulus expands the logarithmic transformation so as to encompass zero and negative values. Given variable x, the log-modulus consists of using

$$\operatorname{sgn} x \log(|x| + 1) \qquad (6)$$

instead of x (Figure 3). In this way, accumulations or subtractions of accumulations, no matter their sign, become statistically well-behaved.

The log-modulus transformation considerably reduces the frequency of missing values in random samples. Missing values are a source of bias because the probability that a reported number is missing often is correlated to the attribute being predicted. For instance, it is frequent to find values of zero in Dividends and other accounts. When ratios are formed with such values in the denominator, as is the case of the ratio "Changes in Dividends in relation to the Previous Year", a missing value is created; and such missing value is correlated with the paying or not of dividends, a predictor of future Earnings' changes. Other changes in relation to the previous period will suffer from the same difficulty. But after the log-modulus transformation, such ratios become subtractions:

$$\delta \log x = \log x_{t-1} - \log x_t \qquad (7)$$

where t and $t-1$ express subsequent time periods and the operator log may refer to (6) in the case of positive- and negative-signed x. Changes expressed as in (7) no longer increase the number of missing values. Incidentally, unlike ratios, transformed values cannot have two meanings. In ratios, negative-valued numerators and denominators lead to the same ratio sign as positive-valued numerators and denominators.

The coming sections show that models using log-modulus transformed accounts as predictors perform better than those using ratios; but where ratios cannot be avoided, then the modelling algorithm is capable of extracting ratios with optimal predicting characteristics from logarithmic and log-modulus transformed accounts.

III. Methodology

The application described here makes use of the following methodologies: Web-mining of financial statements; the use, as input, of logarithmic-transformed monetary amounts directly taken from such statements; pre-selection of model input variables amongst a wider set of monetary amounts; the specific architecture and training of three MLPs so that internal representations similar to financial ratios are formed; and finally, the interpretation of such MLP's internal representations via a features' map. This section briefly discusses such methodologies.

A. *Web-mining of financial statements*

Until recently, financial statements were published in a variety of formats including PDF, MS Word and MS Excel. Such variety, forced users and their supporting tools into a significant amount of interpretation and manual manipulation of meta-data and led to inefficiencies and costs. From 2010 on, the Securities and Exchange Commission (SEC) of the US, as well as the United Kingdom's Revenue & Customs (HMRC) and other regulatory bodies, require companies to make their financial statements public using the XML-based eXtensible Business Reporting Language (XBRL). Users of XBRL now include securities' regulators, banking regulators, business registrars, tax-filing agencies, national statistical agencies plus, of course, investors and financial analysts worldwide [26]. XML syntax and related standards, such as XML Schema, XLink, XPath and Namespaces are all incorporated into XBRL, which can thus extract financial data unambiguously. Communications are defined by metadata set out in taxonomies describing definitions of reported monetary values as well as relationships between them. XBRL thus brings semantic meaning into financial reporting, promoting harmonization, interoperability and greatly facilitating ETL tasks. Web-mining of financial data is now at hand.

The initial module of the application carries out Web-mining of XBRL content. The user first introduces a selection criteria, namely a company name or code, such as the "Central Index Key" (CIK) and the period. Then, the search of pre-existing indexes will identify Web locations containing the required statement. In the US, for instance, such location is the Securities and Exchange Commission repository (known as "EDGAR") containing "fillings" of companies' statements and other data.

The Electronic Data Gathering, Analysis, and Retrieval (EDGAR) repository performs automated collection, validation, indexing, acceptance, and forwarding of submissions by companies and others who are required by law to file forms with the SEC. Its primary purpose is to increase the efficiency and fairness of the securities market for the benefit of investors, corporations, and the economy by accelerating the receipt, acceptance, dissemination, and analysis of time-sensitive corporate information filed with the agency. The SEC's File Transfer Protocol (FTP) server for EDGAR filings allows comprehensive access by corporations, funds and individuals.

The actual annual statement of companies need not be submitted on EDGAR, although some companies do so voluntarily. However, a report on a standardised format, known as "Form 10-K", which contains much of the same information, is required to be filed on EDGAR; and since recently filers are also required to submit documents in XBRL format. Besides the 10-K form, other widely used form is the 10-Q, which refers to quarterly statements. Rules established by the SEC offer guidelines for the content and format, including which data may be provided as part of an Interactive Data document, and the relationship to the related official filing.

An extremely helpful resource for FTP retrieval is the set of EDGAR indices listing the following information for each filing: company name, form type, CIK of the company, date filed, and file name (including folder path). Four types of indexes are available:

1) company, sorted by company name
2) form, sorted by form type, 10-K or 10-Q
3) master, sorted by CIK code
4) XBRL, list of submissions containing XBRL financial files, sorted by CIK code.

The application described here uses the package "XBRL" from the R language [27] to access and retrieve SEC filings. The XBRL package offers access to functions to extract business financial information from a XBRL instance file and the associated collection of files that defines its Discoverable Taxonomy Set (DTS).

When the report from a given company and period is requested by a user, an index is searched and the corresponding document is retrieved from its Web location on EDGAR. Next, the relevant information is put in place. Functions provided by the XBRL package return readily available data, complete with standard descriptions, including taxonomies. As published taxonomy files are immutable and are used by most filers, the package offers the option of downloading them only the first time they are referred, keeping a local cache copy that can be used from then on.

B. *Data description and variable selection*

Financial analysts base their diagnostic on several concurring pieces of evidence, in favour or against *a priori* hypotheses. On the other hand, the extant research on financial statements' manipulation suggests that fraudulent numbers lead to detectable imbalances in financial features. For instance, income may increase without the corresponding increase in free cash. In order to respond to the need, in the part of analysts, to examine concurring facts, the application, besides predicting fraud, also predicts the state of two other attributes mentioned in published research [4][5] as capable of detecting such imbalances.

Therefore, after Web-mining and the log-transformation of monetary amounts as described in Subsection II-D, three MLP are set to separately predict three financial attributes known to widen fraud propensity space, namely:

- Trustworthiness, comprising two classes (states): fraudulent (manipulated, misstated) vs non-fraudulent statement [4][5][7];
- Going Concern, comprising two classes: bankrupt vs solvent [19][28][29];
- Unexpected Increase in Earnings One Year Ahead, comprising two classes: Earnings' increase vs Earnings' decrease one year ahead [20][30].

Trustworthiness and Going Concern are the two basic attributes of financial analysis, directly influencing the way all other attributes are interpreted. As for Earnings' direction one year ahead, it is, amongst the attributes occupying a place further down in the hierarchy, one often scrutinized by investors.

So far, Going Concern is the only predictable attribute. In spite of the large research effort devoted to improving Trustworthiness prediction, until now, as mentioned, results are below the feasibility level, at 75% out-of-sample correct classification at best, for large, non-homogeneous samples. Besides being meagre, such results are unbalanced: one of the states is significantly better predicted than the other. All the previously cited authors use ratios as predictors.

Instances employed in the training and testing of the three MLP and the corresponding input and target attributes are extracted from the following sources:

- UCLA-LoPucki Bankruptcy Research Data [31] as well as a list of bankrupt companies kindly provided by Professor Edward Altman (New York University), covering the period 1978-2005.
- The collection of Accounting and Auditing Enforcement Releases (AAER) resulting from investigations made by the SEC against a company, an auditor, or an officer for alleged accounting and/or auditing misconduct, identifying a given set of accounts as fraudulent [5], covering the period 1983-2013. This data is made available by the Centre for Financial Reporting and Management of the Haas School of Business (University of California at Berkeley) [32].
- The "Compustat" repository of financial data by Standard & Poor's, where monetary amounts are collected, and from which unexpected Earnings increases and decreases are estimated [20][30].

Input to each of the three MLP are logarithms or log-modulus, (6), of accounts pre-selected amongst all the aggregated accounts in published statements. Accounts are taken from two consecutive statements of a company, forming instance j of actual period, t, and of previous period, $t-1$. Log-differences in relation to such previous period, (7), are computed and included in the pre-selection process.

Pre-selection of input variables is carried out using the "Forward Selection" algorithm attached to most Logistic regressions [33]. Accounts and log-differences selected in this way are then used as input to the corresponding MLP.

TABLE I. BK = BANKRUPTCY, FR = FRAUD, EA = EARNINGS.

Log	Cash and Short Term Investments	Bk	Fr	
Log	Receivables (total)		Fr	
Log	Assets (total)		Fr	Ea
Log	Long-Term Debt		Fr	
Log	Liabilities (total)	Bk	Fr	Ea
Log	Liabilities (total) change		Fr	
Lmd	Retained Earnings	Bk		Ea
Lmd	Retained Earnings change			Ea
Log	Common Stock (equity)		Fr	
Log	Revenue (total)		Fr	
Lmd	Gross Profit			Ea
Lmd	Gross Profit change			Ea
Lmd	Tax Expense	Bk		Ea
Lmd	Cash-Flow from Operations	Bk		Ea
Lmd	Dividends per Share			Ea
Lmd	Dividends per Share change			Ea

Table I lists the 16 variables that were pre-selected using such method, together with the attribute they predict and the type of transformation applied in each case: "log" for the logarithmic transformation (positive-only accounts) and "lmd" for the log-modulus transformation (accounts which may take both positive and negative values).

C. MLP architecture and training

When analysing attributes, such as Trustworthiness, financial analysts need to know which ratios are at work, their position in relation to industry standards and in which direction they are moving. In order to respond to the first of such demands, MLP architecture and training are designed so that internal representations similar to financial ratios are formed in hidden nodes. Before training, MLP architecture consists of:

1) A total of 41 input nodes corresponding to the 16 variables listed on Table I plus 24 dummies, one for each of the "Global Industry Classification Standard" (GICS) groups [34] (each instance belongs to one such industrial group), plus a constant-valued dummy.
2) one hidden layer with 10 nodes in each of which an internal representation similar to a ratio may be formed;
3) two output nodes where outcomes are symmetrical about zero, plus the corresponding "biases" assigned to the constant value of 1 and -1. Symmetry and output node duplication is not required, in theory, but it may facilitate training.

Hyperbolic tangents (threshold functions symmetrical about zero) are used as transfer functions in all nodes.

Given the inclusion of 24 dummies, hidden nodes' biases assigned to the constant value of 1 should be redundant. But since, during training, MLP connections (weights) are subject to a stringent pruning whereby most connections disappear, the constant bias often is the sole remaining dummy.

MLP training is carried out in the usual way until a minimum is found. Then a popular weight pruning technique known as "Optimal Brain Surgeon" [35] is applied. The result is a significant reduction in the number of connections. Typically, all of the industry dummies, plus a significant number of input variables and, often, entire hidden-layer nodes are discarded at this stage.

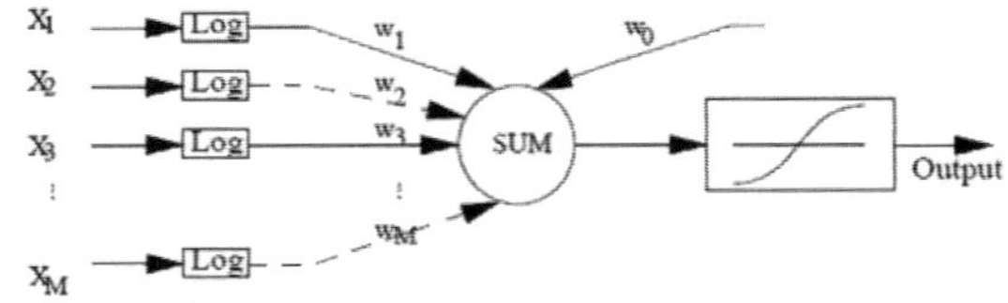

Figure 4. Given values x_k and x_i, the ratio x_{kj}/x_{ij} from statement j, is formed in an MLP hidden node as $\log x_{kj} - \log x_{ij}$ when $w_k = -w_i$.

The next training step consists of an extremely crude penalisation of synaptic weights linking inputs, the $\log x_i$ in (1), to hidden nodes: each epoch reduces the absolute value of weights by a small margin, typically 0.001. This leads to a kind of competition for survival amongst weights; and it is verified that some weights are resilient in the sense that they regain their values while others are non-resilient, quickly decaying to zero, and are pruned.

Then, beginning with the most significant node, all but the two largest-valued input weights are pruned. The pruning is repeated in the other nodes, one at a time, while synaptic weights linking input variables to all hidden nodes keep on being subject to the described penalisation. When the relationship being modelled is strong, as is the case of bankruptcy prediction, this procedure is sufficient to bring about internal representations similar to ratios; in the case of weak relationships, the procedure requires trial and error in the choice of the first hidden nodes to be subject to the forced pruning of all but two weights.

Instances used in MLP training greatly differ in size while the predicted variable is indeed predictable. Hidden nodes, therefore, have a tendency towards self-organizing themselves into size-independent variables, which are, at the same time, efficient in explaining the attribute being modelled. This is basically the definition of a financial ratio; and the described procedure simply avoids ratios with more than one numerator and denominator.

According to (5), in a nearly size-independent predicting context, synaptic weights tend to survive in each node so that their summation is nearly zero. And if nodes are further forced into having two weights only, then such two weights will be symmetrical (opposite signs and approximately similar absolute values). Internal representations thus mimic the logarithm of ratios and can be interpreted similarly to ratios (Figure 4). Note that the term "internal representation" refers to values assumed by each hidden node after summation (SUM in Figure 4) but before transfer function.

In some hidden nodes, only one weight survives, not two. This may happen where input variables are themselves ratios, such as Dividends per Share or changes from the previous- to the current-year account (7). This may also happen when the relationship to be modelled requires the presence of size as a predictor.

Although absolute values of the two surviving weights in each hidden node are not much different from one another, they differ across nodes. Such difference, together with the magnitudes of synaptic weights linking them to output nodes, crudely reflects the importance of each node for the final classification performance. In the final step of training,

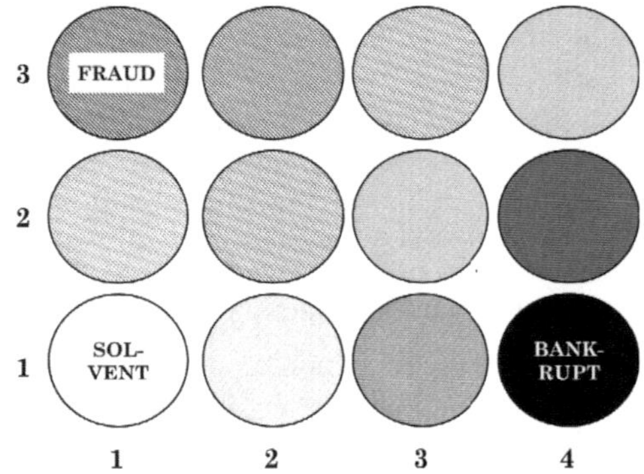

Figure 5. Position of financial attributes' classes in 4 by 3 features' map.

the less important hidden node is also tested for pruning using trial and error, the pruning criterion being non-significant reduction in performance. The final result is a parsimonious model with meaningful internal representations.

After appropriate ratios are selected, analysts interpret their observed, company-specific deviations from expectation. In this way, expected μ_i from (1) are also modelled and accounted for inside such node. Since node outputs and attributes' classes are both balanced, the effect of industry dummies is to subtract industry-specific log-ratio standards from internal representations thus making them similar to a difference of two ε_i in (1). Such difference is, in log space, what analysts seek when they compare a ratio with its expectation. As mentioned, for the modelling tasks at hand, industry dummies are not significantly distinctive.

D. *Graphical interpretation of results*

Internal representations from the three MLP are input to a 2-dimensional features' map [36] with 4 by 3 nodes. When self-organisation has taken place, specific nodes or groups of nodes in the map become associated with classes of attributes, such as fraud and bankruptcy (Figure 5). Visual examination of the features' map facilitates interpretation, both proximity to a given node and trajectories towards or away from nodes, being informative. In this way, analysts observe in which direction attributes move and whether a company is approaching nodes where fraud, bankruptcy and unexpected changes in Earnings are likely.

The self-organised map aims at facilitating the graphical interpretation of representations created by the three MLP; no inferential role is attributed to it.

IV. Results

For the three MLP, this section lists the input weights which survive pruning, the ratios formed from them in hidden layers and their relative importance for explaining the outcome. Test-set classification accuracy is also reported. MLP performance is compared with that of Logistic regression classifiers using similar data-sets and MLP's surviving inputs as predictors. In this way, the performance of models using the newly discovered ratios as predictors is compared with that of models using ratio components as predictors. The section concludes by showing the self-organised features' map at work.

A. *Bankruptcy prediction*

From a total of 2,997 cases of US bankruptcy filings, and after discarding bankruptcies but the first in each company as well as cases about which detailed financial figures are not available, two random samples of nearly 900 different cases each are drawn. The two samples contain companies listed in US exchanges and present in the Standard & Poor's "Compustat" database. They span the period 1979-2008. The deciles of the logarithm of Assets (total) are used as a discrete size measure, all sizes being represented in samples. Similarly, all the 24 GICS groups are significantly represented in samples. Cases in the two samples are then matched with an equal number of records from non-bankrupt companies. Pairing is based on the GICS group, on size decile and on year. Among financial statements fulfilling the pairing criteria, one case is randomly selected for matching and then such case is made unavailable for future matching. Although the same case is not used to match more than one bankruptcy case, other cases from the same company in different years remain available for matching. The two matched samples have nearly 1,800 cases each. One of the two samples, always the same, is used as the learning-set and the other as the test-set. Due to missing observations, samples contain less than 1,800 cases:

Learning-set: non-bankrupt	845 (50.1%)
Learning-set: bankrupt	841 (49.9%)
Test-set: non-bankrupt (N)	837 (49.8%)
Test-set: bankrupt (P)	845 (50.2%)

When the MLP learning process is concluded, only 4 hidden nodes persist. In each of these, the two input weights which survive pruning are of a crudely similar magnitude and opposite sign. Therefore, the MLP has formed 4 internal representations, B1 to B4, which are similar to financial ratios in log space. When ordered by magnitude of the weight leading to output nodes, a rough measure of predictive importance, such ratios are:

- B1 ratio of Cash and Short Term Investments to Liabilities (total)
- B2 ratio of Retained Earnings to Liabilities (total)
- B3 ratio of Cash-Flow from Operations to Cash and Short Term Investments
- B4 ratio of Tax Expenses to Liabilities (total)

All industry-specific weights are also pruned away during training, denoting no significant influence of the industrial group on bankruptcy prediction. Therefore, the final MLP model has 5 inputs (detailed in Table I), 4 hidden nodes and 2 symmetrical but otherwise identical outputs.

Test-set performance of the MLP using the above 4 log ratios (internal representations) formed from 5 inputs, is reported in Table II together with the performance of a Logistic regression using the same 5 inputs as predictors.

As mentioned, bankruptcy prediction is the sole case of successful modelling of financial attributes. This is probably due to the fact that statements were perfected so as to warn against solvency problems. Therefore, the relationship is strong. Performance reported here is not inferior to that found in the literature while balance increases markedly.

TABLE II. BANKRUPTCY PREDICTION CLASSIFICATION RESULTS.

Bankruptcy predicting models	MLP (4 ratios)	Logistic (5 variables)
Non-bankrupt correct (TN)	822 (98.2%)	822 (98.2%)
Non-bankrupt incorrect (FP)	15 (1.8%)	15 (1.8%)
Bankrupt correct (TP)	811 (96.0%)	814 (96.3%)
Bankrupt incorrect (FN)	34 (4.0%)	31 (3.7%)
Precision: TP / (TP + FP)	98.18%	98.19%

The number of variables and synaptic weights engaged in modelling is less than that reported in the literature. Robustness is therefore higher. When predictors are ratio components rather than ratios (Logistic regression), performance increases slightly.

B. Fraud detection

The methodology used in the building of fraud-detecting samples is similar to the bankruptcy-prediction case. Data used for learning and testing consists of a collection of 3,403 AAERs. It contains enforcement releases issued between 1976 and 2012 against 1,297 companies, which had manipulated financial statements. After removing cases for which no detailed financial data is available, the database contains 1,152 releases. Manipulated statements from the same company in different years are not removed from the sample. Enron, for instance, was the object of 6 releases and all of them are included. Two random samples of nearly 550 different cases each are then drawn. They span the period 1976-2008. All sizes and all GICS groups are significantly represented. The two samples are matched with an equal number of statements from companies that are neither the object of releases throughout the period nor bankrupt in the year of the release. Matched samples have nearly 1,100 cases each. One of the two samples, always the same, is used to build models and the other to test performance of models. Due to missing observations, the size of samples available for model-building and model-testing ends up being less than 800 cases each:

Learning set: non-fraud cases	335	(45.7%)
Learning set: fraud cases	398	(54.2%)
Test set: non-fraud cases (N)	353	(46.2%)
Test set: fraud cases (P)	411	(53.8%)

When the MLP learning process is concluded, 6 hidden nodes persist. Five of these 6 nodes have two surviving input weights with a relatively similar magnitude and opposite sign. The remaining node, F5, has only one surviving weight. The MLP has formed 5 internal representations, F1 to F4 plus F6, which are similar to financial ratios in log space. The following list displays the representations in the 6 hidden nodes ordered by magnitude of weight leading to the output node, a rough measure of predictive importance:

- F1 ratio of Liabilities (total) to Assets (total)
- F2 ratio of Cash and Short Term Investments to Revenue (total)
- F3 ratio of Long Term Debt to Common Stock (equity)
- F4 ratio of Receivables (total) to Common Stock (equity)
- F5 Change in Liabilities (total)
- F6 ratio of Revenue (total) to Common Stock (equity)

TABLE III. FRAUD DETECTION CLASSIFICATION RESULTS.

Fraud predicting models	MLP (6 ratios)	Logistic (8 variables)
Non-fraud correct (TN)	299 (84.7%)	303 (85.8%)
Non-fraud incorrect (FP)	54 (15.3%)	50 (14.2%)
Fraud correct (TP)	369 (90.0%)	371 (90.5%)
Fraud incorrect (FN)	41 (10.0%)	39 (9.5%)
Precision: TP / (TP + FP)	87.2%	88.1%

All industry-specific weights are pruned away during training. Therefore, the final MLP model has 8 inputs (detailed in Table I), 6 hidden nodes and 2 symmetrical but otherwise identical outputs.

Test-set performance of fraud-detecting MLP using 8 inputs and 6 hidden nodes is reported in Table III together with the performance of the Logistic regression using the same 8 inputs. The model shows a substantial increase in out-of-sample performance, of more than 10% in relation to previous studies using large, diversified samples, while imbalance in the recognition of classes is reduced. Type II error (the most expensive in this case) is clearly subdued. When predictors are ratio components rather than ratios (Logistic regression), performance increases.

C. Earnings prediction

The task of predicting Earnings' changes one year ahead is generally considered as having theoretical rather than practical interest: it is indeed possible to predict Earnings but, so far, the attained increase in accuracy over the tossing of a coin is barely 10% [20].

Samples used in the prediction of the sign of unexpected changes in Earnings (in fact Earnings per Share, EPS) one year ahead, are not matched: classes to be predicted are estimated from data available in each set of accounts [20]. In the present case, after withdrawing cases with missing values in the predicted dichotomous variable (Earnings increase vs Earnings non-increases) or in predictors, a total of nearly 140,000 cases remain, where some 90,000 are non-increases and 50,000 are increases. The size of the sample is higher than in previous cases and classes are unbalanced: after adjusting for expectation, non-increases are more frequent than increases. Other methodological details are the same as in previous cases. The final number of cases in the learning- and test-set is:

Learning set: EPS non-increases	41,851	(64.3%)
Learning set: EPS increases	23,275	(35.7%)
Test set: EPS non-increases (N)	41,750	(64.4%)
Test set: EPS increases (P)	22,811	(35.6%)

Class proportions are significantly dissimilar in this case.

When the MLP learning process is concluded, 10 hidden nodes persist, 5 of which have only 1 synaptic weight. In the remaining 5 nodes the two surviving input weights are of a relatively similar magnitude and opposite sign. The MLP has formed 5 internal representations, E2, E3, E5, E6 and E7, which are similar to financial ratios in log space. The following list displays the 10 representations formed in hidden nodes ordered by the magnitude of weight leading to the output node, a rough measure of predictive importance:

TABLE IV. EARNINGS PREDICTION CLASSIFICATION RESULTS.

Earnings predicting models	MLP (10 ratios)	Logistic (10 variables)
EPS non-increases correct (TN)	35,783 (85.7%)	35,783 (85.7%)
EPS non-increases incorrect (FP)	5,967 (14.3%)	5,967 (14.3%)
EPS increases correct (TP)	16,153 (70.8%)	16,153 (70.8%)
EPS increases incorrect (FN)	6,658 (29.2%)	6,658 (29.2%)
Precision: TP / (TP + FP)	73.02%	73.02%

E1	Dividends per Share
E2	ratio of Cash-Flow from Operations to Tax Expenses
E3	ratio of Retained Earnings to Liabilities (total)
E4	Change in Gross Profit
E5	ratio of Retained Earnings to Tax Expenses
E6	ratio of Gross Profit to Cash Flow from Operations
E7	Assets (total)
E8	ratio of Tax Expenses to Assets (total)
E9	Change in Retained Earnings
E10	Change in Dividends per Share

All industry-specific weights are pruned away. The final MLP model has 10 inputs (detailed in Table I), 10 hidden nodes and 2 symmetrical but otherwise identical outputs.

Test-set performance of the MLP Earnings-predicting model using the 10 input just mentioned, is reported in Table IV together with the performance of the Logistic regression model using the same 10 inputs differently organised: instead of ratios, ratio components are used as input. Performance is, in this case, similar for ratios (MLP) and their components (Logistic regression).

One of the internal representations is not a ratio but the logarithm of Assets (total). This introduces in the modelling of Earnings' changes the effect of size, required by this particular relationship.

Classification results should be interpreted in the light of the strong class imbalance observed in the training-set [37], which is nearly 14% in this case. Namely, a classification accuracy of 73%, obtained from an initial class imbalance of 14% means a gain, in relation to a classification made at random (without any previous information) of $9\% = 73\% - (50\% + 14\%)$. Contrary to published results [20][30], the final classification imbalance is not worsened by the modelling process. In the present case, imbalance is similar to that of the sample used to build models while performance is significantly increased by 4% in relation to such previously reported performance.

D. The features' map

Data employed to self-organise the features map contains instances used in the learning and testing of two of the MLP, namely bankruptcy-prediction and fraud-detection data. Classes, such as fraud, bankruptcy and their opposites may occur together in some instances; and all instances include the two classes of unexpected Earnings' increases and decreases. The total number of instances is 5,369.

When self-organised, the 4 by 3 nodes in the features' map are sensitive to distinct financial attributes. Considering the lattice of 12 nodes defined as x, y where $x = 1, \dots 4$ and $y = 1, \dots 3$, the strongest sensitivities observed are as follows:

- Fraud in node $x = 1, y = 4$
- Bankruptcy in node $x = 4, y = 1$ and its opposite, Solvency, in node $x = 1, y = 1$
- Earnings' decrease in nodes $x = 1, y = 1$ and $x = 1, y = 3$

Figure 6 compares the frequencies associated with, respectively, fraud, bankruptcy and unexpected Earnings' decreases in the self-organised map.

Besides graphically locating the financial position of companies with reference to fraud and bankruptcy, the self-organised features' map shows the trajectory drawn by companies, from the previous into the current year. Figure 7 illustrates the yearly evolution of the accounts of some, well-known, financial scandals and failures, as mapped into the self-organised lattice.

V. ARCHITECTURE, OUTPUT AND DEPLOYMENT

The most informative result provided by the application is the set of three probabilities obtained from MLP outputs. After being adjusted so as to become 0-1 variables, such outputs may be interpreted as conditional probabilities of observing the associated input values when the predicted class is fraud, bankruptcy and Earnings decrease respectively. And when combined with Prevalence numbers (prior probabilities of fraud, bankruptcy and Earnings decrease), MLP outputs become posterior probabilities of fraud, bankruptcy or Earnings decrease given the values observed in input variables. Posterior probabilities are then made available to users as outputs. Output node representations (after summation but before the transfer function) can also be used as scores.

Each analysed company generates two sets of results corresponding to time periods $t-1$ and t. Output to analysts consists of the following:

1) Three posterior probabilities: fraud, bankruptcy and Earnings' decrease, with a sign indicating the direction of their change from $t-1$ to t.
2) The respective scores.
3) The 9 most significant values internal representations assume at period t, three from each MLP, with a sign indicating the direction of change from $t-1$ to t. Values are labelled as the respective ratio.
4) Graphical description of financial position in the self-organised features' map and trajectories from $t-1$ to t, allowing the detection of trends towards a given class.
5) Names, year and attributes of three instances from the learning- and test-set, which are closest to the instance being investigated respectively regarding fraud, bankruptcy and unexpected Earnings' decrease. The proximity criterion used in the three cases is the value of the internal representation formed in one of the output nodes.

The application uses a variety of packages and languages, namely the R-language; it has been set-up, tested and deployed in two versions, stand-alone and Web-based, the latter having no training capability. The stand-alone version is a Java-based set of modules, as depicted in Figure 8.

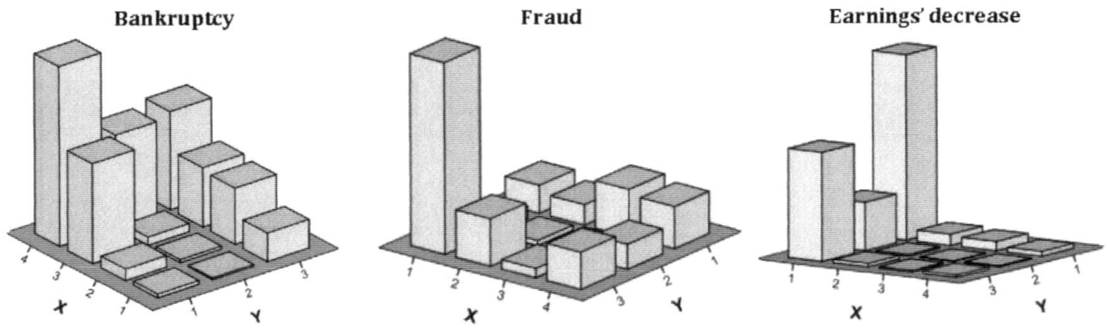

Figure 6. Class frequencies in features' map. Node $x = 4, y = 1$, bankruptcy; node $x = 1, y = 3$, fraud; nodes $x = 1, y = 1$ to 3, Earnings' decreases.

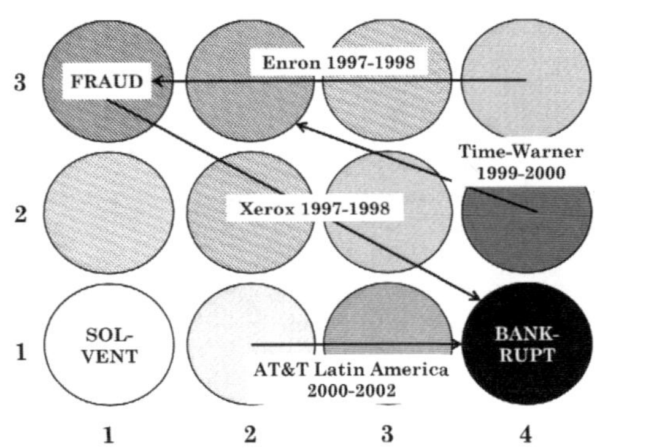

Figure 7. Trajectories drawn by well-known cases in the features' map.

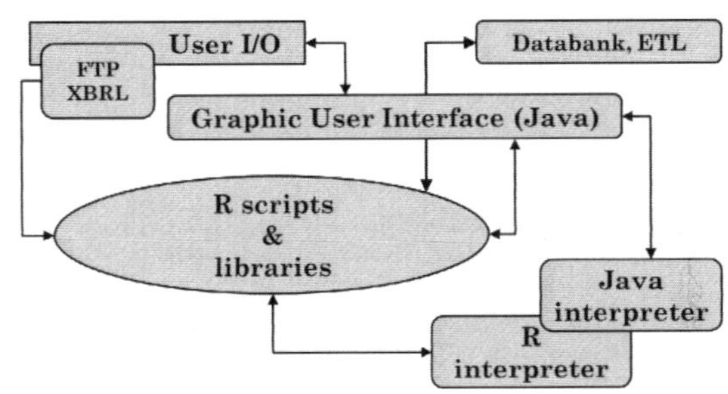

Figure 8. Modular architecture of the stand-alone application deployed.

VI. Conclusion

Notwithstanding the abundance of research devoted to the subject, until now, the surge in marketed Financial Technology applications did not contemplate software to support the detection of fraud in published financial statements. This is due to difficulties in extracting and put in place of the required input data and also due to the "black box" nature of researched solutions. The application presented here aims at solving both problems, producing automated Web-mined input and interpretable diagnostics. In the hands of analysts, the application's output is self-explanatory, not just pointing out companies likely to have committed fraud but showing, rather than hiding, financial attributes that are capable of supporting such diagnostic.

Limitations of ratios highlighted in the paper, some of which persist after appropriate logarithmic or log-modulus transformations, are not sufficient to erode performance significantly. Experiments reported in the paper show that log-ratio use, as an alternative to log-transformed accounts, is acceptable for predictive modelling purposes. This probably stems from the fact that such log-ratios are discovered by the optimisation algorithm, rather than being pre-selected by analysts. In this way, the most performance-damaging ratios will not be selected, meaningful as they may seem to be. Ratios, in turn, bring with them some noteworthy advantages, namely diagnostic interpretability and size-independence, including much needed currency-independence.

The application illustrates a case of close alignment between users' needs and algorithmic characteristics. The application is also an example of knowledge-discovery, whereby explanatory variables are discovered amongst many candidates so that a predicting task is carried out with optimal performance. The choice of the algorithm, the MLP, was dictated solely by its ability to form meaningful internal representations. Neither algorithmic performance nor the testing of novel algorithmic capabilities was the goal here. Out-of-sample classification results obtained are more than 10% above those reported by other authors for large-non-homogeneous samples; but such increase in performance is obtained simply by using, as input variables, log-transformed accounts rather than previously-defined ratios. Appropriately transformed variables, not algorithms, led to the discovery of log-ratios and then to parsimonious, precise, balanced and robust prediction.

The final goal is to build a usable tool, an apparently simple task but which, in this particular subject area, has eluded research effort during the last 20 years. Thus, the ultimate test is yet to be carried out, namely whether analysts will use the application or not.

Acknowledgments

This research is sponsored by the Foundation for the Development of Science and Technology (FDCT) of Macau, China.

References

[1] D. Trigueiros and C. Sam, "Streamlining the Detection of Accounting Fraud through Web Mining, and Interpretable Internal Representations," in Proc. IMMM 2015: The Fifth International Conference on Advances in Information Mining and Management, Brussels, June 2015, pp. 23–26, ISBN: 978-1-61208-415-2.

[2] M. Nigrini, Forensic Analytics: Methods, and Techniques for Forensic Accounting. John Wiley, and Sons, 2011.

[3] W. Albrecht and M. Zimbelman, Fraud Examination. Mason, South-Western Cengage Learning, 2009.

[4] M. Beneish, "The Detection of Earnings Manipulation," Financial Analysts Journal, vol. 55, no. 5, pp. 24–36, 1999.

[5] C. Dechow, G. Weill, and R. Sloan, "Predicting Material Accounting Misstatements," Contemporary Accounting Research, vol. 28, no. 1, pp. 17–82, 2011.

[6] E. Ngai, Y. Hu, Y. Wong, Y. Chen, and X. Sun, "The Application of Data Mining Techniques in Financial Fraud Detection: a Classification Framework, and an Academic Review of Literature," Decision Support Systems, vol. 50, no. 3, pp. 559–569, 2011.

[7] A. Sharma and P. Panigrahi, "A Review of Financial Accounting Fraud Detection Based on Data Mining Techniques," International Journal of Computer Applications, vol. 39, no. 1, 2012.

[8] K. Phua, V. Lee, and R. Gayler, "A Comprehensive Survey of Data Mining-Based Fraud Detection Research," Clayton School of Information Technology, Monash University, 2005.

[9] U. Flegel, J. Vayssire, and G. Bitz, "A State of the Art Survey of Fraud Detection Technology," in Insider Threats in Cyber Security, ser. Advances in Information Security, C. W. Probst, J. Hunker,, and M. Bishop, Eds. Springer US, vol. 49, pp. 73–84, 2010.

[10] E. Kirkos, S. Charalambos, and Y. Manolopoulos, "Data Mining Techniques for the Detection of Fraudulent Financial Statements," Expert Systems with Applications, vol. 32, p. 995–1003, 2007.

[11] W. Zhou and G. Kapoor, "Detecting Evolutionary Financial Statement Fraud," Decision Support Systems, vol. 50, pp. 570–575, 2011.

[12] P. Ravisankar, V. Ravi, G. Rao, and I. Bose, "Detection of Financial Statement Fraud, and Feature Selection Using Data Mining Techniques," Decision Support Systems, vol. 50, no. 2, pp. 491–500, 2011.

[13] F. Glancy and S. Yadav, "A Computational Model for Financial Reporting Fraud Detection," Decision Support Systems, vol. 50, no. 3, pp. 595–601, 2011.

[14] S. Huang, R. Tsaih, and F. Yu, "Topological Pattern Discovery and Feature Extraction for Fraudulent Financial Reporting," Expert Systems with Applications, vol. 41, no. 9, pp. 4360–4372, 2014.

[15] https://www.quora.com/What-are-the-biggest-FinTech-trends-in-2015 Retrieved: May 2016.

[16] http://blog.dwolla.com/12-companies-pushing-fintech/ Retrieved: May 2016.

[17] https://letstalkpayments.com/applications-of-machine-learning-in-fintech/ Retrieved: May 2016.

[18] http://www.capterra.com/financial-fraud-detection-software/ Retrieved: May 2016.

[19] E. Altman, "Financial Ratios, Discriminant Analysis, and the Prediction of Corporate Bankruptcy," The Journal of Finance, vol. 23, no. 4, pp. 589–609, 1968.

[20] J. Ou and S. Penman, "Financial Statement Analysis, and the Prediction of Stock Returns," Journal of Accounting, and Economics, vol. 11, no. 4, pp. 295–329, 1989.

[21] S. McLeay and D. Trigueiros, "Proportionate Growth, and the Theoretical Foundations of Financial Ratios," Abacus, vol. XXXVIII, no. 3, pp. 297–316, 2002.

[22] D. Christodoulou and S. McLeay, "The Double Entry Constraint, Structural Modeling and Econometric Estimation," Contemporary Accounting Research, vol. 31, no. 2, pp. 609–628, 2014.

[23] W. Beaver, "Financial Ratios as Predictors of Failure," Journal of Accounting Research, Suplement. Empirical Research in Accounting: Select Studies, vol. 4, pp. 71–127, 1966.

[24] D. Trigueiros, "Incorporating Complementary Ratios in the Analysis of Financial Statements," Accounting, Management, and Information Technologies, vol. 4, no. 3, pp. 149–162, 1994.

[25] J. John and N. Draper, "An Alternative Family of Transformations," Journal of the Royal Statistical Society, Series C (Applied Statistics), vol. 29, no. 2, pp. 190–197, 1980.

[26] T. Dunne, C. Helliar, and R. Mousa, "Stakeholder Engagement in Internet Financial Reporting: The diffusion of XBRL in the UK," The British Accounting Review, vol. 45, no. 3, pp. 167–182, 2013.

[27] R. Bertolusso and M. Kimmel, "XBRL: Extraction of Business Financial Information from XBRL documents," 2015, CRAN repository, https://cran.r-project.org/web/packages/XBRL/index.html Retrieved: May 2016.

[28] E. Altman, Corporate Financial Distress. Wiley (New York), 1983.

[29] M. Bellovary and D. Giacomino, "A Review of Bankruptcy Prediction Studies: 1930-present," Journal of Financial Education, vol. 33, pp. 1–42, 2007.

[30] J. Ou, "The Information Content of Non-Earnings Accounting Numbers as Earnings Predictors," Journal of Accounting Research, vol. 28, no. 1, pp. 144–163, 1990.

[31] http://lopucki.law.ucla.edu/ Retrieved: May 2016.

[32] http://groups.haas.berkeley.edu/accounting/faculty/aaerdataset/ Retrieved: May 2016.

[33] D. Trigueiros and C. Sam, "Log-modulus for Knowledge Discovery in Databases of Financial Reports." in Proc. IMMM 2016: The Sixth International Conference on Advances in Information Mining and Management, Valencia, May 2016, pp. 26–31, ISBN: 978-1-61208-477-0.

[34] https://www.msci.com/gics Retrieved: May 2016.

[35] G. Hassibi and D. Stork, "Optimal Brain Surgeon, and General Network Pruning," in Proc. IEEE International Conference on Neural Networks, San Francisco, CA, 1993, vol. 1, pp. 293–299.

[36] T. Kohonen, Self-Organization, and Associative Memory. Springer Verlag (Berlin), 1984.

[37] N. Chawla, "Data Mining for Imbalanced Datasets: an Overview," in Data Mining, and Knowledge Discovery Handbook, O. Maimon, and L. Rokach, Eds. Springer US, pp. 853–867, 2005.

International Journal on Advances in Software, vol 9 no 1 & 2, year 2016, http://www.iariajournals.org/software/

Coordinated Task Scheduling in Virtualized Systems: Evaluation and Implementation Details

Jérémy Fanguède, Alexander Spyridakis and Daniel Raho
Virtual Open Systems
Grenoble - France
Email: {j.fanguede, a.spyridakis, s.raho}@virtualopensystems.com

***Abstract*—Task scheduling is one of the key subsystems of an operating system. Generally, by providing fairness in terms of processor time allocated to tasks, the task scheduler can guarantee low latency and high responsiveness to applications. In this paper, we demonstrate that specific problems can occur in virtualized environments, where virtual core scheduling on the host can negatively affect process scheduling in the guest. More precisely, there is a need to implement a communication channel between the host and guest task scheduler, particularly when full-virtualization techniques are used, in order to avoid latency issues and loss of responsiveness in virtual machines, especially when processors execute excessive workloads. After having analyzed the potential problems in virtual machines, experiments were performed with real world and benchmarking applications. In this work we detail possible solutions to solve the issue previously highlighted, and describe the proposed implementation, which is based on a coordinated scheduling mechanism between the host and guest systems. For testing, an embedded ARMv7 Linux-based platform and two different task schedulers were used, with a benchmark suite specifically designed for virtualized environments, with which application responsiveness and latency are measured and compared.**

***Keywords*—KVM/ARM; embedded virtualization; coordinated scheduling; embedded systems; task scheduling; CFS; BFS; para-virtualization**

I. INTRODUCTION

Virtualization technology offers a way to increase efficiency and adaptability both in general purpose and embedded systems, but to get an efficient virtualization solution, latency of virtual machines and responsiveness of applications should be guaranteed at a reasonable level. For instance, an interactive application launched in a virtual machine should not have much worse performance in terms of responsiveness and latency than one executed in a host machine in the same conditions.

In previous work, we showed that latency issues can occur with task schedulers under some conditions [1]. We have already experimented with this objective in mind, for storage-I/O, which led us to the implementation of Virtual-BFQ [2][3], a Linux I/O scheduler based on the Budget Fair Queuing (BFQ) scheduler [4]. The work described in this paper, instead targets process scheduling, so that it could be used as a complementary approach. The solution described in this paper is based on a coordinated scheduling mechanism. This type of solution has already been implemented specifically to make real-time hypervisors [5][6], while in this work we extend coordinated scheduling also to non real-time tasks.

In this paper, we provide the following contributions:

A. Contributions of this paper

We highlight that in virtualized environments there are latency problems with task scheduling, where a missing link between the guest and the host scheduler can affect performance negatively. In fact, there is a need to implement a coordinated communication channel between schedulers in virtual machines and the host task scheduler. As a consequence, latency of a guest operating system can be higher, especially in a system with many CPU-bound tasks. This results in degraded responsiveness of applications in virtual machines, compared to similar conditions for non-virtualized systems. To show this problem, through experimentation, we use two different Linux task schedulers.

Then, experimental results are reported; these results confirm that, in virtualized environments, when a process requires a high portion of the processor's time in both the guest and host system, the latency and the responsiveness of the guest application is not guaranteed.

A solution, described in this paper, based on a coordinated mechanism, solves the problem highlighted previously, it is based on the default Linux scheduler, CFS, which stands for *Completely Fair Scheduler*, the implementation is described in detail. Experimental results are reported for this extended version of CFS, which includes the coordinated scheduling mechanism.

An ARM-based embedded system was used to run the experiments, it aims to be representative of modern embedded systems and consumer devices, which have relatively small amount of CPU resources. Finally, the virtualization platform selected for this implementation is Kernel-based Virtual Machine (KVM) of Linux together with Quick EMUlator (QEMU), which are among the most popular solutions in embedded virtualization.

B. Organization of this paper

The paper is organized as follows. In Section II, a description of the two task schedulers used is provided. Then, in Section III latency problems and the lack of responsiveness is highlighted. After describing the benchmark suite and the experimentation methods in Section IV, the results are reported in Section V. In Section VI, possible solutions are detailed in order to solve the issue highlighted. Then, in Section VII the description of a solution based on a coordinated scheduling mechanism for the CFS scheduler is provided. Finally, in Section VIII we report our results for the same experiments, but with the coordinated scheduling mechanism developed for CFS.

II. Linux Task Schedulers

The task scheduler, also named process or CPU scheduler, is the part of an operating system that decides which task runs when, and on which core. The job of a scheduler is to share the CPU time between processes that require CPU resources, to pick a suitable task to run next if required, and to balance processes between the different CPUs in a multi-core system.

Two Linux task schedulers were used, CFS [7], which stands for *Completely Fair Scheduler* and is the default scheduler of the Linux kernel, and BFS [8] (see the acronym in [8]), which is a popular alternative.

By default, Linux can handle real-time and non real-time policies, which are implemented by the selected scheduler. Both CFS and BFS schedulers implement their own non real-time and share the same real-time policies. By extension, with the term CFS or BFS we refer to both the included scheduling policies of these schedulers, as well as the entirety of their implementation.

BFS, which is not part of the Linux mainline kernel [9], could be considered as an alternative, it is designed for desktop interactivity on machines with few cores [8], and its source code has a smaller footprint and is by design simpler. For these reasons, BFS was also selected in the experimental results as a comparison to CFS, in case where different behavior is observed.

A. The Completely Fair Scheduler

The default Linux kernel scheduler, named *Completely Fair Scheduler* [7], is modular and permits to use different policies for different tasks. Linux has two main types of scheduling policies: a real-time one for real-time task and a normal one named *fair policy* for all other tasks.

Among the real time scheduling, Linux distinguishes three policies: SCHED_FIFO, a first-in, first-out policy; SCHED_RR, a round robin policy; and SCHED_DEADLINE, a policy implementing the earliest deadline first algorithm (since kernel v3.14). Additionally within the fair scheduling policies: SCHED_NORMAL, the default Linux time-sharing policy, and SCHED_BATCH, a policy for "batch" processes.

Linux defines the static priority of a task by a value, which ranges from 0 to 99, while the real-time scheduling class uses values from 1 (lowest priority) to 99 (highest priority). Processes using the fair scheduling class have necessarily a static priority of 0. In order to determine which thread (or process) should be run next, the Linux scheduler maintains a list of runnable processes for each possible static priority, and it selects the head of the list with the highest static priority. In other words, a thread, with a higher static priority than the current running thread which becomes runnable, will necessarily preempt the current process. For the fair scheduling class, the kernel uses a priority called dynamic priority, which from a user's point of view is also better known as the *nice value*, and it ranges from -20 (highest priority) to +19.

CFS is used as the default Linux scheduler since kernel version v2.6.23, it replaced the old scheduler: *O(1)*. And implements a completely fair algorithm (hence the name). The algorithm is based on the concept of an ideal multi-tasking processor. With such a processor, each runnable task would run at the same time, sharing the processor power. Of course, this behavior is not possible, but an equivalent behavior, would be to run each runnable task for an infinitesimal amount of time with full processing power. Due to task switching cost, CFS only approximates this behavior.

For that purpose, CFS stores the runtime value of each task in a variable called *vruntime* (stands for virtual runtime) and tries to keep all *vruntime* values the closer to each other. So the runnable task that has the lower *vruntime* value is chosen to be the next task to run. The priority of a task (the dynamic priority, i.e., the nice value) influences the way vruntime is increased.

To handle interactive tasks, CFS does not use complex heuristics. In fact, the concept of fair scheduling is enough to maximize interface performance. For example, consider a processor-bound task (e.g., an encryption calculation, a video encoder, etc.) and a I/O-bound task (e.g., a terminal, a text editor, etc.), which will be the interactive task. In that situation, the scheduler should give to the interactive task a larger share of the processor time to enhance the user experience. In fact, this is what CFS will do: CFS wants to be fair, so each time the interactive task become runnable, CFS will see that this task consumed significantly less processor time than the CPU-bound task. So, the interactive task will preempt the other, and will be executed until its runtime reaches the value of the processor-bound task or be blocked from an I/O request.

B. BFS - The Alternative

BFS is an alternative to CFS, it was written by *Con Kolivas*. It is not in the mainline kernel and is available as source code patches [9].

BFS focuses on a simplistic design (about 2.5 times fewer lines of code than CFS) and aims for excellent desktop interactivity and responsiveness on personal computers with a reasonable amount of cores [8]. It uses a single work-queue, $O(n)$ look-up for all cores unlike CFS, and implements the *earliest eligible virtual deadline first* algorithm for non real-time policies.

BFS, like CFS, provides real-time task policies: SCHED_FIFO and SCHED_RR, and also two others policies for normal tasks: SCHED_ISO and SCHED_IDLEPRIO. The first, SCHED_ISO (for isochronous) is designed to provide "near real-time" performance to unprivileged users. And SCHED_IDLEPRIO scheduling policy can be used to run tasks only when the CPU would be idle otherwise.

The design of BFS makes it efficient when the number of running processes is small (inferior than the number of CPUs), which is normally, according to its author [8], a common use case for a desktop computer.

III. Potential Problems in Virtualized Environments

In a virtualized environment a guest system is seen, from the host scheduler, as just one, or more additional jobs to

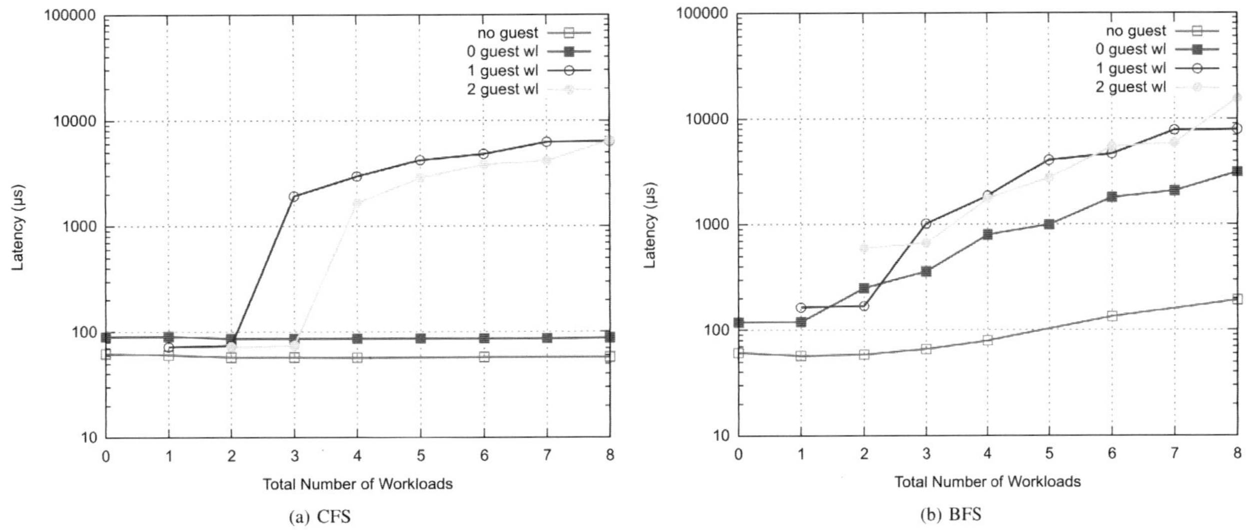

Figure 1. Latency results

schedule, without any awareness from the host of the fine-grained requirements of the corresponding guest scheduler. For example, a new spawned task in the guest system could be scheduled in a different way by the guest scheduler, but this information is not visible on the host side. Under certain conditions, this could lead to undesired behavior.

To highlight the problem we can consider a system, with two physical CPUs and a guest with one virtual CPU. Two CPU-bound workloads are launched in the host (one per CPU) and one in the guest (one per virtual-CPU). In this situation, the task scheduler will share fairly the processor time between the vCPU thread (which runs a workload) and the two workloads in the host, since these three tasks are quite similar in terms of CPU time demand.

When an interactive task is started in the guest system, the guest scheduler will *detect* this new task and assign a substantial amount of the vCPU time compared to the workload running in the same guest. On the host side though, the scheduler sees only three processes that request a large amount of CPU time for only two CPUs. So, the host scheduler has absolutely no reasons to privilege the vCPU thread compared to other processes (workloads). Additionally, the latency of this interactive task will probably be higher than in a host system with the same number of workloads (aside from the constant overhead of KVM/QEMU). This problem persists for whatever value the priority of the interactive task in the guest is set to (could be a real-time one), since the priorities and policies are not made aware to the host system.

IV. Experiment Method and Benchmark Suite

To highlight the problem described above, we set up a benchmark suite in order to measure, in particular, the latency of the system. We used the tool, *cyclictest*, which is usually used to measure latency on a *Real Time Linux* (i.e, patched with *rt* patches) [10]. Generally, *cyclictest* is used to measure the latency of real-time thread/process (schedule with SCHED_FIFO or SCHED_RR), but it can also be used with *normal* (SCHED_NORMAL) threads. For each latency measurement *cyclictest* is run twice, each one with a 100000 loop, which means that the latency provided by the benchmark is the average of 200 thousands measurements. The following command line is used "cyclictest -q -n -l 100000 -h 5000" to generate the results, and the latency histogram is also retrieved (*-h* option) in order to analyze in more detail.

The second kind of benchmark measures the *start-up time* of an application. We simply measured how long it takes from when an application is launched to when an application is ready. This benchmark gives an idea of the *responsiveness* of an application. The start-up time is measured with hot caches, to avoid any I/O perturbations. For each configuration (i.e., number of workload in the host and guest), 100 measurement iterations are performed, and the average, as well as the standard deviation are retrieved.

As workload, we used a simple program that does an *infinite loop* and, therefore has a very low memory footprint.

V. Experimental Results

We executed our experiments on a Samsung Chromebook equipped with an ARMv7-A Cortex-A15 processor (dual-core, 1.7 GHz) and 2 GB of RAM. Both the host and the guest run upstream Linux v3.17 with the *PREEMPT* configuration option enabled.

A. Latency

In order to measure latency, we used the *cyclictest* tool and the number of workloads is kept the same as in the start-up time test. The result of this experiment is shown in Figure 1, where latency is measured in microseconds and represented in a logarithmic scale on axis Y.

For the host and guest system we employed up to 8 and 2 workloads, respectively. Axis X corresponds to the total number of workloads, i.e., host plus guest workloads. The output of the results are four different curves:

no guest: No virtual machine, serves as reference, the application is launched in the host

N guest wl: With N workloads in the guest, the application is launched in the guest. With N ranging from **0** to **2**.

We can notice that, with the CFS scheduler (Figure 1a), as soon as there are more workloads than physical cores (total of two cores in the system, latency increases significantly for the critical curves, which are *1 guest wl* and *2 guest wl*) and with at least one workload in the guest. By adding more workloads, this behavior persists until values are not suitable for interactive usage. This kind of result confirms the issue highlighted in Section III, where an interactive application in a virtualized system can have an extremely high latency.

Also, it worth noting that the latency is better with *2 guest workloads* than with *1 guest workload* when the total number of workloads is high. This behavior is perfectly explainable due to the difference in the number of workloads in the host. For instance, in the specific case of 4 total workloads, when we have *1 guest workload* the host system *sees* four main processes requesting a high amount of CPU time for only two CPUs, but when we have *2 guest workloads*, there are only three processes that still share two CPUs. In the latter case, the process corresponding to the vCPU has more CPU time: this could lead, depending on the efficiency of the guest scheduler, to a better latency compared to the former case.

With BFS (Figure 1b), the results are less obvious, but we can still notice the difference between virtualized and normal environments, and between the curves of 1 or 2 guest workloads and the curve of 0 guest workloads.

Although our objective is not to purely compare the two schedulers, which has already been done [11], we can remark that even with no virtual machines (curve *no guest*), latency with BFS increases steadily, contrary to CFS. This is probably due to the fact that BFS is not designed to be efficient when the number of running tasks is higher than the number of physical cores [8].

We can also analyze the histogram provided by the *cyclictest* results to compare the distribution of latency. Figure 2 shows the two latency histograms on a virtual machine without any workload. We can notice that even if the average value is slightly lower with CFS, the BFS case exposes more converged values with a lower maximum.

In Figure 3, two cases are compared for CFS latency measured in a virtual machine. Both test cases have the same amount of CPU-bound workloads, but distributed in a different manner. In the first case all workloads reside in the host, while in the second, one of the workloads is reserved for the guest. Although the distribution of samples for low latency is quite similar for both cases, in the case where one of the workloads is in the guest, we still observe a significant amount of samples in the range of 200 to 5000 μs. This is different from the first case, where almost all samples are around the 100 μs mark.

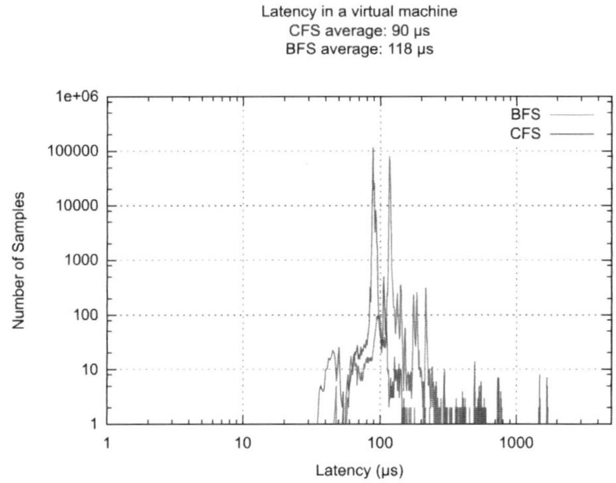

Figure 2. Guest Latency compared between BFS and CFS

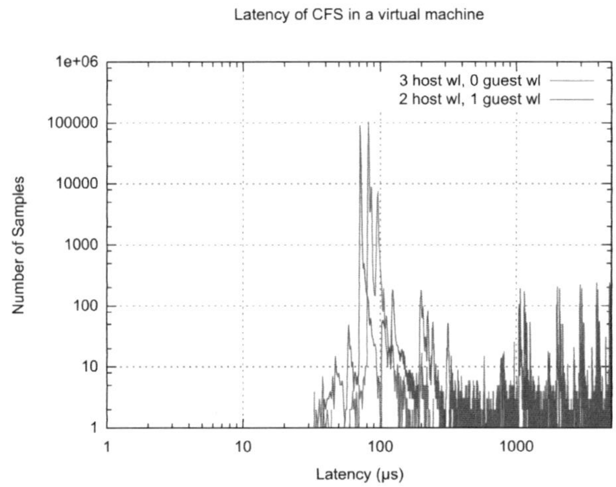

Figure 3. CFS latency in a virtual machine, compared between 3 host workloads and 2 host and 1 guest workloads

B. Start-up Time

Next, we measure the start-up time of an application. We choose the *xterm* application because its start-up time can be easily measured. In addition, this application was also selected to measure performance of the BFQ and Virtual-BFQ I/O scheduler [2] [3] [4].

As we can see in this Figure 4a, which represents the startup time measured with the CFS scheduler, the curve corresponding to a measurement in the host (*no guest*) has a slightly positive constant slope. This increase is not unexpected because CFS tries to guarantee only fairness: an increase in the number of CPU-bound can negatively affect the start-up time of a new application. Curve *0 guest wl* corresponds to the case in which there is no workload in the guest, but only in the host. We can see that this curve almost follows curve *no guest*, where a constant overhead is observed.

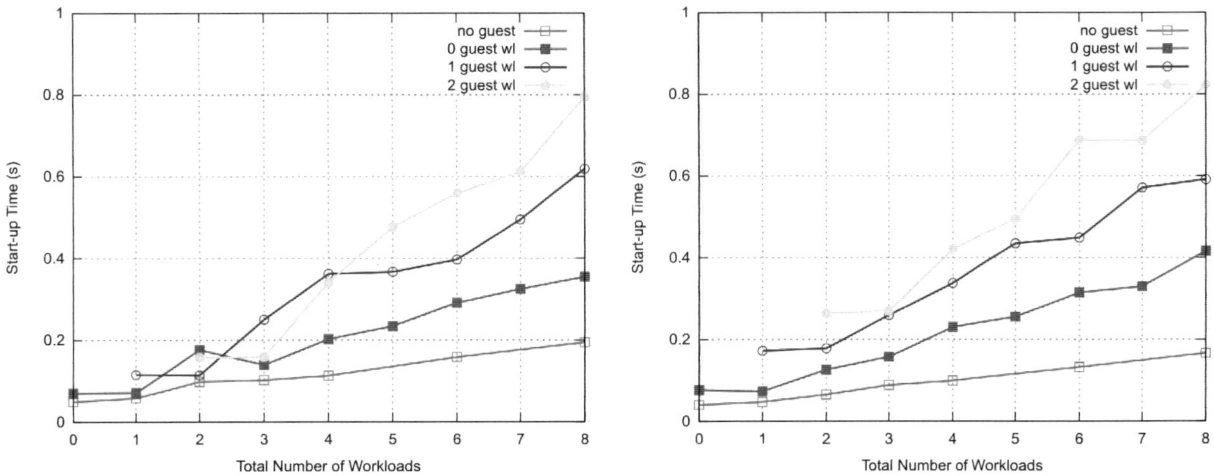

(a) CFS (b) BFS

Figure 4. Start-up time results

In view of the problem highlighted above, the critical scenarios are the ones corresponding to the curves *1 guest wl* and *2 guest wl*, more particularly when the number of workloads in the host is equal or greater than number of physical cores (in our case 2). In fact, when vCPU threads are allowed to use all available cores, the results are acceptable as the start-up time remains quite low (case *1 guest wl* with a total workload of *1* and *2*, and with *2 guest wl* with *2* and *3* total workloads). To summarize our test case results, when the number of workloads in the host is higher than two, the start-up time increases significantly.

With the BFS scheduler (Figure 4b), although the appearance of the curves seems quite different, we have the same behavior: higher start-up times when there are too many workloads.

To sum up, our results are coherent both for start-up times as well as latency. Moreover, they clearly prove that, in scenarios where a workload is present in both the guest and host, the responsiveness of an application in the guest can not be guaranteed.

VI. Solutions

For the scheduling problem described in the previous chapters, there are two possible solutions that are proposed below. First, scheduling via a simple static prioritization policy and second, a coordinated solution that enables communication between the schedulers of the host and guest systems.

A. Static prioritizing

A straightforward solution could be a static prioritization scheme, by simply increasing the priority of the QEMU vCPU threads, or by changing the scheduling policy to a real-time one. This solution will allow QEMU/KVM to avoid interference from other tasks in the host system (if there are no other real-time threads). This method will result in a better latency, in particular a reduction of the maximum latency [6]. With this solution though, the guest is always privileged even when it does not execute an interactive program. This solution can be useful for simple use cases, i.e., when a guest system which executes soft real-time applications needs to be prioritized compared to other guests or applications. But in more demanding use cases, where efficiency is required, statically raising the priority of a vCPU is not an option.

B. Coordinated scheduling

Instead of prioritizing QEMU threads statically, another solution could be to *boost* these threads only when it is necessary, i.e., temporary increasing the priority or changing the scheduler policy, when the guest system requests it. It is a sort of dynamic prioritizing with a coordinated scheduling mechanism: the guest kernel detects when it needs higher priority, and informs the host system about it. This *co-scheduling* mechanism was already implemented successfully for Virtual-BFQ [3], therefore, the communication mechanism could be equivalent to the one developed for that storage I/O scheduler.

This type of solution has already been implemented and evaluated, especially to make KVM a real-time hypervisor [5] [12] on the *x86* architecture. Such attempts mainly focused to run a real-time Linux OS as a guest, thus, when a guest executes a real-time thread it informs the host of its current scheduling policy and priority, the host system then has to pass on this policy and priority to the affected QEMU thread.

In order to extend this coordinated scheduling mechanism also to non real-time applications, a mechanism to detect interactive applications in the guest system is needed. Heuristic algorithms have to be added for this purpose.

The communication mechanism between the host and guest scheduler, is a crucial part, it needs to be fast or at least not too frequent. The solution chosen in the Virtual-BFQ [3] I/O scheduler is to use, a special ARM instruction, *HVC*, that results in a hypervisor *trap*. Moreover, the cost of calling this instruction, around 2000 CPU cycles (for an ARM Samsung Chromebook), is not very expensive and can fit the requirement of a task scheduling coordinated mechanism.

VII. Coordinated Scheduling Proof of concept for CFS

We choose to implement a coordinated mechanism for the CFS scheduler as a proof of concept for ARM processors. A similar mechanism has been also developed for the BFS scheduler, but for the sake of clarity and simplicity only the CFS implementation and its results are detailed, since they are very similar to BFS. This implementation is based on the *HVC* instruction as a communication mechanism between the guest and the host. The virtual machine is able to inform the host when it wants to be prioritized, depending on the real-time or interactive tasks that are executed, as well as when it does not need any prioritization anymore, i.e., a "deboost". This communication mechanism, using *HVC*, is wrapped around the "paravirt"[13] and "hypercall" infrastructure of Linux. Since this "paravirt" and "hypercall" infrastructure does not exist, yet, for *KVM on ARM*, we had to implement it. This implementation is described in the following sections.

A. Paravirt ops interface for ARM

Linux already provides a way to perform some paravirtual actions through an infrastructure named `paravirt-ops` (`pv-ops` for short)[13]. This API is used to run para-virtualized virtual machines on multiple hypervisors with the same kernel binary. This means that the same kernel binary can run on bare hardware, or on hypervisors such as VMWARE VNI or Xen, and it can be para-virtualized or fully virtualized[14].

This infrastructure exists for multiple architectures and hypervisors, but not for *KVM on ARM*, the virtualization solution we use. Therefore, a basic `paravirt-ops` implementation was developed. It is based on a patch series that enables `paravirt-ops` for Xen on ARM/ARM64[15], thus, only the KVM related part was developed.

The paravirtual functions require a hypercall implementation, to be able to send information to the host system. Therefore, hypercall functions specific to KVM have been implemented into the KVM code base of the Linux kernel. These functions use the *HVC* instruction of the ARM architecture, with the immediate argument of the HVC instruction being a constant integer used to recognize a *paravirt* call (from a PSCI call, for instance, which can also use an *HVC* instruction[17]). The parameters of the hypercall are passed through the scratch registers, *r0* contains the identification number of the hypercall and registers *r1* to *r3* represent the potential arguments for this hypercall. Figure 5 details the implementation of the `kvm_hypercall1`, which is the hypercall implementation for hypercalls with one parameter.

Those hypercalls are called from the `paravirt-ops` implementation of each paravirtualized subsystem. In our case, it simply consist of pointers to functions, stored in a structure that represent the paravirt subsystem. Those functions are

```
static inline int kvm_hypercall1(u32 num, u32 arg1)
{
    register u32 n asm("r0"); /* Hypercall ID */
    register u32 r asm("r0"); /* Returned value */
    register u32 a1 asm("r1"); /* First argument */

    n = num; /* Hypercall ID is stored in r0 */
    a1 = arg1; /* The first argument is stored
        in r1 */
    __asm__ __volatile__(
      __HVC(KVM_IMM)
      : "=r" (r) : "r" (n), "r" (a1) : "memory"
      ); /* Inline assembly to call HVC
          instruction */

    return r;
}
```

Figure 5. Source code for the hypercall "1" of KVM on ARM

called if the `paravirt-ops` infrastructure is enabled for the hypervisor on which the virtual machine is running.

For our needs a *paravirt-ops* interface named `pv_cosched_ops` was added. Along with a new hypercall named `KVM_HC_COSCHED`. The `pv_cosched_ops` paravirt interface contains three functions:

- **New task**, `new_task()`
  Called each time a new process is created. We use this function to implement a heuristic mechanism to detect which are the tasks that need to be prioritized. This function is called from `wake_up_new_task()` in the Linux kernel code (kernel/sched/core.c)[16].
- **Activate task**, `activate_task()`
  Called each time a task becomes runnable. That is to say, each time a task that was waiting voluntary or due to an I/O wait becomes runnable again. We also use this function for the detection mechanism of the task to prioritize. This function is called from the function `activate_task()` in the Linux kernel (kernel/sched/core.c).
- **Schedule**, `schedule()`
  Called each time a new task is scheduled. It is in this paravirt function that the hypercall `KVM_HC_COSCHED` is performed; to request a *boost* or a *deboost*. This function is called from `__schedule()` in the Linux kernel code (kernel/sched/core.c).

On the host side, *HVC* instructions executed by the guest are trapped by KVM (in function `handle_hvc()` in arch/arm/kvm/handle_exit.c), and thus, can be handled correctly, the immediate argument of the *HVC* instruction is also checked to be sure that it is a hypercall and not something else. Then, KVM can perform the corresponding action to this hypercall according to the value retrieved from `r0`.

For the hypercall we added, `KVM_HC_COSCHED`. It takes only one argument, which is an integer set to `1` if the guest needs to be prioritized and `0` if it does not need this anymore.

B. Host side

The modifications done in the host side are located in the KVM and scheduler code base of Linux. We had to implement the "backend" of the `KVM_HC_COSCHED` hypercall, which retrieves the argument of the hypercall and performs the corresponding actions. Thus, according to the argument, which could be `0` or `1` the hypercall handler will finally invoke the functions `coshed_boost_task()` or `coshed_deboost_task()` on task `current`. The task `current` is always a vCPU thread in that case.

The added function `cosched_boost_task()` lives in the scheduler code base of Linux (kernel/sched/core.c), it takes a `struct task_struct` as an argument, which is the task to prioritize (although in our case this function is always called with `current` as an argument). It boosts the priority of all threads associated to this task, i.e., the potential other vCPU threads and the I/O threads. We choose to prioritize those processes with a `SHED_RR` policy of priority 1. For this purpose, it invokes the function `sched_setscheduler_nocheck()` to change the scheduling policy of these tasks.

The function `cosched_deboost_task()` does the reverse operation, that is to say it *deboosts* all the threads related the virtual machine, so that the policy of the processes is re-set to `SCHED_NORMAL`.

C. Guest side

On the guest side the modifications consist of calling the hypercall to request a *boost* or a *deboost* at the right time. Therefore, the `schedule()` paravirt function of `pv_coshed_ops` is called from the core `__schedule()` function (in kernel/sched/core.c)[16] equipped with the next task to schedule as a parameter. A test on this future process to run is performed to determine if this process needs to be prioritized or not, according to this information the hypercall is executed with the correct argument (*boost* or *deboost*).

Importantly enough, the time needed to perform a hypercall is not negligible, especially because of the *HVC* instruction, trapped by KVM. We estimate that the guest to host plus host to guest context switch, is around 2.1K cycles for the *Samsung ARM Chromebook* with Linux kernel v3.17. Thus, if the number of hypercalls is too frequent the performance will be worse than without the co-scheduling mechanism due to this overhead. So, in order to solve this problem, the guest will request a boost for a process, for at least a minimal period of time, i.e., the guest guarantees that it will not require a prioritization period inferior of the minimal boost time. The pseudo-code of this paravirtual `schedule()` function is detailed in Figure 6.

Function `need_to_be_boosted()` determines whether a task deserves to be prioritized or not. All tasks managed by a real time policy (i.e., `SCHED_FIFO`, `SCHED_RR` and `SCHED_DEADLINE`) are qualified for being "boosted", it corresponds to all the tasks that have the `prio` field of the `struct task_struct` strictly inferior to `100`. For tasks managed by the fair policies (i.e., `SCHED_NORMAL` and `SCHED_BATCH`), a linked list of all tasks to prioritize is maintained, this is where the two other paravirt functions are useful: *New task* and *Activate task*.

```
function pv_cosched_ops.schedule(next_task):
static start_time /* Time on which a task
    needed a boost */
static boosted = false /* Static variable that
    stored the state of the guest */
  if need_to_be_boosted(next_task):
     start_time = current_time() /* Time is
         updated */
     if not boosted:
        /* Ask for a boost */
        kvm_hypercall1(KVM_HC_COSCHED, 1)
        boosted = true
  else if boosted:
     now = current_time()
     /* Check if enough time has been spent
         on boost */
     if (start_time + MIN_BOOST_TIME) <= now:
        /* Ask for a deboost */
        kvm_hypercall1(KVM_HC_COSCHED, 0)
        boosted = false
```

Figure 6. Pseudo-code of the paravirtual "schedule" function

Each time a new task is created the paravirt function `new_task()` adds this task to the *prioritized list of tasks* and each task has a counter associated and initialized to a positive value. This paravirt function is called form `wake_up_new_task()` in Linux (kernel/sched/-core.c). Each time a task of this list is scheduled, its counter is decremented (in the `schedule()` paravirt function), and when it reaches 0 the task is removed from the list. The counter is incremented each time a task is woke-up from a voluntary sleep, that is to say, a sleep caused by the task itself, e.g., a wait for a I/O job or a timer, this is done in paravirt `activate_task()`, which is called from `activate_task()` in Linux (kernel/sched/core.c).

VIII. Experimental Results with Coordinated Scheduling

We repeated the same experiments as in Section V, but with the co-scheduling mechanism previously described. We report the results for the CFS scheduler, including latency and start-up time tests. The testing platform is once again *Samsung's ARM Chromebook* with version 3.17 of the Linux kernel.

A. Latency

The selected application to measure latency while testing is *cyclictest*. The minimal prioritization time (minimal boost time) selected is *500* μs, which according to our tests corresponds to the best compromise between performance and granularity in the coordination mechanism.

The results are compared to the ones reported in Section V, Figure 1a. The first four curves are kept the same for reference, and the results corresponding to co-scheduling are curves: *0 guest wl with co-sched*, *1 guest wl with co-sched* and *2 guest wl with co-sched*. The same *cyclictest* command line is used (two times, 100000 measurements, with a default interval of 1 ms).

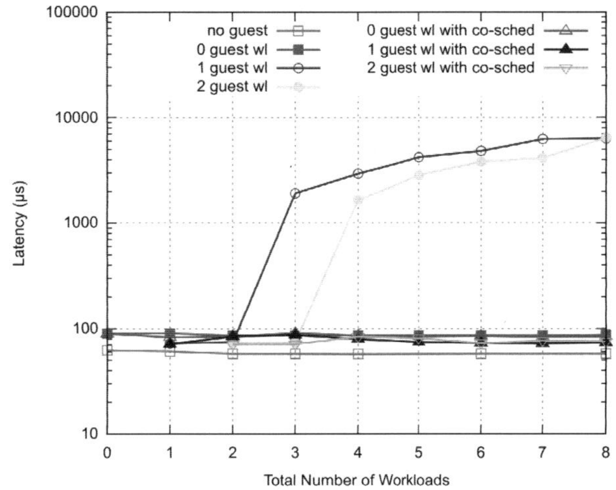

Figure 7. CFS latency results with and without coordinated scheduling mechanism

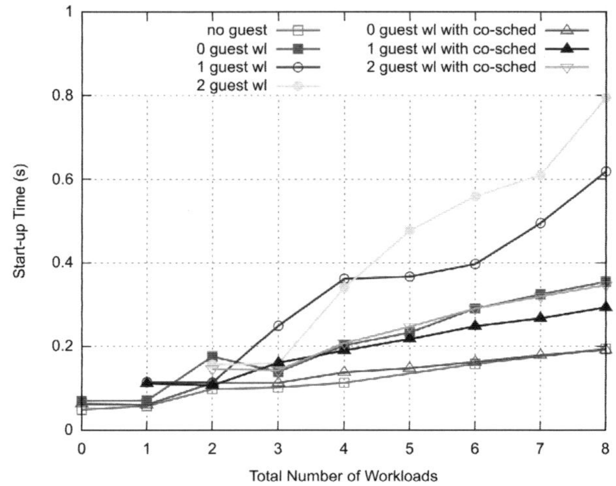

Figure 9. CFS start-up time results with and without coordinated scheduling mechanism

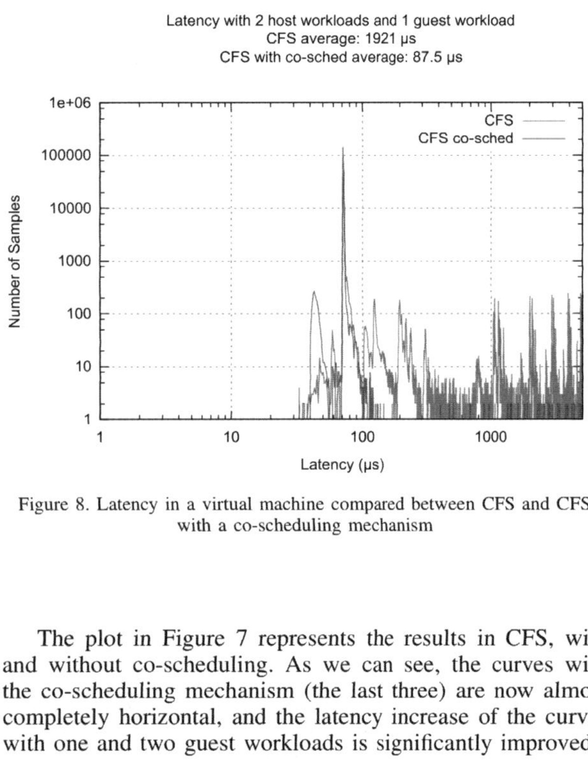

Figure 8. Latency in a virtual machine compared between CFS and CFS with a co-scheduling mechanism

The plot in Figure 7 represents the results in CFS, with and without co-scheduling. As we can see, the curves with the co-scheduling mechanism (the last three) are now almost completely horizontal, and the latency increase of the curves with one and two guest workloads is significantly improved.

Figure 8 represents the histogram of the distribution of the latency measured by *cyclictest* for the case where the system is loaded with two host workloads and one guest workload. First, we notice than the average latency with coordinated scheduling is now close to the average latency of a system without workloads, given the high value for CFS without coordinated scheduling (1921 μs). The distribution of latency is also better since there are less overall values in the high range.

B. *Startup Time*

The start-up time measurements were also tested with the coordinated scheduling mechanism, where latency measurements are compared to the initial tests found in Figure 4a.

The plot in Figure 9 shows the start-up time results of *xterm*, with and without the coordinated scheduling mechanism in CFS. The minimal prioritization time used is also kept at 500 μs. We can observe a significant improvement since the curves with the coordinated scheduling mechanism have, a lower slope, and the difference with the *no_guest* curve is almost constant.

IX. CONCLUSION AND FUTURE WORKS

In virtualized environments, we highlighted that the task scheduler in the host, can fail to preserve low latency for the guest environment, and thus to maintain responsiveness when the system is loaded with CPU-bound programs in certain conditions. The behavior of an interactive application inside a guest will be masked by other processes requiring a lot of CPU time in the host, and the attempts of the guest scheduler to enhance the responsiveness of this application may be ineffective. This issue mostly occurs when the number of CPU-bound processes is higher than the number of physical cores in the system.

Furthermore, from this work, it is shown that a coordinated scheduling mechanism can be used for process scheduling, as a way to achieve lower latency and high responsiveness in an over-committed virtual environment. The target platform used for the implementation and testing of this mechanism was based on an ARMv7 embedded system with the KVM hypervisor. Additionally, a new paravirtual interface for the scheduler was introduced, which makes easier the implementation and deployment of a coordinated scheduler.

The presented implementation of coordinated scheduling is still a proof of concept, and further optimization and regression testing is needed, especially in the area of task detection heuristics. Finally, an extension for tests with more complex scenarios, including more than one virtual machines and multiple vCPUs, is under way.

ACKNOWLEDGMENT

This research work has been supported by the Seventh Framework Programme (FP7/2007-2013) of the European Community under the grant agreement no. 610640 for the DREAMS project.

REFERENCES

[1] J. Fanguède, A. Spyridakis, and D. Raho, "Towards Coordinated Task Scheduling in Virtualized Systems," ADVCOMP 2015, The Ninth International Conference on Advanced Engineering Computing and Applications in Sciences, 2015, pp. 106-111.

[2] A. Spyridakis and D. Raho. "On Application Responsiveness and Storage Latency in Virtualized Environments," CLOUD COMPUTING 2014, The Fifth International Conference on Cloud Computing, GRIDs, and Virtualization, 2014, pp. 26-30.

[3] A. Spyridakis, D. Raho, and J. Fanguède, "Virtual-BFQ: A Coordinated Scheduler to Minimize Storage Latency and Improve Application Responsiveness in Virtualized Systems," International Journal on Advances in Software, vol 7 no 3 & 4, 2014, pp. 642-652.

[4] P. Valente and M. Andreolini, "Improving application responsiveness with the BFQ disk I/O scheduler," Proceedings of the 5th Annual International Systems and Storage Conference (SYSTOR'12), June 2012, p. 6.

[5] J. Kiszka, "Towards linux as a real-time hypervisor," In Proceedings of the 11th Real-Time Linux Workshop, 2009, pp. 215-224.

[6] R. Ma, F. Zhou, E. Zhu, and H. Guan, "Performance Tuning Towards a KVM-based Embedded Real-Time Virtualization System," Journal of Information Science and Engineering 29.5, 2013, pp. 1021-1035.

[7] "CFS scheduler," [retrieved: February 2016]. Available: http://lwn.net/Articles/230501/

[8] C. Kolivas, "BFS FAQ," [retrieved: February 2016]. Available: http://ck.kolivas.org/patches/bfs/bfs-faq.txt.

[9] C. Kolivas, "BFS Patches," [retrieved: February 2016]. Available: http://ck.kolivas.org/patches/bfs/3.0/.

[10] "Cyclictest," [retrieved: February 2016]. Available: https://rt.wiki.kernel.org/index.php/Cyclictest

[11] T. Groves, J. Knockel, and E. Schulte. "Bfs vs. cfs scheduler comparison," 2009.

[12] M. Aichouch, J-C. Prevotet, and F. Nouvel, "Evaluation of an RTOS on top of a hosted virtual machine system," In Design and Architectures for Signal and Image Processing (DASIP), 2013 Conference on. IEEE, 2013, pp. 290-297.

[13] "Linux kernel paravirt_ops documentation," [retrieved: February 2016]. Available: http://lxr.free-electrons.com/source/Documentation/virtual/paravirt_ops.txt

[14] "Xen Paravirt ops," [retrieved: February 2016]. Available: http://wiki.xen.org/wiki/XenParavirtOps

[15] S. Stabellini, "Xen ARM/ARM64 CONFIG_PARAVIRT patch series" [retrieved: February 2016]. Available: http://lists.xen.org/archives/html/xen-devel/2014-01/msg00851.html

[16] "Linux process scheduler core code file," [retrieved: February 2016]. Available: http://lxr.free-electrons.com/source/kernel/sched/core.c

[17] "PSCI Linux documentation," [retrieved: February 2016]. Available: http://lxr.free-electrons.com/source/Documentation/devicetree/bindings/arm/psci.txt

Enterprise Integration Modeling

A Practical Enterprise Integration Solution Featuring an Incremental Approach via Prototyping

Mihaela Iridon
Cândea LLC
Dallas, TX, USA
e-mail: iridon.mihaela@gmail.com

Abstract*— As larger and more complex line-of-business (LoB) software systems emerge and grow within an organization so does the need for such systems to interact with each other and exchange data, making it imperative to design flexible, scalable integration architectures and frameworks to support a robust and well-performing enterprise system. System integration is a multi-faceted undertaking, ranging from low-level data sharing (Shared Repository or File Sharing), to point-to-point communications (Remote Procedure Invocation via Service Orientation), to decoupled data exchange architectures (Messaging). It is not uncommon to build entire integration sub-systems responsible not only for exchanging information between systems (commands and notifications) but also for potentially more complex business logic orchestration across the entire enterprise (Message Broker). Moreover, implementing large integration solutions carries a considerable amount of risk so it is imperative that such solutions be validated by releasing functional prototypes to a smaller client bases in order to ascertain the benefits of - and perhaps the clients' interest in - delivering new features. This paper is contemplating a practical data notification and synchronization integration solution that allows multiple enterprise domains to share data that is critical for business operations. The solution features an incremental delivery approach based on initial prototyping that allowed for additional market analysis and a gradual integration. The article presents the architecture achieving this business objective, together with the corresponding system models and design artifacts. It described the data integration solution realized using a broker-based messaging approach employing various enterprise integration patterns, as well as the initial synchronous functional prototype and the many benefits of software system prototyping in general.

Keywords-enterprise integration; system modeling; data integration; canonical model; integration patterns; prototyping; simulation; testing.

I. INTRODUCTION

Within an enterprise, system integration solutions are usually designed and implemented as an afterthought, as an attempt to build or to expand a new or existing enterprise architecture comprised of heterogeneous legacy system. It may be safe to say that most companies do not start with an integrated enterprise architecture but rather a core domain (also referred to as a vertical), which will eventually grow and become part of a larger enterprise system as the industry case described in [1]. In many cases, such integration is achieved by employing various off-the-shelf integration products, such as Microsoft's BizTalk [2] or TIBCO's Integration Platform [3].

Software system integration comes in different flavors, depending on the business objectives, the overall enterprise architecture, and ultimately the realization approach chosen. In Section II, we will investigate these driving factors and then present a concrete implementation approach and its models in Section III, as it has been proposed and adopted by a provider of the nation's largest portfolio of benefit and payroll products and services designed to help more than 200,000 small and medium-sized businesses [1].

The beginning of Section III also examines the motivation behind this paper by attempting to set the right expectations with the reader and to rationalize the purpose of the technical artifacts gathered here. It strives to provide relevant context and comprehension that underscores the focal point of this document: a practical application of integration patterns and system integration modeling towards building a concrete industry solution, with the intention of sharing experience, approaches, challenges, and design artifacts that are neither trivial nor stereotypical.

The present article is an elaboration of the "Enterprise Integration Modeling: A Practical Enterprise Data Integration and Synchronization Solution" paper presented at IARIA's First International Conference on Fundamentals and Advances in Software Systems Integration (FASSI 2015) [1]. This paper focuses on architectural modeling applied in a real-case enterprise implementation, but also captures relevant aspects regarding prototyping as a tool for analysis and risk mitigation that enabled a phased market release.

The central topic described in this paper represents a data integration and synchronization blueprint aimed at implementing the "Maintain Data Copies" data integration pattern [4] by means of a decoupled integration mechanism realized on a custom broker-based messaging architecture [1] [5] [6]. The data payloads exchanged between the loosely coupled sub-systems abide to a *ubiquitous* integration language, referred to as the *canonical model* [7] and is described in Section IV. This model is the unified abstraction of the data structures that must be shared and synchronized between these systems.

Section V describes the functional prototype that was initially implemented and released to a reduced client base. It features a synchronous messaging approach as a generalization of the larger integration vision. The purpose of the prototype was to provide the necessary tools for a deeper analysis, both of the market reception and feature usability, as well as of the overall integration challenges and effort.

Section V concludes by presenting various aspects and benefits of software system prototyping – as identified in this particular implementation – with emphasis on prototyping for system integration. It also discusses how prototyping and building synthetic components helped alleviate some of the challenges encountered, including distributed teams' collaboration, component development, and unit and system integration testing.

Concluding remarks and highlights of the information shared in this paper are summarized in the final section.

II. System Integration Perspectives: Comparing and Contrasting Functional and Data Integration

When building a large enterprise software system by bringing together multiple domain applications, it is important to first identify the level of abstraction at which the integration specifications are being defined: Do the integrating sub-systems only need the data that allows them to carry out their own functions, or do they also require access to cross-domain exposed functional features? In other words, should a system expose data only or features as well?

The answers to these questions will determine the type of integration that must be realized: data or functional integration, and, perhaps even further, it will help discern between the need of a flexible, lightweight, loosely-coupled integration architecture and one that adds enterprise features and interactions, transcending domain system boundaries.

It is also possible that, in some cases, a hybrid approach will be pertinent, either to realize a quick and simple integration with a narrower scope (e.g., a pilot or test product implementation), or to overcome deep architectural and data model discrepancies between the existing systems. In this case, the solution must fulfill some imperative enterprise needs - whether they are related to exposing new system features in a short amount of time or at a lower cost until further market research proves the worthiness of additional funding for a comprehensive, scalable, extensible, and suitable solution. These considerations are primarily relevant when contemplating a phased delivery to the customer base in order to reduce the amount of risk that larger, more complex integration solutions usually incur.

A. Functional Integration

This type of integration involves exposing data and behavior [8] to systems that participate in the integration in order to trigger or invoke business features exposed by these systems. Usually, a pure Service Oriented Architecture (SOA) [9] [10] would be the simplest architectural approach that could realize this requirement, but it would introduce system coupling and would also lead to serious scalability concerns [11]. However, a synchronous point-to-point integration solution is perfectly suitable in many cases, and – as it will be presented here – would make perfect candidate for an initial system prototype. Web Services implement in effect the Remote Procedure Invocation integration pattern paradigm [7] and this implies mutual awareness of the presence of – and the functionality provided by - each of the integrating systems.

Complexity becomes apparent when more than two systems must interact at a logical and/or functional level of abstraction by invoking these exposed features and generating chattiness across the network, or when systems evolve, possibly threatening the stability of the integration contracts and hence of the solution. Several options are available to alleviate these problems, from architectural ones to following best practices, proper functional decomposition, and service encapsulation, and eventually to making the proper technology choices [10].

B. Data Integration

This type of integration assumes that the various integrating systems were not designed to work together [12], and that they do not have direct access to the entire enterprise data but only to that which they provision directly. These systems were built in order to fulfill certain functional and business requirements, rather than architectural ones. It is also possible that some systems were acquired later (e.g., corporate mergers, third-party software acquisitions, etc.)

Given that the systems evolved independently, enabling them to interoperate using multiple copies of the enterprise data (i.e., multiple data sources) while providing enterprise-level business features in a unified fashion is problematic, since there is no single source of truth and, potentially, no single source of data entry. Multiple applications may allow users to enter the same type of data from different user interfaces that sit atop of different business/logic layers and, consequently, different data sources.

Achieving this type of data integration can rely on either the delivery of custom solutions (for example, involving an enterprise service bus), or commercial tools (such as implementations of a Master Data Management system), which may expedite the time-to-market of such an integration, in some cases at lower costs than custom solutions [7] [13].

III. A Practical Data Integration and Synchronzation Solution

A. Setting the Expectations

1) This Paper Is Not a Comparative Study Including Integration Solutions and Approaches

The solution described in this paper is an actual integration design created for a client that had very specific requirements for bringing together a couple of business verticals and lay the foundation for adding a new vertical to the mix. The integration involved both legacy systems as well as a newly released one, and presented unique challenges that required extensive analysis and prototyping before the final custom solution was considered as a viable candidate. Enterprise integration always caters to very specific needs, as unique as the systems that they attempt to bring together.

This paper does not compare the solution designed for this particular client with other enterprise integration solutions but rather focuses on a particular implementation for an actual client who elicited this solution and who delivered the initial prototype to their client base. Some of the reasons for not pursuing a comparative study against the solution presented here are described next.

Although at a high level architectural styles may be compared and contrasted, including the technologies employed, it is rather uncommon to come across detailed technical specifications of actual integration solutions from various industries to conduct such a comparative study. In some cases, enterprise system architecture is shown as very high-level, in the form of block diagrams, to the extent that they are relevant from a Business and/or Sales view. Component diagrams, architectural layers, interfaces and frameworks are usually handled as proprietary technical documentation and artifacts rather than being exposed for public evaluation.

It is also understandable why such artifacts are not publicized. Unless the company's software is going to be acquired by some other entity, the internal architecture of that software system is not necessarily relevant to potential consumers. Instead, its exposed features –functional and perhaps non-functional – are shared – up to a certain degree of detail. From a client's perspective, a software system – especially one that sits behind a service interface, will be treated as a black box whose features are exposed via rich user interfaces - web applications in most cases – whether the software system is self-hosted (by the client's infrastructure) or vendor-hosted, cloud-based or on premise. An adequate level of technical detail for other industry implementations is rather scarce and difficult to come by in order to assemble a meaningful comparison of behavior and/or performance.

One last important fact that prohibits the development of a proper and relevant comparison analysis of integration solutions is that various companies, even if they cater to similar domains (e.g., payroll service providers), they may adopt highly specialized system models and architectural approaches to building their enterprise integration, as dictated by the features they provide to their clients. Not uncommon, dealing with legacy systems is also a relevant aspect of modeling new features and/or adding integration capabilities to existing domains, since the complexity of such tasks increases significantly. This is primarily due to the difficulty of bringing together old and new technologies and practices. In any case, specific domain models are not usually shared openly; and they may vary greatly from one enterprise to another, despite the realization of similar functionality.

For this reason, any meaningful comparison with such enterprise systems would not carry a significant value, assuming that the specific solution's topology details and/or performance specs are disclosed and available for evaluation.

2) This Paper Does Not Introduce Groundbreaking Ideas for Solving Integration Problems

Many books and online resources on software system design and software system integration are very useful tools for understanding the many ways in which one can build robust, extensible, maintainable, scalable software [5] [7] [9] [11]. Patterns, principles, and best practices are always emphasized and more or less extensive examples are provided. However, usually such books have a very precise and well-organized agenda that they follow, introducing and/or elaborating on various technologies, architectural and/or integration styles, leaving it up to the reader to absorb all that knowledge and apply it in ways that are best suitable for the system that they are building. Rarely, if ever, is there a "one size fits all" approach to software design. Nevertheless, it takes skill, experience, and a good understanding of the problem and the domain to devise the appropriate architecture, layers, components, and how they interact with each other to build the system that is required. Moreover, in many if not most cases, architects and technical leads deal with various departmental, organizational, and technological constraints that may render the best solution unfeasible.

What this paper shows, however, is how various approaches, practices and industry recommendations were selected and chosen to build a practical solution for a client with clear requirements and constraints, that would enable their isolated business domains to share data.

B. The Businss Domains

Consider three major business domains, Human Resources (HR), Payroll, and Benefits. The common ground for all three is the demographic data that defines the companies (or clients) that these systems are servicing and their employees. As is quite often the case, neither domain was built with a true enterprise vision in mind, neither architecturally, nor functionally. Yet the main enterprise data on employees and clients served must be shared across all domains when multiple data copies exist, one per domain. These data sources were designed for a very specific purpose, making it prohibitively expensive to refactor the systems' layers and the business applications so that they rely on a single source of truth – a unified data source across the enterprise. A solution employing Master Data Management (MDM) tools has been evaluated but the business requirements did not warrant such elaborate implementations for this particular case. The proposed and agreed upon solution was to implement the "Maintain data copies" data integration pattern [4] by means of a custom scalable and extensible middleware architecture (or integrating layer [5]), reusable frameworks and models, and carefully-chosen technologies, to fulfill the business need of providing multiple services (HR, payroll, and benefits) to an array of small to large size clients.

The following sub-section presents the main models of the proposed integration solution, where data notifications are being exchanged between the various domains via a broker-based messaging architecture, using various enterprise integration patterns, also depicted later in the EAI pattern-mapping diagram in Figure 4. The data payload for these messages is wrapped inside a context-based notification model, allowing participating systems to take the appropriate action – based on their own domain rules – using the data received from the message broker. The individual domain systems are not aware of each other, only of the message broker through which they communicate.

C. The Structural and Behavioral Integration Models

All models, structural and behavioral, included in this paper are excerpts from the technical design specifications document created on behalf of the client's Enterprise Integration Solution [6] and they are being used hereby with permission from this client.

1) Structural Models: High-Level Enterprise Integration Architecture and Components

The integration middleware was designed as an extensible, highly responsive, and scalable broker-based topology through which the formerly isolated domain systems will exchange data notifications in near real-time and in a loosely coupled fashion. The middleware is built on durable messaging frameworks, such as an enterprise service bus (ESB), queues, an entity mapping/correlation infrastructure, and various service endpoints (SOA).

The high-level component diagram (Figure 1) shows the three business verticals as clients to the enterprise services that provide access to features that implement cross-cutting concerns (logging, SSO, audit) while indirectly exchanging data notification messages among each other.

This message exchange is intended to take place without reciprocal system awareness or knowledge of the features they provide, using the integration middleware exposed via a service endpoint (i.e., the Data Notification Receiver Service).

This design ensures system scalability and plasticity of the integration scope (data or functional), while hiding the actual technology specifics from the participating systems.

2) Object/Data Models: The Canonical Model

The data notifications exchanged between the systems via the service-broker integration middleware are structured as a two-layered object model. One is the actual data payload represented by the integration ubiquitous model, also referred to as the Canonical Model [7], and the second is the notification model which is wrapping (or encapsulating) the canonical model payload, adding context, source, and target details to the communication messages.

This allows for a reusable notification model, where - by employing generic data types for the payload wrapped within the notification together with the appropriate inheritance (generic type inheriting from the non-generic type) – we can design any number of notification schemata that could encapsulate any business entity models inside a generic payload. The payload is domain-specific (or enterprise integration-specific in this case), whereas the notification model is domain-agnostic. This is depicted in the object model in Figure 2. The generic type T of the payload can be represented by any domain entity. Section IV describes the standalone object model used for the enterprise integration solution presented here.

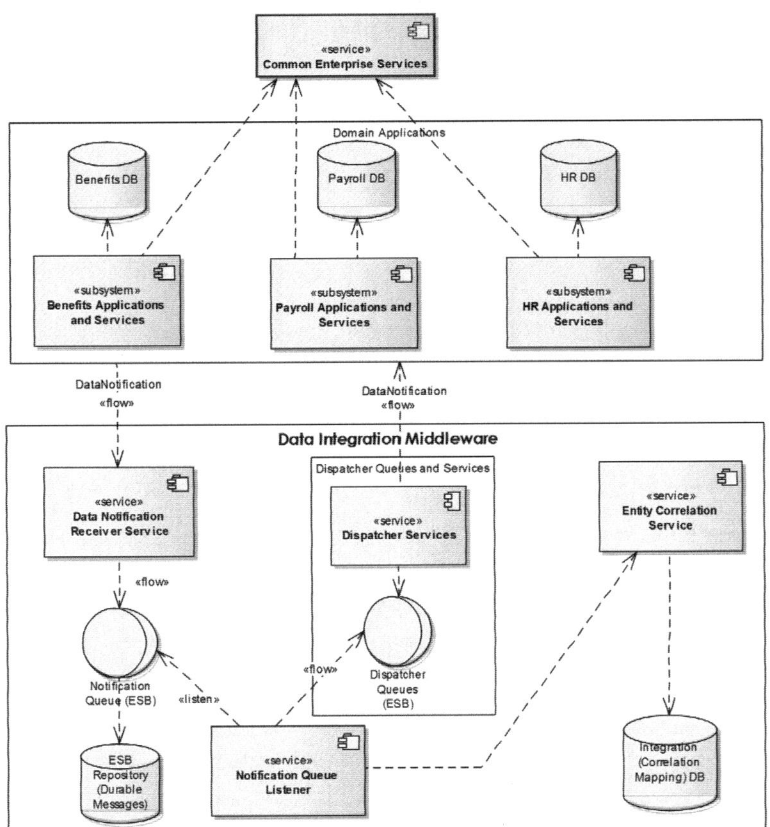

Figure 1. Overall enterprise integration topology: business verticals and integration middleware

This allows for a reusable notification model, where - by employing generic data types for the payload wrapped within the notification together with the appropriate inheritance (generic type inheriting from the non-generic type) – we can design any number of notification schemata that could encapsulate any business entity models inside a generic payload. The payload is domain-specific (or enterprise integration-specific in this case), whereas the notification model is domain-agnostic. This is depicted in the object model in Figure 2. The generic type T of the payload can be anything that one would define for a given domain: employee, client, address, benefit, participant, dependent, etc. In fact, a separate object model for the enterprise integration has been defined and is used in the implementation of this solution (see Section IV for further details).

3) Behavioral Models: The Communication Model Describing the Enterprise Data Synchronization Process

For the implemented solution, the data notification exchange follows a very simple path through the hub-and-spoke (or star) integration middleware topology (Figure 3). However, the main challenge that had to be overcome is associating the business entities from one system to business entities in other systems, without introducing direct dependencies between these systems or awareness of other domains or domain-specific identifiers that – semantically – tie these enterprise entities together. For this purpose, an entity correlation service was introduced, using a separate repository of entity IDs that represent logically - or semantically - identical entities across the enterprise. Such correlations will be specified during an initial data setup process by administrative users or via custom automation tools and import/export facilities.

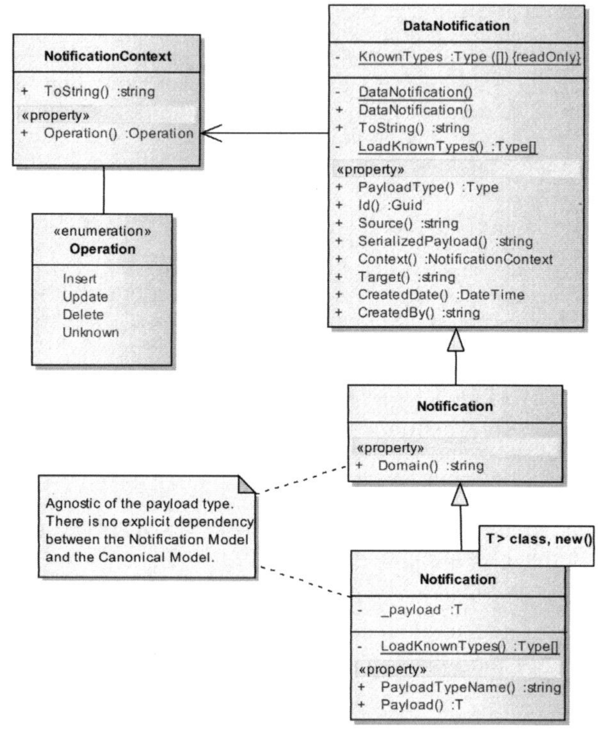

Figure 2. Data notification object model

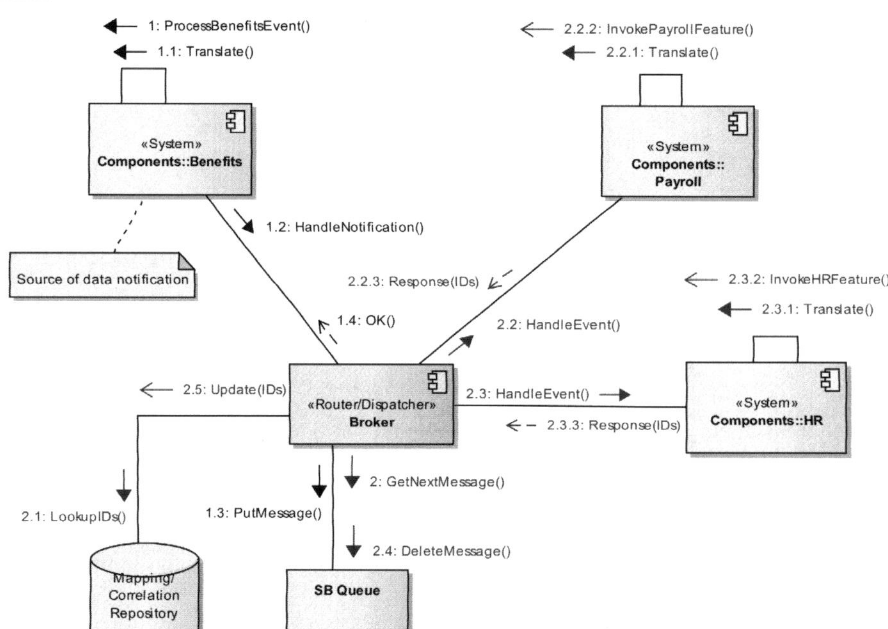

Figure 3. High-level integration communication model mapped to the service broker (star) topology

D. Integration Architecture Feature Highlights

Noteworthy features of this integration solution are compiled below. They are grouped into functional and non-functional characteristics. Several design details are included to impart to the reader additional context and comprehension of the architectural and technical approaches chosen.

1) Key Functional Attributes

a) Enterprise Data Coherence

Maintaining multiple data copies synchronized, all integrators become symmetrical systems of record for the core/common enterprise data.

All systems participating in the integration are able to notify the enterprise about relevant data updates in a particular line of business system without being aware of the other systems that might need this information or of the way in which this data will be consumed. They will do so by raising notifications with the integration middleware alone.

Consequently, the systems will be notified of relevant data updates occurring across the enterprise by receiving such notifications that encapsulate data payloads following a normalized model. These notifications are dispatched by the integration middleware, potentially based on specific integration rules and constraints.

This notification mechanism will in turn allows the integrating systems to keep their own data copy synchronized with the data across the enterprise, while continuing to provision it independently, according to the domain's business rules.

b) Enterprise Functional Coherence

Specialized domain services offered to clients will continue to be managed and augmented within each individual vertical, without the need to cross domain boundaries, since all necessary data is available at the domain level, nearly real-time consistent with the enterprise data.

Decoupled and asynchronous notifications exchanged via the messaging broker keep systems unaware and independent of each other, while allowing the enterprise to grow as needed. Additional applications may be added; if these applications require their own data copy, they will start listening to notifications from the middleware services. If they also support or require data updates that must be synced with other applications' data sources, then the new participants will also start sending notifications to the broker to be dispatched and consumed throughout the enterprise, as needed.

2) Key Quality Attributes

Large integration undertakings - as the one described here – can carry significant risks, require substantial effort to realize, and are built with a very long-term plan in mind. For this purpose, multiple non-functional features of the proposed solution have been identified and analyzed. A subset of all those considered with the client, mainly the critical ones, are presented next.

a) Scalability

Without any architectural changes to the integration framework or the domain systems, new systems can be added to this topology and can be enabled to participate in the integration (assuming they also use their own data source(s) that require continuous or occasional synchronization with the enterprise data).

The two main requirements for these systems are (a) to expose a data notification service endpoint that will handle enterprise notifications from the middleware (i.e., to react to notifications from the broker) and (b) to have the ability to raise such data notifications appropriately, while being aware of the canonical model as the lingua franca of the enterprise integration.

b) Testability

Although additional testing frameworks for the integration components must be designed and built, individual systems will continue to be tested independently of each other or the integration middleware.

Components that simulate/generate notification traffic through the integration framework can be built to allow for independent testing of the service broker and the integration infrastructure.

c) Maintainability

The basic SOLID design principles employed, and most importantly the "separation of concerns" (or SoC) principle, ensure a highly maintainable architecture and codebase due to overall high cohesion and low coupling [5] [11].

Domain rules do not escape the boundaries of the system to which they belong, and similarly integration logic is isolated to the broker components and services.

d) High Availability

By employing load balancing and clustering around the integration services and the choice of technology (e.g., Service Bus Farm), the deployment topology was designed to ensure high availability as far as the integration components are concerned.

e) Performance

Assuming appropriate technology choices, the integration framework ensures a high throughput of notifications with minimal integration logic (i.e., entity correlation map lookup) required between the moment of receiving a notification and that of dispatching one.

For example, Microsoft's Windows Server Service Bus 1.1 (on premise) can process 20k messages/second (based on 1K message size) with an average latency of 20-25ms [14].

f) Stability

The integration middleware and the canonical model had to be built in such a way that the overall system would not require changes over time. Moreover, the middleware had to be impervious to individual client failures. For this reason, a lot of thought and design hours were spent on the various models presented here, so that they can withstand various changes (and potential failures) of the integrating systems.

E. Enterprise Integration Patterns Mapping

Hohpe and Woolf compiled an excellent collection of asynchronous messaging integration patterns in their book [7]. Furthermore, their practical advice on designing such integration systems and the various examples provided helped with the design of this messaging architecture, while it also facilitated the selection of the appropriate topology and

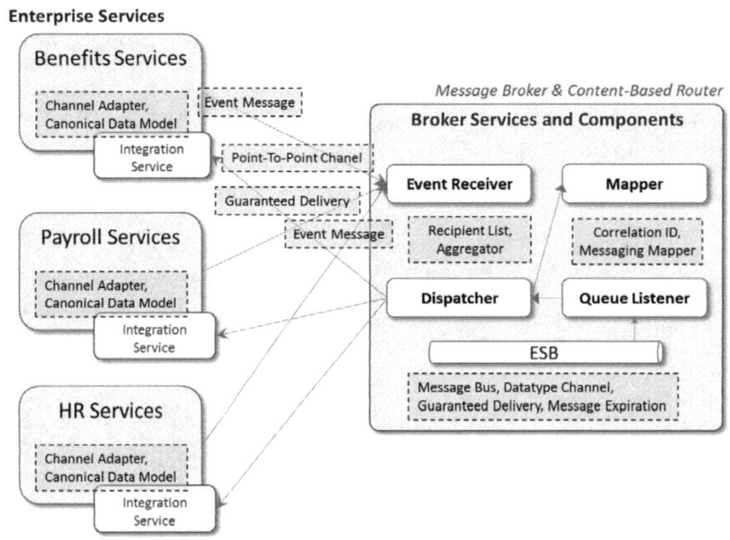

Figure 4. Mapping of enterprise integration patterns to domain systems and to integration middleware components

patterns that were fundamental to the delivery of an effective system integration solution.

It is interesting to see how the key integration patterns employed in the design and realization of the integration architecture directly map to the business verticals and integration middleware components. This mapping is shown as an overlay atop the simplified enterprise system block diagram in Figure 4.

IV. SUPPLEMENTAL INTEGRATION MODELS

A. The Canonical Model's Base Class Details

The Canonical Model integration pattern [7] has been the central theme of the solution implemented and is the only integration element that was allowed to permeate the enterprise (at each system's integration endpoints). This model can be envisioned as the ubiquitous integration language, which describes entities that are shared across the various domains of the enterprise. However, these entities in turn share data elements that are best modeled separately, as properties on base classes, using elemental inheritance, aggregation, and composition modeling concepts. For the domains in the presented case study, the need to support entity identifiers of different types, active timeframes, and traceability/audit features, led to the design of the model in Figure 5 where all domain entities inherit from the abstract class *EntityBase* shown in the center of the class diagram.

B. The Canonical Model and the Main Integration Entities

The main (aggregate root) entities in the integration's lingua franca are Group and Employee. They reflect the primary integration objective: keep Employee and Group demographics data in sync among all enterprise systems, by allowing each system to maintain and operate on their individual copy of the data. The model shown in Figure 6 is specific to the integration solution proposed for the client, aiming at integrating Benefits, Payroll, and Human Resources domains, more specifically for achieving the business goal of cross-selling services to various clients.

Noteworthy here is the fact that if we consider the canonical model as the domain of the integration, then it is following the anemic domain model design anti-pattern [15]. This is because these are simple data containers and do not encapsulate functionality as the integration framework's domain itself is behavior-less. The model's only purpose is to capture and transport data notifications across systems –so, from this (proper) perspective the model is abiding to the Data Transport Object (DTO) pattern of enterprise application architecture [11].

Generic functionality is exposed in the form of service operation contracts for handling notifications (whether a domain system raises a notification or must handle one), but no enterprise features are being implemented here, hence data representation and modeling is of essence and imperatively affects the success of the proposed system integration solution.

C. The Integration Activity Model

The overall system integration flow is modeled in the activity diagram in Figure 7, where the various integrating systems and the broker components are bounded by the vertical swim lanes, to indicate where activities and actions cross system boundaries. The diagram also shows how the correlation service is being employed to allow the integration framework to associate the same (logical) clients across domains by looking up and populating the appropriate domain identifiers, as part of the context that wraps the notification data payload passing through the broker.

Behind the broker services, multiple queues were utilized as a durable and priority-based messaging mechanism, in order to decouple the various processes that take place at the integration framework level: receiving messages, processing notifications, and dispatching them to targets.

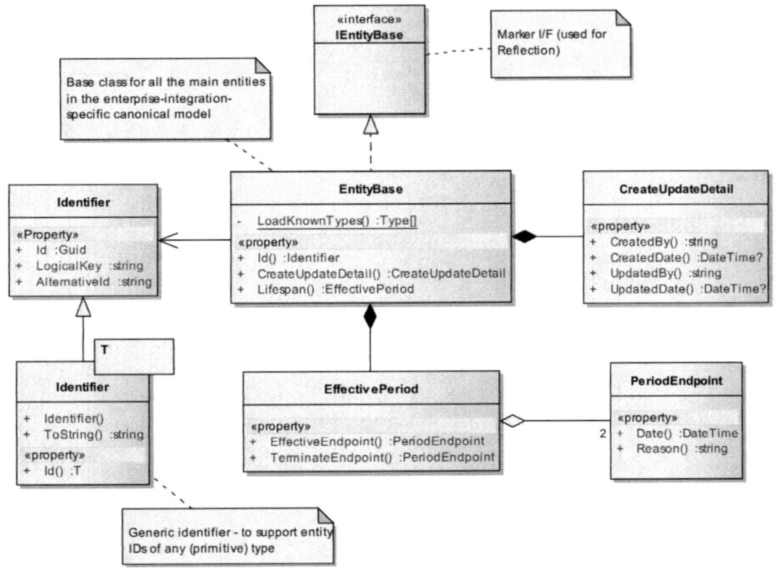

Figure 5. Base class and common elements for the canonical model types

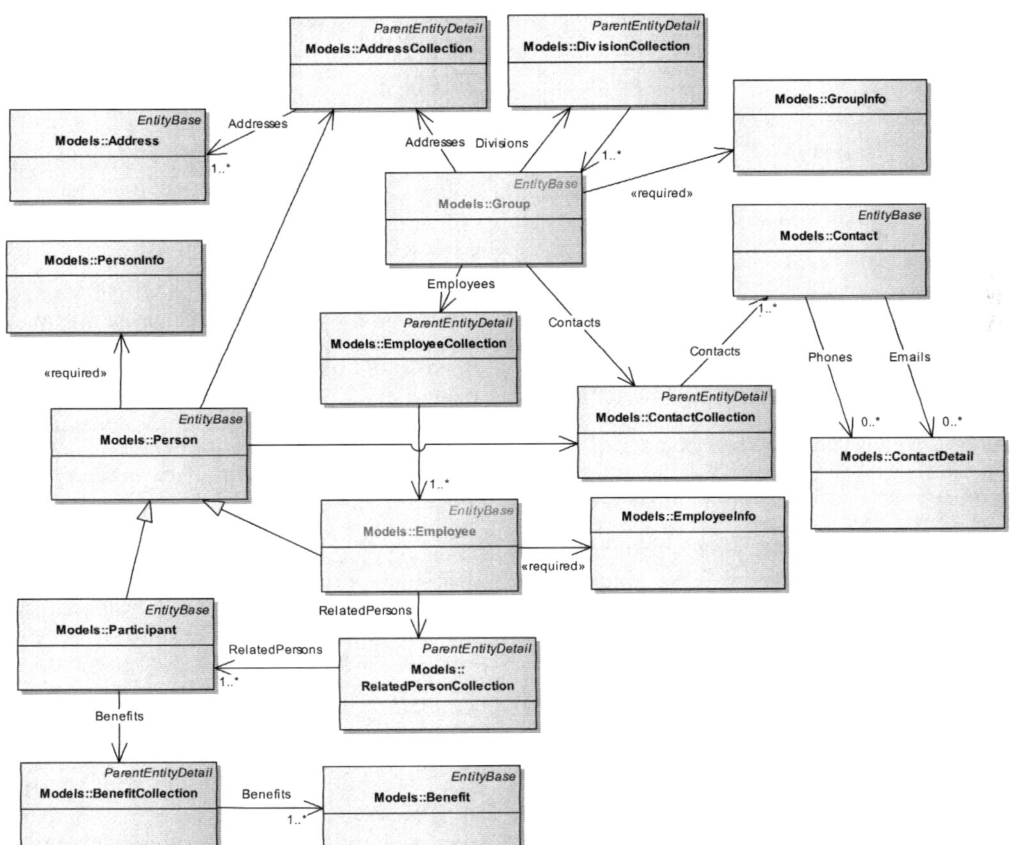

Figure 6. Canonical model's main entities: the payload of the data notifications

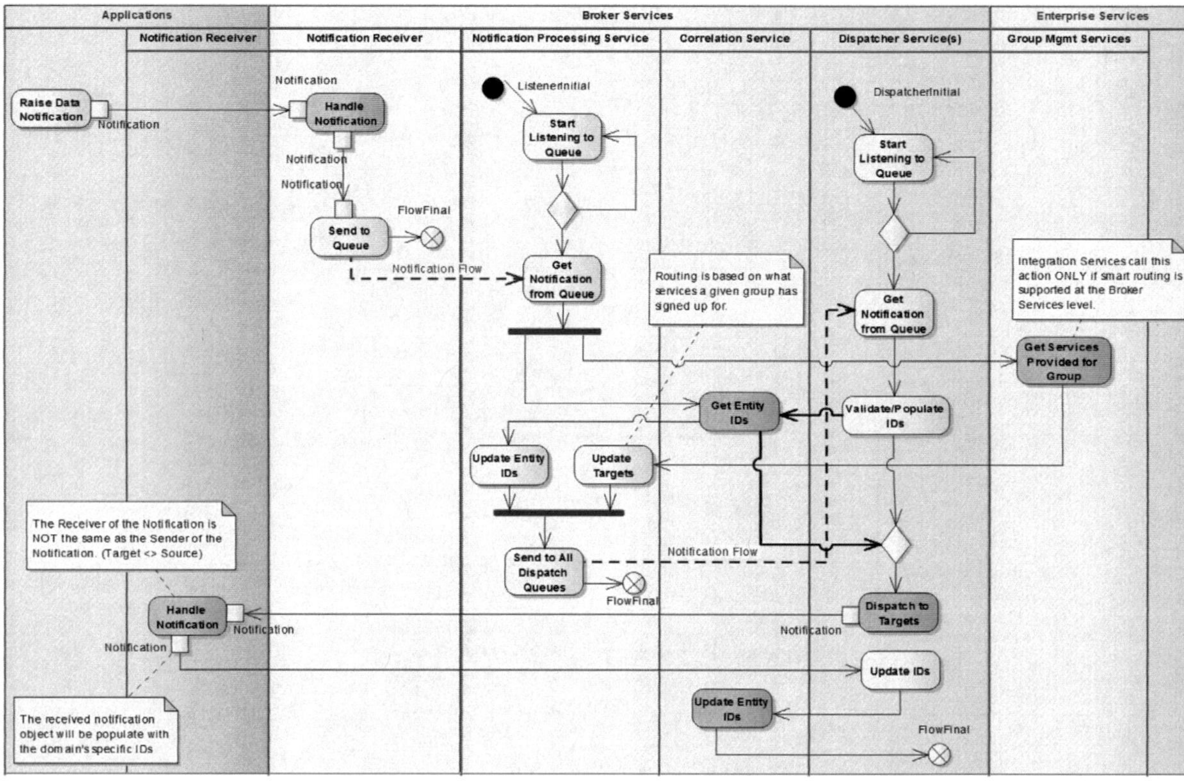

Figure 7. Enterprise integration activity model

V. A Phased Delivery via Prototyping

A. The Enterprise Integration Pilot Release

All of the artifacts presented so far are describing the asynchronous enterprise integration solution proposed and adopted by the client. It is important to note however, that this design was preceded by the implementation of a synchronous services middleware prototype, smaller in footprint and scope than the original design. This prototype was exposed only to a small set of customers, mainly in order to gain a deeper understanding of the data integration needs, the customer traction and adoption that such integration would yield, and the overall value it would bring to the Business.

Although early on it became evident that without such domain integration, independent systems would be forced to duplicate data and functionality, leading to potentially hazardous and undesired side effects as well as duplication of effort, a pilot version of the data integration was requested by the client, was implemented, and successfully released to the market.

Aside from the business value mentioned above, the prototype also allowed the teams to work out the means to a successful collaboration, to get familiar with each other's development processes and expectations, and to support each other during the system integration testing phase.

B. A Synchronous SOA-Based Prototype

For a faster turnaround, a combination of functional integration and data integration using synchronous services built around Microsoft's Windows Communication Framework (WCF) was designed and implemented as the pilot release. This prototype enabled two distinct business domains (benefits and payroll) and three isolated enterprise applications (one very large benefits application, a legacy payroll application, and a newly released, smaller payroll system) to share data common across multiple customers that these systems were actively servicing.

These customers for which common data required sharing and synchronization across systems, are provisioned via a lightweight web interface through which administrators have the ability to enable or disable the main integration facilities provided by the prototype – features that are specific to one or the other of the two domains. Since the initial set of customers to which this integration product was released was rather small (up to 50), a semi-manual provisioning activity was deemed acceptable. The web tool – developed as a Single Page Application (SPA) using Angular, Bootstrap, and JavaScript – just to mention a few of the technologies employed - also allowed power users to settle any customer identity (or reference) clashes that could not be automatically resolved via logical key matching.

Following a pure SOA approach and employing the industry-recommended SOA design patterns [9] [13], an integration middleware layer was implemented as part of this prototype solution, which included the correlation service and integration feature activation service along with a small database used to persist the data required by these services.

The middleware's purpose is to enable access to integration correlation data and resolve access queries against the unifying customer reference tables. It is responsible for activating or deactivating integration features for the targeted customers, and it also serves as an operational service layer to the provisioning web application.

At a high level, the architecture of the prototype and the communication paths between the integrating systems and the integration middleware are shown in Figure 8.

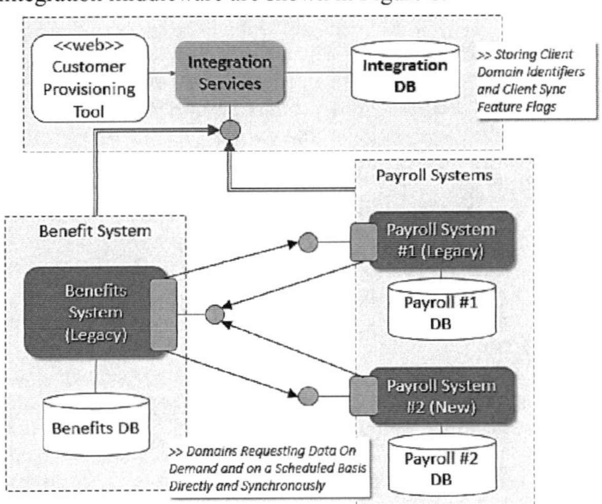

Figure 8. SOA-Based Synchronous Integration Prototype

The three integrating domains communicate directly with each other via service calls that encapsulate along with the payload, the correlation ID in order to reference a given customer. The ID is obtained from the Correlation Service (part of the integration services layer).

The service contracts designed for the domain-exposed endpoints (shown as horizontal lollipops in Figure 8) are simple yet symmetric (identical), allowing for a unified and consistent mechanism for requesting and exchanging data.

To overcome some of the architectural shortcomings of one of the legacy systems, changes to certain data required for synchronization had to be captured at the data layer (i.e., the database). For this purpose, a custom service component was designed using Microsoft's Change Tracking solution, which constitutes a lightweight implementation of the Data Change Tracking (DCT) solution.

This enabled monitoring and capturing the data updates from a standalone service component, without having to make changes to the domain services of the integrating system. Given the ease of implementation and ability to build it in isolation of other components, if was suggested as an alternate solution to the other integrating systems to compensate for the absence of reusable domain services, where and if applicable.

C. Key Benefits of Prototyping

Identifying specific areas of integration challenge and collecting valuable market insight from building and deploying a low-risk integration pilot (prototype) - even after high-level design effort and some middleware prototyping for the larger integration solution had already been wrapped by up the architecture team – were compelling enough arguments for the Product Management team.

Hence, the decision to spend the additional effort towards building a simplified synchronous functional integration pilot was made. As teams mobilized in the design elaboration and realization of this interim solution, several immediate benefits emerged, both for the development groups as well as for the decision-making entities.

Some of these benefits – relevant for this particular implementation – are captured below.

1) Refinement of the Integration Models and Contracts

Once concrete implementation artifacts started to take shape around the proposed models and interfaces, various gaps were identified and flagged with the design team. Such gaps included missing data fields for certain key domain entities – required for one system but not the others, ancillary lookup data mismatch across systems, and the stringent need for refining the composite logical (natural) keys used for uniquely identifying critical data entities (specifically, the aggregate roots) targeted for synchronization.

2) Identification of Edge-case synchronization issues

Certain customer data in one of the systems were found to have multiple representations in that system and such representations had to be handled accordingly by that system during the synchronous data exchange. This raised questions about handling data synchronization failures, both for the synchronous as well as the asynchronous implementation, which eventually lead to customizations to the durable message design realized by the service bus implementation, and the provisioning of nightly scheduled jobs that would retry sending or queuing failed notifications.

3) Defining Cross-Team Collaboration Processes

Multiple geographically dispersed teams were involved in the realization of the integration solution. Each system that would participate in the integration already had its own development team structure in place, its technical Subject Matter Experts (SMEs) and leads, its own practices and approaches to developing software.

Although all three teams involved in the original pilot implementation and delivery were following agile methodologies, the iteration schedules, task sizes and assignments, and even the way scrum meetings were run, differed quite a bit among them. Some effort was involved to iron out these differences and bring the teams to work together, to "speak the same language", to set the right expectations, and to meet the deliverables.

Moreover, issue escalation channels were established and the need to allow teams to *independently* test the integration points and, evidently, their own systems as they react to integration notifications became a critical item on everyone's list. This fact points us to the next benefit of prototyping – especially relevant in the case of systems' integration.

4) Building Synthetics

In general, when one thinks of software prototyping, perhaps throwaway and/or wireframe prototypes come to mind. Although some of the modules of the prototype presented here had to be modified or replaced in order to accommodate the larger integration solution, a big part of the middleware and components that encapsulated the production and consumption of notifications were fully reusable for the larger integration. However, in order to test those components while other teams were implementing their own handlers and dispatchers –without having to wait on everyone else to complete their implementation – specialized components that targeted the production of synthetic data and behavior – had to be built: both notification generators as well as mock notification handlers.

The idea behind the need for these synthetics is the distinction between unit testing and system integration testing; whereas the latter should not be allowed to proceed before independently validating first the integrating systems, the new components and frameworks, in isolation from each other.

Not only did these additional components provide a consistent testing framework for all teams, but also these synthetics would continue to be used and enhanced as needed, to support all ongoing unit and integration testing needs, including regression testing. These components greatly helped developers in catching integration point failures early on, before system integration testing (SIT) would commence. It identified the type of information that had to be monitored and captured to facilitate troubleshooting integration bugs, and made the overall integration testing much less painful than it would have been otherwise.

Although such simulators and data generators do not have a place in the final product, they are an absolute necessity in developing systems that must interact with each other – whether these systems are developed by the same company or are involving third party components. It is imperative to relieve individual component and/or system testing from any external dependencies in order to ensure proper validation of the system being built. Arriving at situations where it is unclear what the origin of the failure is or, worst, slowing down the development of your own system because of a faulty or unavailable external system, should always be avoided.

5) Aiding the Quality Assurance (QA) Teams with the Gradual Development of Integration Test Cases

Familiarizing themselves with a simpler system, the synchronous service-based prototype, gave the QA team ample time to prepare for the larger integration solution, identifying gradually the appropriate tests to be developed. This lead to a better comprehension of the key features of the integration that were mission-critical from an overall system perspective.

Finally, just as was the case for the development teams, multiple testing teams were assembled, facing similar challenges. Although with some additional effort and time, the QA teams successfully identified and implemented the necessary processes towards coordinating their testing efforts, preparing the test data, and collaborating effectively in order to validate the entire enterprise integration solution.

VI. CONCLUSION

Depending on the scope of system integration as well as the functional and non-functional requirements, creating the right frameworks and sub-systems that allow isolated domain systems to seamlessly share key enterprise data between them is a challenging undertaking. A variety of technology choices, architectural and modeling approaches and patterns exist, but features and limitations of the integrating systems, along with organizational, budgetary, technical, and technological constraints can make the integration task even more difficult. Generally speaking, in multi-domain enterprise systems, data integration and synchronization can be achieved in various ways. One of them – as the one presented here and in [1] – involves custom integration frameworks and components, using various enterprise integration patterns.

This paper presented an actual industry integration solution, explained via several structural and behavioral system models, and provided details on how the "maintain data copies" data integration pattern would be realized via a broker-based messaging middleware. The data exchanged between the various domains is encapsulated by the canonical model, which is the common data abstraction across the enterprise. This in turn is wrapped inside a context-based, generic, and reusable notification model, allowing systems to react to these notifications based on their own business rules.

This paper also captured essential enterprise integration patterns chosen for this solution and how they were employed, as well as the architectural topology designed to address specific functional and non-functional requirements. Central to the solution proposes here, the paper presented the common integration model and described how this model played the role of the semantic glue that unified the data exchange mechanism between the various integrating systems and components.

Following industry-recommended patterns and practices – yet custom-tailored to meet the specific client integration needs, the resulting architecture features scalability, extensibility, and high-availability – to mention just a few quality attributes. Concerning performance, it supports near-real-time data synchronization between systems and allowing them to operate without awareness of each other, while using their individual data formats, features, and domain rules.

Finally, the paper introduced a generalized integration prototype that was released to a reduced customer base as a pilot implementation, in order to test the market response to the new features enabled via integration. The prototype development proved valuable in several ways, as discussed in this article. The development of synthetics, in order to facilitate the imperative unit testing of all systems and components as a prerequisite to system integration testing, proved to be an invaluable byproduct of prototyping system integration.

A. Future Work

One of the benefits of being in the consulting business is the exposure to a diverse array of problems and challenges, leading the way by designing custom solutions, releasing the product to the market, and then moving on to new problems waiting to be solved. For the author of this paper, the solution presented here has been a goal in itself, and it has been accompanied by a successful release to the market of the initial prototype, as well as the client's adoption of the extended asynchronous integration solution shown here. The responsibility of maintaining the integration middleware, as well as enhancing existing systems while adding new domains (such as Human Resource (HR) vertical(s) and Time and Attendance applications) into the integration mix stayed with the client for which the solution presented here was prototyped and delivered.

REFERENCES

[1] M. Iridon, "Enterprise Integration Modeling - A Practical Enterprise Data Integration and Synchronization Solution," FASSI 2015 : The First International Conference on Fundamentals and Advances in Software Systems Integration, pp. 23-30, August, 2015.

[2] Microsoft BizTalk Integration Platform. [Online]. Available from: https://www.microsoft.com/en-us/server-cloud/products/biztalk/ [retrieved: June, 2016]

[3] TIBCO Integration Platform. [Online]. Available from: http://www.tibco.com/products/integration [retrieved: May 2016]

[4] Microsoft, Data Integration. [Online]. Available from: https://msdn.microsoft.com/en-us/library/ff647273.aspx [retrieved: June, 2016]

[5] Microsoft, Integration Patterns. [Online]. Available from: https://msdn.microsoft.com/en-us/library/ff647309.aspx [retrieved: June, 2016]

[6] M. Iridon, "Technical Design Specifications for Enterprise Integration Solution," 2015, unpublished/internal document.

[7] G. Hohpe and B. Woolf, "Enterprise Integration Patterns; Designing, Building, and Deploying Messaging Solutions," Addison-Wesley, 2012.

[8] Microsoft, Functional Integration. [Online]. Available from: https://msdn.microsoft.com/en-us/library/ff649730.aspx [retrieved: June, 2016]

[9] T. Erl, "SOA Design Patterns," Prentice Hall, 2009.

[10] T. Erl et al., "Next Generation SOA: A Concise Introduction to Service Technology & Service-Orientation," Prentice Hall, 2014.

[11] M. Fowler, "Patterns of Enterprise Application Architecture," Addison-Wesley Professional, 2002.

[12] T. Erl, "Service-Oriented Architecture: A Field Guide to Integrating XML and Web Services," Prentice Hall, 2004.

[13] T. Erl, "Service-Oriented Architecture (SOA): Concepts, Technology, and Design," Prentice Hall, 2005.

[14] Microsoft, Service Bus for Windows Server Quotas. [Online]. Available from: https://msdn.microsoft.com/en-us/library/dn441429.aspx [retrieved: June, 2016]

[15] M. Fowler, Anemic Domain Model. [Online]. Available from: http://www.martinfowler.com/bliki/AnemicDomainModel.html [retrieved: June, 2016]

Facial Part Effects Analysis using Emotion-evoking Videos focused on Smile Expression Process

Kazuhito Sato and Hirokazu Madokoro
Department of Machine Intelligence and Systems Engineering,
Faculty of Systems Science and Technology, Akita Prefectural University
Yurihonjo, Japan
e-mail: {ksato, madokoro}@akita-pu.ac.jp

Momoyo Ito
Institute of Technology and Science,
Tokushima University
Tokushima, Japan
e-mail: momoito@is.tokushima-u.ac.jp

Sakura Kadowaki
Smart Design Corp.
Akita, Japan
e-mail: sakura@smart-d.jp

Abstract - **This study specifically examines the expressive process of "happiness" related facial expressions after giving a stress stimulus. In addition, it presents a quantitative analysis of expressive tempos and rhythms using mutual information. By acquiring image datasets of facial expressions under states of pleasant-unpleasant stimulus for 20 participants, we calculated the information in three region of interests (ROIs): ROI 1, the whole face and the upper face; ROI 2, the whole face and the lower face; and ROI 3 between the upper face and the lower face. Additionally, we tried to express complexity and ambiguity objectively during facial expressions because of human psychological states. The results clarified the possibility of estimating the impression of facial expressions from the magnitude relation and order relation of mutual information of each ROI. More than male participants, female participants were able to create facial expressions of "happiness" easily and intentionally, and were less susceptible to discrepancy expressions. Finally, we discussed the differences of expressive paths between intentional and spontaneous facial expressions based on the order of the mutual information of the ROIs. As a result, we figured out the validity of our hypotheses concerning to the individual expressive path of each facial expression.**

Keywords - Psychological stress measures; Intentional facial expression; Machine learning approaches; Behavior modeling

I. INTRODUCTION

Human faces are often described as a window by which one can discern information of various types such as the state of a person's mind and health condition. Especially, facial expressions can reveal aspects of internal psychology, reflective emotions such as delight, anger, sorrow, pleasure, and the existence of stress. In contrast, humans can feel rhythms from all of their personal surroundings that are moving, especially any emitting sound. Additionally, they feel rhythms from engaging in daily life, such as rhythms related to conversation and rhythms of human life. To clarify the relevance between psychological states and facial expressions, we have been studying a dynamical framework that specifically examines actions to repeat intentional facial expressions after giving a stress stimulus [1].

Attractive smiles attract people and represent a symbol of happiness, soothing another person's mind. Smiles are therefore effective as a lubricant of human communication. According to a study [2] that analyzed geometric features with respect to charming smiles, the most attractive part of smiles in both men and women is perceived as the eye, followed by the mouth. In addition, facial parts associated with the eyes and mouth, such as the corners of the eyes and mouth, are reportedly more important as attractive factors of smiles. In attractive smiles, the existence of a golden ratio was observed in the aspect ratio of the expression rectangle. Furthermore, Yamada et al. [3] investigated the relevance between the whole and partial impression formed from facial parts and pointed out the following points. Eyes play an extremely important role in forming impressions of others. It is possible to some degree to illustrate the overall impression by adding and coupling the partial impression formed from each part. However, they suggest that individual differences exist in the information of the parts which are expected to be related to emphasis. Assessing male and female viewpoints of smile expressions specifically, women are said to tend to expose smiles more than men [4]. Moreover, smiles are natural for women: women are better at making smiles than men. Particularly, women have excellent skills to adjust positive emotional expressions. Such natural expressions can elicit positive effects on a person viewing the smile (recipient). Nevertheless, for the creation of intentional facial expressions, different facial muscles are said to move in conjunction with natural facial expressions [5]. Particularly examining the expressive process, the deformation degree, and operation timing of facial parts creating smiles are expected to vary slightly.

To clarify the relevance between facial expressions and psychological states to date, as a result of verifying the relevance between psychological stress and facial expressions using the framework of Facial Expression Spatial Charts (FESCs), we demonstrated that the degree of stress accumulation can be easily ascertained from facial expression types and expressive processes [6] [7]. Additionally, we proposed a framework of rhythms and tempos that specifically examines actions to repeat intentional facial expressions after giving a stress stimulus [8]. We define one rhythm as one tempo repeated several times. In addition, regarding one tempo as the period during which facial expressions transform from a neutral face (i.e., expressionless) to the next neutral face, we found that the variation in unpleasant stimulus became greater than that in pleasant stimulus, addressing the variation of the number of frames constituting one tempo. Furthermore, using Bayesian networks, we constructed a graphical model of the relation between these three facial expressions and psychological stress factors. Results show that facial expressions displaying the effects of psychological stress easily were "happiness" and "sadness." Additionally, we showed the possibilities that facial parts (such as the eyes and mouth) easily differed by facial expression type [9] [10] [11].

In this study, particularly addressing the expressive process of "happiness" facial expression after giving a pleasant-unpleasant stress stimulus by emotion-evoking videos, we strove objectively to express complexity and ambiguity through facial expression because of human psychological states, by quantitative analysis of expressive rhythms from the viewpoint of mutual information.

This paper is presented as follows. We review related work to clarify the position of this study in Section II. Section III presents a definition of a new framework of exposed rhythms and tempos for analyzing relations of psychological stress and facial expressions. Section IV describes a method to capture facial expression images, in addition to preprocessing, classification of facial expression patterns with self-organizing maps, integration of facial expression categories with fuzzy adaptive theory, and quantification of expressive rhythms using mutual information. We explain our originally developed facial expression datasets including stress measurements in Section V. In Section VI, based on the calculation results of mutual information in a time-series change of ELs for each facial region, we analyze the respective trends exhibited by men and women. Additionally, we discuss the effects of a pleasant-unpleasant stimulus which would give the expressive rhythm of facial expressions from the perspective of mutual information. Finally, we present conclusions and intentions for future work in Section VII.

II. Related Works

In spite of increasing or decreasing attractiveness of a "smile" with changes in expressive process, many conventional studies have examined the shape of a post-expression face. Case studies examining the expressive process are few [12]-[15]. Regarding impression formation of friendly and thoughtful smile expressions, Ishi et al. [12] described the following. A continuous video presentation, such as expression levels from a neutral face become the maximum, is the most effective. Hanibuchi et al. [13] proposed a smile training method that specifically examines facial expressions process. Through impression evaluation experiments, they demonstrated the validity of goal setting with the actor's perspective. In addition, particularly addressing a natural smiling face, Fujishiro et al. [14] [15] investigated how eye, cheek, and mouth movements contribute to the impression formation of natural smiles in the expressive process. Results revealed moderate correlation between the behavioral termination of the eyes and cheek and the impression formation of natural smiles. Nevertheless, the authors did not report the psychological state of the actor when viewing a "natural smile" and "forced smile," such as a disagreement expression or expression suppression. Particularly, they were unable to come up to address impression formation based on the timing structure of facial parts.

For a good impression on the face of a conversation partner, Kampe et al. [16] revealed that the good impression was more emphasized with matching of each other's eye-gaze. Using anthropomorphic agents, Kuroki et al. [17] indicated the following. The combination of eye-gaze and facial expressions affects emphases of impressions. The impressive transmission of friendship properties can be emphasized particularly. Moreover, by analyzing brain activities using functional magnetic resonance imaging (fMRI) as physiological indices, an activation is observed in the prefrontal cortex responsible for higher cognitive functions such as emotional processing, motivation, and reasoning. Furthermore, the same activation is observed in the amygdala associated with emotions and rewards. Therefore, the formation of a good impression shows that the prefrontal cortex and the amygdala play mutually important roles [18]. However, impression evaluation has not been done subjectively for overall impressions of the face. Moreover, dealing with impression formation based on the timing structure of facial parts has not been achieved.

III. Framework of Exposed Rhythms and Tempos

As an index for quantifying individual facial expression spaces, we proposed a framework of expression levels (ELs) [6]. The ELs include both features of the pleasure and

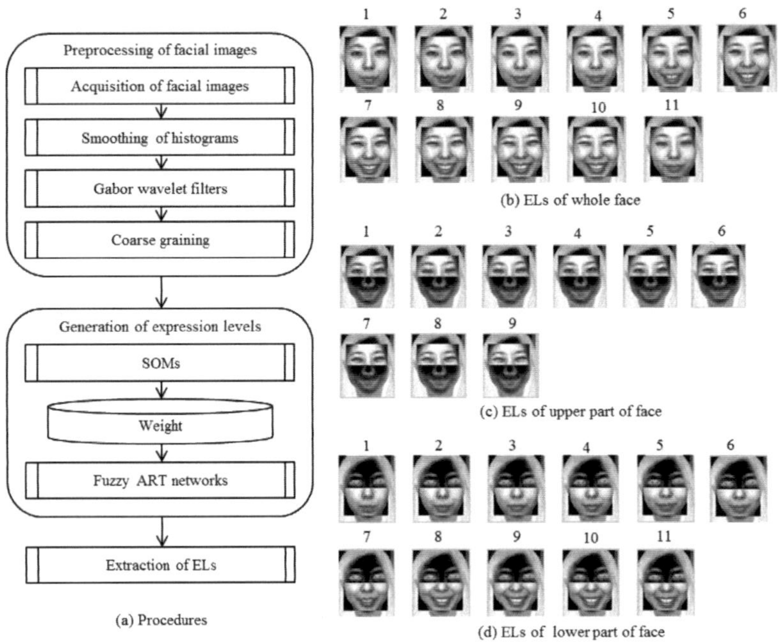

Figure 1. Overview of the procedures used for our proposed method.

arousal dimensions based on the arrangement of facial expressions on Russell's circumplex model [19]. Specifically, we extract the dynamics of topological changes of facial expressions of facial components such as the eyes, eyebrows, and mouth. Topological changes show the structure defining the connection form of the elements in the set. The ELs obtained in this study are sorted to categories according to their topological changes in intensity from expressions that are regarded as neutral facial expressions. As discussed above, the ELs in this study include features of both pleasure and arousal dimensions. In Russell's circumplex model, all emotions are constellated on a two-dimensional space: the pleasure dimension of pleasure-displeasure and arousal dimension of arousal-sleepiness. In the intentional facial expressions covered in this study, direct handling of the facial expressions for the influence of pleasure dimension is difficult. As a method of measuring the transitory stress response, we conduct an evaluation using the salivary amylase test during the task of watching emotion-evoking videos causing a pleasant-unpleasant state. Specifically examining the values of salivary amylase activity before and after watching videos, we can effectively perform stress measurements using salivary amylase tests to assess the stress state transiently. Consequently, we target the intentional facial expressions under pleasant and unpleasant stimulation states.

In this study, using temporal variation of ELs, we intend to visualize rhythms and tempos of facial expressions that humans create. We defined one rhythm as a tempo that is repeated several times. One tempo is the period during which facial expressions are transformed from a neutral state to the next neutral state. Facial expressions exhibited intentionally by humans form an individual space based on the dynamic diversity and static diversity of the human face. Facial expression dynamics can be regarded as "topological changes in time-sequential facial expression patterns that facial muscles create." Static diversity is individual diversity that is configured by the facial component position, size, and location, consisting of the eyes, nose, mouth, and ears. In contrast, dynamic diversity denotes that a human can move facial muscles to express internal emotions unconsciously and sequentially or to express emotions as a message. After organizing and visualizing topological changes of face patterns by ELs, we attempt to use the framework of rhythms and tempos with expressions to examine ambiguities and complexities of facial expressions attributable to a psychological state.

IV. Proposed Method

Facial expression processes differ among individuals. Therefore, adaptive learning mechanisms are necessary for modification according to individual characteristic features of facial expressions. In this study, our target is intentional facial expressions. We use self-organizing maps (SOMs) [20] to extract topological changes of facial expressions and for normalization with compression in the direction of the temporal axis. After classification by SOMs, facial images are integrated using Fuzzy ART [21], which is an adaptive

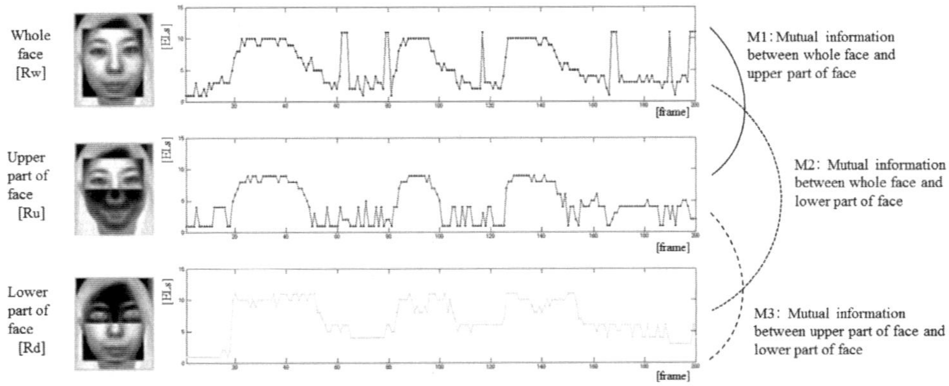

Figure 2. Each mutual information among time-series changes of facial parts.

learning algorithm with stability and plasticity. In fact, SOMs perform unsupervised classification input data into a mapping space that is defined preliminarily. In contrast, Fuzzy ART performs unsupervised classification at a constant granularity that is controlled by the vigilance parameter. Therefore, using SOMs and Fuzzy ART, time-series datasets showing changes over a long term are classified using a certain standard. Figure 1 presents an overview of the procedures used for our proposed method. In the following, we describe extraction of time-sequential changes of ELs, and also explain quantification of expressive tempos and rhythms by mutual information.

A. Acquisition of Time-series Variation of ELs

We set the region of interest (ROI) to 90 × 80 pixels, including the eyebrows, which all contribute to the impression of a whole face as facial feature components. With preprocessing, brightness values are normalized for time-series images of facial expressions. The influence of brightness values attributable to illumination conditions is thereby reduced. Moreover, smoothing the histogram is useful to adjust contrast and clarify the images. In addition, using the orientation selectivity of Gabor Wavelets filtering as a feature representation method, the facial parts characterizing the dynamics of facial expressions are emphasized, such as the eyes, eyebrows, mouth, and nose. By down-sampling (i.e., 10 × 10 pixels) time-series facial expressions converted with Gabor Wavelets filtering [22], the effects of a slight positional deviation when taking facial images were minimized. Then data size compression was conducted.

First, SOMs are used to learn the time-series images of facial expressions with down-sampling. The face images showing topological changes of facial expressions that are similar are classified into 15 mapping units of SOMs. Next, similar units (i.e., Euclidean distances of the weight vectors are close) among 15 mapping units of SOMs are integrated into the same category using Fuzzy ART. By sorting the facial expression categories integrated by Fuzzy ART from neutral facial expression to the maximum of facial expression, we obtain ELs labeled as expressive intensities of facial expressions quantitatively. The integrated category sorting procedure is based on the two-dimensional correlation coefficient of the average image of the facial expression images classified into each category. Finally, we conduct correspondence of ELs with each frame of the facial images to assess a time-series dataset of variation of ELs.

B. Quantification of Exposed Rhythms using Mutual Information

Mutual information [23] [24] can express changes between signals with the entanglement and synchrony. It can be regarded as an amount that represents linear and nonlinear dependence between the two time-series datasets. Moreover, it represents information flows and dynamically coupled rings between two signals. Mutual information between these two signals is zero if the two systems for observation target differ completely from independent ones. Applying this scheme to the facial expression process, it is possible to quantify the synchronicity and functional connectivity between facial parts. Figure 2 presents one example of time-series changes of ELs in the "Whole face," "Upper part of face," and "Lower part of face" obtained in Section IV.A. In this study, three ROIs listed below are calculated as the mutual information among facial parts in the expressive process. The time-series changes of ELs with respect to the "Whole face," "Upper part of face," and "Lower part of face" respectively represent $R_w = R_w(t)$, $R_u = R_u(t)$, and $R_d = R_d(t)$. Then, mutual information of each ROI is obtained as described below.

Mutual information between the "Whole face" and "Upper part of face" is $I(R_w; R_u)$:

$$I(R_w;R_u) = H(R_w) + H(R_u) - H(R_w,R_u) \quad (1)$$

Mutual information between the "Whole face" and "Lower part of face" is $I(R_w;R_d)$:

$$I(R_w;R_d) = H(R_w) + H(R_d) - H(R_w,R_d) \quad (2)$$

Mutual information between the "Upper part of face" and "Lower part of face" is $I(R_u;R_d)$:

$$I(R_u;R_d) = H(R_u) + H(R_d) - H(R_u,R_d) \quad (3)$$

In that equation, $H(R_w)$, $H(R_u)$, and $H(R_d)$ respectively represent the entropy of $R_w(t)$, $R_u(t)$, and $R_d(t)$. $H(R_w,R_u)$, $H(R_w,R_d)$, and $H(R_u,R_d)$ respectively denote the joint entropy of both.

V. DATASETS

For this study, we constructed an original and long-term dataset for the specific facial expressions of participants. Details of the experimental protocols are the following. One experiment comprises three steps: step 1 is conducted under a normal state; step 2 is done during viewing of a pleasant video; and step 3 is done during viewing of an unpleasant video. We gave participants the task of watching emotion-evoking videos, causing a pleasant-unpleasant state, and took stress measurements by salivary amylase tests to assess the stress state transiently. In addition, the watching time is about 3 min for each emotion-evoking video. We prepared unpleasant videos (i.e., implant surgery and cruel videos) and pleasant videos (i.e., comedy videos of three types). The subjective assessment of five stages was also conducted at watching videos. For all participants, we fully explained the experiment contents in advance, based on the research ethics policy of our university, and also obtained the consent of experiment participants in voluntary writing of participants. Moreover, from each, we received agreement to publish facial images as part of their experimental participation.

A. Facial Expression Images

Open datasets of facial expression images are open to the public through the internet from universities and research institutes. However, the specifications vary among datasets because of imaging with various conditions. As static facial images, the dataset presented by Ekman and Friesen [25] is a popular dataset comprising collected various facial expressions used for visual stimulation in psychological examinations of facial expression cognition. As dynamic facial images, the Cohn-Kanade dataset [26] and Ekman-Hager dataset [27] are used widely, especially in experimental applications. In recent years, the MMI Facial Expression Database presented by Pantic et al. [28] and the CK+ dataset [29] have become a widely used open dataset containing both static and dynamic facial images. These datasets contain a sufficient number of people as horizontal datasets. However, facial images are taken only once for each person. No dataset exists in which the same person has been traced over a long term. Therefore, we created original and longitudinal datasets that include collections of the specific facial expressions of the same person during a long term.

The six basic facial expressions proposed by Ekman et al. [25] are "happiness," "anger," "sadness," "disgust," "fear," and "surprise." Among those six basic facial expressions, we specifically examined the facial expression of "happiness," which is believed to be most likely to be exhibited spontaneously. As the target facial expression of "happiness" under pleasant and unpleasant stimulation states, we acquired the facial expressions of 20 people. As a stimulation method, we pre-selected emotion-evoking videos that elicit pleasant or unpleasant emotions, with all participants expressing facial expressions of "happiness" immediately after viewing them. Participants, all of whom were university students, were 10 men, whom we designated as A-J (J was 20 years old; B, G, H, and I were 21; A, E, and F were 22; C and D were 23) and 10 women whom we designated as K-T (K, M, O, and P were 20 years old; L, Q, R, S, and T were 21; N was 23). The imaging period was three weeks at one-week intervals for all participants. The imaging environment for facial expressions was an imaging space partitioned by a curtain in the corner of the room. We took frontal facial images with conditions including the head of the participant in each image. In advance, we instructed each participant to expose the facial expression with no head movement. Consequently, imaging the face region to fit within the scope was possible. However, with respect to extremely small changes caused by body motion, we used template-matching methods to trace the face region by setting the initial template to include facial parts. By consideration of the application deployment and ease of imaging in future studies, we used commercially available USB cameras (QcamOrbit; Logicool Inc. [30]). When taking images of each facial expression, the same expression was repeated three times based on the neutral facial expression during the image-taking period of 20 s. We had previously instructed all participants to express an emotion three times at their own timing according to a guideline for 20 s. One dataset consisted of 200 frames with the sampling rate of 10 frames per second.

B. Stress Measurement Method

Because types of psychological stress are regarded as affecting facial expressions, we assessed transient stress and chronic stress. Chronic stress is that which humans have on a daily basis, whereas transient stress is that caused by a temporary stimulus. To assess transient stress stimulus to the participants in this study, we applied the salivary amylase test, which measures transient stress reactions. As a biological reaction, salivary amylase activity is detected as a low value if one is in a pleasant state. In contrast, the value

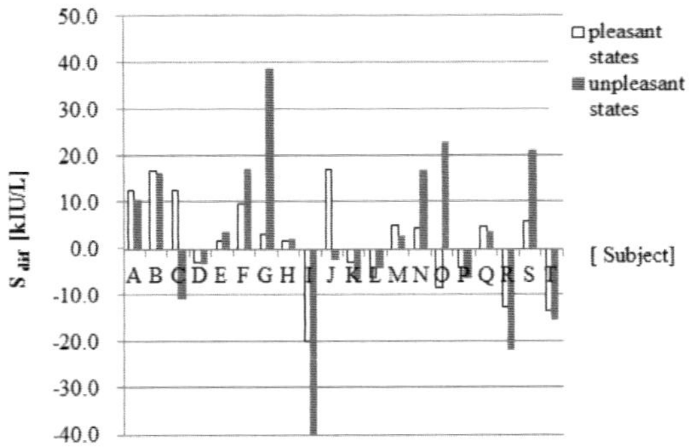

Figure 3. Results of S_{dif} obtained for target to the 20 subjects of A-T.

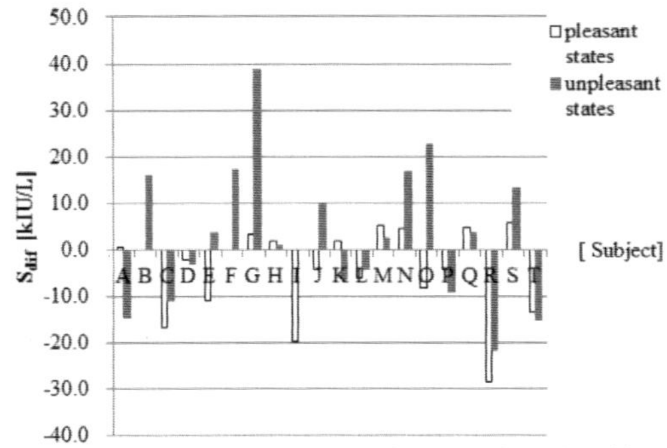

Figure 4. Results of S_{dif} addressed only the score of 4 and 5 with subjective evaluations.

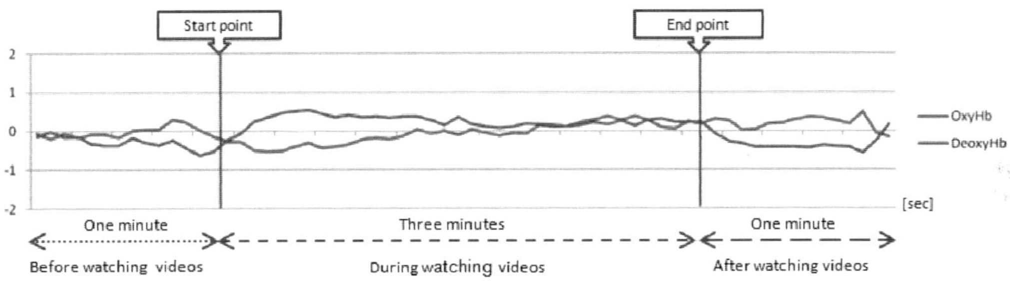

Figure 5. NIRS signals at pleasant stimulus for whole subjects.

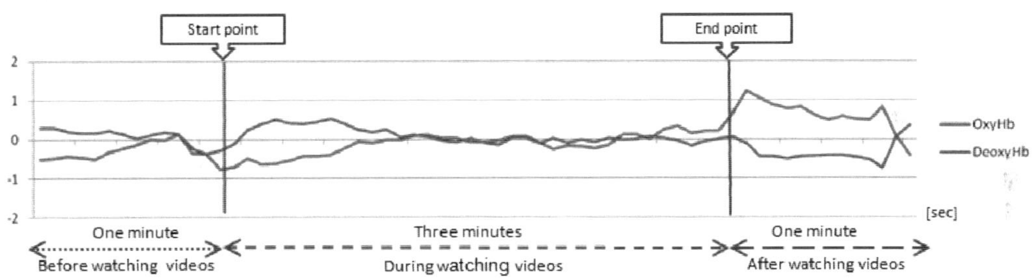

Figure 6. Changes of NIRS signals at unpleasant stimulus for whole subjects.

is high if one is in an unpleasant state. As stress reactions when subjected to external transient stimulus, Yamaguchi et al. [31] confirmed that salivary amylase activity is an effective means of stress evaluation. For this study, using emotion-evoking videos as an external transient stimulus, we used the salivary amylase test method to measure stress reactions immediately after participants watched the videos.

We verified the validity of emotion-evoking videos, which give a pleasant-unpleasant stimulus. Using the salivary amylase test, we examined the validity of emotion-evoking factor in watching the video used as a pleasant-unpleasant stimulus. The following were shown for salivary amylase activity. The value of salivary amylase activity is reduced if in a pleasant state. In contrast, its value is increased if one is in unpleasant circumstances [31]. Accordingly, letting S_{normal} be the value of salivary amylase activity at normal state, and letting S_{stimu} be the value of salivary amylase activity after watching the video, then the difference of salivary amylase activity between the normal state and after watching video (S_{dif}) is defined by the following equation.

$$S_{dif} = S_{stimu} - S_{normal} \quad (4)$$

$S_{dif} < 0$ (i.e., after watching pleasant videos)

$S_{dif} > 0$ (i.e., after watching unpleasant videos)

Figure 3 presents results of S_{dif} obtained for target to the 20 subjects of A-T. As noted previously, this figure

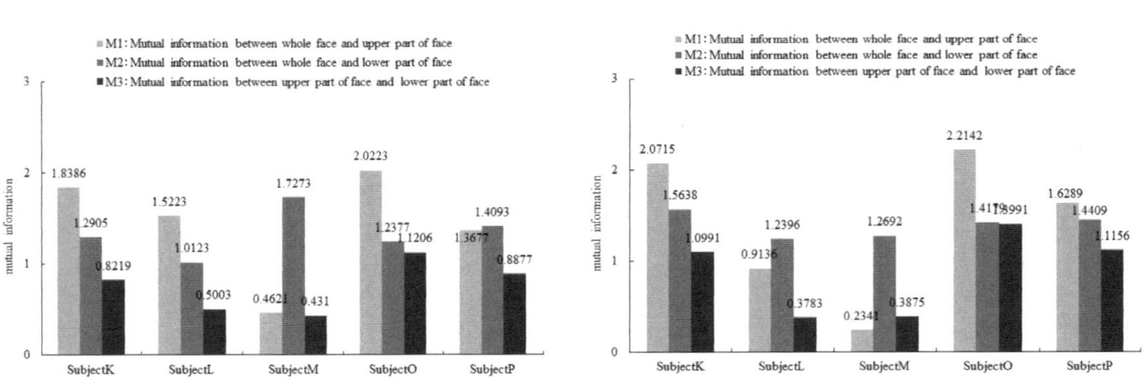

(a) Pleasant stimulus with emotion-evoking videos

(b) Unpleasant stimulus with emotion-evoking videos

Figure 7. Mutual information results among each facial part for female.

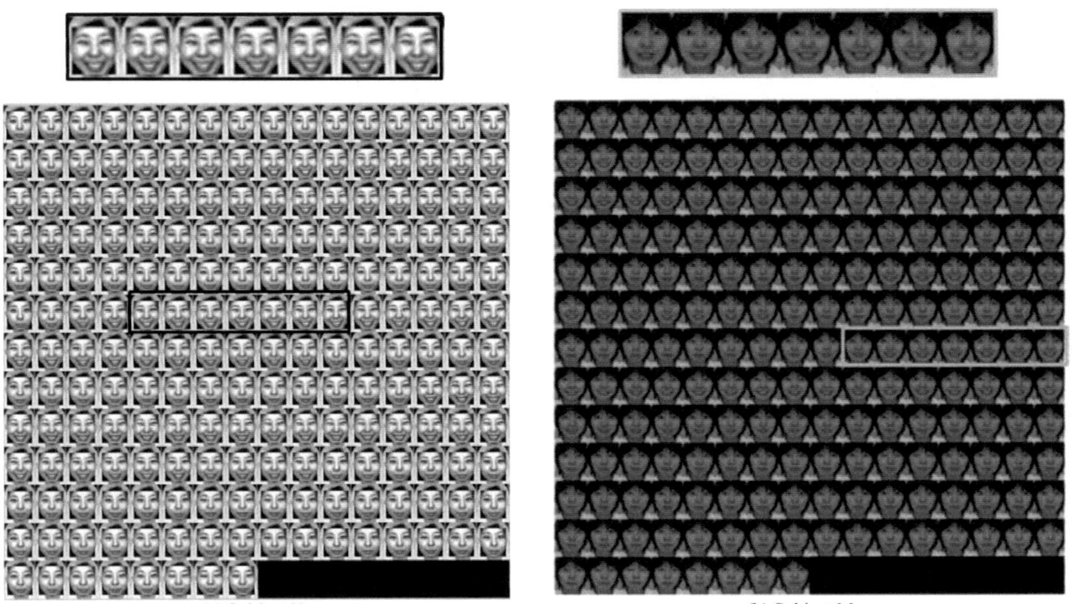

(a) Subject K

(b) Subject M

Figure 8. Time-series changes of smile facial expression with pleasant stimulus for specified subjects of female.

indicates each average value of three pleasant videos (i.e., comedy videos of three types) and three unpleasant videos (i.e., implant surgery and cruel videos). Generally, it is known that increase or decrease of the salivary amylase activity is well consistent with the enhancement and calm down of sympathetic nerve activity. If all of these videos might be effectively acting on each subject, the value of salivary amylase activity should be reduced if in a pleasant state. In contrast, its value should be increased if in an unpleasant state. However, we are unable to confirm such a significant tendency in Figure 3. In this case, the perception for the pleasant-unpleasant videos differs slightly among subjects, so this fact might cause the results of salivary amylase activity of C and B differ with previous studies [31]. Therefore, we decided to calculate the salivary amylase activity only for data for which subjective evaluation of the subject is high. The subjective evaluation receives a score of 1-5, score 1 (i.e., not at all), score 5 (i.e., strong) at watching each emotional video. Figure 4 presents results of salivary amylase activity in the case of particularly addressing only the score of 4 and 5 because we consider that the emotional video is effectively working as a pleasant-unpleasant stimulus. Based on this result, the average of all S_{dif} indicates -2 [kIU/l] at a pleasant state, 5 [kIU/l] at an unpleasant state.

Furthermore, using NIRS (Near-Infrared Spectroscopy: OEG-16; Spectratech Inc. [32]), we measured the activation states of brain for three periods: i.e., 1 minute before

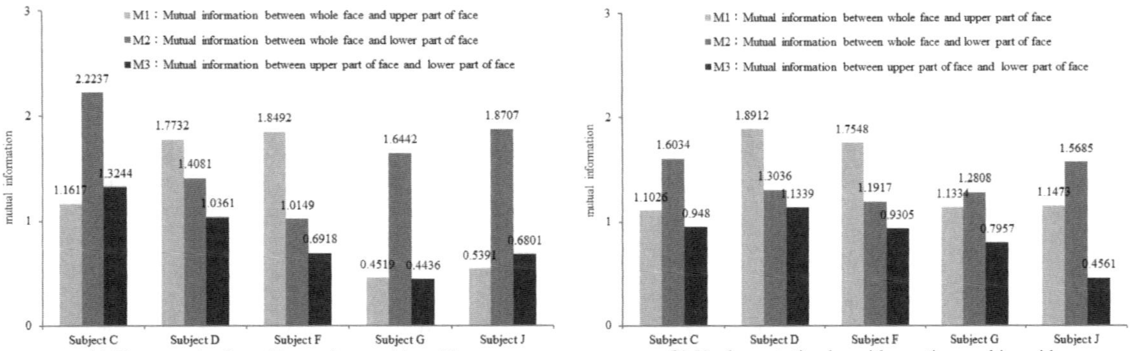

(a) Pleasant stimulus with emotion-evoking videos (b) Unpleasant stimulus with emotion-evoking videos

Figure 9. Mutual information results among each facial part for male.

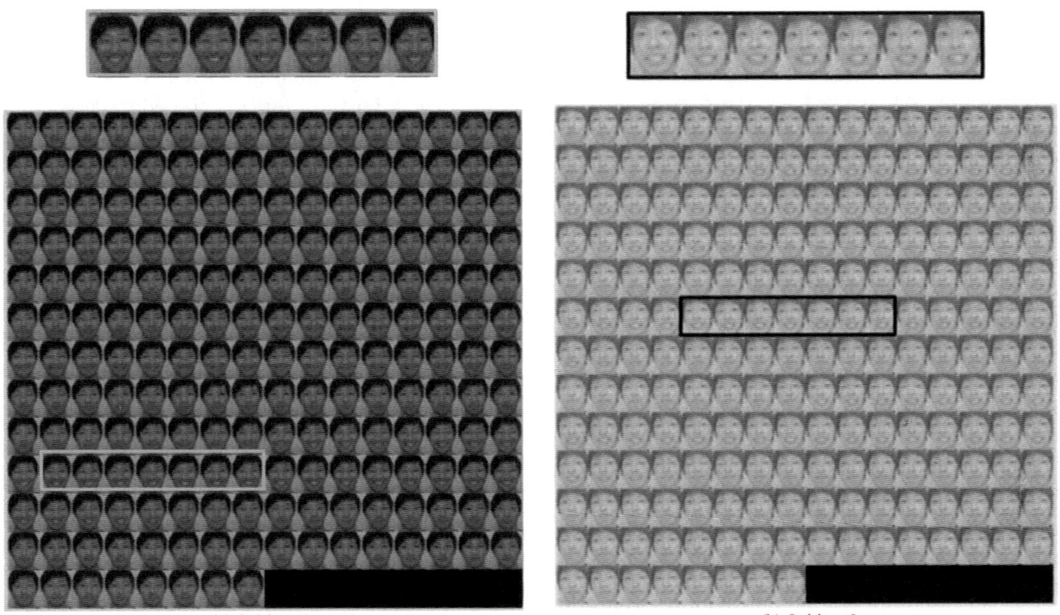

(a) Subject D (b) Subject J

Figure 10. Time-series changes of smile facial expression with pleasant stimulus for specified subjects of male.

watching each video, 3 minutes during watching each video, and 1 minute after watching each video. As a new functional brain analysis method, NIRS for measuring the cerebral blood volume changes locally non-invasively is also attracting attention as a stress measuring method, which indicates that the activity of the prefrontal cortex is changed significantly [33]. Generally, when the brain is activated, the following findings are reported: i.e., the oxygenated hemoglobin (Oxy-Hb) in the brain would increase. Conversely, the deoxygenated hemoglobin (Deoxy-Hb) should decrease [34]. In addition, because NIRS signals indicates the relative changes on the basis of the time of measurement start, we separated the noise to signal components by multiresolution analysis, and we carried out the standardized scoring (Z) using the following equation. Here, X is the NIRS signal, μ is the average, ρ is the standard deviation.

$$Z = \frac{X - \mu}{\sigma} \tag{5}$$

After standardized scoring, we calculated the average of all subjects. Then, we compared the activated state of brain at the pleasant-stimulus and the unpleasant-stimulus. These results are shown in Figure 5 and Figure 6. Although the signals of Oxy-Hb and Deoxy-Hb during watching videos are varied little by little, after watching videos, it indicates that the value of Oxy-Hb is higher than Deoxy-Hb obviously, which represents the state of brain are activated. Consequently, we convinced that the emotion-evoking videos used as pleasant-unpleasant stimulus in this study might be act effectively. Particularly, we considered that the unpleasant videos would be more effective than the pleasant videos as a transient stress stimulus. Therefore, these results show that the emotion-evoking video functioned as a pleasant-unpleasant stimulus.

VI. EXPERIMENT

Based on the calculation result of mutual information in a time-series change of ELs for each facial region, we analyzed the respective male and female trends. Finally, we discussed the effects of a pleasant-unpleasant stimulus which would give the expressive rhythm of facial expressions from the perspective of mutual information.

A. Analysis of Female Participants

Figure 7 depicts the calculation results of mutual information of five cases of female participants K, L, M, O, and P. The results show the mutual information of the time-series variation of ELs in each face region described in Section IV.B. Figure 7-(a) presents the calculation results obtained after giving a pleasant stimulus. Figure 7-(b) shows calculation results obtained after giving unpleasant stimulus. As an overall trend of female participants, we confirmed the following. For K, L, O, and P, the value of the mutual information is reduced to the order of "ROI 1: between the whole face and upper face," "ROI 2: between the whole face and lower face," and "ROI 3: between the upper face and lower face." The value of "ROI 2: between the whole face and lower face" is clearly larger than those for other ROIs in M. For K, M, and O, we were unable to recognize a marked change in the trend of mutual information by pleasant-unpleasant stimulus. However, for L and P, we detected a specific change in the trend of the mutual information after giving pleasant-unpleasant stimulus. Particularly, the tendency of L is remarkable. In pleasant stimulus, the value of the mutual information is reduced to the order of "ROI 1: between the whole face and upper face," "ROI 2: between the whole face and lower face," and "ROI 3: between the upper face and lower face." Otherwise, "ROI 2: between the whole face and lower face" shows a large value for the unpleasant stimulus. In the unpleasant stimulus, the value of the mutual information is reduced to the order of "ROI 1: between the whole face and upper face," "ROI 2: between the whole face and lower face," and "ROI 3: between the upper face and lower face." However, in pleasant stimulus, the order relation of mutual information of P is reversed with L because the value of "ROI 1: between the whole face and upper face" is reduced. Next, although the same trend is apparent for both pleasant and unpleasant stimuli, we compare K to M, for which the order relation of the mutual information in each facial region is markedly different. For K in both pleasant and unpleasant stimuli, the mutual information value of "ROI 1: between the whole face and upper face" is larger than "ROI 2: between the whole face and lower face." In addition, particularly addressing "ROI 3: between the upper face and lower face," the value of K is larger than M. However, for M with both pleasant and unpleasant stimuli, the mutual information value of "ROI 2: between the whole face and lower face" is markedly larger than others. Furthermore, particularly addressing "ROI 1: between the whole face and upper face" and "ROI 3: between the upper face and lower face," the values of M are clearly smaller than those of K. For K and M, thumbnail images representing the time-series changes of "happiness" in pleasant stimulus are shown in Figure 8. Figures 8-(a) and 8-(b), respectively present thumbnail images of K and M. The top of each figure shows the characteristic section during exposed facial expression of "happiness." Comparing the thumbnail images shown in Figure 8 to the calculation result of mutual information shown in Figure 7, for K exposed "happiness," we can recognize the change of facial expression in the upper face such as the brow and the area around the eyes, and in the lower face such as the mouth. Otherwise, for M, we can not observe any change of facial expression in the upper face. However, only the corner of mouth in the lower face has changed significantly. Actually, K has the characteristics which the upper part and lower face change both synchronized during facial expressions. Staying on the subjective impression of the experimenter, the result for "happiness" looks more natural facial expressions. In contrast, for M, only the corner of the mouth in the lower face has been changed. Therefore, we have an uncomfortable feeling about the unnatural facial expression of "happiness."

B. Analysis of Male Participants

Figure 9 presents calculation results of mutual information of five cases of male participants. Figure 9-(a) presents the calculation results after giving pleasant stimulus. Figure 9-(b) shows the calculation results after giving unpleasant stimulus. As an overall trend of male participants, we confirmed the following. For D and F, the value of the mutual information is reduced to the order of "ROI 1: between the whole face and upper face," "ROI 2: between the whole face and lower face," and "ROI 3: between the upper face and lower face." The value of "ROI 2: between the whole face and lower face" is markedly larger than those of other ROIs in C, G, and J. For male participants C, D, F, G and J, we were unable to recognize a marked change in the trend of mutual information by pleasant-unpleasant stimulus.

Next, regarding male participants, we compare D to J, for whom the order relation of the mutual information in each facial region is significantly different. For D, in both

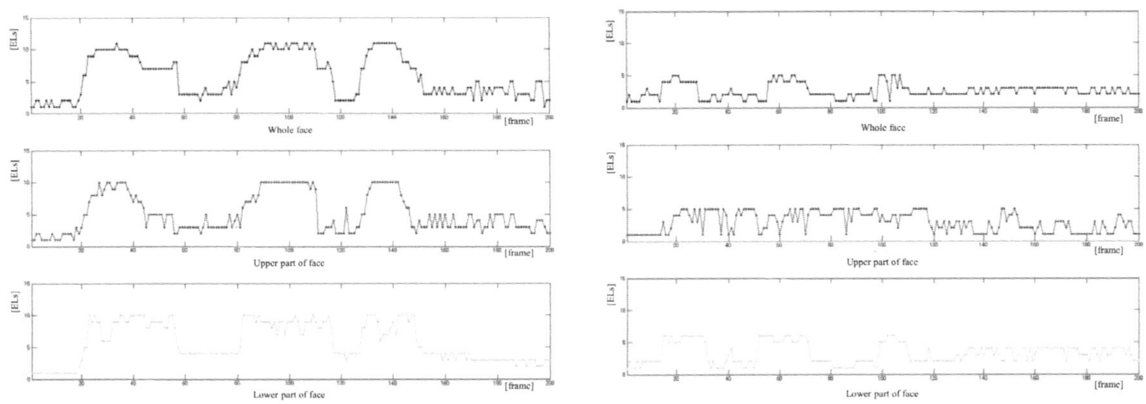

(a) Subject K

(b) Subject M

Figure 11. Comparison of time-series changes of ELs with unpleasant stimulus.

pleasant and unpleasant stimuli, the mutual information value of "ROI 1: between the whole face and upper face" is larger than "ROI 2: between the whole face and lower face." In addition, particularly addressing "ROI 3: between the upper face and lower face," the value of D is larger than that of J. However, for J in both pleasant and unpleasant stimulus, the mutual information value of "ROI 2: between the whole face and lower face" is markedly larger than others. In addition, particularly addressing "ROI 1: between the whole face and upper face" and "ROI 3: between the upper face and lower face," the values of J are clearly smaller than those of D. For D and J, the thumbnail images representing the time-series changes of "happiness" in pleasant stimulus are portrayed in Figure 10. Figures 10-(a) and 10-(b) respectively present thumbnail images of D and J. The top of each figure shows the characteristic section during exposed facial expression of "happiness." Comparing the thumbnail images shown in Figure 10 to the calculation result of mutual information shown in Figure 9, for D exposed "happiness," we can recognize the change of facial expression in the upper face such as the brow and around the eyes, and in the lower face such as mouth. Otherwise, for J, no change of facial expression can be observed in the upper face. Only the corner of the mouth in the lower face has changed substantially. Actually, D has characteristics by which the upper part and lower face change at the same time during facial expressions. Therefore, the exposing result of "happiness" looks more natural facial expressions. In contrast, for J, only the corner of the mouth in the lower face has been changed. Therefore, we have an uncomfortable feeling about the unnatural facial expression of "happiness." These results underscore a common tendency between male and female participants and can be anticipated as a new index for quantification of the impression during facial expressions based on the mutual information of the time-series change of each face region.

C. Effects of Pleasant-unpleasant Stimulus on Mutual Information

The discrepancy expression in facial expressions means to expose the emotions that do not match one's own feelings when experiencing certain emotions, such as having a smile, even though one might be in a sad mood. In previous studies, being positive emotional expressions during negative emotional experiences has been shown to engender the following: an amplification of actor's sympathetic nerve activities [35], an increase of subjective emotional experiences, and some memory loss [36]. The discrepancy expression can easily take cognitive loads for expressive person. Additionally, it can potentially give bad effects to the mental health of actors. Furthermore, the expressive suppression in facial expressions indicates an emotional suppression by facial expressions when experiencing a certain emotion, such as to stifle crying when in a sad mood. Expressive suppression is reportedly associated with social support, closeness with others, and reduction in social satisfaction [37]. In comparison to men, women are more skilled at making smiles and excellent adjustments of positive emotional expressions. Moreover, women show similar effects such as natural expressions to recipients [4].

Exposing facial expressions related to "happiness" after viewing an unpleasant video is equivalent to a discrepancy expression. In contrast, exposing the facial expression of "happiness" after viewing a pleasant video is a matching expression. For female participants K and M, such order of mutual information was markedly different; Figure 11 presents their facial expression rhythms. In the impression analysis of Section VI.B, the smile of K gave us a natural impression. In contrast, we received an unnatural impression from the smile of M. Focusing on an expressive rhythm of each facial part, the expressive rhythm of K indicates a time-series change such as to work together in each facial

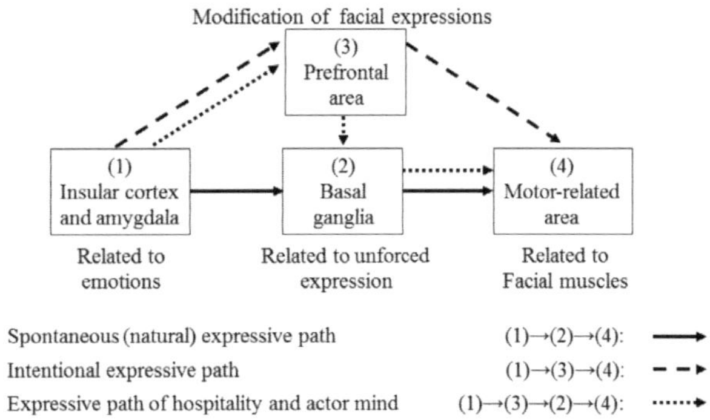

(a) Block diagram of expressive paths based on four brain domains

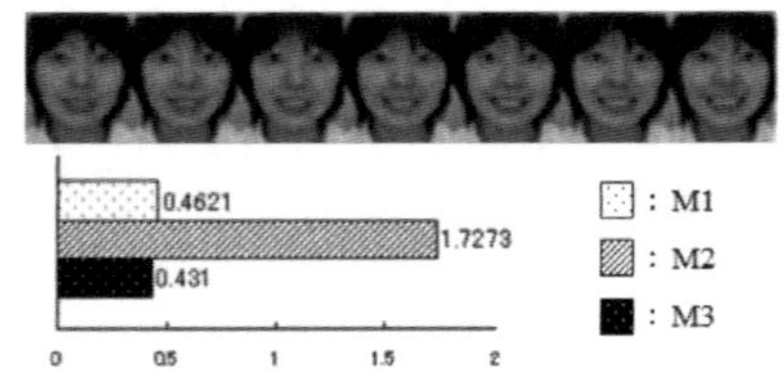

(b) The order of mutual information values corresponding to "Intentional expressive path"

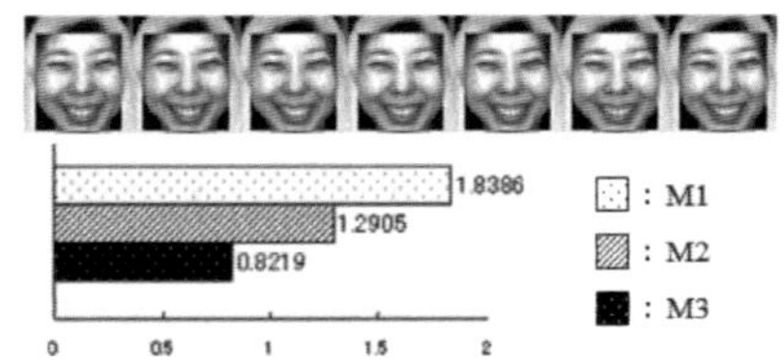

(c) The order of mutual information values corresponding to "Spontaneous expressive path"

Figure 12. Differences of expressive paths between intentional and spontaneous facial expressions focusing on the order of the mutual information values, i.e.,M1, M2, and M3.

part. In contrast, we were unable to recognize cooperative movements at all in the expressive rhythm of M because the upper face and the lower face are independent. The mutual information of the ROIs (i.e., ROI 1, ROI 2, and ROI 3) effectively expresses the degree of similarity and synchronization of signal waveforms in facial expression rhythms. These mutual information values can be interpreted as quantified indices of the timing structure indicating the synchronization between the upper face (e.g., the eyebrows and eyes) and the lower face (e.g., mouth), which contribute the impression formation to the whole face. We should comprehensively consider the analysis results of Sections VI.B and VI.C. By particularly addressing the magnitude relation between ROI 1 and ROI 2 with respect to the mutual information, we were able to interpret "Eyes say things sufficient to mouth" quantitatively. Around the value of ROI 3 quantifying the timing structure between the upper face and the lower face, noting the magnitude relation and order relation between the values of ROI 1 and ROI 2, it is effective as an index for quantifying the degree of spontaneity and artificiality in facial expressions. Furthermore, more than male participants, the female participants easily created facial expressions of "happiness" intentionally. Then we assumed that result was only slightly affected by the discrepancy expression.

D. *Consideration for Differences of Expressive Paths*

From a viewpoint of the order of the mutual information values, we try to discuss differences of expressive paths between intentional and spontaneous facial expressions. Blair [38] has reported that, for facial expressions, four brain domains are mutually related: (1) parts producing feelings (insular cortex and amygdala), (2) parts forming facial expressions involuntarily (basal ganglia), (3) parts embellishing facial expressions according to the surrounding circumstances (prefrontal area), and (4) motor-related areas actually moving mimic muscles. As presented in Figure 12, in cases where facial expressions are embellished intentionally or spontaneously, time-sequential differences exist based on the route through which facial expressions are revealed. According to specific brain waves of four brain area, nerve cells of each brain area are used to work cooperatively, in the case of the repetition process of facial expressions under a pleasant-unpleasant stimulus particularly. Mimic muscles are activated by coordination of nerve cells with different speed, a unique expression is exposed through the individual path of each facial expression, such as the intentional or spontaneous expressive path described in Figure 12-(a). Therefore, the order of the mutual information of the ROIs (i.e., ROI 1, ROI 2, and ROI3) is able to figure out the expressive paths between intentional and spontaneous facial expressions. Figure 12-(b) indicates the order of mutual information values corresponding to "Intentional expressive path." In contrast, Figure 12-(c) presents the order of mutual information values corresponding to "Spontaneous expressive path." Even an intentional smile, it seems to strike a natural impression (e.g., hospitality smile), if exposing through "Expressive path of hospitality and actor mind" described in Figure 12-(a).

VII. Conclusion and Future Work

In this study, by quantitative analysis of expressive rhythms from the viewpoint of mutual information, particularly addressing expressive processes of "happiness" facial expression after giving a pleasant-unpleasant stress stimulus by emotion-evoking videos, we objectively strove to ascertain complexity and ambiguity when making facial expressions because of human psychological states. Using evaluation experiments examining 10 participants (i.e., 5 men, 5 women), we analyzed the information of time-series changes in ROIs (i.e., ROI 1, ROI 2, and ROI 3), revealing the following points. By particularly addressing the expressive rhythm of each face region, one can estimate the impression of facial expressions from the magnitude relation and order relation of mutual information of each ROI. Additionally, the mutual information of expressive rhythms is effective as an index for measuring degree of spontaneity and artificiality during facial expressions. Female participants were better able to create facial expressions of "happiness" easily and intentionally than male participants were. Moreover, they were less susceptible to discrepancy expressions. Finally, we discussed the differences of expressive paths between intentional and spontaneous facial expressions based on the order of the mutual information of the ROIs. As a result, we figured out the validity of our hypotheses concerning to the individual expressive path of each facial expression. In future work, by quantifying fluctuations of expressive tempos in facial parts upon the impression formation, and analyzing their timing structure, we intend to clarify differences of expressive paths between intentional and spontaneous facial expressions.

ACKNOWLEDGMENT

The authors thank the 20 students at our university who participated by letting us take facial images over such a long period. This work was supported by the Japan Society for the Promotion of Science (JSPS) KAKENHI Grant Number 25330325 and the Cosmetology Research Foundation.

REFERENCES

[1] K. Sato, M. Ito, H. Madokoro, and S. Kadowaki, "Facial Part Effects Analysis using Emotion-evoking Videos: Smile Expression," Proceedings of the Tenth International Multi-Conference on Computing in the Global Information Technology (ICCGI2015), pp. 30-39, Oct. 2015.

[2] T. Iguchi, "Geometrical Features of the Attractive Smile: -Attractive Production by Kansei X Technology = Kanseiweab-," The Institute of Electronics, Information, and Communication Engineers, Technical Report, pp. 51-56, Mar. 2007.

[3] T. Yamada and I. Sasayama, "A Study of the Correlation between the Impression Formed from Each Features and the Impression Formed from Face," Bulletin of Fukuoka University of Education, vol. 48, no. 4, 1999, pp. 229-239.

[4] L. Ellis, "Gender differences in smiling: An evolutionary neuroandrogenic theory," Physiology and Behavior, vol. 88, pp. 303-308, 2006.

[5] K. M. Prkachin, "Effects of deliberate control on verbal and facial expressions of pain," Pain, vol. 114, pp. 328-338, 2005.

[6] H. Madokoro, K. Sato, and S. Kadowaki, "Facial expression spatial charts for representing time-series changes of facial expressions," Japan Society for Fuzzy Theory, vol. 23, no. 2, pp. 157-169, 2011.

[7] H. Madokoro and K. Sato, "Facial Expression Spatial Charts for Representing of Dynamic Diversity of Facial Expressions," Journal of Multimedia, vol. 6, no. 1, pp. 1-12, Jan. 2007.

[8] K. Sato, H. Madokoro, and S. Kadowaki, "Transient Stress Stimulus Effects on Intentional Facial Expressions," Japan Society for Fuzzy Theory, RJ-005, pp. 29-36, 2012.

[9] K. Sato, H. Otsu, H. Madokoro, and S. Kadowaki, "Analysis of Psychological Stress Factors on Intentional Facial Expressions," Japan Society for Fuzzy Theory, RJ-002, pp. 21-28, 2013.

[10] K. Sato, H. Otsu, H. Madokoro, and S. Kadowaki, "Analysis of Psychological Stress Factors and Facial Parts Effect on Intentional Facial Expressions," Proceedings of the Third International Conference on Ambient Computing, Applications, Services and Technologies, pp. 7-16, Oct. 2013.

[11] K. Sato, H. Otsu, H. Madokoro, and S. Kadowaki, "Analysis of Psychological Stress Factors by Using Bayesian Network," Proceedings of 2013 IEEE International Conference on Mechatronics and Automation, pp. 811-818, Aug. 2013.

[12] H. Ishi, M. Kamachi, and J. Gyoba, "Effect of Facial Motion on Impression of Smile," The Institute of Electronics, Information, and Communication Engineers, Technical Report, pp. 25-30, Dec. 2004.

[13] S. Hanibuchi, K. Ito, and S. Nishida, "Analysis of Transformed Impression of Smile Process: - An Approach to Supporting Facial Expression Process Training -," The Institute of Electronics, Information, and Communication Engineers, Technical Report, pp. 35-40, Oct. 2009.

[14] H. Fujishiro, A. Maejima, and S. Morishima, "Natural Smile Synthesis Considering Impression of Facial Expression Process," The Institute of Electronics, Information, and Communication Engineers, Technical Report, pp. 31-36, Mar. 2011.

[15] H. Fujishiro, A. Maejima, and S. Morishima, "Analysis of Relation between Movement of Smile Expression Process and Impression," The Journal of the Institute of Electronics, Information, and Communication Engineers, vol. J95-A, no. 1, pp. 128-135, 2012.

[16] K. W. Kampe, C. D. Frith, R. J. Dolan, and U. Frith, "Reward value of attractiveness and gaze," Nature, vol. 413, Oct. 2001.

[17] Y. Kuroki, S. Shiraishi, N. Mukawa, M. Yuasa, and N. Fukayama, "Interaction between Human and Human-like Agent with Gaze and Facial Expression for Human Computer Interaction," The Institute of Electronics, Information, and Communication Engineers, Technical Report, pp. 49-54, Mar. 2005.

[18] Y. Kuroki, S. Shiraishi, N. Mukawa, M. Yuasa, and N. Fukayama, "Impression of Human-like Agent with Gaze and Facial Expression: -Brain Activity Analysis of HCI using fMRI-," The Institute of Electronics, Information, and Communication Engineers, Technical Report, pp. 43-48, Mar. 2006.

[19] J.A. Russell and M. Bullock, "Multidimensional Scaling of Emotional Facial Expressions: Similarity from Preschoolers to Adults," Journal of Personality and Social Psychology, vol. 48, pp. 1290-1298, 1985.

[20] T. Kohonen, Self-organizing maps, Springer Series in Information Sciences, 1995.

[21] G. A. Carpenter, S. Grossberg, and D.B. Rosen, "Fuzzy ART: fast stable learning and categorization of analog patterns by an adaptive resonance system," Neural Networks, vol. 4, pp. 759-771, 1991.

[22] M. Haghighat, S. Zonouz, and M. Abdel-Mottaleb, "Identification Using Encrypted Biometrics," Computer Analysis of Images and Patterns, Springer Berlin Heidelberg, pp. 440-448, 2013.

[23] T. Ikeda, H. Ishiguro, and M. Asada, "Moving Signal-Source Tracking Based on Mutual Information Maximization," The Transactions of the Institute of Electronics, Information, and Communication Engineers D, vol. J90-D, no. 2, pp. 535-543, 2007.

[24] T. Kikuchi, K. Kishi, and J. Miyamichi, "An Automatic Data Classification Algorithm Adjusted by Mutual Information, " The Transactions of the Institute of Electronics, Information, and Communication Engineers D, vol. J82-D, no. 4, pp. 660-668, 1999.

[25] P. Ekman and W. V. Friesen, "Unmasking the Face: A Guide to Recognizing Emotions from Facial Clues," Malor Books, 2003.

[26] T. Kanade, J. F. Cohn, and Y. L. Tian, "Comprehensive database for facial expression analysis," Proc. of the Fourth IEEE Int. Conf. on Automatic Face and Gesture Recognition, pp. 46-53, 2000.

[27] M. Bartlett, J. Hager, P. Ekman, and T. Sejnowski, "Measuring facial expressions by computer image analysis," Psychophysiology, vol. 36, pp. 253-264, 1999.
[28] M. Pantic, M.F. Valstar, R. Rademaker, and L. Maat, "Web-based Database for Facial Expression Analysis," Proc. IEEE Int'l. Conf. Multimedia and Expo, Amsterdam, The Netherlands, Jul. 2005. doi: 10.1109/ICME.2005.15214.
[29] P. Lucey et al., "The Extended Cohn-Kanade Dataset (CK+): A complete expression dataset for action unit and emotion-specified expression," Proc. of the Third Int. Workshop on CVPR for Human Communicative Behavior Analysis, pp. 94-101, 2010.
[30] QcamOrbit; Logicool Inc., http://www.logicool.co.jp/ja-jp/webcam-communications/webcams [retrieved: June, 2016]
[31] M. Yamaguchi, T. Kanamori, M. Kanemaru, Y. Mizuno, and H. Yoshida, "Correlation of Stress and Salivary Amylase Activity," Japanese Journal of Medical Electronics and Biological Engineering: JJME, vol. 39, no. 3, pp. 46-51, Sep. 2001.
[32] OEG-16; Spectratech Inc., http://www.spectratech.co.jp/product/16me/ [retrieved: June, 2016]
[33] I. Akirav and M. Maroun, "The role of the medial prefrontal cortex-amygdala circuit in stress effects on the extinction of fear," Neural Plast. Published online 2007 Jan. doi: 10.1155/2007/30837.
[34] K. Yanagisawa, H. Tsunashima, Y. Marumo, S. Hirose, T. Shimizu, M. Taira, and T. Haji, "Measurement and Evaluation of Higher Brain Function Using Functional Near-Infrared Spectroscopy (fNIRS)," Journal of Human Interface Society, vol.11, no.2, pp.21-29, 2009.
[35] J. L. Robinson and H. A. Demaree, "Physiological and cognitive effects of expressive dissonance," Brain and Cognition, vol. 63, pp. 70-78, 2007.
[36] W. Sato, M. Noguchi, and S. Yoshikawa, "Emotion elicitation effect of films in a Japanese sample," Social Behavior and Personality, vol. 35, pp. 863-874, 2007.
[37] S. Srivastava, M. Tamir, K. M. McGonigal, O. P. John, and J. J. Gross, "The social costs of emotional suppression: A prospective study of the transition to college," Journal of Personality and Social Psychology, vol. 96, pp. 883-897, 2009.
[38] R.J.R. Blair, "Facial expressions, their communicatory functions and euro-cognitive substates," Philos. Trans. R. Soc. Lond., B358, pp. 561-572, 2003.

International Journal on Advances in Software, vol 9 no 1 & 2, year 2016, http://www.iariajournals.org/software/

Infinite Horizon Decision Support For Rule-based Process Models

Michaela Baumann*, Michael Heinrich Baumann†, Dominik Franz-Xaver Gruber‡, and Stefan Jablonski*
*Institute for Computer Science, University of Bayreuth, Germany
†Institute for Mathematics, University of Bayreuth, Germany
‡Faculty of Computer Science, Hochschule Kempten – University of Applied Sciences, Germany
email: {michaela.baumann, michael.baumann, stefan.jablonski}@uni-bayreuth.de, dominik.f.gruber@stud.fh-kempten.de

Abstract—**In recent years, process models tend to turn away from common procedural models to more flexible, rule-based models. These models are characterized by the fact that in each execution step users usually have to decide between several rule-consistent tasks to perform next. Precise execution paths are not given, which is why adequate execution support needs to be provided. Simulation is one means to facilitate the users' decisions. In this context, we suggest an execution simulation tool with an infinite horizon, i.e., in each (simulated) step, users are informed about the tasks that in any case still need to be done to properly finish one process instance, and about tasks that may no longer be executed. The forecasts consider an actual or a simulated history of the process instance and the rules given by the model. In contrast to systems that show consequences of decisions for the next 1, 2, 3, ... steps, our system deals with impacts until the end of the process instance, independent of the length of the instance, i.e., the number of steps, which is what we call "infinite horizon."**

Keywords–Process execution; Rule-based process models; Process decision support;

I. INTRODUCTION

This paper is based on the ICCGI 2015 contribution [1].

In many fields of economy, industry, and research, process models are used for supporting the execution of operating processes, for designing work steps, for documentation purposes, and so on [1]. Usually, these process models are a sort of procedural process models, where the execution order of the process steps is prescribed through the control flow. Notations for this kind of process models are, for example, Event-driven Process Chains (EPCs) [2], the Business Process Model and Notation (BPMN) [3], and petri nets [4]. See the left side of Figure 1 for an imperative process model example in BPMN. Other execution orders than the prescribed ones are not provided. This is why computational offloading ("the extent to which differential external representations reduce the amount of cognitive effort required to solve informationally equivalent problems" [5]) is quite well achieved in procedural process models. For rule-based process models, this is not the case [6], as they take a different modeling and representation approach. They are typically used when procedural process models are too restrictive or get too complicated when complex facts shall be displayed. The approach of rule-based process models is to provide a set of tasks, firstly without stating any execution order, and then to restrict all possible execution orders by adding rules or constraints that should be met during the execution. An example for such a rule could be: "If task A has been executed, afterwards task C needs to be eventually executed, too." See Figure 2 or the right side of Figure 1 for an example of a graphically represented rule-based process model in the ConDec language [7] whose elements will be explained in Section III. In some related work ConDec is also called DECLARE [8], but the term DECLARE is also used for a constraint-based system that supports LTL-based models like ConDec.

The two notations of Figure 1 express the same circumstance, namely that task A has to be executed at least two and at most five times in one process instance. As [9] states, declarative process models may be transformed into imperative ones, but the resulting model will probably look like a so-called "spaghetti-model" as the number of execution paths is incredibly large [10]. An example of such a transformation is given in Figure 1. Especially for rule-based process models, guidance for the user through the process is necessary, as the execution sequences leading to a proper process completion are not easy to see [11]. The paper at hand provides one mechanism for such a guidance through rule-based process models.

The work proceeds as follows: Section II briefly describes the research question in contrast to related work. Section III presents the declarative modelling language ConDec, which is based on linear temporal logic and considered in the further course of this paper. Section IV introduces the basic idea of the infinite horizon decision support whereas Section V then presents the concrete mechanism through deriving so-called status values out of the declarative process rules. Section VI briefly introduces a prototypical implementation. Section VII

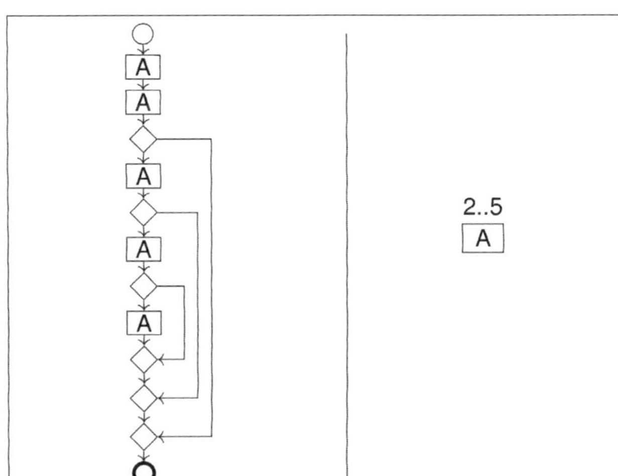

Figure 1: The same process model: on the left hand side an imperative representation, on the right hand side a declarative one.

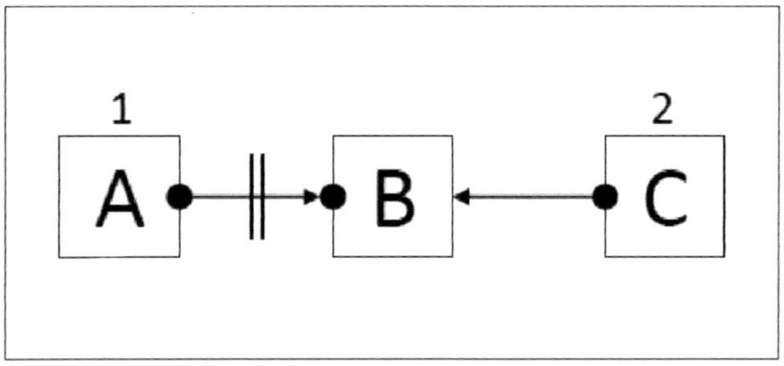

Figure 2: An example process model where ν has to look forward intelligently.

provides an exemplary process execution with infinite horizon status indicators and Section IX concludes the paper with topics for ongoing research.

II. Related Work and Research Question

For imperative process models a variety of execution support tools are available [12], like Workflow Management Systems (WfMSs) and electronical or paper-based checklists [13]. These support tools help the user to proceed the process adequately and can be based on the underlying process models but also on log data gained from previous process instances [14]. This is typically done by telling the user which tasks he has to perform or is allowed to perform next, or which tasks still have the possibility to be performed and which are no longer allowed due to previous decisions. Also, advice and frequently performed task orders together with some kind of evaluation may be provided to the user. For declarative process models, the basic functions of execution support tools are the same. However, due to the differences in the modelling approaches, there may be differences in the tools as well, for example the handling of the high level of flexibility when executing declarative process models [15]. In the work at hand, a mechanism for answering the following list of questions when processing a declaratively modelled process shall be presented:

(a) Which tasks still need to be executed during the process instance? How many times?
(b) Which tasks still can be executed during the process instance (but do not have to)? Is there a maximum number of executions?
(c) Which tasks are no longer allowed to be executed during the process instance?
(d) What changes take place for (a), (b), and (c) if a certain task would be performed next?

We do not want to answer the question, which tasks may be executed in the next step (finite horizon with step size 1). This has been done in other work, e.g., in [16] for ConDec models via automata. Instead, we want to look at the infinite horizon, i.e., a possibly infinite number of future steps, to give hints about process activities *valid for an indefinite future time frame*, exactly as specified in (a)-(d). To the best of the authors' knowledge, such a feature is not yet available. However, we assume that there is a mechanism ν available, like the one of [16], that chooses tasks for the next step in a way that every resulting process history is model conform and that dead ends are avoided. Furthermore, we need process models that do not contain conflicting constraints, i.e., that there is at least one possibility to finish the process successfully (satisfiability of the model) and that do not contain dead activities [16].

Our approach is in general independent of the underlying modelling language, i.e., also independent of the underlying logic the rules are based on, e.g., linear temporal logic or predicate logic. One reason, why we cannot use state automata for answering the above questions (a)-(d) is that it is not clear whether all declarative process models can be expressed as finite state automata at all [17]. If it is possible to express a model via an automaton, then for realistic models the automata usually suffer from a state explosion [18] and their computation gets very costly [19]. Furthermore, we want to be able to express exact numbers of activity recurrences (see (a) and (b)).

For run-time support, recommendations for effective execution [15] can be given. However, these recommendations are usually based on past experiences and need a specific goal, i.e., a rating of experiences in terms of desirability [8], as input. Due to this preselection, parts of the executable tasks are hidden from the executing agent. The decision support we head for is somehow different as we do not intend to give recommendations based on a specific goal (as input into the system) but to provide an overview over *the impact of each of his decisions* to the process participant. He can then decide, according to the overview and a goal (which is only in his mind), which step to execute next. The system and the model do not need to be changed, which may cause history-based violations when done at run-time [8]. As in declarative process models there is not necessarily a limit of steps till the end of an instance for answering questions (a)-(d), we talk of *infinite horizon* in this context. A use case for this approach could be the following example situation: in one section of a company problems have occurred (e.g., power failure, machine failure). Now, all processes that are executed until the problem is fixed shall be proceeded without consulting this section. A change of the workflow system is not needed as the problem can be fixed any time.

III. The Declarative Process Model

At first we have to specify the process model that will serve as input for the execution support tool. As already mentioned in Section II, the model shall be declarative, i.e., based on certain rules. One declarative modelling language is ConDec [7], a language based on LTL. It is usable in the DECLARE system [8], but it only allows for rules considering the tasks, i.e., the functional perspective of a process model in the five perspective approach of [20]. Rules for the other process perspectives like the data perspective, the operational perspective, or the organizational perspective are not covered. The control-flow perspective regarding the tasks is induced by the rules themselves. The limitation to the functional and the control-flow perspective through the use of ConDec simplifies the presentations but still makes clear the method of our apporach. As our approach is not dependent on ConDec but ConDec is just an example, we can extend the infinite horizon decision support to other rules involving other process perspectives as well. This extensibility comes from the fact that we do not directly use the particular modelling language's elements but the meaning behind the specific constructs, which can be called dependency patterns or *generic activity relationships*, a

TABLE I: LTL symbols and their meanings, taken from [24].

$\wedge, \vee, \neg$	Common logical operators (AND, OR, NOT)
$\Rightarrow, \Leftrightarrow$	Abbreviations for expressions formed with above operators (IMPLICATION, EQUIVALENCE)
$\bigcirc\phi$	ϕ has to hold next in the process history (NEXT)
$\Box\phi$	ϕ has to hold always in the subsequent process history (ALWAYS)
$\Diamond\phi$	ϕ has to hold eventually in the subsequent process history (EVENTUALLY)
$\phi \cup \psi$	ϕ has to hold in the process history at least until ψ holds where ψ holds eventually in the process history (UNTIL)

term used in [21]. Examples for other declarative modelling languages are the Case Management Model and Notation (CMMN) [22] specification of the Object Management Group (OMG) or the textual Declarative Process Intermediate Language (DPIL) [17]. The model elements of CMMN are to some extent very particular and exceed the scope of our approach, which is why we did not consider CMMN. DPIL is at that time not yet fully established, but it contains rules also for the other perspectives as well as cross-perspective rules. As ConDec is very common, we illustrate our approach with this graphical notation.

Independently of the underlying modelling language we have tasks $A, B, C, \ldots \in \mathcal{A}$ that may be executed in one process instance. The rules applied on the tasks of $\mathcal{A}$ are summarized in set $\mathcal{R}$. In the ConDec language there exist 19 basic rule types, also representable in linear temporal logic (LTL) [23], which will be considered further on. The basic LTL elements are listed in Table I.

The 19 basic rules of ConDec are the following ones. Every rule has a textual macro, an LTL representation indicated in square brackets, and a graphical representation, see [24]. The graphical representations are in Figures 3 and 4.

i) $existence(A, m)$: Task A has to be executed at least m times, $0 < m < \infty$
$[\Diamond(A \wedge (\bigcirc existence(A, m-1)))$ where $existence(A, 1) = \Diamond A]$
ii) $absence(A)$: Task A may not be performed
$[\neg existence(A, 1)]$
iii) $absence(A, n+1)$: Task A may only be executed up to n times, $0 < n < \infty$
$[\neg existence(A, n+1)]$
iv) $exactly(A, n)$: Task A has to be performed exactly n times, $0 < n < \infty$
$[existence(A, n) \wedge absence(A, n+1)]$
v) $init(A)$: Each process instance has to start with the execution of task A
$[A]$
vi) $respondedExistence(A, B)$: If task A appears in the process instance, then task B has to appear at some point, too
$[\Diamond A \Rightarrow \Diamond B]$
vii) $coExistence(A, B)$: If task A appears in the process instance, then task B has to appear at some point, too, and vice versa
$[\Diamond A \Leftrightarrow \Diamond B]$
viii) $response(A, B)$: If task A appears in the process instance, then task B has to appear after A, too
$[\Box(A \Rightarrow \Diamond B)]$
ix) $precedence(A, B)$: Task B can only be executed if task A has already been executed, i.e., already appears in the process history
$[(\neg B \cup A) \vee \Box(\neg B)]$
x) $succession(A, B)$: If task A shall be executed, then task B needs to be executed at some point afterwards and if B shall be executed, A needs to be performed in advance
$[response(A, B) \wedge precedence(A, B)]$
xi) $alternateResponse(A, B)$: If task A appears in the process instance, then task B has to appear after A, too, and A may not appear a second time before B
$[\Box(A \Rightarrow \bigcirc(\neg A \cup B))]$
xii) $alternatePrecedence(A, B)$: Task B can only be executed if task A has already been executed and between two executions of B at least one execution of A has to appear
$[precedence(A, B) \wedge \Box(B \Rightarrow \bigcirc(precedence(A, B)))]$
xiii) $alternateSuccession(A, B)$: Task A has to be followed by B and B has to be preceded by A and two executions of A need to have an execution of B before the second A and two executions of B need to have an execution of A after the first B
$[alternateResponse(A, B)$
$\wedge\ alternatePrecedence(A, B)]$
xiv) $chainResponse(A, B)$: Every execution of task A has to be directly followed by B
$[\Box(A \Rightarrow \bigcirc B)]$
xv) $chainPrecedence(A, B)$: Every execution of task B has to be directly preceded by A
$[\Box(\bigcirc B \Rightarrow A)]$
xvi) $chainSuccession(A, B)$: Every execution of task A has to be directly followed by B and every execution of task B has to be directly preceded by A
$[\Box(A \Leftrightarrow \bigcirc B)]$
xvii) $notCoExistence(A, B)$: Once task A is executed the first time, task B may not be executed any more and vice versa
$[\neg(\Diamond A \wedge \Diamond B)]$
xviii) $notSuccession(A, B)$: Once task A is executed, task B may not be executed any more after A
$[\Box(A \Rightarrow \neg(\Diamond B))]$
xix) $notChainSuccession(A, B)$: Task B may not be executed directly after A
$[\Box(A \Rightarrow \bigcirc(\neg B))]$

Graphical representations of the constraints are presented in Figure 3 and 4. These representations correspond to that ones shown in [16]. However, rules i)-iv) or i)-v) may be combined into the following two rules that are also shown in Figure 3 with $0 \leq m \leq n \leq \infty$ and $m < \infty$. We consider rules i') and ii') instead of the original ones in the further course of the paper.

i') $existence(A, m, n)$: Task A has to be performed at least m times but not more than n times
ii') $initExistence(A, m, n)$: Task A has to be performed at least m times but not more than n times and every process instance has to start with the execution of A

The LTL representation of each of these templates implies that formal model checking and verification can be applied. This is done via a translation to automata [16]. We require that set $\mathcal{R}$ is executable, i.e., that the underlying set of LTL formulas is satisfiable. Rules i)-v) or i') and ii'), resp., are also known as existence templates, rules vi)-xvi) as relation

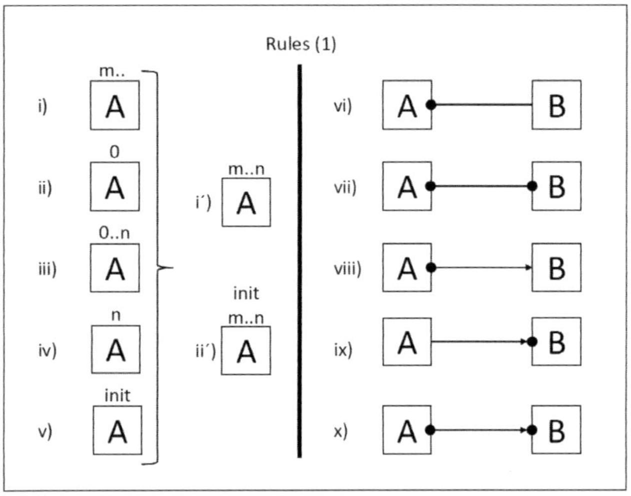

Figure 3: ConDec rules i)-x) and rules i') and ii').

templates and rules xvii)-xix) as negative relation templates. A fourth group of rules, choice templates, has been skipped like in [24] where the first three groups are referred to as basic rule types. In [16], LTL formulas for the choice templates are listed. However, as the rules base on LTL expressions, arbitrary rules can be added or existing rules modified or removed. The templates are always evaluated regarding their LTL expression, not their shortcut or graphical representation that are only used for better readability.

IV. Concept of the Infinite Horizon Decision Support

We already stated in Section I that a function or machine called ν exists that correctly returns all tasks that are executable in the next step. This means that according to every given and rule-consistent history $h \in \mathcal{H}$, where $\mathcal{H}$ is the space of all admissible histories, function $\nu : \mathcal{H} \rightarrow \mathcal{P}(\mathcal{A})$ returns those tasks that will not inevitably lead to an erroneous instance state. From every task supposed by ν at least one correct path, i.e., a rule-consistent task sequence, to a successful process completion has to exist. Regard Figure 2 for an example. Three tasks, namely A, B, and C may be executed during an instance of this example process. More precisely, task A has to be executed exactly once and task C exactly twice. However, after the execution of A, task B may no longer be executed. But after any execution of C task B must eventually be executed. Let $h = \odot$ be the empty history at the beginning of a process instance. Then $\nu(\odot) = \{B, C\}$ and not $\{A, B, C\}$ because if A would be executed at the very beginning, task B may no longer be executed. But the execution of task C, and C has to be executed even twice, requires at least one execution of B afterwards. This is a contradiction and would lead to a non-correct process completion. This is why function ν may not suggest task A as first task in the process instance.

The example in Figure 2 also illustrates the possibly infinite length of a process instance. A valid process execution would be to do task C twice, then B, then A: $h = C.C.B.A$. This is indeed the shortest possible execution. But it would also be valid to do B ten times: $h = C.C.B.B.B.B.B.B.B.B.B.B.A$, or even a hundred times, as the number of executions of task B is not restricted. If the user of a process support system has insight only into the tasks executable in the next step, he will not be able to recognize the impact of his decisions more than one step and possibly infinite steps ahead. For answering the questions (a)-(d) from Section I we introduce two counters for each task. One counter for the mandatory executions of a task and one for the optional executions. If the mandatory counter of a task has value $a \geq 0$, this means that no matter which decisions are made from now on, this task has to be executed at least a times. If the optional counter of a task has value $b \geq 0$, this means that from now on there is no path through the process where this task may be executed more than b times. It always holds that the mandatory counter is less than or equal to the optional counter. Furthermore, the optional counter cannot increase during the execution, otherwise the previous counter value would have been wrong. If the optional counter value is zero, the corresponding task may no longer be executed during this process instance. Mandatory counters can only decrease through the execution of a task. A process can only be successfully finished when the mandatory counters of all tasks are zero.

According to the declarative nature of the process model, the initial values of the counters are zero for the mandatory counters and infinite for the optional counters. Thus, the initial status of every task is $status(A) = (man(A), opt(A)) = (0, \infty)\ \forall A \in \mathcal{A}$. The initial status of the process of Figure 2 when subsuming the statuses of all tasks into one matrix would be the following:

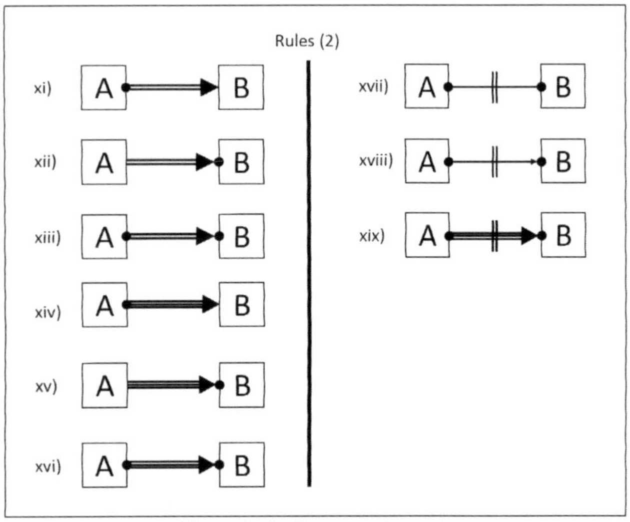

Figure 4: ConDec rules xi) - xix).

TABLE II: Initial status table for the example process of Figure 2; $h = \odot$.

Task	$mandatory$	$optional$
A	0	∞
B	0	∞
C	0	∞

In the next step, these status values must be updated

according to the process model rules given in $\mathcal{R}$. Every process model rule implies several status update rules. The specific update rules are derived in Section V, but we can state several general conditions for the change of a status value. For all model rules, we check these general conditions whether they apply for a model rule and determine the consequences. The possible conditions are the occurrences of the following events:

- The process instance has just been started ($start$)
- A certain task has just been executed ($exec(task)$ with $task \in \mathcal{A}$)
- The mandatory value of a certain task is greater than zero ($man(task) > 0$ with $task \in \mathcal{A}$)
- The optional value of a certain task is equal to zero ($opt(task) == 0$ with $task \in \mathcal{A}$)
- The optional value of a certain task is finite ($opt(task) \neq \infty$ with $task \in \mathcal{A}$)
- A certain task appears somewhere in the instance history ($task \in h$ with $task \in \mathcal{A} \wedge h \in \mathcal{H}$)
- A certain task appears on the last place in the instance history ($task = \ell(h)$ with $task \in \mathcal{A} \wedge h \in \mathcal{H}$ and ℓ a one-input function returning the last element of the history)
- A certain task appears more recently in the instance history than another task ($\ell(h, task, anothertask) = task$ with $task, anothertask \in \mathcal{A} \wedge h \in \mathcal{H}$ and ℓ a three-input function returning the more recent element of two of the history)
- A certain task does not appear somewhere in the instance history ($task \notin h$ with $task \in \mathcal{A} \wedge h \in \mathcal{H}$)
- A certain task does not appear on the last place in the instance history ($task \neq \ell(h)$ with $task \in \mathcal{A} \wedge h \in \mathcal{H}$ and ℓ a function returning the last element of the history)

The statuses $man(task) == 0$ and $opt(task) == \infty$ for $task \in \mathcal{A}$ do not have any consequences as theses statuses are the default ones. Of course, a condition can also be the conjunction of several of the above events. The possible consequences are the following events:

- The mandatory value of a certain task is reduced by one if it is greater than zero ($man(task) \leftarrow \max\{0, man(task) - 1\}$ with $task \in \mathcal{A}$)
- The mandatory value of a certain task is set to a fixed value ($man(task) \leftarrow n$ with $task \in \mathcal{A} \wedge n \in \mathbb{N}$)
- The mandatory value of a certain task is set to at least one or the value it was before ($man(task) \leftarrow \max\{1, man(task)\}$ with $task \in \mathcal{A}$)
- The mandatory value of a certain task is set to at least the mandatory value of another task (maybe increased or decreased by one) and the value it was before ($man(task) \leftarrow \max\{man(task), man(anothertask[\pm 1]\}$ with $task, anothertask \in \mathcal{A}$)
- The optional value of a certain task is reduced by one if it is greater than zero ($opt(task) \leftarrow \max\{0, opt(task) - 1\}$ with $task \in \mathcal{A}$)
- The optional value of a certain task is set to a fixed value ($opt(task) \leftarrow n$ with $task \in \mathcal{A} \wedge n \in \mathbb{N}$)
- The optional value of a certain task is set to zero ($opt(task) \leftarrow 0$ with $task \in \mathcal{A}$)
- The optional value of a certain task is set to at most the optional value of another task (maybe increased or decreased by one) and the value it was before ($opt(task) \leftarrow \min\{opt(task), opt(anothertask[\pm 1])\}$ with $task, anothertask \in \mathcal{A}$)

The reduction of the mandatory and the optional value of a certain task by one is only done when this task is executed.

If $exec(A)$: $\max\{0, man(A) \leftarrow man(A) - 1\}$;
If $exec(A)$: $\max\{0, opt(A) \leftarrow opt(A) - 1\}$;

Setting the mandatory and optional values to a fixed value is only done once at the beginning when existence rules are evaluated. For the remaining consequences it holds that the optional value of a task never increases and the mandatory value of a task never reaches infinity during the execution of the process.

For every process rule we now have to check which conditions imply which consequences for the involved tasks, i.e., we have to find the specific status update rules for every process rule.

V. Task Status Update Rules

For deriving the update rules we begin with the existence rules as these are the first ones to be evaluated after starting a process. The relation rules come next but without the chain rules, as these require a more thorough investigation. As third we examine the negation rules again without the negated chain rule. Finally, we analyze the relation and negation chain rules and observe particular behaviour for these rules because they do not directly influence the infinite horizon by definition. The derivation of the update rules is accompanied by the example process of Figure 2.

A. Existence Rules

The ConDec existence rules are equivalent to rules i') and ii'). These rules only change the status values of the tasks at the beginning of the process. After $start$ they are evaluated once and for the rest of the execution they are no longer relevant. What the update rules do is that they set the mandatory and optional values to the fixed values of the existence template that state that a task has to be executed at least m times and at most n times. If a value is not specified it remains the inital mandatory or optional value of 0 and ∞, respectively.

Rule i)':
$\forall\ existence(A, m, n) \in \mathcal{R}$:
If $start$: $man(A) \leftarrow m$;
If $start$: $opt(A) \leftarrow n$;

Whether a task has the $init$ property or not does not affect the infinite horizon, thus rule ii') is exactly the same regarding the status update values. Of course, if a task is marked as $init$, its mandatory value has to be at least one and there may only exist at most one $initExistence$ rule.

> Rule ii)':
> $\forall$ $initExistence(A, m, n)$: $existence(A, \max\{1, m\}, n)$

The example in Figure 2 has two existence rules, namely $existence(A, 1, 1)$ and $existence(C, 2, 2)$. According to the update rules above the status matrix in Table II changes to the matrix shown in Table III.

TABLE III: Status table for the example process of Figure 2 after evaluating the update rules resulting from existence rules; $h = \odot$.

Task	$mandatory$	$optional$
A	1	1
B	0	∞
C	2	2

B. Relation Rules without Chain Rules

The ConDec relation rules are rules vi)-xiii) plus $chainResponse$, $chainPrecedence$, and $chainSuccession$, but we consider the $chain$ rules not until Section V-D. We start with the $response$ rule. As $response(A, B)$ states that after A has been executed, B has to be eventually executed, too, the execution of A sets the mandatory value of B to at least one. But we also know that if A still has to be executed (not matter how often), B also has to be executed at least once. And we know that if B can no longer be executed, A must be prevented from execution, too, by setting $opt(A) == 0$. The $response$ rule is not history dependent.

> Rule viii):
> $\forall$ $response(A, B) \in \mathcal{R}$:
> If $exec(A)$: $man(B) \leftarrow \max\{man(B), 1\}$;
> If $man(A) > 0$: $man(B) \leftarrow \max\{man(B), 1\}$;
> If $opt(B) == 0$: $opt(A) \leftarrow 0$;

In contrast to the $response$ rule, $precedence$ is history dependent. We do not want to state that for rule $precedence(A, B)$, if A has already been executed, B may be executed in the next step, but we want to give long-range information. That means, if A has not yet been executed (is not in h) and can no longer been executed, the optional value of B has to be set to zero, because the prerequisites for executing B can never be fulfilled. The other way round, if B still needs to be executed and A is not yet executed, its mandatory value has to be at least one.

> Rule ix):
> $\forall$ $precedence(A, B) \in \mathcal{R}$:
> If $opt(A) == 0 \wedge A \notin h$: $opt(B) \leftarrow 0$;
> If $man(B) > 0 \wedge A \notin h$: $man(A) \leftarrow \max\{man(A), 1\}$;

For $succession$ both the update rules of $response$ and $precedence$ hold.

> Rule x):
> $\forall$ $succession(A, B) \in \mathcal{R}$:
> $response(A, B) \wedge precedence(A, B)$

$respondedExistence$ is a variant of $response$ and causes the same update rules as $response$ in case that the second input task not already appears in the history. If this task already appears in the history, then the $respondedExistence$ process rule has no implications on the status values.

> Rule vi):
> $\forall$ $respondedExistence(A, B) \in \mathcal{R}$:
> If $exec(A) \wedge B \notin h$: $man(B) \leftarrow \max\{man(B), 1\}$;
> If $man(A) > 0 \wedge B \notin h$: $man(B) \leftarrow \max\{man(B), 1\}$;
> If $opt(B) == 0 \wedge B \notin h$: $opt(A) \leftarrow 0$;

For $coExistence$, the update rules of $respondedExistence$ with the tasks in original order and transposed order hold.

> Rule vii):
> $\forall$ $coExistence(A, B) \in \mathcal{R}$:
> $respondedExistence(A, B)$ $\wedge$
> $respondedExistence(B, A)$

The status update rules implied by the ConDec $alternate$ rules make use of the function $\ell : \mathcal{H} \times \mathcal{A} \times \mathcal{A} \rightarrow \mathcal{A}$ that returns the more recent task out of two tasks under the current history h. If only one of the two tasks is in History h then ℓ returns this task. If none of the tasks is in h, it returns $NULL$. The update rules implied by the $alternate$ rules are similar to that of $response$, $precedence$, and $succession$, except that for two of the update rules, a case differentiation based on the current history has to be made. The $alternateResponse$ is, in contrast to the $response$ rule, history dependent:

> Rule xi):
> $\forall$ $alternateResponse(A, B) \in \mathcal{R}$:
> If $exec(A)$: $man(B) \leftarrow \max\{man(B), 1\}$;
> If $opt(B) \neq \infty \wedge \ell(h, A, B) == A$:
> $opt(A) \leftarrow \min\{opt(B) - 1, opt(A)\}$;
> If $opt(B) \neq \infty \wedge \ell(h, A, B) == B$:
> $opt(A) \leftarrow \min\{opt(B), opt(A)\}$;
> If $\ell(h, A, B) == A$:
> $man(B) \leftarrow \max\{man(B), man(A) + 1\}$;
> If $man(A) > 0 \wedge \ell(h, A, B) == B$:
> $man(B) \leftarrow \max\{man(B), man(A)\}$

The second and third as well as the fourth and fifth update rule can be combined via an indicator function. This is in line with the possible $NULL$ return of ℓ if neither A nor B appears in h:

> Rule xi):
> $\forall$ $alternateResponse(A, B) \in \mathcal{R}$:
> If $exec(A)$: $man(B) \leftarrow \max\{man(B), 1\}$;
> If $opt(B) \neq \infty$:
> $opt(A) \leftarrow \min\{opt(B) - \mathbb{I}_{\ell(h,A,B)==A}, opt(A)\}$;
> If $man(A) + \mathbb{I}_{\ell(h,A,B)==A} > 0$:
> $man(B) \leftarrow \max\{man(B), man(A) + \mathbb{I}_{\ell(h,A,B)==A}\}$;

Also for $alternatePrecedence$, the usual $precedence$ can be applied modified by another history dependency:

Rule xii):
$\forall$ $alternatePrecedence(A, B) \in \mathcal{R}$:
If $opt(A) \neq \infty$:
$opt(B) \leftarrow \min\{opt(B), opt(A) + \mathbb{I}_{\ell(h,A,B)==A}\}$;
If $man(B) - \mathbb{I}_{\ell(h,A,B)==A} > 0$:
$man(A) \leftarrow \max\{man(A), man(B) - \mathbb{I}_{\ell(h,A,B)==A}\}$;

The update rules implied by $alternateSuccession$ are the conjuction of the update rules of $alternateResponse$ and $alternatePrecedence$:

Rule xiii):
$\forall$ $alternateSuccession(A, B) \in \mathcal{R}$:
$alternateResponse(A, B) \land$
$alternatePrecedence(A, B)$

C. Negation Rules without Chain Rule

Like the relation rules, the negation rules xvii) and xviii) are at first considered without the $chain$ rule, in this case without the $notChainSuccession$ rule xix. For $notSuccession(A, B)$ it holds that as soon as task A is executed, task B may no longer be executed, i.e., the optional status value of B becomes zero. The fact that as long as B has to be executed ($man(B) > 0$) prohibits A from execution cannot be considered in the infinite horizon but this restraint has to be realized in ν but this is not focussed in this paper.

Rule xviii):
$\forall$ $notSuccession(A, B) \in \mathcal{R}$: If $exec(A)$: $opt(B) \leftarrow 0$;

For the $notCoExistence$ rule the fact that a mandatory value of one of the tasks is greater than zero influences the infinite horizon status update rules as there is no time dependency for this rule.

Rule xvii):
$\forall$ $notCoExistence(A, B) \in \mathcal{R}$:
If $exec(A)$: $opt(B) \leftarrow 0$;
If $exec(B)$: $opt(A) \leftarrow 0$;
If $man(A) > 0$: $opt(B) \leftarrow 0$;
If $man(B) > 0$: $opt(A) \leftarrow 0$;

We can now futher analyze the model of Figure 2 and its implications on the status update table. Table III shows the statuses after $start$ of the process. The update rules implied by the relation and negation process rules have to be checked next, still before having executed the first task. We have to consider the following update rules, induced by $response(C, B)$ and $notSuccession(A, B)$:

- If $exec(C) : man(B) \leftarrow \max\{man(B), 1\}$;
- If $man(C) > 0 : man(B) \leftarrow \max\{man(B), 1\}$;
- If $opt(B) == 0 : opt(C) \leftarrow 0$;
- If $exec(A) : opt(B) \leftarrow 0$;

Clearly, the update rules activated by $exec$ have not effect at the moment. Only one update rule ($man(C) > 0$) is activated. The status changes are in Table IV. The mandatory value of B has increased by one. Note that the status update rules excluding that ones with $exec$ and $start$ can in general influence each other. The order of processing them does not matter but they have to be processed as many times until nothing more changes.

TABLE IV: Status table for the example process of Figure 2 after evaluating all update rules without having executed a task; $h = \odot$.

Task	$mandatory$	$optional$
A	1	1
B	1	∞
C	2	2

Tasks executable next (the output of function ν with respect to history $h = \odot$) are B and C. The execution of B implies the following changes: B is executed and thus $man(B) \leftarrow 0$ and $opt(B) == \infty$ (reducing ∞ by one is still ∞). Then the update rule $man(C) > 0$ activates and the mandatory value of B is again set to one. The situtation is as before. When executing C, $h = C$, the statuses change according to Table V.

TABLE V: Status table for the example process of Figure 2 after execution of C: $h = C$.

Task	$mandatory$	$optional$
A	1	1
B	1	∞
C	1	1

Now, we have $\nu(C) = \{B, C\}$. Executing B in the second step would again lead to no changes, but executing C will result in a status table as shown in Table VI.

TABLE VI: Status table for the example process of Figure 2 after execution of C again; $h = C.C$.

Task	$mandatory$	$optional$
A	1	1
B	1	∞
C	0	0

The output of ν under $h = C.C$ is now only B, thus, task B needs to be executed next. This results in statuses as seen in Table VII. The output of ν under $h = C.C.B$ is now A and B.

TABLE VII: Status table for the example process of Figure 2 after execution of B; $h = C.C.B$.

Task	$mandatory$	$optional$
A	1	1
B	0	∞
C	0	0

As soon as A is executed, the process has successfully finished as all mandatory values have reached zero. Furthermore, all optional values are zero as well, which means that no task may be executed again as well, see Table VIII. Before executing A, B can be executed arbitraritly often without changing the status values.

D. Relation and Negation Chain Rules

The $chainResponse$ behaves similar to the $alternateResponse$ with the difference that in the sequence of several tasks A and B, B has to directly follow A. Therefore, the update rules of $alternateResponse$ can be

TABLE VIII: Status table for the example process of Figure 2 after execution of A; $h = C.C.B.A$.

Task	$mandatory$	$optional$
A	0	0
B	0	0
C	0	0

modified through considering $\ell(h)$ instead of $\ell(h, A, B)$ with $\ell : \mathcal{H} \to \mathcal{A}$ returning the most recent task in instance history h.

Rule xiv):
$\forall\ chainResponse(A, B) \in \mathcal{R}$:
If $exec(A)$: $man(B) \leftarrow \max\{man(B), 1\}$;
If $opt(B) \neq \infty$:
$$opt(A) \leftarrow \min\{opt(A), opt(B) - \mathbb{1}_{\ell(h)==A}\};$$
If $man(A) + \mathbb{1}_{\ell(h)==A} > 0$:
$$man(B) \leftarrow \max\{man(B), man(A) + \mathbb{1}_{\ell(h)==A}\};$$

The same modifications hold for $chainPrecedence$.

Rule xv):
$\forall\ chainPrecedence(A, B) \in \mathcal{R}$:
If $opt(A) \neq \infty$:
$$opt(B) \leftarrow \min\{opt(B), opt(A) + \mathbb{1}_{\ell(h)==A}\};$$
If $man(B) - \mathbb{1}_{\ell(h)==A} > 0$:
$$man(A) \leftarrow \max\{man(A), man(B) - \mathbb{1}_{\ell(h)==A}\};$$

For $chainSuccession$, the update rules of $chainResponse$ and $chainPrecedence$ are conjuncted.

Rule xvi):
$\forall\ chainSuccession(A, B) \in \mathcal{R}$:
$chainResponse(A, B)\ \wedge\ chainPrecedence(A, B)$

Rule xix): $notChainSuccession$ has no direct implications on the status update rules but affects them indirectly. We address these indirect consequences in Section V-F.

E. Additional $notSuccession$ and $notChainSuccession$ caused by $chainResponse$ and $chainSuccession$

For $chainResponse$, as well as for $chainSuccession$ as it includes the $chainResponse$, we can make another observation. As soon as A is executed, B has to be executed next, and so all status changes B causes are actually already caused through the execution of A. For the status update rules, this transfer caused by a $chainResponse$ resp. $chainSuccession$ is already done indirectly except for the $notSuccession$ and $notChainSuccession$ rules. The

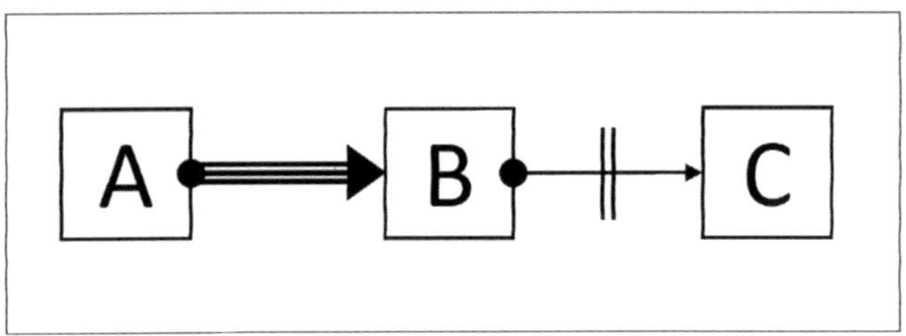

Figure 5: ConDec model where $notSuccession(B, C)$ causes the addition of $notSuccession(A, C)$ because of $chainResponse(A, B)$.

$notSuccession$ only has one update rule, which is triggered by the execution of a certain task, the $notChainSuccession$ has no update rules at all. Figure 5 shows a situation where a $notSuccession$ causes the addition of another rule. Task A has to be directly followed by B and then, after the execution of B, C may no longer be executed because of the rule $notSuccession(B, C)$. The update rule implied by the $notSuccession$ is, however, If $exec(B)$: $opt(C)$ $==$ 0 although it is already clear when executing A, C can no longer be executed. We want the update rule If $exec(A)$: $opt(C)$ $==$ 0. This can be achieved by including a $notSuccession(A, C)$ in addition to the original $notSuccession(B, C)$. Similar to this, it holds for $notChainSuccession$: $chainResponse(A, B)\ \wedge\ notChainSuccession(B, C)$: add $notChainSuccession(A, C)$ to the model. The addition of a $notChainSuccession$ may look like a redudant thing to do because the $chainResponse$ prohibits all other tasks except the responding task in the next step, but the problem gets clear with another observation described in Section V-F.

The $chainPrecedence$ is only history dependent and does not imply additions of process rules.

F. Infinite horizon implications of $notChainResponse$

At a first glance, the $notChainSuccession$ rule does not affect the infinite horizon as it prevents the execution of a certain task only in the next step (which would be a matter for ν). But indeed, it can have a considerable impact on the infinite horizon. See Figure 6 for an example of the infinite horizon effect of a $notChainSuccession$. The model consists only of three tasks, A, B, and C, where A needs to be executed at least once and C may not be executed directly after A. As soon as B is executed, C may no longer be executed. When starting with A, there is no direct infinite horizon status change for C. The $notSuccession$ causes no status changes at this point as well, as it only triggers through the execution of B. But in fact, C may no longer be executed as the next task after A is again A or B (C is prohibited through the $notChainSuccession$). Executing A again implies no changes, but the execution of B sets the optional value of C to zero. That means, through $exec(A)$ is should have followed immediately $opt(C) == 0$.

The detection of such a connection can be very complicated as it can involve any number of steps. A helpful approach is to conduct a review of the $notChainSuccession(A, B)$ rules under the current history if A is executed. In our example in Figure 6, the $notChainSuccession$ implies the same process behavior when executing A as a $notSuccession$ under $h = \odot$, i.e., it actually affects the infinite horizon statuses. So, for the situation $h = \odot$ the $notChainSuccession$ rule is translated into a $notSuccession$ implying all status update rules of the $notSuccession$. We call these translated $notChainSuccession$ rules $deFactoNotSuccession$ rules. They turn back to $notChainSuccession$ after one process step as their transformation is history dependent. That is, the status update rules implied by a $deFactoNotSuccession$ only hold for one turn. Figure 7 shows a situation where the $notChainSuccession$ not necessarily turns into a $notSuccession$. Before execution, the rule $notChainSuccession(A, D)$ has to be added to the original model because of $chainResponse(A, B)$ and

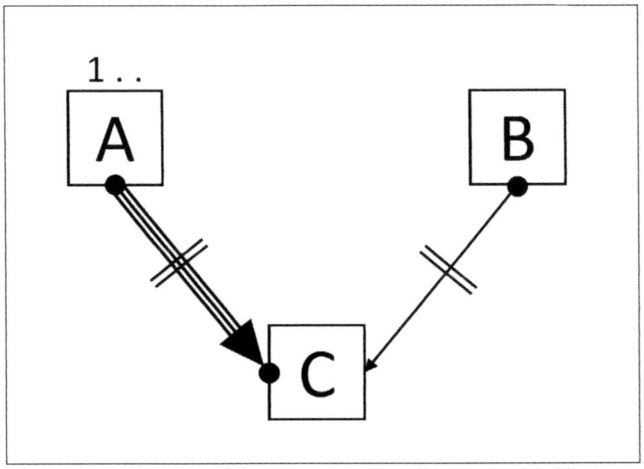

Figure 6: ConDec model where $notChainSuccession(A, C)$ is a $deFactoNotSuccesion(A, C)$.

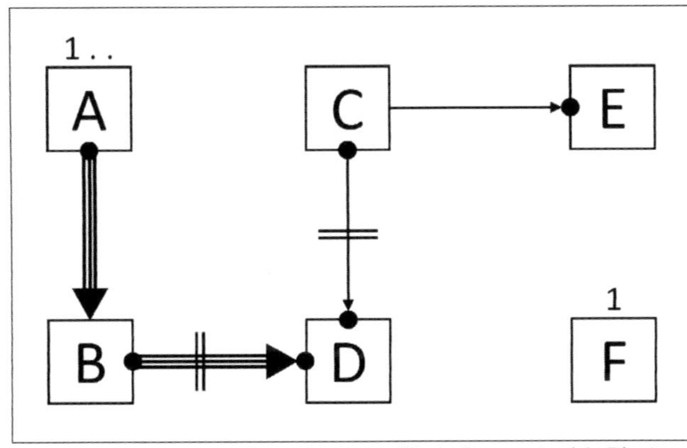

Figure 7: ConDec model where $notChainSuccession(A, D)$ is a $deFactoNotSuccesion(A, D)$ with underlying history $h = F$.

$notChainSuccession(B, D)$. It is possible, to start the process with execution of A: $h = A$. Now it has to be checked, if task D is only locked for the next step because of $notChainSuccession(A, D)$ or if it is a $deFactoNotSuccession(A, D)$ setting $opt(D) == 0$. With history $h = A$ we find the following path to execute D afterwards: task B has to follow immediately: $h = A.B$. But also here, D is not allowed at least in the next step and we also have to check for $deFactoNotSuccession(B, D)$. Task E requires C, but C immediately prohibits any further execution of D. Instead, task F can be executed: $h = A.B.F$. After execution of F, execution of D does no longer conflict with $notChainSuccession(A, D)$ and $notChainSuccession(B, D)$ and thus, D can be executed next. However, if we consider the situation where F is executed first and then A, we are no longer able to find a way to executed D afterwards. The only possible way to executed D after A was to do F, but it has exact execution number of one, i.e., its mandatory and optional values have turned to zero after the first process step. So, with history $h = F.A$ the execution of A causes the rule $notChainSuccession(A, D)$ to transform to a $notSuccession(A, D)$ and the optional value of D is immediately reduced to zero. When executing B afterwards, rule $notChainSuccession(B, D)$ does not need to be checked for being a $deFactoNotSuccesion(B, D)$ as already $opt(D) == 0$.

> Rule xix):
> $notChainSuccession(A, B)$: As this rules points exactly one task execution into the future, it has no direct implications for the infinite horizon. When A is executed, it must be checked whether it is an actual $notChainSuccession$ or a $deFactoNotSuccession$, which applies the status update rules of a $notSuccession$, depending on the current history.

This possible translation of $notChainSuccession$ rules into $deFactoNotSuccession$ rules is the reason why $notChainSuccession$ rules have to be added due to $chainResponse$ rules as described in Section V-E. The conduction whether a $notChainSuccession$ is a $deFactoNotSuccession$ or an actual $notChainSuccession$ can be done via model verification: For $notChainSuccession(A, B)$ simulate the execution of A based on the current history h (simulated history: $h' = h.A$) and check the model for freeness of conflicts when adding the rule $response(A, B)$. If the original model was conflict-free and now a conflict occurs, it means that B cannot be executed after A and thus, the $notChainSuccession(A, B)$ is a $deFactoNotSuccession(A, B)$.

VI. IMPLEMENTATION

In this section, we demonstrate the functioning of the derived infinite horizon status update rules with a prototypical proof-of-concept implementation of the infinite horizon system in Java. This implementation is a stand-alone program reflecting the infinite horizon mechanism and can be integrated into existing process execution systems. Figure 8 presents a reduced UML class diagram that shows the structure of the infinite horizon update rule system. The rules not shown in Figure 8 indicated through the "incomplete" annotation are included in the same way as the respresented ones. The update rules derived in Section V are implemented as methods in the respective rule classes.

Because we did not implement interfaces yet in the prototype, the process models we checked were entered by hand. If necessary, we added transferred $notSuccesion$ and $notChainSuccession$ rules. The derivation of those tasks that are executable next, i.e., the functionality of ν, can be achieved with an automaton based approach as described in [8]. The same automaton based approach can be used when checking for $deFactoNotSuccessions$ as described in Section V-F: for every $notChainSuccession(A, B)$, history $h = history.A$ with $history$ being the status of the process instance so far and the model has to be entered into the verification system. Additionally, the rule $response(A, B)$ is needed to check whether there are any conflicts or not, i.e., whether B is eventually executable or not. If a conflict occurs, the $notChainSuccession(A, B)$ is a $deFactoNotSuccession$ and the respective update rule has to be added into our system.

Basically, the procedure of the update rules trigger mechanism is the following where start-update rules (s-update rules)

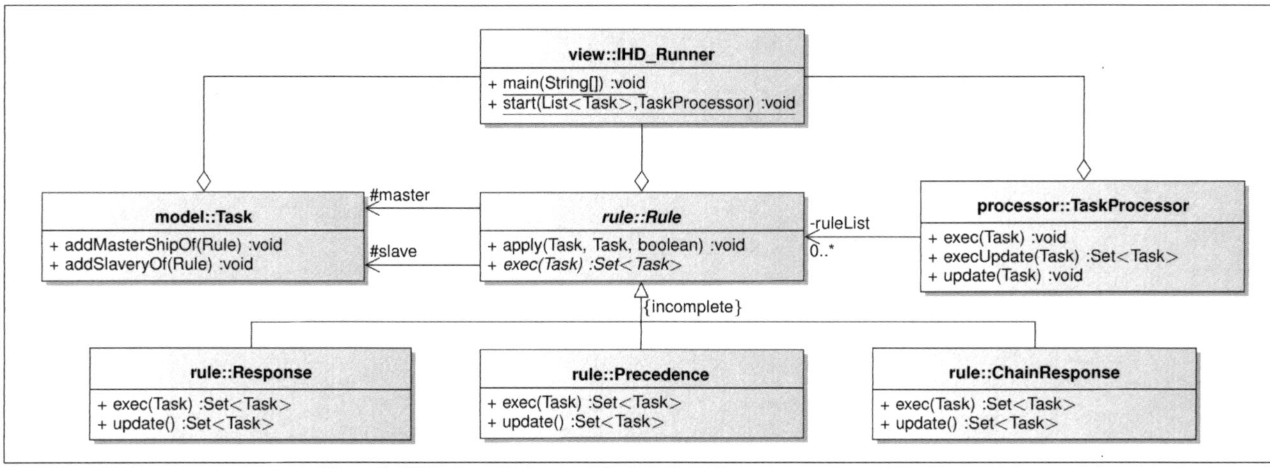

Figure 8: UML class diagramm of the infinite horizon status update rule system.

are those beginning with "If $start$" and execution-update rules (e-update rules) are those beginning with "If $exec(\cdot)$":

1) $h \leftarrow \odot$;
   initialization of status table (mandatory values zero, optional values ∞);
2) start process:
   go through s-update rules once;
   go through other update rules (except e/s-update rules) as many times until nothing more changes;
3) execution of $task \in \nu(h)$:
   $h \leftarrow task$;
   go through e-update rules once;
   go through other update rules (except e/s-update rules) as many times until nothing more changes;
4) execution of $task \in \nu(h)$:
   $h \leftarrow h.task$;
   go through execution-update rules once;
   go through other update rules (except e/s-update rules) as many times until nothing more changes;
5) etc.

The order of the rules when going through s-update rules, e-update rules, or all other update rules is not important, as long as the other update rules are processed until in one run no changes apply to the status values. We tested the behavior of the infinite horizon status update mechanism with several distinct process models and always reached the desired, correct behavior of the status updates. One such execution example is provided in Section VII to illustrate the functionality of the implemented prototype.

VII. Example

As an illustrational example of the infinite horizon decision support we take the process given in Figure 9 representing a (fictional) clinical diagnosis process. The example contains three $precedence$ rules, one $response$ rule, one $respondedExistence$ rule und one $notChainSuccession$ rule. In this example, the $notChainSuccession$ rule never turns into a $deFactoNotSuccession$ rule as task "magnetic resonance tomography" can always be executed. Thus, the $notChainSuccession$ rule has no influence on the infinite horizon. With the abbreviations MRT (magnetic resonance tomography), $assistant$ (assistant physician's round), $blood$ (blood test), $head$ (head physician's round), and $Xray$ (X-ray examination) for the tasks and the status rules applied after initializing the states the table for history $h = \odot$ looks like Table IX.

TABLE IX: Diagnosis process: status table with history $h = \odot$.

Task	$mandatory$	$optional$
MRT	1	∞
$blood$	0	1
$assistant$	1	∞
$Xray$	0	∞
$head$	0	1

Regarding the console output of our prototype in Figure 10, we get the same result.

Table IX says that there are two tasks that need to be done in any case, even in every instance of this process as the history is empty at the moment, namely tasks MRT and $assistant$. All other tasks may be done at some point during an instance, however, not necessarily all tasks in one instance. Now imagine that there is a patient for whom a diagnosis has to be made without performing the X-ray examination in this particular case. Is there a possibility to perform the diagnosis process without this specific task? Table IX states "yes" as the $mandatory$ value of $Xray$ is 0. This means, there is at least one successful execution without having to perform the X-ray examination.

Possible tasks in the first step give by $\nu(\odot)$ are MRT, $blood$ and $XRay$. When executing $blood$, the output of the prototype is shown in Figure 11.

Summarized in a status table, the status values for $h = blood$ are represented in Table X. The status values reveal that if the blood test is done then the X-ray examination eventually needs to be done, too. This is not desired for our patient, so the blood test should not be the choice in the first step.

Instead of the blood test the MRT is executed in the first step (this task has to be executed anyway during the process), so we have history $h = MRT$. The prototype output of Figure

TABLE X: Diagnosis process: status table with history $h = blood$.

Task	$mandatory$	$optional$
MRT	1	∞
$blood$	0	0
$assistant$	1	∞
$Xray$	1	∞
$head$	1	1

TABLE XI: Diagnosis process: status table with history $h = MRT$.

Task	$mandatory$	$optional$
MRT	0	∞
$blood$	0	1
$assistant$	1	∞
$Xray$	0	∞
$head$	0	1

12 and the summarized status table in Table XI show that this choice is fine since the X-ray examination is still optional, but not mandatory.

The only remaining mandatory task is $assistant$. If this task is performed next, then the diagnosis process can be finished successfully as all $mandatory$ values are 0. This is apparent from both Figure 13 and summarized status Table XII.

So, the answer to the question if the process can be performed without having to do the X-ray examination can be given directly after initializing the tasks' states, but the concrete steps that have to be taken to reach this goal can only be detected through simulation. However, the execution $h = MRT.assistant.end$ is one possibility to finish the process under the given constraints. There may exist others as well.

VIII. Inclusion of the Next Function

The function that returns the tasks executable in the next step is not in the focus of this paper. However, to obtain a satisfactory decision support tool, the functionality of such a mapping ν has to be integrated into the system. At the moment, the output of function ν is generated externally. We

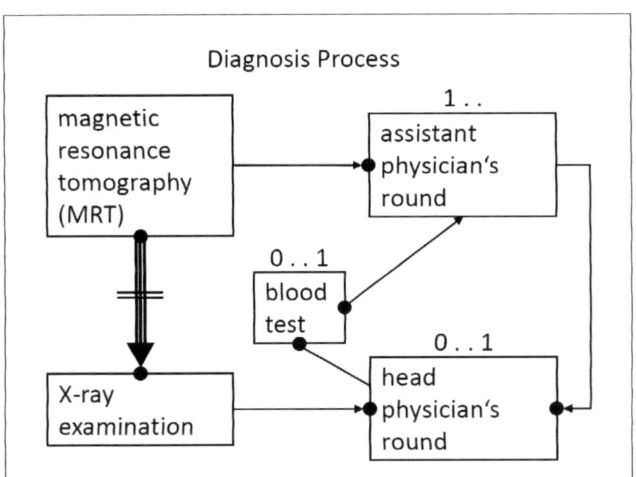

Figure 9: A fictional clinical process model representing a diagnosis process.

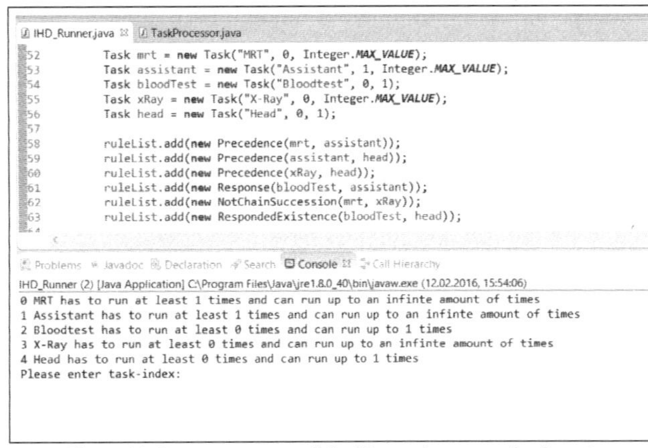

Figure 10: Prototype output of the Diagnosis process for $h = \odot$.

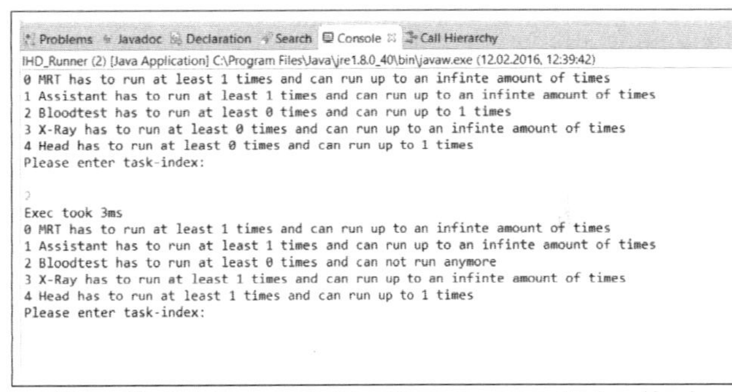

Figure 11: Prototype output of the Diagnosis process for $h = blood$.

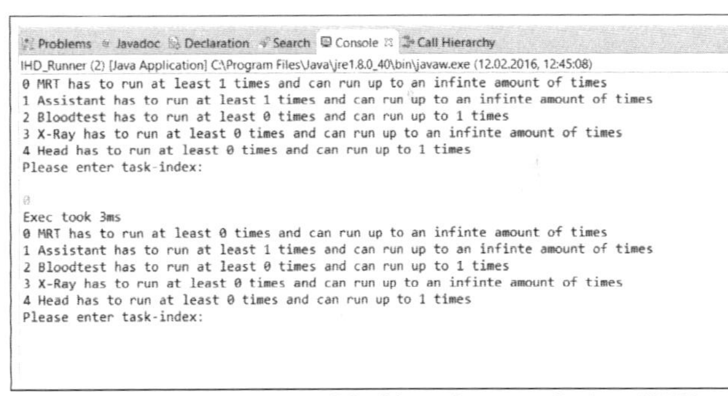

Figure 12: Prototype output of the Diagnosis process for $h = MRT$.

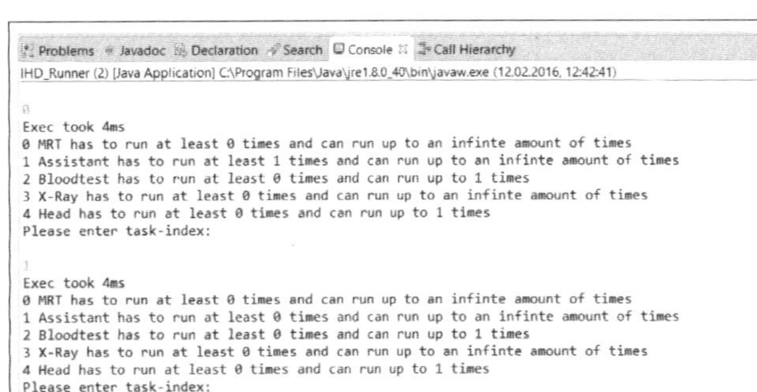

Figure 13: Prototype output of the Diagnosis process for $h = MRT.assistant$.

TABLE XII: Diagnosis process: status table with history $h = MRT.assistant$.

Task	$mandatory$	$optional$
MRT	0	∞
$blood$	0	1
$assistant$	0	∞
$Xray$	0	∞
$head$	0	1

TABLE XIII: Diagnosis process: user decision support with next executable tasks and their implications with $h = \odot$.

	$mandatory$	$impossible$
Current	MRT, $assistant$	
MRT	$assistant$	
$blood$	MRT, $assistant$, $Xray$, $head$	$blood$
$Xray$	MRT, $assistant$	

are currently working on the inclusion of ν in the same manner as the mandatory and optional values are generated. We add a third type of status value to each task indicating whether a task is locked by certain process rules or not. The update rules have to be extended by locking rules.

The $response$ rule does not have any influence on the locking of tasks, but for the $precendence$ rule, we have to add the following status update rule: $\forall\ precedence(A, B) \in \mathcal{R}$: If $A \notin h$: $lock(B)$. This functionality could be realised with a map in Java to ensure that a lock is released only once as one task may have several locks from different process rules. This locking mechanism wourld detach the dependency on process models representable as finite state automata (see, e.g., [16]) but extent the set of possible process models.

A schematical representation of the user decision support with next executable tasks is depictured in Table XIII. The process is that one of Figure 9 with an empty history. Table XIII shows the current mandatory/optional values not with their concrete values but only distiguishes between a value of 0 or > 0. This current state is shown in the row above the double horizontal line: MRT and $assistant$ have to be executed somewhen to finish the process under the current situation. There are not any non-executable tasks at the beginning. The tasks executable next, i.e., in the first step, are shown in the left column below the double horizontal line as well as their implications on the infinite horizon in the respective rows: the tasks that are mandatory after the execution of one of the next executable tasks and the tasks that are impossible to execute in the further process instance. For example, if $blood$ is executed in the next, i.e., first, step, then it cannot be executed any more but $Xray$ and $head$ get mandatory, too. MRT and $assistant$ remain mandatory as they have not been executed yet. The optional values are indirectly given. If a task has an optional value of zero, it is listed in column $impossible$. For example, $blood$ gets impossible for all future steps after execution of $blood$ in the first step.

IX. Conclusion and Ongoing Research

The work at hand presents a possibility for decision support for declarative process models. The presented decision support applies to an infinitely long forecast horizon. It makes use of the process rules and their implications to the states of the tasks they refer to. The rules considered in this paper only concern the sequence flow of a process so an extension to other rule types, e.g., concerning roles and agents, is worthwhile. Furthermore, the tasks are only points in time, i.e., only their final execution is registered. However, due to concurrency issues it would be beneficial to split one task into different events, at least into $taskstarted$ and $taskfinished$. According to these events, the update rules need to be adjusted. Furthermore, tasks can also serve as containers implying subprocesses, like activities marked as subprocesses in BPMN do. For such nested process models the update rules can also be nested, meaning, the execution of a container task initializes a separate set of update rules for the subprocess. For larger process models, the status value tables can be stored via a hash key once they are computed to reduce runtime.

The mechanism presented in this paper can be seen as an extension for existing decision support systems or process navigation tools where it can be embedded into. Interfaces for the respective target system have to be built then, but the mechanism, i.e., the logic of the task status update rules, can be taken one to one.

Acknowledgement

The work of Michael Heinrich Baumann is supported by a scholarship of "Hanns-Seidel-Stiftung (HSS)", which is funded by "Bundesministerium für Bildung und Forschung (BMBF)." The authors wish to thank Josef Noll (Basic Internet Foundation and University of Oslo, University Graduate Center (UNIK), Norway), session chair at The Tenth International Multi-Conference on Computing in the Global Information Technology (ICCGI 2015) October 11 - 16, 2015 - St. Julians, Malta.

References

[1] M. Baumann, M. H. Baumann, and S. Jablonski, "An idea on infinite horizon decision support for rule-based process models," in *ICCGI 2015, The Tenth International Multi-Conference on Computing in the Global Information Technology*, H. Kaindl, K. György, and D. Tamir, Eds. Think Mind, 2015, vol. 5, pp. 73–75.

[2] A.-W. Scheer, O. Thomas, and O. Adam, "Process modeling using event-driven process chains," *Process-Aware Information Systems*, pp. 119–146, 2005.

[3] P. Wohed, W. van der Aalst, M. Dumas, A. ter Hofstede, and N. Russell, "On the suitability of bpmn for business process modelling," in *Business Process Management*, ser. LNCS, S. Dustdar, J. Fiadeiro, and A. Sheth, Eds. Springer Berlin Heidelberg, 2006, vol. 4102, pp. 161–176.

[4] J. Desel, "Process modeling using petri nets," *Process-Aware Information Systems: Bridging People and Software through Process Technology*, pp. 147–177, 2005.

[5] M. Scaife and Y. Rogers, "External cognition: how do graphical representations work?" *International Journal of Human-Computer Studies*, vol. 45, no. 2, pp. 185–213, 1996.

[6] S. Zugal, J. Pinggera, and B. Weber, "Creating declarative process models using test driven modeling suite," in *IS Olympics: Information Systems in a Diverse World*, ser. LNBIP, S. Nurcan, Ed. Springer Berlin Heidelberg, 2012, vol. 107, pp. 16–32.

[7] M. Pesic and W. van der Aalst, "A declarative approach for flexible business processes management," in *Business Process Management Workshops*, ser. LNCS, J. Eder and S. Dustdar, Eds. Springer Berlin Heidelberg, 2006, vol. 4103, pp. 169–180.

[8] M. Pesic, H. Schonenberg, and W. van der Aalst, "DECLARE: Full support for loosely-structured processes," in *Enterprise Distributed Object Computing Conference, 2007. EDOC 2007. 11th IEEE International*, 2007, pp. 287–287.

[9] D. Fahland, D. Lübke, J. Mendling, H. Reijers, B. Weber, M. Weidlich, and S. Zugal, "Declarative versus imperative process modeling languages: The issue of understandability," in *Enterprise, Business-Process and Information Systems Modeling*, ser. LNBIP, T. Halpin, J. Krogstie, S. Nurcan, E. Proper, R. Schmidt, P. Soffer, and R. Ukor, Eds. Springer Berlin Heidelberg, 2009, vol. 29, pp. 353–366.

[10] C. Günther, S. Schönig, and S. Jablonski, "Dynamic guidance enhancement in workflow management systems," in *Proceedings of the 27th Annual ACM Symposium on Applied Computing*, ser. SAC '12. New York, NY, USA: ACM, 2012, pp. 1717–1719.

[11] W. M. van der Aalst, M. Weske, and D. Grnbauer, "Case handling: a new paradigm for business process support," *Data & Knowledge Engineering*, vol. 53, no. 2, pp. 129 – 162, 2005.

[12] S. Jablonski, "Do we really know how to support processes? considerations and reconstruction," in *Graph Transformations and Model-Driven Engineering*, ser. LNCS, G. Engels, C. Lewerentz, W. Schäfer, A. Schürr, and B. Westfechtel, Eds. Springer Berlin Heidelberg, 2010, vol. 5765, pp. 393–410.

[13] M. Baumann, M. Baumann, S. Schönig, and S. Jablonski, "Enhancing feasibility of human-driven processes by transforming process models to process checklists," in *Enterprise, Business-Process and Information Systems Modeling*, ser. LNBIP, I. Bider, K. Gaaloul, J. Krogstie, S. Nurcan, H. Proper, R. Schmidt, and P. Soffer, Eds. Springer Berlin Heidelberg, 2014, vol. 175, pp. 124–138.

[14] W. van der Aalst, T. Weijters, and L. Maruster, "Workflow mining: discovering process models from event logs," *Knowledge and Data Engineering, IEEE Transactions on*, vol. 16, no. 9, pp. 1128–1142, Sept 2004.

[15] W. van der Aalst, M. Pesic, and H. Schonenberg, "Declarative workflows: Balancing between flexibility and support," *Computer Science - Research and Development*, vol. 23, no. 2, pp. 99–113, 2009.

[16] M. Pesic, "Contraint-based workflow management systems: Shifting control to users," Ph.D. dissertation, Technische Universiteit Eindhoven, 2008.

[17] M. Zeising, S. Schönig, and S. Jablonski, "Towards a common platform for the support of routine and agile business processes," in *Collaborative Computing: Networking, Applications and Worksharing (CollaborateCom), 2014 International Conference on*, Oct 2014, pp. 94–103.

[18] E. Clarke, O. Grumberg, S. Jha, Y. Lu, and H. Veith, *Informatics: 10 Years Back, 10 Years Ahead*. Springer Berlin Heidelberg, 2001, ch. Progress on the State Explosion Problem in Model Checking, pp. 176–194.

[19] M. Montali, "Specification and verification of declarative open interaction models – a logic-based framework," Ph.D. dissertation, Alma Mater Studiorum Universitá di Bologna, 2009.

[20] S. Jablonski and C. Bussler, *Workflow management: modeling concepts, architecture and implementation*. International Thomson Computer Press, 1996.

[21] P. Dourish, J. Holmes, A. MacLean, P. Marqvardsen, and A. Zbyslaw, "Freeflow: Mediating between representation and action in workflow systems," in *Proceedings of the 1996 ACM Conference on Computer Supported Cooperative Work*, ser. CSCW '96. ACM, 1996, pp. 190–198.

[22] Object Management Group, "Case management model and notation version 1.0," 2014. [Online]. Available: http://www.omg.org/spec/CMMN/1.0/PDF/ [accessed: 2015-07-19]

[23] F. Maggi, M. Montali, M. Westergaard, and W. van der Aalst, "Monitoring business constraints with linear temporal logic: An approach based on colored automata," in *Business Process Management*, ser. LNCS, S. Rinderle-Ma, F. Toumani, and K. Wolf, Eds. Springer Berlin Heidelberg, 2011, vol. 6896, pp. 132–147.

[24] F. Maggi, A. Mooij, and W. van der Aalst, "User-guided discovery of declarative process models," in *Computational Intelligence and Data Mining (CIDM), 2011 IEEE Symposium on*, April 2011, pp. 192–199.